FURIOUS IMPROVISATION

FURIOUS IMPROVISATION

How the WPA and a Cast of Thousands
Made High Art out of Desperate Times

Susan Quinn

Walker & Company
New York

Published by Walker Publishing Company, Inc., New York
Distributed to the trade by Macmillan

All papers used by Walker & Company are natural, recyclable products made from
wood grown in well-managed forests. The manufacturing processes conform to
the environmental regulations of the country of origin.

Library of Congress Cataloging-in-Publication Data

Quinn, Susan, 1940–
Furious improvisation : how the WPA and a cast of thousands made high art out of
desperate times / Susan Quinn.
p.   cm.
Includes bibliographical references.
ISBN-13: 978-0-8027-1698-9 (alk. paper)
ISBN-10: 0-8027-1698-9 (alk. paper)
1. Federal Theatre Project (U.S.).   2. United States. Work Projects Administration.
I. Title.
PN2270.F43Q56 2008
792.0973—dc22
2008001274

Visit Walker & Company's Web site at www.walkerbooks.com

First U.S. edition 2008

1   3   5   7   9   10   8   6   4   2

Typeset by Westchester Book Group
Printed in the United States of America by Quebecor World Fairfield

To DHJ

CONTENTS

AUTHOR'S NOTE

Because the Federal Theatre Project and many other institutions and individuals used the British spelling of *theatre* during the 1930s, I have opted to do so here.

PROLOGUE

One day in January 1931, a white tenant farmer named H. C. Coney who lived near the little town of England, Arkansas, reached the limit of his patience. He and his wife and children struggled in the best of times, in a cabin with newspaper on the walls and a wood stove for heat. But the drought of 1930, coinciding with the greatest depression in the nation's history, had devastated the farms of the South. Without a harvest of corn or cotton, the situation had grown desperate. Coney couldn't even find anyone to buy his truck for the deflated price of $25, and there weren't enough clothes among all the family members, as he later told a reporter, "to wad a shotgun proper."[1] The stingy ration of lard, flour, and beans, given out to drought victims by the Red Cross, kept the family constantly on the edge of starvation. Then, on January 3, 1931, a neighbor lady told Coney that her children hadn't eaten in two days. That sent him into action.

Coney and his wife jumped into his truck and drove to the nearby home of a landowner named L. L. Bell, the local chairman of the Red Cross. There Coney found a crowd of hungry neighbors, all demanding food. The chairman refused aid because the office had run out of forms and couldn't proceed without them. (Red Cross officials worried about "impostors" hoarding supplies.) Coney yelled to some of the crowd to jump on his truck and drive to the nearby town of England, where the stores were, to demand food and, if necessary, to take it. By the time they reached England, a crowd of some five hundred white and black farmers had gathered, shouting, "We're not going to let our children starve," and, "We want food and we want it now."[2]

The Lonoke County drought chairman, a prominent lawyer and plantation owner named G. E. Morris, stood up before the crowd and promised

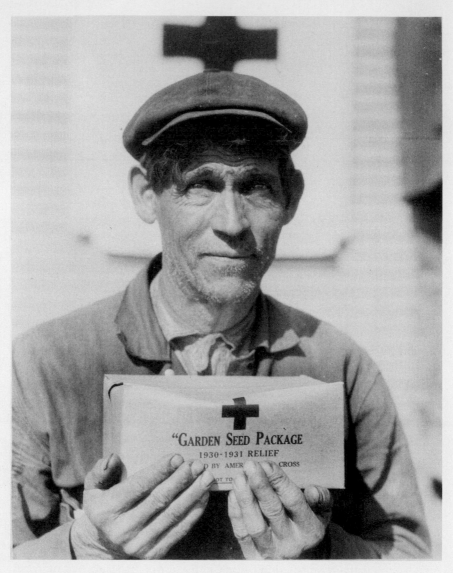

Arkansas farmer with seed package, 1930–31 (Library of Congress, Prints and Photographs Division)

that he would get them food if they would just be patient. Morris made frantic phone calls to Red Cross authorities in Little Rock, which finally resulted in the distribution of $2.75 worth of rations, meant to last for two weeks, for each of five hundred families in need. It wouldn't have taken much to provoke a violent showdown, Coney said afterward, but "they doled out the feed and we all idled back here without nobody gettin' hurt."[3] Thus ended "the England riot."

Reactions to the January 3 incident in England, Arkansas, varied wildly. The *New York Times* called it an "invasion of armed and hungry farmers and their wives." The Red Cross spokesman minimized the incident, insisting that the trouble was incited by "about 40 men from one section of the county, causing only temporary excitement but no damage to property or persons."[4] Some in Congress denounced the farmers as Communist instigators, a charge that even Red Cross county chairman Morris denied. "I knew the crowd to whom I spoke," Morris said. "All of them were poor, illiterate Americans, having made share crops around England for years. They never heard that Russia had a revolution."[5] Will Rogers, humorist and lecturer, put it more succinctly during a tour of the drought region: "In this little town where I am going tomorrow there ain't no reds," he said. "A red can't live there because he can't eat, and therefore he can't holler."[6]

Communists had nothing to do with the desperate actions of the hungry farmers in England, Arkansas. But the discontent of farmers in the South, and the impotence of the federal government in the face of it, created opportunities for Communist organizers. Not long after the England event, the Communist Party distributed leaflets in the drought area charging that "the Red Cross, headed by Hoover, is deliberately starving toiling people to death."[7] In March, a young party member named Whittaker Chambers used the event as the basis for a short story in the leftist monthly *New Masses* called "Can You Make Out Their Voices?" And that story, in turn, became the basis of a play written and staged by the fiery and energetic director of experimental theatre at Vassar College, a woman named Hallie Flanagan. Flanagan, along with co-writer Margaret Clifford, called their play *Can You Hear Their Voices?* and turned it into a less preachy and more powerful evocation of the desperate plight of farmers.

The main character of their play, Ed Wardell, is a self-professed Communist, and some of his neighbors resist him as a troublemaker. But as their cows die and their families grow hungrier, many come around to his point of view. The climactic moment comes when a young mother, unable to find milk for her baby, smothers it in a blanket rather than see it "tortured to death by inches." When they can stand it no longer, Wardell and his supporters sweep into town in their flivvers and stop in the middle of the street. The men with their guns and the women with their babies storm the Red Cross relief office, the stores, and the landowner's barn for food and milk.

To increase the impact of the play on their middle-class Vassar audience, Flanagan and Clifford introduced a parallel story, involving a very rich congressman named Bageheot and his daughter, Harriet, who is about to come out at a debutante party costing $250,000. Harriet Bageheot is a social butterfly, but not without some awareness of what is going on in the world. She finds her parents' plans for her coming-out party excessive. "Look here, Father," she says at breakfast, "doesn't it seem a little incongruous to be giving parties with the country in the state it is? With people standing in bread lines and dying of hunger?"

Her father's reply is that it would be selfish not to spend. "The thing to do is to keep money in circulation."

In her final scene, at the debutante ball, Harriet rises drunkenly to speak. The crowd, thinking she's going to announce her engagement, shouts out, "Who's the lucky man?"

"No, there's nothing tender about this," she says. "I want to tell you something important. I want to tell you about the drought."

The crowd responds, "Hurrah! The drought! Is there a drought?"

"There's a drought," Harriet insists. "In the United States—In the South. It's a terrible thing—It's killing the crops—It's making people hungry—It's making people thirsty—And you know what it is to be thirsty, my children."

There are cries of "Give the girl a drink!" and "Let's all have a drink!"

But Harriet continues, "We're the educated classes. We're the strength of the nation! What're we going to do about it? What're we going to do about the drought?"

Harriet's friends say nothing. Finally, the orchestra ends the awkward silence, striking up the tune "Just a Gigolo."

The final scene takes place in the drought-stricken South. Ed Wardell and his wife, fearing retribution from government troops for the attack on the food supply, send their two young sons away to keep them from trouble. "Try to remember all you've seen here," Ed Wardell tells his sons. "Remember that every man . . . ought to have a right to work and eat. Every man ought to have a right to think things out for himself."

The lights fade out, and a final message appears on a screen: "These boys are symbols of thousands of our people who are turning somewhere for leaders. Will it be to the educated minority? CAN YOU HEAR THEIR VOICES?"[8]

The Vassar production of *Can You Hear Their Voices?* in May 1931 came just a few months after a historic debate in Washington about how to deal with the growing desperation of people on farms and in cities throughout the country. On one side were President Herbert Hoover and his allies, who insisted that private charity could handle the problem. Hoover looked to the past for reinforcement, quoting President Grover Cleveland's dictum that "though the people support the government, the government should not support the people." Government loans, which promoted self-help, were all right, but direct aid to hungry people was dangerous. The "dole," Hoover insisted darkly, would lead to an "abyss of reliance in future upon government charity."[9]

Hoover had powerful allies in Congress. "Isn't it better," asked Senator Hiram Bingham of Connecticut, "to follow the regular American procedure and give the people a chance to feel the joy of giving voluntarily?"[10] If federal aid was given, argued House Republican floor leader James Q. Tilson, the "principled . . . will cripple themselves . . . in an attempt to repay it, and the idle and shiftless . . . will live off the Federal Government as long as the opportunity exists." Besides, Tilson insisted, the drought was a temporary setback, which "a sturdy class of Americans possessing . . . an indomitable will" could overcome in a matter of months.[11]

On the other side of the debate were those who believed the federal government had an obligation to its citizens in time of need. In the words of Senator Alben Barkley, "The people have the right to relief from the treasury which they have helped to fill."[12] These Democrats and insurgent Republicans argued that the situation required extraordinary measures. "We have just gone through the most devastating drought in history," Senator T. H. Caraway of Arkansas told his colleagues, "and are in the throes of the greatest depression since the Civil War."[13]

The position of Hoover and his allies led them to absurd extremes. They were willing to support a bill that gave millions in farm loans for purchasing seed and food for livestock, while vetoing a measure that would feed farmers. As one senator observed during the proceedings, "You cannot rehabilitate farms with dead farmers."[14]

The national chairman of the Red Cross, Judge John Barton Payne, was perhaps the most outspoken opponent of federal grants, insisting that the $10 million he could raise from private individuals would be more than adequate to meet the problem. When the Congress temporarily allocated $25 million to the Red Cross for hunger relief, Judge Payne refused to take it. "Leave us alone," he told Congress.[15] But the insistence on private aid, with an emphasis on self-help, was a cruel joke in the face of starvation. Photographs of gaunt and tattered farmers holding Red Cross seed kits for kitchen gardens dramatized the Red Cross's failure to come to grips with the problem. The Red Cross was run by the elite—in the South that meant the planters—and their charity was top-down and inadequate, as the "England riot" demonstrated. The charity they gave kept everyone, the poor white sharecroppers and their even poorer black counterparts, in their place.

Desperate farmers took the law into their own hands that winter, and not only in England, Arkansas. In Oklahoma City, a crowd of hungry men and women raided a grocery story near city hall. In Minneapolis, several hundred men and women smashed grocery store windows and grabbed bacon and ham, fruit and canned goods. Similar "food riots" took place in cities from San Francisco to St. Louis. Many observers believed, as *Can You Hear Their Voices?* implied, that the country was ripe for revolution. No one would ever know, General Hugh S. Johnson said later, "how close we were to collapse and revolution. We could have got a dictator a lot easier than Germany got Hitler."[16] Even Congressman Hamilton Fish Jr. of New York, a patrician of the old school, argued in 1932 that major changes were necessary. "I am trying to provide security for human beings which they are not getting," he said. "If we don't give it under the existing system, the people will change the system. Make no mistake about that."[17]

Apparently Franklin Delano Roosevelt sensed this, too. After his huge victory against the out-of-touch Herbert Hoover in November 1932, Roosevelt returned to his childhood home in Hyde Park, New York, to work out his plans for rescuing the country from the worst depression in its history. A visitor to Hyde Park told him that he could go down as the greatest American president if he succeeded and the worst American president if he failed. "If I fail," Roosevelt answered, "I shall be the last one."[18]

chapter one

ON THE TRAIN

On July 25, 1935, a small, energetic woman with a head of firmly curled auburn hair and a tall, gaunt man with a perpetual cigarette met at Union Station in Washington, D.C., and boarded a westbound train. She was Hallie Flanagan, director of a groundbreaking and widely admired theatre program at Vassar College. He was Harry Hopkins, a former social worker now running the Works Progress Administration (WPA), Franklin Delano Roosevelt's program to provide desperate people with meaningful employment. Harry Hopkins and Hallie Flanagan were old friends: They had grown up together in Grinnell, Iowa, and graduated a year apart from Grinnell College. Now, many years later, they were traveling back to Iowa to launch a daring new venture: a federal program to put artists back to work.

The Works Progress Administration was less than three months old but had already dispensed billions for practical undertakings: Hundreds of thousands had jobs building bridges and dams and roads. Now that summer had come, Harry Hopkins decided it was time to announce the most daring of all WPA gambits: a four-part program called Federal One, which would employ writers, visual artists, musicians, and theatre workers in four separate projects. Hallie Flanagan had agreed to head up the Federal Theatre Project.

It was Hopkins's idea to launch the Federal Theatre Project in the Midwest. For one thing, it would serve to emphasize that the theatre program was not going to be confined to Broadway or even to the major cities. But it also happened that a national theatre conference was taking place in Iowa City that week: Many of the participants were directors of the regional

Riding the rails, 1940 (National Archives and Records Administration)

theatres that would form the backbone of the federal theatre network Hallie Flanagan planned to develop. Besides, it was familiar territory for Hallie and Harry. Hallie was well known and respected among regional theatre directors coming to the gathering. And of course Iowa was home for both Harry and Hallie.

The train picked up speed as it chugged out of Union Station, steaming west through the verdant Virginia hills, up over the Allegheny mountain range, through the mining regions of West Virginia and the foothills of the Appalachians in southern Ohio, then heading north toward the great railway hub in the heart of the country: Chicago. Outside the train windows, Hallie and Harry saw plenty of evidence that the Depression stubbornly persisted, despite the efforts of the Roosevelt administration. On the outskirts of towns, flimsy shacks clustered near the tracks, often at the site of a stream or pond. Railyards in larger cities along the way had become a last refuge: People who had been evicted from their homes built up whole villages there of shacks and huts constructed of scavenged materials—packing boxes, barrel staves, pieces of corrugated iron for roofs, an occasional stolen door or window frame.

Hallie and Harry were riding west in comfort, in one of the varnished fliers that were the pride of the railroads in the thirties. But there were hundreds of thousands who were riding in boxcars or on top of gondola cars full of sand or steel pipes, squeezed inside the ice containers of "reefers" (refrigerator cars), or "riding the blinds," wedged into the narrow space just outside the accordion joints that connected the walkways between passenger cars. In 1932, the Southern Pacific Railroad reported ejecting over 780,000 transients from its cars. Other railroads stopped counting or even trying to interfere, finding it cheaper to add on empty boxcars than to have riders breaking in or hanging on outside, where they lost limbs or even died in frequent accidents. Almost all were looking for work, heading sometimes west and sometimes east, following the harvests or rumors of jobs.

For the crowds riding the rails, and for the many more who stayed behind looking for work, the Depression had come as a complete surprise. First the stock market collapsed, then the banks closed, then ordinary people began to lose their jobs. On average, companies fired twenty thousand workers every day of the work week, every week for three years following the Crash in 1929. In some cities, unemployment was 30 percent; in others, including Cleveland, Akron, and Toledo, it rose to 50 percent. "Our country was on the brink of hell," recalled Jim Mitchell, who left his home in Kenosha, Wisconsin, as a teenager to ride the rails and look for work. "All of a sudden the bottom fell out. Why? No one had the answer."[1]

The new economic era, so confidently predicted by Presidents Coolidge and Hoover, came to a premature end on Wall Street on "Black Thursday," October 24, 1929. But the groundwork for the collapse had been laid in the late twenties. The causes were multiple. As the stock market boomed, more and more people got caught up in the possibility of making a fast buck. Scam artists went unnoticed in the bull market: People bought stock in "investment trusts" that owned nothing but a reputation. The huge utility empire of Samuel Insull was one of many built on paper, sweeping thousands into bankruptcy.

By the time of the 1932 presidential election, Herbert Hoover had become so unpopular that he was greeted by angry mobs at campaign stops. Some noted that anyone still breathing could have defeated him. Franklin Roosevelt, who waged a vigorous campaign in which he visited thirty-eight states, radiating his charm and optimism, won by a landslide, carrying all but six states. Will Rogers observed that the whole country was with Roosevelt, "just so he does something. Even if what he does is wrong they are with him . . . If he burned down the Capitol, we would cheer and say, 'Well, we at least got a fire started anyhow.' "[2]

Once in office, FDR acted quickly. At his behest, Congress embarked on the most extraordinary session in the country's history, passing, in a few short months in 1933, bills that repealed Prohibition, regulated Wall Street, protected small bank depositors, and, for the first time in American history, established a federal system to bolster local relief efforts through the Federal Emergency Relief Act (FERA). To run FERA, Roosevelt chose the man who had succeeded in running a similar program for him when he was governor of New York State: Harry Hopkins.

The initiatives undertaken in the first hundred days of the Roosevelt administration began to turn things around. A year and a half later, national income was up by $9 billion, nearly 25 percent, over 1933. Unemployment was down by over two million. And a whole raft of legislation promised to bring some measure of humanity to employment practices, to provide some security for homeowners, farmers, and old people, and to enforce new controls over financial institutions. FERA, and its offshoot the Civil Works Administration (CWA),[3] provided relief in the form of food, allowances, and some jobs.

But Roosevelt was troubled by the make-work nature of his administration's early relief efforts under FERA. In 1935, he told Congress that "the Federal Government must quit this business of relief. I am not willing that the vitality of our people be further sapped by the giving of cash, of market baskets, of a few hours of weekly work cutting grass, raking leaves or picking up papers in the public parks . . . To dole out relief in this way is to administer a narcotic, a subtle destroyer of the human spirit . . . We must preserve not only the bodies of the unemployed from destitution but also their self-respect, their self-reliance and courage and determination." Out of this resolve was born the most expensive program ever launched by any government anywhere in the world: the Works Progress Administration, designed to provide meaningful work instead of make-work and charity. To run it, FDR turned once again to Harry Hopkins.

Hopkins was a man full of nervous energy, impatient with red tape and formalities and eager to get things done. His speech was pithy, often sarcastic, sometimes profane. Though frequently humorous, he also had flashes of indignation. He was quick to speak his mind about the plight of the poor and what the New Deal was doing about it: "The last Republican administration let people starve," he told a reporter. "We fed them. They divided relief money among political henchmen. We stopped this racket."[4] That was typical Hopkins-speak, blunt and to the point.

Somehow or other, perhaps because of his liberal arts education at Grinnell, Hopkins had a profound respect for artists. Even in the early months of the New Deal administration, when he was putting people to work building roads and schools, Hopkins had found employment for three thousand writers and artists. "Hell!" he said in his typically combative style. "They've got to eat just like other people."[5]

The train trip to Iowa City took the better part of two days, giving Hallie and Harry plenty of time to talk about their goals for the Federal Theatre Project. For Harry Hopkins the hope, first and foremost, was that the Federal Theatre would provide jobs for thousands of unemployed and hard-pressed theatre workers, onstage and behind the scenes. But he also hoped the project would expose ordinary people all over the country to affordable live theatre for the first time. As he and Hallie conceived it, the Federal Theatre also had the potential to take on the country's deep-seated racism, by fostering Negro[6] companies and requiring integrated audiences for all performances.

Hallie Flanagan had even greater ambitions. She viewed the Federal Theatre Project as a chance to innovate on an unprecedented scale. It might be possible to make theatre history, mounting cutting-edge productions that were too risky for the profit-bound theatre. It might even be possible to create a whole new kind of theatre that addressed people's everyday struggles in these difficult times. The project had the potential, in Hamlet's phrase, to "hold the mirror up to nature . . . to show the very age and body of the time his form and pressure." Or so Hallie imagined, as she and her old friend Harry traveled west together.

Hallie had already seen the transforming power of the New Deal when she visited her aunt, who ran a settlement house in an impoverished area of Detroit. "You know how you sometimes see," she wrote Harry, "reflected in a drop of water, a whole landscape—sky, trees, a world in little? Melville House is such a microcosm."

Melville House, she explained, had done admirable work before the Depression hit, providing adult education for the many immigrants in the area—Poles, Hungarians, Macedonians. There were classes for the men, most of whom worked in the "Ford's factory," and for their wives and children. It was, she said, "one of the most remarkable organizations I had ever seen . . .

"Then," Hallie continued, "everything changed." After the 1929 Crash, the men began to lose their jobs, the school board cut support for classes. "Year by year when I would come, Melville House would be bleaker and more shabby. The house and the streets were full of unemployed men growing increasingly bitter against the government. It used to terrify me . . . to hear nightly in this book-filled old room, wild talk of anarchism, communism and hatred of the status quo. Not that I blamed the men. Watching the waste and terrible contrast between rich and poor, I often wondered why they didn't smash up Ford's factory and die splendidly instead of gradually."

The letter continues: "Then—as our first Grinnell movies used to say, came the dawn. One of the men here in the house got a CWA job: the board of education began to pay a little again—the night classes picked up. The spirit of hopefulness is very marked. The belief in the administration is 100% strong—the interest in Perkins [Frances Perkins, secretary of labor], Wallace [Henry Wallace, secretary of agriculture], above all, Hopkins is almost religious in its fervour. Out of a class of women I visited, . . . fourteen of the 20 said they had a wage earner 'for Hopkins' in the family . . . The change from complete hopelessness to renewed courage in this house is only symbolic of the situation throughout the country—and I want to say that I think the work you are doing is superb."[7]

Not everyone shared Hallie's enthusiasm. Hopkins's nemesis Governor Eugene Talmadge of Georgia had pronounced the entire New Deal "a combination of wet-nursin', frenzied finance, downright communism and plain damn foolishness." Talmadge claimed that "the only way to have an honest government is to keep it poor."[8]

In the past, Americans rarely encountered the federal government, except when they went to the post office. But as they rode west together, Hopkins pointed out to Hallie that there were other precedents. The government had given free land to war veterans, rights-of-way to railroad entrepreneurs, and protective tariffs to infant industries. Now the New Deal was expanding the tradition by giving of the nation's resources to the unemployed in the form of jobs, so that they could build a better America. It was the right thing to do. And it was the right thing, as he said on numerous occasions, to include artists. "Artists," he told a reporter, "were suffering . . . acutely in many cases. The WPA theory is that this human skill and talent should be preserved and the wealth of the nation added to materially by those who possess it."[9]

Harry and Hallie's train conversation was frequently interrupted at stops along the way, as reporters and photographers hopped on to catch Hopkins and ask him questions. "Can't I have peace, even when the train's in motion?" Hopkins groused.

Just outside Chicago, in Englewood, the regional administrator of the WPA, Howard Hunter, got on and rode with them into the city, complaining along the way about red tape in Washington.

Hunter thumped his bulging briefcase. "I've got questions that ought to have been answered six weeks ago," he told Hopkins. "Seventy-five thousand people can't get paid until those questions are answered. And Washington sits back on its haunches and does absolutely nothing."

Money was at the root of most of Hopkins's problems in trying to get the WPA up and running: how to free money from bureaucratic entanglements, how to keep the politicians from misusing it, and finally how to fend off the critics who inevitably accused him of waste and corruption when he did spend it.

Compared with overall WPA expenditures, the budget of Federal One was laughably small, and the Federal Theatre Project's was even smaller: a mere tenth of 1 percent of the WPA's overall expenditures. But Harry knew from experience that money was going to rule Hallie's life as director of the Federal Theatre. As he gazed out the train window at the gray tenements of Chicago, he suddenly asked:

"Can you spend money?"

Hallie, who loved nice clothes, luxurious travel, and elegant houses, was taken aback at first. She told Harry that "the inability to spend money is not one of my faults."

But Harry was thinking on a larger scale. "It's not easy. It takes a lot of nerve to put your signature down on a piece of paper when it means that the government of the United States is going to pay out a million dollars to the unemployed in Chicago. It takes decision, because you'll have to decide whether Chicago needs that money more than New York City or Los Angeles.

"You can't care very much what people are going to say," he warned Hallie, "because when you're handling other people's money whatever you do is always wrong. If you try to hold down wages, you'll be accused of union-busting and of grinding down the poor; if you pay a decent wage, you'll be competing with private industry and pampering a lot of no-accounts; if you scrimp on production costs, they'll say your shows are lousy and if you spend enough to get a good show on, they'll say you're wasting the taxpayers' money. Don't forget that whatever happens you'll be wrong."[10]

Hopkins spoke from bitter experience. Most frustrating of all was the constant accusation of corruption in the dispersing of funds. The word *boondoggle*, used to describe make-work provided in exchange for political support, ran rampant in newspaper attacks on the new program. The acerbic critic H. L. Mencken, writing that month in the *Baltimore Sun*, described the $4.8 billion WPA budget as a "slush fund" designed to buy votes for FDR's 1936 reelection. "They have the taxpayer down at last," wrote Mencken, "and when they let him up there will be nothing left of him save his identification tag and a couple of knuckles."[11]

Even newspapers sympathetic to the New Deal insisted that there was no way to keep politics out of WPA operations. One cartoon showed the heavy boot of "POLITICS" kicking open the door marked "RELIEF"; another had a hungry Democratic donkey lusting for the clover growing just beyond the sign reading "Relief jobs: KEEP OUT."[12]

Much of the press was hostile to the New Deal. Iowa, Hallie and Harry's home territory, was no exception. The *Des Moines Register* regularly ran stories about New Deal spending programs with such headlines as NO END IN SIGHT. A commentator for the paper described the WPA arts programs as "boondoggling on a gigantic scale."

"The thing is incredible," wrote Frank R. Kent. "Millions are to be spent giving piano lessons to the children of those on relief. Millions more will pay 7000 men to write a guide book of America . . . Though the usual face-saving pretense of progress will be kept up, clear-headed men generally recognize now the whole scheme is doomed to be the most ghastly and tragic flop of the New Deal regime."[13]

Some Iowans, already benefiting from New Deal programs, were natural allies. Lorena Hickok, a journalist who was informing Harry Hopkins on conditions around the country, reported that thousands in Des Moines, hired under the CWA to labor with picks and shovels, "lined up and got paid—MONEY. They took it with wide grins and made bee-lines for the grocery stores."[14] But many Iowa farmers had been evicted from their land, in judgments rendered by the government, and had yet to see positive results from Roosevelt's farm policies. Also, small-town opinion makers favored self-reliance over what they saw as the lavish spending of the New Deal.

When Harry Hopkins and Hallie Flanagan got off the train in Iowa City on that Friday in July 1935, they had two very different constituencies to win over. One was a distinguished group of regional theatre directors. They liked and admired Hallie, but they were suspicious of the federal government's ability to tolerate challenging, cutting-edge theatre. Hopkins was reassuring. "I am asked whether a theatre subsidized by the government can be kept free from censorship," he told a dinner audience of theatre folk, "and I say, yes, it is going to be kept free from censorship. What we want is a free, adult, uncensored theatre."[15] It was a large promise. Hallie Flanagan, for one, was not going to let him forget he'd said it, out loud and in public.

The other constituency was a general cross section of Iowa voters, many of them hardworking farm people who shared the *Des Moines Register's* suspicion that the WPA in general and the theatre program in particular were a colossal waste of their tax dollars. Before a skeptical audience of seven thousand on the Iowa University campus, Hopkins defended the New Deal programs in his usual combative style. "The way we let people live, and the dog houses we let them live in are a scandalous disgrace," he told his listeners. The opponents of the New Deal, he charged, were selfishly protecting their interests. "They don't want brains—competent people—in government . . . What they want is political eunuchs." As for Hoover, he "didn't spend any money on 'em [the unemployed]—he talked rugged individualism and gave it to 'em for breakfast." This comment elicited loud applause from the crowd.

Hopkins mixed his hard-hitting remarks with Iowa humility that charmed even his critics. "On the speaking platform," reported the *Des Moines Register*, "the works progress administrator was something to behold. Not only was his entire address slangy and plugged with wisecracks . . . when the spirit moved him, he injected whatever happened to come to his mind. 'Prosperity for who?' he boomed at one point and then quickly asked—'or is it whom? Doggone, I always forgot that word.'"[16]

"It was a hot night," Hallie Flanagan recalled, "and the farmers were in their shirtsleeves." As Hopkins expatiated on what the WPA could do, someone in the crowd shouted up toward the podium, "Who's going to pay for all that?"

Hopkins looked out over the crowd. He took off his jacket, unfastened his tie, and rolled up his sleeves. "The crowd," Hallie wrote, "got perfectly still. Then he said 'You are.' His voice took on urgency. 'And who better? Who can better afford to pay for it? Look at this great university. Look at these fields, these forests and rivers. This is America, the richest country in the world. We can afford to pay for anything we want. And we want a decent life for all the people in this country. And we are going to pay for it.' "[17]

chapter two

HARRY

When Harry Hopkins arrived in Washington in 1932 to attack unemployment, he began, in the words of journalist Marquis Childs, "a furious improvisation; he was playing by ear on a giant organ with all the stops pulled out. It is the record of his entire career in Washington," Childs added, "improvisation at the center of a tornado."[1]

Harry Hopkins had never been much of an actor. According to the Grinnell College *Scarlet and Black*, his portrayal of Captain Jinks suffered from "rigid poses and gestures" and "an over emphasis . . . on facial expressions."[2] But he had always had a gift for improvisation, perhaps because he came from a family that required alternating allegiances to virtue and vice. Harry was the fourth of five children born to Anna Pickett Hopkins, a tall, thin, dignified woman who required her offspring to attend services at Grinnell's imposing stone Methodist church twice on Sunday and to gather around the pump organ at home to sing hymns on a regular basis.

Harry's father, on the other hand, was the popular and social owner of a harness shop in town, well known to Grinnell College students because he dispensed magazines and candy as well as harness and because he made a point of remembering every student's name. He was also a highly skilled bowler who liked to bet on his games. Al, a friend noted, "would bowl anyone anytime for money, marbles or chalk."[3] Harry remembered the time his father took him to the basement and showed him $500 he had just won. Al admonished his son not to tell Anna Hopkins about the money, knowing she would turn it over to the missionary fund.

Even as a high school boy, Harry excelled in a crisis. A classmate named Dwight Bradley, son of the college president and a natural target for bullies,

Harry Hopkins (Library of Congress, Prints and Photographs Division)

remembered the day a gang tied him to a telephone pole, started a fire near his feet, and told him they were going to burn him at the stake.

"I was scared stiff," Bradley recalled years later, "but before the smoke had quite suffocated me Harry rushed forward with his jack-knife and cut me loose."[4]

At Grinnell College, Harry was a mediocre student. But he seems to have been captivated by a new theological alternative to his mother's severe Methodism. He excelled in the classes taught by Grinnell professors Jesse Macy and Edward Steiner, a kind of one-two punch in the teaching of the social gospel.

Jesse Macy was an internationally known professor of English history with Iowa humility. Once, when a prominent visitor to his home from England left his shoes outside the door in the evening for the servant to polish, Macy polished them himself, without mentioning it in the morning. In class, Macy emphasized that the old history, which told only of the ruling classes and ignored the slaves and workers, was obsolete. "What we call Grecian history," Macy wrote, "is only the history of the masters . . . As we become more scientific and more Christian," he asserted, much of past history will need to be discarded because of its "political prejudice and hypocrisy."[5]

Edward Steiner, a bold theologian who held the Grinnell chair in "applied Christianity," was the voice of tolerance, teaching his students "how to look at the unlike and learn to like them."[6] Steiner himself had traveled to America from Europe in steerage, then repeated the journey in steerage on numerous occasions in an attempt to assess and improve conditions.

The Steiner/Macy influence was evident by the time Harry Hopkins reached his senior year. HOPKINS GIVES PITHY TALK AT Y.M.C.A., read the headline in the college paper. "Hoppy," the paper reported, "pointed out how necessary it is for us to have ideals in our life here but maintained that we should carry them out to make them worth anything to us and to others."

"Every man," said Hopkins, "has the spark of Christianity in him, and it is our duty to help him develop it."[7]

But the popular "Hoppy" had another side. Like his father, he was a competitor, the "bright and shining light" of the basketball team, according to the school newspaper, but capable, according to opponents, of playing a little rougher than the rules allowed. He was also an inveterate practical joker and a sometime troublemaker: Although his role didn't come out at the time, Hopkins was involved in plotting the use of stink bombs during one of the annual freshman-sophomore battles at Grinnell, a plot that sent several students to the infirmary and precipitated an official inquiry.[8] After he became admired and famous, a friend wrote to him, threatening to "tear off the veil."[9]

After college, Hopkins followed his own advice about living out Christian ideals and went to work at Christodora House, a settlement house in the midst of the greatest concentration of immigrants in the United States, on the Lower East Side of Manhattan. It was a strange new world, not just for migrants from distant shores, but also for a young man from a small town on the Iowa plains. The families he encountered in his unpaid role as "friendly visitor" were dealing with disease, danger, extreme overcrowding, and often hunger as well. As he climbed the inner stairs of the five- and six-story walk-ups, Hopkins encountered the stench of the water closets, often one or two to a floor housing several dozen people. The apartments were crowded with families of five or more and with unrelated boarders as well, brought in to help pay the rent. Often one room would be given over during waking hours to piecework—young and old would gather around a table and share the repetitive tasks of assembling clothing or rolling cigars or packaging nuts. The rooms, stacked one behind the other, let in little light and were crowded with the necessities of living. In the warm weather, everyone inside spilled out onto fire escapes and front stoops for sleeping.

Christodora House was unusual among the settlement houses established by reformers in large cities just before the turn of the century. Most, like Lillian Wald's Henry Street in New York City and Jane Addams's Hull House in Chicago, tolerated and even celebrated religious diversity. But when the founders of Christodora, Christina MacColl and Sarah Carson, established their settlement house on Avenue B in 1897, they chose a name that meant "Christ's gift" and gave implicit endorsement to the belief that Protestant Christianity was the one true faith. There was rejoicing among the Christodora House settlement workers when a Jew or Catholic in their flock embraced Protestantism.

Before long, Harry met and fell in love with one of the holdouts, a petite dark-haired Jewish immigrant from Hungary named Ethel Gross. Ethel was four years older than Harry and had far more experience of the world. She had traveled in steerage to America with her mother and four siblings and, despite dropping out of school in eighth grade, had taken on increasingly challenging secretarial jobs. She had also endured the suicide of her mother, who never truly adjusted to life in America. In a photograph from the period, Ethel, dressed in white and wearing a VOTES FOR WOMEN sash, looks both stylish and confident beneath her plumed hat; her flashing eyes and half-smile suggest she is a woman with her own opinions.

When Ethel and Harry decided to marry, their frequent letters were full of worry, laced with amusement, about how their families would deal with the decision. Harry's marriage to Ethel, as he later noted, had the advantage of shocking the good Methodists back home. When the fateful day arrived, Harry and Ethel chose to be married at the secular Ethical Culture Society, whose founder, Felix Adler, was a rabbi's son and a social reformer. Not long after that, Hopkins told a Grinnell classmate that he had "left the Church" altogether. "The chief thing in my mind," he told his friend, "is to work toward the founding of an ideal state, in this earth, based on social justice which will make for happiness for us all."[10]

Not surprisingly, Hopkins soon grew unhappy with Christodora House. "If this house is on the side of the Lord," he wrote Ethel during their courtship, "then I am going to straightaway apply below."[11] By 1913, he had left Christodora House for a job with John Kingsbury at the Association for Improving the Condition of the Poor (AICP). Times were hard. Unemployment in New York was rising at an alarming rate, and Hopkins was disturbed by the sight of hundreds of men "walking aimlessly from factory to factory looking vainly for work."[12] He was frustrated with the weak solutions offered by both Democrats and Republicans and cast a vote—later used against him by congressional critics—for a Socialist candidate for mayor, Morris Hillquit.

It was during the 1915 recession that Hopkins first revealed his skills as an improviser in troubled times. Many of the unemployed sought help from the AICP, insisting they wanted jobs, not charity. In response, Hopkins tried an innovative approach that he would replicate many times over. As it happened, there was a project at the Bronx Zoo that needed workers. Hopkins, along with colleague William Matthews, offered to supply workers using the funds of the AICP. The parks commissioner, who wanted to improve the zoo but had no public funds at his disposal, accepted the offer. Before nightfall on the day he got the news, Hopkins was writing letters to a hundred men, offering them "real work at real wages." Even though the pay was only $2 a day, and even though the men were limited to working three days a week, the Bronx Zoo project became a model.

By the time of the Great Depression, Hopkins had assumed the well-paid and influential post of director of the Tuberculosis and Health Association. Then in 1930, in time left over from the director's job, Hopkins and his former co-worker Matthews once again used the Bronx Zoo idea to put people back to work. After raising $6 million from private sources, and with the cooperation of Mayor Jimmy Walker and the New York parks commissioner, they were able to put a hundred thousand men to work on city projects. The pay was only $5 a day and the work week was, once again, only three days long. But it was better than nothing. In 1915 and again in 1930, Hopkins was doing on a small scale, with private funds, what he would do on a vast scale, with federal funds, a few years hence. He was also learning to shrug off his critics, who disapproved of handing out jobs willy-nilly to whoever asked, without sorting out the deserving from the undeserving. Hopkins, according to colleague Dr. Jacob Goldberg, said the naysayers could "go to hell."[13]

But Harry Hopkins's successes in work were not replicated in his life as a husband and father of three sons. Ethel had felt for years that Harry's devotion to desperate people in the larger world took precedence over her needs and those of the family. During one summer when he was taking care of flood victims for the Red Cross in New Orleans and Ethel was back in New York with their first child, she wrote him with questions about domestic arrangements, adding, "I know too that you are busy and haven't time to bother too much about these things. But I'm sure you took care of the Guatemala refugees and the homeless at Lake Charles much better."[14] Harry responded with news of what he was doing, never addressing Ethel's complaints.

By the time of the Depression, Harry's marriage to Ethel was at a breaking point. He had fallen in love with Barbara Duncan, a nurse ten years younger than him who worked at the Tuberculosis and Health Association. Harry told a friend that cultural differences were part of the problem in his marriage. Certainly Barbara Duncan's WASP background was closer to his own. More important, Barbara seemed to have been more willing than Ethel to accept Harry's workaholic ways and to admire him without reservation.[15] But Hopkins was torn between his duty to Ethel and the children and his new love. He went into Freudian analysis. He also looked for answers in the works of Carl Jung and Alfred Adler. And he had long talks with his older sister Adah and with close friends. He even took a steamship journey to Europe, hoping distance would bring some resolution. Everyone, including the psychoanalyst, advised him to remain in his marriage for the sake of his wife and three young sons, aged sixteen, nine, and five.

But in 1930, Harry Hopkins left his wife and sons anyway to marry Barbara Duncan. Such behavior was considered highly reprehensible at the time. Twelve years earlier, Franklin Roosevelt had considered divorce after Eleanor discovered his affair with Lucy Mercer, but he had been persuaded against it: Divorce would have spelled the end of his career in politics. Hopkins didn't yet have political ambitions, but he paid a price nonetheless. His trusted sister Adah, whose example had led him into social work, stopped speaking to him. So, for a time, did his most important mentor, John Kingsbury. Kingsbury had given Hopkins his first paying job in New York and had become a close friend and ally in the fight to reform the field. Kingsbury was with Hopkins on his soul-searching steamship journey to Europe and had spent many hours discussing his marital problems. Hopkins had assured Kingsbury then that there was "no woman in the case," a lie that only worsened his colleague's opinion of his behavior.[16]

But by the time his divorce was finalized and his new marriage begun, in June 1931, Hopkins had been given another chance to prove himself in a time of crisis and to find redemption in the eyes of his disapproving friends. Franklin Delano Roosevelt, elected by a huge majority to a second term as governor of New York, was among the first to address mushrooming unemployment. He established the Temporary Emergency Relief Administration (TERA) in October 1931. Shortly after, the newly appointed TERA board offered Harry Hopkins the job of executive director. He was not the board's first choice, and may not even have been their second, but he accepted the job immediately and eagerly.

Hopkins first shook hands with Roosevelt when he was running for governor in 1928. To FDR, Hopkins was just another enthusiastic stranger, but Hopkins never forgot that first brief encounter during all the years of friendship that were to follow. Hopkins had been impressed by Roosevelt's eloquent nomination of Al Smith for president at the Democratic convention. The "Happy Warrior," as Roosevelt styled Smith, was Hopkins's hero at the time.

FDR was a reluctant candidate for governor the year Hopkins met him. In 1921, following a term as assistant secretary of the navy in Woodrow Wilson's administration, he had been stricken with polio. Seven years later, he still believed that he might be able to regain the use of his legs if he continued to devote himself to the task of rehabilitation in Warm Springs, Georgia. What's more, he and his closest political adviser, Louis Howe, didn't think 1928 was going to be a Democratic year. When Al Smith himself urged a run, Roosevelt told him, "As I am only 46 years of age, I feel that I owe it to my family and myself to give the present constant improvement a chance to continue."[17] In the end, however, Smith and those around him won the day. Roosevelt ran for governor and won a two-year term by a narrow margin. Al Smith lost badly to Herbert Hoover in the presidential race and watched with increasing chagrin as his younger protégé took center stage, first in state and then in national politics.

During his nine months as director of TERA in 1931 and 1932, Harry Hopkins had a formal, businesslike relationship with Governor Roosevelt, speaking with him in person perhaps a dozen times. Hopkins wasn't part of the "brain trust" Roosevelt was beginning to develop in the early thirties, as the possibility grew of a run for the presidency. Although he did attend the Democratic convention in Chicago in 1932, Hopkins watched from the sidelines as Democrats, in one of the rowdiest and most contentious gatherings in their history, made their momentous choice.

Chicago, in the summer of 1932, was a microcosm of the nation: There were huge areas of lifeless factories as well as overgrown parks and rows of vacant stores with blackened windows. Armies of the unemployed, numbering fifty thousand or more, lined up for food and gathered in makeshift Hoovervilles. Yet the Republicans, who held their convention in Chicago just before the Democrats, persisted in the belief that their man could win a second term. Their convention, renominating Hoover, contained no surprises.

The Democrats' convention, on the other hand, was full of them. Even before it started, the Democratic delegations brought their regional color to the embattled city. There were the supporters of Oklahoma's "Alfalfa Bill" Murray, for instance, who brought along an all-girl band in thigh-high kilts. And there were the Tammany bosses, who arrived by special train from New York with seventy cases of "ginger ale" (Prohibition was still in force) and took up residency on five floors of the elegant Drake Hotel on the Gold Coast. Will Rogers noted: "If this convention stopped right now, two days before the voting starts, it's been a better convention than the Republican one."

The convention itself lived up to the preamble. Roosevelt's closest advisers had been preparing the way for his nomination since the day after he won a second term for governor in a landslide. James Farley, who had managed that campaign, told the press right after the gubernatorial victory: "The Democrats in the nation naturally want as their candidate for President the man who has shown himself capable of carrying the most important state in the country by a record-breaking majority. I do not see how Mr. Roosevelt can escape becoming the next Presidential nominee of his party, even if no one should raise a finger to bring it about."[18]

It wasn't going to be that easy, however. At the start of the convention, there were ten contenders for the nomination, including Al Smith and John Nance Garner of Texas, the seasoned and crusty Speaker of the House. And in the days before television dictated the schedule, the delegates who gathered in the barnlike Chicago Stadium that June were ready and willing to sit through long speeches and loud music and to parade through the crowd in raucous, lengthy demonstrations for their candidate. By the time the first vote was taken, at almost five in the morning, Roosevelt was one hundred votes short of the two-thirds majority required for nomination. A second vote, which followed quickly on the first, wasn't much different. By nine-thirty in the morning, exhaustion had set in. The convention adjourned until evening.

The key to a victory for FDR was the Texas delegation, committed to Garner. Farley went to his lieutenant Sam Rayburn and promised that Roosevelt was willing to offer Garner the vice presidency if he would deliver the Texas delegation. Rayburn, resistant at first, finally told Farley "We'll see what can be done." In the end, Garner himself released the delegates. "I think it's time to break this thing up," he told Rayburn. "This man Roosevelt is the choice of the convention." As Texas went, so went the convention. On the fourth and final tally, Roosevelt won the nomination.

In a break with precedent, Roosevelt flew from Albany to the scene of the convention in Chicago to accept the nomination in person, arriving in an open car, surrounded by his wife, Eleanor, and his children. The flight from Albany had taken almost ten hours, yet Roosevelt on the podium, in his double-breasted suit and bow tie, radiated joy, optimism, and, importantly, health. His braced legs were invisible to his audience, and his vigor was undeniable. "This is more than a political campaign," he told the delegates in his robust patrician tones, "it is a call to arms. Give me your help, not to win votes alone, but to win this crusade to restore America to its own people." And speaking for the first time the phrase that would be forever associated with his leadership, he told them: "I pledge you, I pledge myself, to a New Deal for the American people."

On inauguration day, March 4, 1933, Franklin Delano Roosevelt made his way on his lifeless and unreliable legs to the podium, leaning on the arm of his son James, to take the oath of office. The enemy, he declared, was "fear itself—nameless, unreasoning, unjustified terror which paralyzes needed efforts to convert retreat into advance." The loudest applause of all came when he promised to request "broad executive power to wage a war against the emergency, as great as the power that would be given to me if we were in fact invaded by a foreign foe."

Harry Hopkins was back in New York, listening to the speech on the radio, along with the rest of the nation. His success with TERA made him desirable: Herbert Lehman, who succeeded Roosevelt as governor of New York, wanted him to continue as head of TERA for $11,500. And Jesse Straus, president of Macy's and a member of the TERA board, offered to hire him away from Lehman for the princely sum of $25,000 (close to half a million in today's dollars) a year to work for him. Harry Hopkins liked the good life: fine restaurants, speakeasies, and a wager or two. The safe thing, given his tastes as well as the postdivorce demands on his pocket-book, would have been to accept one of the excellent offers at hand.

But the job he wanted was in Washington. "I'd rather have a small job with the President of the United States," Hopkins explained to Lehman, "than a big job with the Governor of New York or anyone else."[19] For weeks, Hopkins looked on restlessly as FDR fulfilled his inaugural promise of "action, and action now," declaring a bank holiday and calling Congress into emergency session, then rushing through emergency legislation to deal with the bank crisis and to reform the budget, followed soon after by the repeal of Prohibition, then by farm bills to address the agricultural crisis. Hopkins had written to FDR early on, with a proposal for a federal program based on the New York model. But Roosevelt initially had reservations about the deficit spending required to provide federal grants to the unemployed millions. Finally, in response to FDR's recommendation, Congress enacted the Federal Emergency Relief Act and funded it with a then enormous $500 million. FERA gave indirect aid to the states, supplementing their efforts to provide food, clothing, small allowances, and jobs in government-generated operations such as manufacturing clothing and mattresses.

It was a momentous new departure: Never before had the federal government provided significant support to individual citizens in need. "It is socialism," a congressman from Massachusetts declared unequivocally. Another, from the Midwest, was nearly speechless. "I can hardly find parliamentary language," declared Simeon D. Fess of Ohio, "to describe the statement that the States and cities cannot take care of conditions in which they find themselves but must come to the Federal Government for aid."[20]

Harry Hopkins, who had managed Governor Roosevelt's TERA so effectively in New York State, was the natural candidate for the FERA job, and FDR asked him to sign on. Hopkins accepted the offer, despite a 40 percent pay cut, on Friday, May 19, 1933. That Sunday, he took the train to Washington and the next morning met with the president. FDR told Hopkins two things: Get speedy and adequate help to the unemployed, and ignore the politicians. Hopkins wasted no time. While his desk was still in the hallway, awaiting the movers, he began dispatching telegrams to state agencies, disbursing $5 million within his first two hours in office. MONEY FLIES, read a headline in the *Washington Post*. Harry Hopkins disguised his zeal behind characteristic humor. "I'm not going to last six months here," he told reporters, "so I'll do as I please."[21]

chapter three

HALLIE

Hallie Flanagan was born Hallie Ferguson, the oldest of three children of Frederic and Louisa Fischer Ferguson, in Redfield, South Dakota, in 1889. The family moved frequently during the depression of the 1890s as Hallie's father lost one sales job after another. For a time he sold harvesting machines, then life insurance, then coal in various towns in South Dakota and Nebraska, in Illinois and Missouri. When Hallie was eleven, the family landed for good in Grinnell, Iowa. Grinnell was chosen, no doubt, because there was family there. But also, like the Hopkins family, the Fergusons were attracted to the town because they hoped for a Grinnell College education for their children.

Hallie's mother was a quiet woman who loved to paint and might have gone to art school in different times. Her father Fred, on the other hand, was gregarious and playful. When Hallie traveled with him on business trips to Chicago, he would be the life of the train car, making hats and boats out of newspaper to cheer crying babies and generally engaging the other passengers in conversation. The Ferguson family's finances remained precarious—Fred invested heavily in a brother-in-law's unsuccessful electric railway company—but Fred kept up a jaunty outward appearance around Grinnell. He had a knack, which his daughter inherited, for turning disappointment into humor and drama.

When the family moved to Grinnell, for instance, Fred brought along several horses from the family farm. But because the neighbors complained, he had to give them up. On the day of parting, Hallie's mother admonished the children to "be very nice to your father" because he was feeling bereft. "This was the first time I ever saw my father depressed," Hallie recalled. But before long, he cheered himself up, announcing, "Oh

Hallie Flanagan (National Archives and Records Administration)

well, I can always ride Rob Roy." Rob Roy was Hallie's favorite stick horse.

"Father was a great person for celebration," Hallie remembered. "Picnics, nutting parties, sleigh rides, Fourth of July, Christmas. All holidays were tremendous affairs." Although neither of her parents had gone to college, they set great store by literature. Many nights, the family gathered to read Dickens or Sir Walter Scott. Perhaps they had an exaggerated idea of what book learning could do: An aunt once asked Hallie's mother if she had told her daughter the facts of life. Her mother replied: "She is reading *Vanity Fair*."

Already, in elementary school, Hallie was beginning to write and to perform as well. She recalled that all the children saved up their scrap paper for her because she was "writing a book" called *Lady Glyde's Revenge*. At recess, she would read everyone the latest installment.

At fifteen, Hallie visited the St. Louis World's Fair with her family and kept a diary that presaged her career as a director and impresario.[1] Like *Lady Glyde's Revenge*, Hallie's vivid description of her final night at the fair was written to captivate an audience:

> It is evening. The great crowds along the banks of the lagoon, facing Festival Hall are suddenly hushed and quiet. The great buildings tower white and impassive against the velvety blackness of the sky . . . But see the tense stillness of the expectant crowds is broken—as we look a million quadrillion tiny bulbs of light on each great building flash forth, transforming the stately palaces into living, throbbing, animate beings. Again there is a stir and murmur. Halfway up Festival Hall the doors swing open and a torrent of water leaps madly down over the cascades between the rows of golden cupids. The rippling water dashes down flashing in the opalescent light . . . as the band plays "Meet me in St. Louis, Louis, meet me at the Fair / Don't tell me the lights are shining anywhere but there."

The description continues for several pages, ending melodramatically: "A lump comes into your throat and tears unbidden to your eyes as you say 'Farewell to St Louis, to the Exposition, the Fairyland which proved conclusively that realization is better than anticipation. Farewell! And may you be enjoyed by millions as thoroughly as you have been by me.' "[2]

Hallie acted in plays in high school and at Grinnell College, but it is surprising how quickly, in a time when women were not encouraged to take charge, she arrived at an understanding of her true gifts as a director and producer.

There is one striking photograph of Hallie in a Grinnell yearbook, playing the part of a captive princess in a production called *Nero*. She reclines at the edge of a throne chair, with her beautifully draped toga cascading downward and folding onto the ground. Her abundant auburn hair is piled high and wrapped in strips of white fabric; her gaze is veiled but seductive.[3]

But often, perhaps because she was small, Hallie was cast as a boy or in comic roles, and this may have contributed to her preference for work behind the scenes, making things happen. By her sophomore year at college, Hallie's unique gifts were coming to light. "Much credit is to be given to Miss Hallie Ferguson," read a note in the Grinnell *Scarlet and Black,* "who is responsible for the excellent stage arrangement, and also for the conversion of a farce into a bit of drama full of color, action, and real living people."[4]

Hallie was almost as busy with extracurricular activities as her friend Harry Hopkins, who entered Grinnell one year after she did. At one social event, according to the college paper, "every one entered into the fun of writing a poem about the person with whom she had last conversed."[5] This may have been the occasion on which Hallie received a poem made up by "the boys of the class who number six," written and signed by, among others, Harry Hopkins.[6]

Somehow, despite the family's shaky finances, the Fergusons had managed to purchase one of the gracious clapboard houses along Grinnell's loveliest street, Broad Street. There, just a block away from the college, Hallie and her parents hosted numerous social events during her college years. Hallie's younger sister remembered a dinner there that included stuffed tomatoes, one of which she dropped accidentally into Harry Hopkins's lap. The *Scarlet and Black* reported on several others. "Hallie Ferguson '11, and Helen Walker, '11, entertained a number of girls at an informal dancing party at the Ferguson home Wednesday night. The rooms were decorated in scarlet salvia, autumn leaves and red shaded lights carrying out the color scheme." Hallie, a hoarder of memorabilia, pasted the cutouts of autumn leaves in her scrapbook.[7,8]

Hallie also remembered vividly that Grinnell, despite professed idealism, shared in the general racism of the time. Grinnell's founder, Josiah Bushnell Grinnell, was a radical Congregationalist minister who was willing to overlook murder in service of the abolitionist cause. When John Brown came to his door in March 1859, having killed a slave owner and stolen away his slaves, Grinnell immediately offered refuge for Brown's party of sixteen and their horses. They slept, with their guns, on Grinnell's parlor floor and moved on only after Grinnell, who was also a wool shipper with connections, could arrange for the slaves to be transported by railcar to Canada.

But nearly fifty years later, when Hallie Ferguson attended the college, the single African American student on campus was looked upon as a problem in the pairing up for the freshman class party. The dean of women recommended that he go to the party either by himself or in a group. "Because he's a Negro," the chair of a student committee explained, "the only one in the College." There was silence at the meeting, according to Hallie, then everyone talked at once about what was to be done about the situation. Hallie wrote:

> I remember suddenly getting very angry and ashamed, though <u>why</u> I don't know—I don't remember that father or mother had ever mentioned race prejudice. Anyway, I said it was all silly and that I would like to go to the party with him. (Of course this may have been just showing off or dramatizing it, but I think the main thing was a revulsion of feeling against injustice.) The committee was horrified, the boys said my parents would object. One boy said "I would never go out with a girl who had gone out with a nigger." I said that no one could sit on our porch and call anyone that.

Hallie never had to make good on her pledge to go to the dance with the boy in question: Not surprisingly, he withdrew from the college not long after.[9]

Four years later, in 1911, Hallie Ferguson graduated from Grinnell College with a combined major in German and English literature. In the college yearbook, a word game used first initials of graduates to describe their salient characteristics. Hallie Mae Ferguson's initials were used to make the phrase *Has Many Friends*. Like most of the female graduates, Hallie planned to go to work at the one job available to women: teaching. She would take a job at the high school in nearby Sigourney, Iowa, for a year. Then, having waited a suitable interval, she would marry the handsome and devoted young man she had been going out with since her freshman year: Murray Flanagan.

Murray Flanagan was "fast, fierce and furious" on the football field, according to the *Scarlet and Black*. He was also a track star, a thespian who could play the villain or a gentleman of "polish and distinction,"[10] and a tenor who sang solos with the Grinnell Glee Club. More than either

Harry Hopkins or Hallie Ferguson, Murray was a committed Christian. In the diary he kept during his senior year, he wrote enthusiastically of his work with the evangelist Billy Sunday, who came to Iowa that year to convert souls. "Three thousand were won to Christ in public," he marveled. "For myself I gained . . . a desire to make my life count for the most in this battle we are here engaged in."

With equal fervor, Murray Flanagan wrote in his diary that year of his growing love for the freshman Hallie Ferguson. Escorting Hallie to a concert, he was "the proudest man in the whole school" because she was "the best-looking girl in the whole chapel . . . She had on a beautiful green gown (made especially to my taste) and her pink roses matched, or rather strove to match her pink cheeks."

By that time, Murray had already taken Hallie for a walk and declared his intentions, writing afterward in his diary, "If the stars should grow cold and dark tonight, and the sun never shine again, and death come upon me, I should never forget this night and what occurred is too sacred to be written, even in my diary. There is only one place wherein it may be chiseled, and it is engraven there, deeply."[11]

Perhaps Murray's reference to death in his diary was based on some sense that his own health was precarious. Boarding that year at the Ferguson household, Murray was comforted, during several bouts of illness, by the hot lemonade and loving care of Hallie's mother. Then that spring, a doctor told Murray he needed to lie down and rest for a month and let his "heart" recuperate and that he might have to give up his plan to go to work the following year for the Cedar Rapids YMCA. Murray, who came from a large, poor family, was devastated. "Good heavens—I can't do that," he wrote in his diary. "I owe too much and my mother needs me too badly."[12] Tuberculosis was never mentioned, although the illness was common enough to be the subject of guest lectures at the college. Still, the warning signs were there, even before he married Hallie in 1912. Later on, when he became very ill, a nurse wrote that he was "like a man who has been tired for years."

But Hallie's scrapbook of the couple's early married years in St. Louis, where Murray got a job in insurance through an uncle of Hallie's, is full of high hopes. Black-and-white photos, pasted on black paper and captioned in white ink, show "our dining room" and "our living room" and "our porch in the treetops." Sentimental poems about "home sweet home" where "the Heart can rest" are scattered throughout.

The gift Hallie and Murray had for laughter is on full display. On one page, entitled "Mixed Nuts," Murray appears in a skirt with a parasol over one shoulder. Another pose features Murray leaning back in a chair and staring out through the clouded glasses of a blind man. In his arms, he holds a small black-and-white terrier. Hallie stands at his side, adorned in a white eyelet lace dress and lampshade hat, with the same parasol over one shoulder and some kind of tall weed in her free hand. The picture is entitled "Wedding Portrait."[13]

As in most families, the photographs tell only the hopeful side of the story. Unseen are tensions in the marriage, apparently over Hallie's utter failure as a cook and housekeeper.[14] Unseen also are Murray's continued illnesses and the devastating news, delivered on the night Hallie returned from the hospital with their second child, that what Murray had been suffering with for some time was in fact tuberculosis. The treatment for TB, before streptomycin, was rest and fresh mountain air. The doctor told Hallie that Murray's best chance for recovery was to travel to a sanitarium in Colorado Springs.

"The next years," Hallie wrote later, "were a nightmare."[15] For a while, she lived at home in Grinnell with her two very young boys, sharing the space with the boarders her parents had taken in to make ends meet. It was best, the doctors assured her, for Murray to recuperate on his own. "Absolute quiescence," she wrote her friend Deborah Wiley, "seems to be part of the cure." Hallie was not yet thirty, and she agonized over every decision. "Sometimes the fear—the loneliness—the sense of responsibility is almost more than I can bear," she wrote her friend.

Leaving her children to be by her husband's side would have been wrenching. Her letters are full of her delight in the two young boys: Frederic, who came into the world in such trying circumstances, was gaining weight rapidly on her breast milk. "I am again rivaling Schumann-Heink [the buxom Wagnerian contralto]!" she wrote. "He smiles almost all the time he is awake. His hair is redder'n ever!! But his chin is a real chin now & I think he's going to be quite a Person." Jack, not yet four, was amazingly verbal and had developed a new interest in listening to music on the Victrola. "You should hear him ask for 'Golden Slipper' and Caruso—I Pagliacci."

At first, the doctors declared Murray's case "a hopeful one," without much lung involvement. But then he began to run high temperatures, and X-rays revealed a larger affected area. "I feel certain that it is going to be a long hard fight," Hallie wrote her friend, "and at times I feel that my duty is so divided between Murray and the children that I am almost desperate . . . We both feel that we must face the separation just as millions of husbands and wives are facing a necessary separation today [in World

War I]—and bring what fortitude we can to bear. I sometimes feel that fortitude is the greatest word in the world except love."[16]

As Murray's condition worsened, the doctor in Colorado wrote to tell Hallie that her husband's only chance of survival was to have her at his side. So she left the boys with their grandparents and moved to Colorado Springs. As usual, she found something "marvelous" in the experience: Murray managed to strike up friendships with the most interesting fellow patients at Glockner Sanitarium—an engineer, a rabbi, a Japanese scholar, a priest. "Conversations around his bed were both profound and gay."

But there was an undercurrent of deep worry, not just about Murray's health, but also about finances and the children. To meet her expenses, Hallie secretly rented a studio and began to teach drama classes. At night, she agonized over the decision to leave her two boys: "I simply couldn't bear to think of them—used to wake up crying." Hallie stayed with Murray at Glockner for a year, but neither her presence nor the society around his bedside was a match for the deadly disease. At the end of that year, Murray Flanagan died.

Many years later, when writing out her curriculum vitae, Hallie described herself as "housewife from marriage 1912 'til death of husband 1919." Had Murray lived, she might have continued to volunteer in amateur theatre—as she had done in St. Louis. His death meant that she had to make theatre her livelihood.

Returning to Grinnell, she used $1,000 from Murray's life insurance policy and built a sleeping porch on the Grinnell house so that she and the children could breathe healthy air and get away from the boarders. And she brought back a nurse from Colorado to care for the children so that she could go back to work.

Very soon, Hallie got work at the local high school teaching drama and discovered she loved it. The following year, she joined the Grinnell faculty as assistant to a new professor from England, who schooled her in voice, fencing, and dance. Hallie had decided by then that she wanted to write plays rather than perform in them.[17] That same year, she wrote *The Curtain*, a morality play with twists and turns of plot worthy of O. Henry or de Maupassant. The play revolves around the issue of facing a painful truth about a loved one—a challenge Hallie knew well from her own experience in dealing with Murray's illness. But in *The Curtain*, the truth concerns a crime committed by a father and denied by a daughter. The daughter in the play tells her father, "If the truth is going to hurt the people I love, I don't believe in telling it."[18] In the end, the father, a forger who has lied to his family about his crimes, convinces her not to fall into his devious ways but rather to tell the truth and turn him in.

Hallie Flanagan didn't think much of *The Curtain* for some reason. Nonetheless, it was published by Samuel French and continued to earn modest royalties for years. More important, it won her a $100 prize that would eventually open the door to George Pierce Baker's prestigious playwriting workshop at Harvard. Things were beginning, it seemed, to "get back into a pattern of happiness."

Then came a second blow, even more devastating than the first. Hallie's older son, Jack, by then a precocious seven-year-old, was brought home from Sunday school one day with spinal meningitis. He died a few days later.

"I remember his beautiful face and his small voice saying, 'A thing of beauty is a joy forever / Its loveliness increases / It will never pass into nothingness,' " she wrote years later. "Jack died. He did not pass into nothingness."

If ever fortitude was needed, it was after the death of her adored older son, Jack.[19] Hallie often broke down in tears after that, provoking Frederic at one point to say, "I should have died instead of Jack."[20] It must sometimes have seemed, after this second loss, as though marriage and motherhood brought nothing but pain. Fortunately, Hallie had another passion, for the theatre. And the theatre, unlike her personal life, seemed to love her back. In July 1923, the year after Jack's death, George Pierce Baker wrote to Hallie in his emphatic hand to inform her that she was admitted to his workshop for the coming year.

Surprisingly, given how torn she had been about leaving the children to go to Murray in Colorado earlier, Hallie seems to have had little hesitation about leaving six-year-old Frederic. Perhaps she simply wanted to leave behind everything associated with her losses. Or perhaps she preferred leaving to the painful experience of being left. Whatever the reason, the pattern of leaving her family was to be repeated often, as her career in theatre gained momentum. Hallie eagerly agreed to attend the Baker workshop, taking along a photograph of Frederic for her dresser in Cambridge but leaving the boy back in Grinnell with his grandparents.

English 47, a Harvard institution more famously known as the Baker workshop, was the first practical playwriting and theatre technique course ever taught in the United States. Since Baker began it in 1904, it had provided American theatre with an astonishing number of critics, playwrights, directors, and producers. Baker's workshop, in the words of playwright, director, and producer George Abbott, "seemed like the open sesame." Eugene O'Neill had attended the workshop, as had playwright S. N. Behrman. The critics Brooks Atkinson, John Mason Brown, Robert Benchley, and Heywood Broun had all tried their hand at writing plays under Baker, before retreating into criticism. There had been many fewer women than men at the workshop. But Theresa Helburn, who became the director of the Theatre Guild, and Dorothy Heyward, coauthor of *Porgy*, were both graduates.[21]

And now there was Hallie Flanagan, encountering for the first time the relative sophistication of the theatre world outside the Midwest. Her journals are filled with her lively reactions to all of it. She loved "the hospitable home of George Pierce Baker, a lived-in looking place, always open to the many who come to Harvard because of the famous 47 Workshop. The large cool living room with a lovely design of green flowering trees on gray walls is Mrs. Baker's reception room, and across the hall a large study literally book-lined from floor to ceiling . . . And heaped high on the massive table which runs down the center of the room . . . Mss. Mss. everywhere. This surely the wonder of the man—that knowing drama as intimately and loving it as well as does Professor Baker, he can still have faith to believe that in the great piles of Mss. he may now and then find one worth entering among the immortals . . . That he also knows that where many are called few are chosen is witnessed by the huge wastebaskets which are amusingly conspicuous."[22]

Hallie studied and wrote extensively during her year at the Baker workshop, but her most visible role was backstage, as an assistant to the producer. This involved such mundane tasks as rolling a large drum across Harvard Square in the rain and in general overseeing everything involved in mounting original plays at Harvard's Agassiz Theatre. At the end of the year, Baker wrote of her that "she has charm poise and tact, and though she had some difficult duties in connection with my 47 Workshop, she closed the year with everybody very friendly."[23]

The influence of the Baker year was apparent in everything Hallie did after she returned to Grinnell. The striking block-printed letterhead of the newly christened "Grinnell Experimental Theatre" echoed Baker's for the 47 Workshop. Inspired no doubt by a production of *Romeo and Juliet* that had moved her in the East, Hallie mounted her own version with the Grinnell Dramatic Club. "Difficult for an amateur production?" she asked rhetorically in her program notes. "Yes, gloriously difficult, for upon the stage the tale must be told swiftly, humanly; it must glow with the ardors of Shakespeare's poetic speech."

Romeo and Juliet is a play of youth; hot blooded riot in the streets with every man quick to give or avenge an insult . . . love scenes in the garden and the chamber where the verse flows like the wine of amorous rapture.[24]

Hallie's clear vision resulted in a *Romeo and Juliet* that the Grinnell year-book described as "the most distinguished contribution of the Dramatic Club in recent years."[25] The opening night audience was less restrained. According to some who were present that night, the audience for *Romeo and Juliet* was stunned when the play ended. When the curtain came down, there was no applause. "I got off the bier," remembers Winifred Parker, who played Juliet, "and walked to the wings in dead silence. Mrs. Flanagan and I stood looking at each other with eyes wide with amazement. Finally the applause burst, tremendous and prolonged."

Privately, Hallie viewed her production of *Romeo and Juliet* as a combination of "all I had learned at Harvard" and "my remembrance of Murray." One line, spoken by Juliet, had special meaning for her: "Alack, alack, that Heav'n should practice stratagems / Upon so soft a subject as myself!"[26]

There is perhaps some poetic justice in the fact that Hallie Flanagan's production, linked in her mind with the cruel losses she had experienced, should be the vehicle for a piece of extraordinarily good luck: One of those in the audience on opening night was Frederick P. Keppel, president of the Carnegie Corporation. Keppel was enchanted by the production and eager to support Hallie Flanagan's work. When she told him she wanted to follow the advice of her mentor, George Pierce Baker, and spend a year abroad studying the theatre, Keppel offered to recommend her to the Guggenheim Foundation. Before 1926, no woman had received a Guggenheim fellowship. That year, four women were chosen. Hallie Flanagan was one of them.[27]

Hallie set off for Europe in the fall of 1926, determined to acquire "first-hand knowledge of the theatres of the world." Once again, she left Frederic behind, although this time reluctantly. She enrolled him in a Swiss school, but the nine-year-old Frederic and her parents convinced her that he was better off staying at his boarding school. As she crossed the Atlantic, she wondered in her journal if it was worth it to leave him for an entire year.

But once she arrived in Europe, Hallie's zeal for her assignment astounded even the director of the Guggenheim Foundation, Henry Moe, who was one of the recipients of her lively reports. "How you have met everybody!" exclaimed Moe.[28] And it was true: She not only met everyone, but seemed to take in every play available in every country. She kept programs, signed by actors and directors, as well as several parallel diaries, personal and professional, full of detailed descriptions of her reading, the people she met, the places she went, and the plays she saw. "I [came] to Europe to imbibe dramatic art and imbibe it I must," she wrote in one of her diaries.[29] When she returned home, she used her notes as the basis for numerous articles and a well-received book, *Shifting Scenes of the Modern European Theatre*.

Sometimes she was disappointed. In London, she put a large dent in her budget by going to the theatre almost every night for two months and came away feeling that English theatre was "a dead thing, totally disassociated from life." She did manage, however, to have tea with John Galsworthy, who was continuing to publish a long series of novels skewering the British upper classes, called cumulatively *The Forsyte Saga*. She called her meeting with Galsworthy "the most thrilling event so far." Like so many of her encounters, this one would pay dividends later on.

Far more exciting than the English sojourn was her journey to Ireland, where Lady Gregory, "the creative power behind the modern Celtic revival," received her at Coole Park and talked of the founding of the Abbey Theatre and of its promising young playwrights, Sean O'Casey and John Millington Synge. She also met AE [George William Russell], William Butler Yeats, and T. S. Eliot, who would later allow her to premiere his work in America.

On the continent, she made the necessary pilgrimages, observing the plays of Henrik Ibsen, performed by the National Theatre of Oslo, and the legacy of August Strindberg in Stockholm. In Italy, a meeting with Luigi Pirandello resulted in a later premiere of one of his plays at Vassar. In Paris, she was made uncomfortable by the French preoccupation with the bedroom. "Don't you tire of the interminable theme?" she asked a French playwright.

" 'That is your American "morality" objecting,' he replied . . . 'It is amusing, this extreme sensitiveness of Americans to the sight of a bed.' "

The Frenchman was right about Hallie's puritanical streak. She was no stranger to the passionate affair and seems to have had male companions, if not lovers, everywhere she went that year. Yet she drew the line at literature that went into detail. "Everybody here talks about Joyce & Ulysses," she wrote in her diary in Paris. "Someone said he was reading the early works of Joyce 'in order to get into the reverential spirit necessary to a reading of Ulysses.' What bunk, what perfect rot. Why enter deliberately to wallow in a sewer, preparing said entrance by a pious petition to be granted grace to understand the smells?"

The contradiction between Hallie's personal code of conduct and her moral strictures was one of several. Another inconsistency was pointed out by a friend when she was enjoying the luxury of a few days on the French Riviera: "You with your love of luxury, your rapture over beauty—your quivering toward scents, sounds, fabrics and your mental acceptance of Russia—new Russia. You're so damned contradictory."

It was true. Without doubt, the high point of Hallie's year abroad was her three-month sojourn in the new Russia, a place of cold and hardship and, in her view, the most exciting and innovative theatre she had ever seen. She was awed by the dedication of Constantin Stanislavski, who continued the work of the Moscow Art Theatre in producing the great classics and who told her, "We are too close to the Revolution to produce art reflecting it." But her greatest excitement was reserved for the new workers' theatres, which were bringing drama to the masses for the first time. She was especially impressed with the work of Vsevolod Meyerhold, who was deeply schooled in the traditions of European theatre, including Stanislavski and commedia dell'arte, but who was at the same time an avowed revolutionary whose goal was to "train a vast audience, unaccustomed to theatre going, in the principles of communism . . . Believing with religious fervor in the theatre as a place where author, actor and spectator are magically fused," she wrote, "he has the power of imbuing others with this belief." After a day of watching Meyerhold directing Nikolai Gogol's *Inspector General*, Hallie concluded that he was "the greatest director I have ever seen."

"Russia, Russia," she wrote in her diary, "here is Russia in all its contradictions and fascinations. If we in America do not recognize Russia, do not understand her, it is <u>our loss</u>." When the anniversary of the October revolution was celebrated on Red Square, Hallie wrote an ecstatic description of "the horsed regiments from all Russia," the children, "little Lenins" waving red flags, and the workers from farm and factory. The account is written with the same feverish excitement as her diary entries at fifteen, describing the World's Fair in St. Louis.[30]

Undoubtedly, Hallie Flanagan's first trip to Russia was colored by an intense affair she had with a remarkable American scientist. Horsley Gantt, who was in Russia working with Ivan Pavlov, was "without exception the most striking looking man I have ever seen—tall, slender—black wavy hair, wonderfully brilliant dark eyes . . . The mouth is . . . beautifully sensuous, full lips with a short upper lip—perfect teeth . . . clothes casual but well-tailored and interesting—a leather coat which is for him the perfect garment."

Horsley Gantt and Hallie took to each other at their very first meeting, and she wound up postponing her departure from Leningrad for two weeks because of him. "Of course I pretend it is because of drama," she wrote. "My life is a tapestry of people and in the tapestry the dark clear thread of him begins."

On her final day in frozen and snowy Leningrad, she and Gantt traveled by sled for miles "across the Neva and out over the steppes." She added, "I am leaving just about in time."

The ecstasy of her final hours in Russia was followed by days of deep despair. Traveling third class across the border, she was stopped by suspicious border guards, who confiscated her diaries and letters of credit. While she was dealing with them in their offices, many of her personal belongings were stolen by fellow passengers on the train. Then, when she arrived in Berlin, she learned that her father was seriously ill. A wire from her mother told her not to come home: Her father didn't want her to change her plans and lose the rest of her precious year abroad. "I am so horribly lonely and depressed that I feel I can't <u>live</u>," she wrote in her diary. "I want to go home. Would it be cowardly? I am worried about Mother and Freder [Frederic, now ten]." Two days later, she received word that her father had died on December 11. "And I never knew. O God." Hallie stayed on but wrote more often of homesickness and concern about her relationship with her son. "He's the only really important thing I have," she wrote. "Am I going to lose him in this year?"[31]

It says a great deal about Hallie's coping mechanisms that she wrote, in the midst of this torment, a hilarious nine-page account of her "Russian frontier episode" for Guggenheim director Henry Moe. "I knew as soon as I saw the head official," she wrote Moe, "that the game was up because he was one of those terrible <u>stone wall</u> looking persons on whose surface nothing can make a dent . . . You can't imagine how furious and helpless I felt in that frontier hut, with the torchlight on all those uncomprehending, hostile faces." And later, "The journey from Riga to Berlin by third class . . . is described by Dante in his jolly little opus <u>Inferno</u>. One goes through what is called the Polish corridor, so designated because it is extremely draughty and also because doors open in Estonia, Lithuania, Poland . . . and at every door officials come in and examine tickets, passports, baggage, until, like the White Queen in <u>Alice in Wonderland</u>, one contemplates suicide from so much pinning and unpinning . . . I arrived in Berlin on Christmas eve in anything but the usual Yuletide spirit."

The letter, written on December 27, makes no mention of the fact that Hallie had received the news of her father's grave illness two days before.[32]

By far the most influential professional relationship Hallie formed during the Guggenheim year was with Gordon Craig, a man who, in her words, was "more responsible than any other person . . . for releasing the stage from the meaningless clutter of the nineteenth century tradition." Craig, son of the great actress Ellen Terry, was the author of *On the Art of the Theatre*, editor of an influential magazine, *The Mask*, and founder of the Gordon Craig School for the Art of the Theatre in Florence, Italy. He was also a groundbreaking set designer.

Hallie first encountered Craig in Copenhagen, where he was producing Ibsen's little-known play *The Pretenders* for the Danish National Theatre. "Being with him for those few days and evenings in Copenhagen," she wrote, was "one of the rarest gifts of my life."[33]

Afterward, she sent him a draft of an article she was working on about him. That was the beginning of a harsh but important education. Craig proceeded to strip her overdecorated prose as he had stripped the Victorian stage. He objected to her ecstatic writing about him, in which she gave him a cape and a twirling cane. "I am not a twirler of canes," he insisted, adding that "it suggests an air I do not possess."

"Don't you see this is what is called *silly*?" he commented on another florid passage. "For your own sake you must not go on writing like this." He suggested a visit to the works of Schopenhauer or Emerson for purification of her writing style.[34]

When Hallie responded that she was "broken to pieces," Craig wrote back playfully, "How can you put a nice hat on pieces?"[35]

Gordon Craig was often insensitive: Once he insulted her by describing her as a "globetrotter," and another time he told her she should be grateful that "you are not an artist," just as he was grateful not to be a woman.[36] But Craig was right about many things, including her penchant for intemperate and uncritical enthusiasms.

On a later visit to Europe, in 1934, Hallie spent a memorable morning with Craig at his villa in Genoa, going over her scrapbook of photographs from her theatre productions at Vassar. Craig had definite opinions about everything. Measuring scale with his thumb, he pronounced one set "beautiful," another "not very nice to look at." He praised actors as strong and sincere in one picture. "These people aren't showing off," he said of one group of actors. Another group he dismissed as all wrong because they were "showing off."

After a while, Craig closed the book and shut his eyes. "Some of these are bad, some are good," he told Hallie Flanagan, "none are indifferent, a few are inspired. Now you have got to decide whether you are going to go on or whether you are going to go churning round and round. You have proved that the theatre is your medium and you can do anything you want with it. Now you must stop experimenting and trying this style and that style. Do the thing you want to do and give reasons to nobody."[37]

★ ★ ★

The Works Progress Administration was the direct result of the Roosevelt leadership's dramatic victory in the midterm congressional elections of 1934. Die-hard Republican opponents in the Senate went down to defeat in that election, and Democrats gained nine more seats in the house, bringing their numbers to 322. A few days later, Harry Hopkins took a rare day off to drive, with several of his subordinates, to the racetrack in Maryland. On the way, he told them, "Boys—this is our hour. We've got to get everything we want—a works program, social security, wages and hours, everything—now or never. Get your minds to work on developing a complete ticket to provide security for all the folks of this country up and down and across the board."[38]

Afterward, Hopkins and his group went to work on a proposal for FDR. And just before Thanksgiving, Harry traveled south to Warm Springs and presented the president with a comprehensive package. Delbert Clark of the *New York Times* reported that "the fire-eating Administrator of Federal Emergency Relief, Harry L. Hopkins, may safely be credited with spoiling the Thanksgiving Day dinners of many conservatives who had been led to believe that President Roosevelt's recent zig to the right would not be followed by a zag to the left."

Hopkins urged FDR to replace FERA with a much larger $4 billion program to put people back to work on useful projects. The WPA would allocate money according to need, would spend promptly, and would privilege wages over large capital costs. The Public Works Administration (PWA) would hire workers to build large bridges and tunnels and dams. The WPA would work on smaller projects and be nimbler, able to start hiring more quickly and to spread the wealth more broadly.

Roosevelt took up Hopkins's proposal and appointed him to head the WPA. Hopkins's personal rival, Secretary of the Interior Harold Ickes, continued as head of the PWA, and the two of them competed for projects. Ickes seethed when Hopkins's WPA got grants for larger projects, like LaGuardia Airport, which he considered his purview. But both programs, WPA and PWA, left a permanent imprint on the American landscape. There are still some sidewalks in America that bear the WPA legend and thousands of dams, bridges, roads, sewers, school buildings, and post offices that were built under the WPA and PWA. But in 1934, what mattered most were the hundreds of thousands of jobs the programs provided to hungry and desperate Americans.

Only a tiny piece of the WPA budget was devoted to the four arts projects—the writers project, visual artists project, music project, and theatre project—grouped under the rubric of Federal One. Despite its relatively small size, Federal One attracted a huge amount of attention. It was a natural target for critics of the New Deal, who saw it as a frill. And artists, who were both needy and vocal, immediately descended on Washington with petitions of every imaginable variety.

All kinds of theatre people paid a visit to Harry Hopkins's spartan office in the Walker-Johnson building. Playwright Elmer Rice came down from New York to ask for $100,000 for the Theatre Alliance. Hopkins's response was, "Oh God, Katharine Cornell has been here, and Frank Gilmore [Actors' Equity] and Edith Isaacs [editor of *Theatre Arts* magazine] and Eva Le Gallienne and they are driving me crazy! Isn't there anyone out there who can rise above their own little project?" Rice knew Hallie Flanagan from a national theatre conference and suggested she might be the one. Apparently, that was the second opinion on his old friend Hallie that Hopkins had been looking for.[39] In February 1934, he called her up.

Harry was his usual informal self on the phone. He was calling from New York, he explained, and wanted Hallie to come in from Poughkeepsie and meet with him about the unemployment situation. "We've got a lot of actors on our hands," he said. "Suppose you come in to New York and talk it over."

Hallie told him she couldn't: She was about to take off for Italy and then circle back to England, where she was planning to spend her sabbatical year directing theatre at a place called Dartington Hall, an idyllic English estate that enlightened aristocrats had turned into a model farm with an arts education program.

Harry told her he didn't see the point. What would an American want to do in English theatre? "Harry Hopkins," she noted, "has a way of saying abrupt things which irritate you at the time and recur to you later."[40]

What Harry didn't know was that Dartington Hall was a pretext for getting out of Poughkeepsie. Hallie was trying to distance herself from the overtures of a Vassar classics professor named Philip Davis. Hallie Flanagan, along with her son, Frederic, had been on their own for twelve years, and she wanted to keep it that way. Or so she believed as she set off for Europe early in 1934. Her first marriage had ended in great loss and pain; her

recovery, in large measure, had come through her work as a theatre director at Vassar. Why should she make any changes?

But as she traveled to Europe aboard the HMS *Escania,* Hallie was in a
state of confusion. What exactly did Harry Hopkins have in mind, and
would it require her to give up her plans for an idyllic sojourn at Dartington Hall, not to mention her rewarding position at Vassar? More important, what should she do about Phil Davis, who was refusing to give up and
go away? Did she dare to risk all and marry again—and become step-
mother to his three children, adding to her responsibility for her own
teenage son, Frederic? "My life," she wrote home from Naples to her
friend Esther Porter, "is a stormy sea at present, very much at variance with
the calm bay of Naples."

Hallie's relationship with Phil Davis began because of a request from
Vassar's president, Henry MacCracken. As Hallie tells it, the president
called her into his office one day and said, "Hallie I want you to do something for me. Put Philip Davis in your play—get him out of this black-
ness." Davis had lost his wife during the birth of the couple's third child
and was in a deep depression. Hallie, who had lost her first husband to tuberculosis fifteen years earlier and her young son not long after that, remembered the feeling "only too well." She gave Davis the part of MAN in
Ernst Toller's *Masse Mensch.* "His face (like something on a Greek coin)
and his voice used to haunt me," Hallie remembered later, "in the scene in
which he faces the whirling planets and says 'Life, life.' "[41]

Philip Davis was slender and handsome, a foot taller and a few years
younger than Hallie. He had a reputation among students as a quiet,
thoughtful listener, "always ready to receive your ideas and never imposing
his own." One student remembered him "reading aloud Greek poetry in
his soft sensitive voice, and making the Ancients live for you."

"You became very honest when talking to Phil Davis," a friend re-
marked, "because everything you said he believed."[42]

In 1930, while Hallie was spending the summer in Europe, Phil Davis
began writing her letters. "I don't believe anyone ever received such letters," she wrote later. "Philosophy, music, art, life and love. In Greek, in
Latin, in French, in drawings. They were an undercurrent of the summer,
but at that time they were not love letters. I attributed them to loneliness."
The "strange courtship" through letters continued, even after she returned
to Vassar, until she decided to "break it all off" in early 1934 before de-
parting for Europe once again, this time with the intention of spending her
sabbatical at Dartington Hall.

"Philip found me in Naples," she recalled. She told him again she wouldn't marry him but agreed on a month in Sicily, which would cure them both. "We went to Sicily and had a divine month. It did not effect a cure."

In the middle of one night in Sicily, she got up and left by herself "in the most melodramatic way" for Tripoli, in northern Africa, without leaving an address. "I had the most wretched time of my life, but I still thought I had made the right decision." When she returned two weeks later to Syracuse to pick up her luggage, Phil Davis was waiting on the dock. He had met every ship since she left. "He had been drinking a lot and looked terrible," she remembered. "When I saw him I knew I was 'like the base Indian who threw a pearl away, greater than all his tribe.' "[43] Hallie gave up her plans to spend the year at Dartington Hall. She and Phil married that April of 1934, in Athens.

In her public version of the story, Hallie's ambivalence ended with the marriage. But in her journals, her profound doubts at what she had done lingered on, even after they repaired to the deserted island of Delos for the honeymoon. Despite her admiration for Davis's "subtle, witty and profound" mind and spirit, Hallie was terrified of a commitment that would require her to subordinate her career to her husband's and to her responsibilities as a wife and mother to three young children, in addition to her adolescent son, Fred.[44]

Delos itself was "strange and beautiful," as she wrote to her theatre group back in Poughkeepsie. "We are the only people on the island, except the Greek family looking after us." It is "the island of Apollo with the terrace of lions, very white in the moonlight, with fields of scarlet poppies, and purple and yellow flowers growing up in the courtyards of the marble palaces where a whole civilization once lived and worked and offered sacrifices to the gods."[45]

Privately, her feelings about Delos fluctuated wildly. "Every day is a cycle with me, emotionally—the dawn, about four, is terrifying. I feel that this place and this marriage are driving me mad. Why did I do it? I have lost my life, my measured, ordered life for which I've fought for ten years. I've lost in a way my identity. I'm no longer Hallie, but Philip's wife. He must increase and I must decrease." Phil went off for hours during the day, collecting and deciphering Greek tablets. "His work, strange and incomprehensible, I can never really grasp. I believe it is wonderful . . . adding to the sum total of human knowledge. But it is of the past—and I am chiefly concerned with the present and the future. Here is this language which I can never learn . . . I have put myself in a position where, with Phil's friends and work, I must always be an outsider. All these things rush through my mind, together with a sense of absolute terror at the new way of life and whether I will be equal to it."[46]

Perhaps her isolation on Delos heightened her terror. In any case, back in Poughkeepsie, after a whirlwind of travel in Europe with her new husband and son Fred, who joined them, Hallie's panic subsided. Phil's children returned from their grandmother's house, accompanied by a nurse they knew well. Her adolescent son, Frederic, got along famously with her new husband. And she and Phil found a big old house in town, which Hallie arranged according to her needs. The largest bedroom, with adjoining bath, was hers. Phil's was the second largest. Since Hallie freely admitted that she could not cook even an egg, cooking was taken over by a cook/housekeeper.[47]

At the college, Hallie continued to ignite her students with her passion for the theatre and to mount demanding, spectacular productions. That fall, the Vassar Experimental Theatre staged Shakespeare's *Antony and Cleopatra*. The opening, in Hallie's version, revisited the themes of passion and dominance that had preoccupied her on Delos. According to Hallie's stage directions:

> Antony, laughing, leaps into view at the top of the ramp, looking back at Cleopatra, who appears in silhouette against space, a vivid, imperious figure, a whip in her hand. To the accompaniment of shouts and laughter from the crowd she lashes him down the ramp. Antony, still laughing, takes the whip, breaks it across his knee and flings it aside . . . The wrestling match starts. Cleopatra watches, Antony looks only at her. She becomes excited. Antony is jealous and sharply orders the wrestlers to stop. The crowd is hushed . . . Cleopatra, furious, whirls on Antony. He laughs, catches her up in his arms and kisses her. From this embrace she gives her first line, "If it be love indeed, tell me how much."

The passionate staging of the opening encounter between the two lovers caused one professor in the audience to walk out, complaining that she felt as if she were "in a brothel." But a Shakespeare scholar at Princeton, Thomas Parrot, wrote to say that the production was "the most lucid, most brilliant exposition of Shakespeare's play that I have encountered. It explained certain obscure passages in a way which gave me a shock of pleasure." Parrot was especially struck by Hallie's use of "the element of heat, of the tropical climate, and its effect on the soldiers. This was something that had never struck me. Now, on rereading I see that you have indis-putable evidence."[48]

Hallie Flanagan was discovering that her recent experience—the flight to North Africa, the sun-baked days on Delos, and above all the give and take of a new relationship—enlarged her work rather than diminishing it. "All this was so rich, full and complete," Hallie wrote later, "that I felt that I could live just this way for the rest of my life."[49]

Then in May 1935, when Hallie's marriage was only a year old, a sec-ond phone call came from Harry Hopkins's office. Hopkins's assistant Ja-cob Baker was on the line. "Mr. Hopkins wants you to come to Washington," he told her, "to talk about the unemployed actors."

Answering Harry's summons, Hallie Flanagan traveled to Washington, entered the great unadorned Walker-Johnson building, and took the rick-ety elevator to Harry Hopkins's tenth-floor office, with its whitewashed walls and exposed pipes. "All the lines of the room," she wrote later, "fo-cused on the clean-swept desk, and on the man behind the desk, whose head and shoulders stood out sharply against the city gleaming from the uncurtained windows back of him. His lean, brown face flashed into a sud-den somewhat satiric smile. 'This is a tough job we're asking you to do.'"

They talked about government-sponsored theatre in Europe, about whether actors on relief would have the ability to do good work, and whether the plays they did could attract audiences. "People ride over roads and bridges built by relief workers," Hopkins said, "but will they ever come to a theatre to see shows put on by relief workers?"

It was clear from the interview that Harry Hopkins had already decided he wanted Hallie for the job. "I'd like to have you stay down a few days," he told her, "go over the whole thing, and then tell me what you think. And then talk it over with Mrs. Roosevelt. She's interested in all these arts projects."

As it happened, there was a party going on that afternoon on the White House lawn, and Harry suggested that Hallie go over and meet the first lady. "Mrs. Roosevelt and a number of Cabinet wives were receiving," Hallie later recalled, "and hundreds of women were strolling about the grounds to the music of a military band." After the crowd had left, Hallie was escorted down a hallway and into an elevator that took her to Eleanor Roosevelt's apartment.

Eleanor Roosevelt asked in particular about costs. Would it be possible to mount attractive productions on a low budget, so that the federal money allotted to the project would go to hiring people? Hallie, a Craig protégée whose productions emphasized ramps and lighting over elaborate scenery and costumes, assured her that it would. As she rose to leave, Mrs. Roosevelt promised to write Vassar president MacCracken and ask him to grant Mrs. Flanagan a leave of absence, so that she could direct the Federal Theatre Project.[50]

But President MacCracken's permission wasn't the problem. Hallie was a new wife, with three young stepchildren and a house to manage. The director's job would keep her in Washington and New York for extended periods and require long trips by train to oversee theatres and productions all across the country. How could she possibly take on this consuming assignment? Yet if she didn't, the fears that had tormented her on Delos would turn out to be real. The marriage would have denied her the greatest opportunity of her life.

When she came back from Washington, Hallie announced to her new husband, "I am not going to do it. You, Fred, the children all need me. And I need all of you—and nothing is as important as that." But as she and Phil were sitting together in the garden that night, he turned to her and said, "You know, darling, don't you? That you will have to do that job. All the forces of your life have led to it."[51]

chapter four

GREAT PLANS FOR MILLIONS

"The congestion in our office," Hallie Flanagan wrote Phil during her first week as director of the Federal Theatre Project, "is equaled by the 6 pm subway crush in Jersey City. But under it all—a surging, thrilling sensation of things starting. Oh, darling—I hope I can do it."[1]

It was summertime in the nation's capital. Hallie was shuttling back and forth between a hot, seedy room at the Hotel Powhatan and a sweltering, gray cell in the Auditorium Building, which, as she wrote Phil, "now houses a small city of several thousand people. Electric fans keep the dead air in motion and we work in a blaze of overhead electric light. Under these conditions Great Plans for Millions are supposed to be made."[2]

Hallie wrote letters home to Phil daily, sometimes even twice a day. From the day of her swearing-in on August 27, 1935, a day that happened to be her forty-sixth birthday, the Federal Theatre Project took up nearly every moment of her days and most of her nights. But she always insisted, reversing the usual cliché, that she could not do it without Phil. Part of this was no doubt her way of flattering and appeasing him: Phil was unhappy about her absence and at times urged her to quit. But in a lonely job, Phil, the good listener, helped her to carry on.

She told him everything about the Federal Theatre, even sent him documents. In part, this was an extension of her own life's habit of keeping a record, of making sense of things by writing and writing and writing. Now, instead of keeping the multiple journals of earlier days, she wrote to Phil. And Phil, for his part, claimed to have a new measure of other people: "If they understand and believe in Federal Theatre, they are good people. If not, they shall be cast into outer darkness."[3]

Eleanor Roosevelt on horseback, 1934 (Franklin D. Roosevelt Presidential Library)

Important ideas often grew out of her weekends, many of which were spent with Phil in Poughkeepsie: "You have been in every second of this day," she wrote him in October, "this exciting day in which plans made in your garden began to take form."[4] Phil, with his love of the ancient Greeks, provided an antidote to her obsession with the here and now. When he wrote her of stargazing in Vermont, she wrote back that "what I need is to go more out on a hill and watch Mars and Jupiter nearing conjunction. Then I might have more perspective on Washington, and on the Federal Theatre."[5] And when she felt especially alone, she wrote Phil that "I try to remember that you think I can do this job."[6]

Some things about Hallie's new job were easier than others. She quickly succeeded in recruiting influential regional theatres to the cause: Directors of the Pasadena Playhouse in California, the North Carolina Playmakers, and the Cleveland Community Playhouse were excited about the possibility of receiving government grants that would allow them to hire actors from relief rolls, along with a limited number (10 percent) of nonrelief workers to oversee productions. Private support for regional theatre was very hard to come by in 1935, and the promise of federal money was new and thrilling.

But the big cities were different. There, the theatrical unions held sway. It took the cooperation of at least twelve unions, for instance, to mount a play on a New York stage. What's more, Harry Hopkins had insisted from the start that "we're for labor, first, last, and all the time . . . We're going to co-operate with all these unions though we can't run a closed shop."[7] The problem was that the WPA wasn't going to be paying anything close to union wages. On the other hand, the WPA would provide jobs to the thousands of union members who were out of work: There were nearly two thousand unemployed stagehands in New York alone. Hallie hoped to persuade the leadership to allow its members to work for less. The president of the stagehands union seemed amenable. "I got my education out of the gutter," he told her at their first meeting, "but I can appreciate the best and we can get down to brass tacks on this proposition."[8]

Three weeks into the project, she met in Washington with a delegation from fifteen trade unions, "hard-faced, successful looking men in business suits, derbys and diamonds," she reported to Phil. "They chew their cigars and ask intelligent and hard boiled questions and altogether are a very good lot."

Hallie went to work: "I never talked so hard and fast as for the first half hour trying to sell them (that really is what it is) the idea that if men accepted these wages lower than union rates, we would try to put them in enterprises that might eventually get them off relief rolls to stay."[9] Hallie seems to have had a knack for working with union men. "My one qualification for this job," she wrote Phil, "is that I like stage hands and stage hands like me."[10] The meeting went on for four hours and ended with the leaders agreeing, at least, to take the first steps toward cooperation. "We parted in the best of spirits," Hallie reported.[11]

Actors' Equity was more resistant. Despite the fact that many of its members were out of work and desperate, the stage actors union wanted nothing to do with recruitment. There was a fear of the taint of amateurish productions with second-rate "relief" actors. The great Eva Le Gallienne told an audience of New Yorkers that she was "terrified by the large sums of money being given by the government to assist dramatic work." Le Gallienne insisted that it was "a vast mistake to feed the people of the nation upon very malnutritious and downright bad food when they can get the best food."[12] The food metaphor seemed particularly inappropriate at a time when many of Le Gallienne's fellow actors were going hungry.

Many New York theatre owners responded to Hallie's overtures with a variation on this refrain that she found especially maddening. At a League of New York Theatres meeting, Hallie heard them argue that the Federal Theatre Project would undercut their business because it would be selling tickets for next to nothing—around fifty cents. At the same time, they argued that the project was going to bring down the quality of theatre in New York. As Hallie pointed out, these two arguments canceled each other out: If Federal Theatre was "doomed to be poor, inept, boring, destructive of all real theatre development" because it employed the "old hacks and trots of the stage world,"[13] why should owners worry about it as a competitor? Even though she agreed to keep Federal Theatre productions on the fringes of the Broadway theatre district, and even though the productions promised to bring new life to theatres that had been dark for years, most New York producers withheld support.

Fortunately, the powerful Lee Shubert saw an advantage to the Federal Theatre Project's arrival on the scene. Shubert had been through some hard times himself. Forced into bankruptcy in 1931, he was surging back by 1935 and assuring Hallie that he was all-powerful. "Lee Shubert can buy and sell anybody in the theatre world," he boasted. At the same time, he was realistic about Hollywood's new power. "We used to be the dog wagging that tail," he told her, "now it's the dog and we're the tail."[14] Shubert believed that "if people who can't pay for our theatres go to Federal Theatres, then they'll want more, and they'll come and buy our cheap seats."[15]

"He pretends to no altruistic idea in this plan," Hallie wrote Phil, "which is the only reason I believe in it."[16]

The biggest obstacle, in the beginning, came not from the outside, but from the federal bureaucracy itself. The overarching goal, of course, was to provide a living wage for the approximately thirteen thousand unemployed theatre workers in the country. The wage itself was very low, even by 1930s standards, beginning at $22.85 a week and going as high as $103 a week for seasoned professionals in New York. But prying those dollars from the federal bureaucracy was turning out, in the early weeks of the Federal Theatre Project, to be the hardest task of all.

The first crisis came when Hallie tried to transfer theatre people who were already on the federal payroll under the previous relief program, FERA. Most of these actors were performing in variety and vaudeville shows, in the camps of the Civilian Conservation Corps (CCC) and in churches and schools around the country. These were people like Violet Dale, who had been acting since childhood but had fallen on hard times when the Depression hit. There followed "many months of great privation," as she later wrote, "of accepting private charity and the help of friends who themselves could ill afford to give." Then one day Violet walked—because she couldn't afford to ride—to midtown Manhattan to interview with a federal official for an acting job. Some weeks later, she got invited to join a tour leaving to perform at a remote CCC camp in the Pennsylvania mountains. "No offer for a Broadway production ever made my heart jump quite so hard."[17]

Now Violet Dale and others like her were in danger of losing their jobs because of bureaucratic delays in transferring them from FERA to the WPA rolls. "Thirty-seven telegrams," Hallie reported to Phil, "all of an immediate nature, from states or cities, saying that unless I took action at once, people on rolls would be in the streets, since their projects end." At first, she responded with instructions to keep people on the rolls for the time being. But her superiors overruled her. Hopkins's assistant Jacob Baker and his number two, Bruce McClure, told her she could do nothing "until their damned procedure slips are drawn up." McClure was now answering all queries and saying, "God knows what. I suppose 'Go to hell until our pimplifaced statisticians get their commas right.' "[18]

Hallie maintained an upbeat attitude in public. "Didn't Nietzsche observe," she asked at an early press conference, "that birth always involved chaos?"[19] What's more, it was probably a good thing for artists to bump up against hard realities. "Of course, we are all baffled by the red tape . . . Being unaccustomed to such involved proceedings, most of us resign either audibly or inaudibly several times a week, as we try to thread our way through the intricacies of man-year cost, requisitions, and regulations of the Procurement Bureau. But actually I think it a rather good thing for us, as playwrights, actors, directors, producers, to leave for the time being the problem of triangular relationships in rectangular settings . . . and to find out something about government; to consider such problems as taxation and how to spend taxpayers' money—our money—so that taxpayers— ourselves—will get the best possible return on it." After all, she pointed out, "the Federal Theatre is a functional theatre springing not from an art theory but from an economic fact. I think we all want to find out whether this limitation is a liability or an asset."[20]

But in private, Hallie was, as she confided to Phil, "trying very hard to keep from exploding with rage at the damnable stupidity of the damnable Mr. So and So's." The so and so who gave her the most trouble was Jake Baker, an inventive engineer who had been working with Hopkins almost since the inception of the New Deal. Baker shared Hopkins's ideals. But even though, according to one newspaper account, he had "once lived in Greenwich Village" and "was considered a great Bohemian,"[21] he had no real background in the arts and little sympathy for Federal One. At the same time, he was under pressure from congressmen, who viewed the WPA as an opportunity to reward loyal constituents with jobs. Congress had even managed to write a provision into the relief bill requiring anyone hired for a salary of $5,000 or more to go through a Senate confirmation hearing.

In particular, Baker was reluctant to hand power over to the four arts directors, all of whom were brimming with ideas for government-subsidized projects. Journalist Henry Alsberg, who headed the Federal Writers' Project, was already planning the *American Guide Series,* a state-by-state inventory of American life that has become a national treasure; Holger Cahill, director of the Federal Art Project, was devising ways to send artists out into the community to paint murals and document American design; and Nikolai Sokoloff, head of the Federal Music Project, believed he could organize symphony orchestras all over the country. Hallie, of course, had her own ambitious plans for innovative theatre productions. If all went well, Federal One would ultimately employ between twenty thousand and thirty thousand.

Baker didn't seem to understand why the model of state control, which had worked for highway projects, couldn't work just as well for Federal One. But the arts directors knew that their projects had to be treated differently: State-controlled programs would be subject not only to local political pressures, but also to local prejudices, resulting in timid and unadventurous art. This was to be a bone of contention between Baker and the arts directors throughout his tenure.

The struggle with Baker had reached a climax just before Hallie returned home to Poughkeepsie on a weekend in September. Hallie learned on Friday that Baker's superior, Colonel Lawrence Westbrook, was forbidding all appointments in the arts programs, right down to the secretarial level, "until political endorsement was secured."[22] That was when Hallie decided to go to the top. She requested a meeting with Eleanor Roosevelt.

Hallie had been imagining a weekend of idleness during her struggle with the bureaucracy in the sweltering confines of her Washington cubicle. "I feel like lying on the cream colored couch," she wrote Phil from Washington after two weeks on the job, "and looking through the arch at flowery panels of delight, with a bowl of garden flowers flaming in a copper bowl. I feel like hearing music, while you sit beside me very tweedy and laughing at me and smoking . . . I feel like having Freder [her son, Frederic, now eighteen] come in from a movie, in one of those outrageous getups of his—and I feel like all of us around the kitchen table eating crackers and cheese . . ."[23]

But the longed-for leisurely weekend in Poughkeepsie wound up being interrupted by Federal Theatre business. That Saturday, September 21, a telegram arrived at her home on Garfield Place: "Mrs. Roosevelt can see you six o'clock today or four o'clock tomorrow at Val-kill Cottage."[24]

And so, on Sunday, Hallie departed Garfield Place to pay a visit to Eleanor Roosevelt at Val-Kill Cottage in nearby Hyde Park. Phil was at the wheel as they traveled north along the Hudson, turning off the main highway and bumping along a dirt road to arrive at Eleanor's secluded retreat.

Val-Kill Cottage was Eleanor Roosevelt's modest alternative to the overstuffed rooms and grand pretensions of nearby Springwood, the big house on the Hudson River where Franklin had grown up and where he now received heads of state. The cottage was an embodiment, in Hudson Valley fieldstone, of Eleanor's independence, not only from Franklin, but also from her domineering mother-in-law, Sara, who couldn't understand in the least why her daughter-in-law insisted on spending so much time there. "Can you tell me *why* Eleanor wants to go over to Val-Kill cottage to sleep every night?" Sara once asked a friend. "Why doesn't she sleep here? This is her home. She belongs here."[25]

But Val-Kill reflected the separate but parallel path Eleanor Roosevelt pursued with increasing confidence during FDR's tenure in the White House—publicly advocating for the causes she believed in through her travels and writing and privately using her leverage with the president and others who would listen when she deemed it necessary. Hallie knew that Federal One was one of her causes and that Harry Hopkins was one of her allies. So it made sense, under the circumstances, to pay Eleanor Roosevelt a visit.

Hallie must have admired the social experiment Eleanor had established on the premises: Val-Kill Industries was a small carpentry shop that provided training and jobs to local people while turning out Colonial reproduction furniture. On the other hand, Hallie didn't share the first lady's homey taste in decorating. Probably she found the pine-paneled rooms and slip-covered furniture of Val-Kill rather shockingly plain.

No record survives of what was said at the meeting. But it is certain that Hallie would have been at her eloquent best, explaining to Eleanor Roosevelt that she and the other arts directors needed the freedom to appoint the best people, regardless of their political affiliations, and that their hands were being tied by considerations that were antithetical to the creative process. Afterward, Eleanor got in touch with Harry Hopkins. And the following Wednesday, back in Washington, Hallie Flanagan witnessed the result.

"I really felt sorry for McClure and Baker before he [Harry Hopkins] got through because he ripped them up and down saying this was always an exceptional project and must be considered as such. He also said, 'Do you or do you not trust the judgment of these four people?'"

When they tried to explain that procedures were not in place, Hopkins responded, "You know damn well that we don't need procedure. We need money in the bank at one end of a telephone wire and a federal theatre or music or art director at the other."

That evening, Harry Hopkins invited Hallie to his house to continue the discussion and made notes on what was needed. The next day, the old rules were set aside and new procedures established. The "Declaration of Independence," as Hallie labeled it, gave the four arts directors "complete and almost terrifying power . . . I feel it is all magnificent, especially the note signed by Hopkins and Roosevelt saying that each federal director is free to appoint personnel without political endorsement.

"But darling," Hallie concluded, "it could never have happened if you had not driven me to Val-kill Cottage on Sunday."[26]

chapter five

ETHIOPIA

The day after his dinner meeting with Hallie, Harry Hopkins left for the West Coast, there to embark on a ten-thousand-mile journey with President Roosevelt on the cruiser USS *Houston*. The twenty-one-day trip was intended to provide Roosevelt and a small congenial group of his aides with a relaxing break, navigating through the Carribean and the Panama Canal to Cocos Island and Hawaii, then back to Portland, Oregon.

FDR was never happier than when he was out on the water, and he relished his hours on board a fishing boat off the *Houston*, testing his physical prowess. He astounded the others with his strength and determination as a fisherman. "The President," Hopkins wrote in his journal on October 11, 1935, "late in the afternoon landed another sailfish (his second) which weighed 134 pounds. The fight for this fish lasted for two hours and twenty minutes. The President's boat was towed nearly five miles to sea into very rough waters."[1]

Harry Hopkins's idea of sport was an afternoon at the racetrack. Yet he seems to have thoroughly enjoyed his time at sea, if only because it gave him a rare interlude away from the office, where he had been working long hours for two and a half years. Hopkins's telegrams back to Washington were full of good humor. HOW ABOUT A PROJECT HUNTING TREASURE ON COCOS ISLAND? he telegraphed his top aide, Aubrey Williams, and added messages for several employees—telling one that the island was A SWELL PLACE FOR TRANSIENTS and another NOT TO LET YOU FELLOWS STEAL THE SILVER PLATE WHILE I'M AWAY."[2]

Back in Washington, the WPA staff was under siege. State after state needed more funds to keep their relief and work programs going. HAVE

Scene from the Living Newspaper *Ethiopia*, with Haile Selassie and drummer, from the
New York Sunday Mirror, March 8, 1936 (New York Public Library at Lincoln Center)

BEEN DELUGED WITH TELEGRAMS, Aubrey Williams wired Hopkins. GOVER-
NORS SENATORS AND CONGRESSMEN DEMANDING ADDITIONAL GRANTS . . . AB-
SOLUTELY NECESSARY TO HAVE PRESIDENT MAKE ADDITIONAL ALLOCATION OF
TEN MILLION IN ORDER TO GET THROUGH MONTH. In staccato language, the
wire warned of dire consequences if money didn't come through: PENN-
SYLVANIA REQUIRED TO DROP TWENTY-FIVE THOUSAND FAMILIES . . . MIS-
SOURI PRESENT FUNDS PERMIT LESS THAN FOUR DOLLARS PER MONTH TO RURAL
FAMILIES OF FIVE . . . SIMILAR DESPERATE SITUATIONS IN TENNESSEE COLORADO
NORTH DAKOTA ILLINOIS . . . [3]

Even as the USS *Houston* navigated seas thousands of miles from home,
Roosevelt and his shipmates couldn't escape for long from the desperation
of Americans back home. But the *Houston* was barely out of port when another kind of news began to come across the wire. "Many dispatches were
received throughout the day," Hopkins wrote on October 3, "reporting
the beginning of hostilities between Italy and Ethiopia."

On that day, Benito Mussolini, after several years of threats and provoca-
tions, invaded Ethiopia from the neighboring Italian colony of Eritrea, while
simultaneously ordering bombs to be dropped on Adowa, an Ethiopian city
where Italian troops had suffered a humiliating defeat thirty-eight years before. Mussolini viewed Ethiopia, with its army of barefoot spear carriers and
camels, as easy prey for Italian military might. Adding Ethiopia to Italian
colonial territory was important to Il Duce, who continued to believe that
colonial reach was a measure of his country's greatness. And in his view, the
defeat at Adowa required retribution.

The sympathy of much of the Western world lined up immediately on
the side of Haile Selassie, the emperor of Ethiopia, an enlightened dictator of a small, courageous state defending its independence in the face of
brutal aggression. On board the USS *Houston*, there was no doubt how
FDR felt. "The President," Hopkins recorded in his log, "said that world
sympathy was clearly with Ethiopia. His certainly are. He scanned the
news dispatches and everything favorable to Ethiopia brought out a loud
'Good.'"

Roosevelt was quick to see the significance of the Italian aggression: the
possibility that the shots fired there would turn out to be, as many historians now assert, the opening volleys in a second global war. At dinner on
board the *Houston*, Roosevelt was impatient with the caution of the State
Department, which advised waiting for the League of Nations before issuing a statement. "They are dropping bombs on Ethiopia—and that is war,"
he complained. "Why wait for Mussolini to say so?"[4]

Yet in the end, Roosevelt's natural impulses to react with strong words and measures had to be subordinated to the political necessity of keeping Congress on his side. At the time, Congress and the American people were still deeply isolationist. The "great mistake of 1917" that precipitated the bloody and senseless Great War was still on everyone's mind. Roosevelt needed those isolationist congressmen to support his domestic agenda.

The Ethiopian war triggered a series of events that would lead eventually to the alliance of Rome and Berlin and to World War II. But in the fall of 1936, the confrontation between the buffoonish Mussolini and the emperor of Ethiopia, in his elaborate gold-encrusted white uniform and blue black beard, seemed to be the stuff of operetta and very remote indeed from Americans' pressing problems.

Back in the United States, the only people paying much attention to the Ethiopian situation were Italian Americans and blacks. Italians, many of whom viewed Mussolini as a reformer and patriot, organized a vast letter-writing campaign urging neutrality. At the same time, some African Americans organized committees to support Ethiopia.

One other person who was paying attention to the war in Ethiopia was Hallie Flanagan. She decided it would make a splendid subject for one of the Federal Theatre Project's very first New York productions. It would be called *Ethiopia* and would be the first in a series of what were to be called Living Newspapers.

The seeds of *Ethiopia* were planted one evening in September 1935, while Hallie was wooing the prominent playwright Elmer Rice. Born Elmer Leopold Reizenstein, Elmer Rice had been forced by economic circumstances to leave school at age fifteen but later managed to obtain a law degree at night, then to mine his brief legal experience as material for a highly successful writing career. His first play, *On Trial,* used the technique of flashback for the first time on an American stage. After that, his well-made and politically prescient plays appeared regularly on Broadway for years. In 1929, he had won the Pulitzer Prize for his play *Street Scene.*

Hallie wanted Elmer Rice to sign on as director of the New York division of the Federal Theatre Project, knowing that his name would go a long way toward silencing the New York skeptics. After "a very fine dinner and much wine" at the Rice apartment, where she admired the spectacular view and the Picassos and Cézannes side by side on the walls, Hallie set off with Rice and his wife to see a murder melodrama by the then unknown Ayn Rand.[5] "The set was mildewed and so was the play," Hallie reported to Phil, "and E[lmer] said if we couldn't do better than that with a relief cast, he was no prognosticator."[6]

After the curtain went down, Hallie and the Rices walked over to Jack

Dempsey's Restaurant for a nightcap. The fighter Jack Dempsey had opened his restaurant earlier that year, but he was definitely bucking the trend. All around the trio, as they walked together that night, was evidence of the Depression's devastating impact on Broadway: Empty storefronts and dark theatres with FOR RENT signs mingled with former theatre palaces now running movie double features and strip shows.

After the Crash of 1929, Broadway found itself at the epicenter of a citywide implosion. Some fifteen thousand people, hit hard by the economic collapse, were living on the streets of the city. In Times Square, much to the consternation of theatre owners, thousands of hungry people, mostly disheartened men, often without overcoats or decent shoes, lined up each dawn for soup and a crust of bread in lines that snaked along for blocks.

The previous Broadway season, according to theatre critic Burns Mantle, had held "little hope for the theatre even among the more optimistic of its followers. Its leading producers had lost all their money. Its more dependable angels were in a state of bankruptcy. Its better playwrights and its better actors had deserted to the motion pictures. Its theatre properties were, for the most part, in the hands of mortgagor bankers." The current season didn't promise to be much better.

In every year since the Depression began, fewer plays had opened. Even producing moguls, including the powerful Shuberts, were forced into bankruptcy. Revivals, at lower ticket prices, proliferated, and burlesque theatres began to creep into the once exclusive Times Square theatre district. "The day of the $3, $4, $5, and $6 theatre is about over," Mantle pronounced.[7]

At Dempsey's, Hallie continued her pitch to Rice. She knew well that the playwright could be cantankerous. After the failure of two of his recent plays, he had told a group of Columbia University students that reviewers were nothing but "nitwits, drunkards, and degenerates" and announced that he was leaving the theatre forever. As Burns Mantle noted, "Mr. Rice retired from the theatre forever and aye, remaining completely aloof for several weeks."[8]

But Hallie Flanagan agreed with Elmer Rice on most issues. When he wrote angry letters to the critics, she wrote to tell him, with characteristic cheek, that she wanted to sign her name to them. "My rage at the asinine and smart aleck reviews of *Judgment Day* was appeased by shall I say our letter in the Sunday *Times*."[9] When they talked about their theatre ideas, Hallie and Elmer Rice found themselves talking "rapidly and almost in unison, 'plagiarizing each other.' "[10] Elmer Rice, as head of the New York division, would signal that the Federal Theatre Project was going to be bolder and better than the relief efforts that had gone before.

But Elmer Rice had all kinds of reasons why he didn't want to sign on. The pay was terrible; he had other commitments in New York and Hollywood. But his main reason was that he didn't think the Federal Theatre Project could possibly hire enough people to make a difference. After all, thousands of actors and backstage workers were out of work in New York alone.

In the late 1920s, Broadway had employed as many as twenty-five thousand theatre workers, onstage and backstage; in 1933, only four thousand still had jobs. Hungry actors survived on the free dinners given out by the Actors' Dinner Club and the Actors' Betterment Association. The Actors' Dinner Club gave out 120,000 free meals to actors in the 1932–1933 season and 200,000 in 1933–1934.

"What could we do with all the actors?" Elmer Rice kept saying. "Even if we had twenty plays in rehearsal at once, with thirty in a cast, that would keep only a fraction of them busy."

"Not wanting to lose Elmer Rice," Hallie remembered later, "I snatched at a straw. 'We wouldn't use them all in plays—we could do Living Newspapers. We could dramatize the news with living actors, light, music, movement.' "[11]

The phrase *living newspaper* was used first in Russia and Germany in the aftermath of World War I to describe a cabaret-style presentation of events in the news, animated by and commented on by actors. In Europe, the Living Newspaper was a Communist propaganda vehicle, calculated to stir up the working classes.[12] While she was at Vassar, Hallie Flanagan had made use of a variant to address a middle-class audience in her play *Can You Hear Their Voices?* Now she suggested to Rice that the Living Newspaper could be used to put hundreds to work presenting an in-depth look at pressing issues of the day.

Elmer Rice, Hallie recalled, "caught the idea in the air. 'I can get the Newspaper Guild to back it.' Acting with his usual velocity once his mind was made up, he accepted the directorship for New York, secured the sponsorship of the Guild, and appointed Morris Watson [vice president of the Guild] to head the Living Newspaper company."[13]

The immediate goal, Hallie and Rice agreed, was hiring. Rice oversaw the process with a combination of determination and rage at the bureaucratic barriers to action. "The most shocking part of the whole business," he wrote Hallie in Washington that November, "is the way the human values are lost sight of in this maze of procedure, routine and politics."

Nonetheless, in New York and all over the United States, the Federal Theatre Project's call to theatre workers had been heard; thousands flocked to Federal Theatre offices to apply for work. "I have put extra steam on here," Rice reported to Hallie, "and requisitions are going through at the rate of several hundred a day."[14]

The New York office was housed, ironically enough, in what had been the United States Bank building, two blocks from Times Square. The main room, where people had come to do business before the bank failed in December 1930, was now crowded with colorful theatre folk, lining up for forms being handed out from behind the bars of the teller windows.

Among the applicants were vaudeville actors and old pros who had spent their lives on the road, as well as eager beginners. There were young and handsome performers like the then unknown Burt Lancaster, who was paired with short, comic Nick Cravat in a "world renowned" triple-bar act called "Lang and Cravat." Burt Lancaster and his partner were assigned to the Federal Theatre circus, one of the holdovers from FERA, in the Bronx. There were also dignified old-timers like the two encountered by New York staffer Francis Bosworth: "She had a large picture hat with a sort of beat-up plume on it," he remembered. "And he had soiled white piping on his vest and he carried a cane. And they spoke a kind of stage English. They wanted to set up their own company. They said 'We had a repertory company for over 12 years and we toured in Newfoundland and the Maritime Provinces.'" The couple described the company repertoire to Bosworth: old chestnuts like *The Gay Lord Quex* and *Lord and Lady Algy*, which had been the staples of road companies in the days before cinema.

Bosworth was curious about one thing: How could a repertory company survive up in the Maritime provinces? The old couple explained: "Well, we only played in the large cities." Although he couldn't oblige with a repertory company, Bosworth found work for the couple in Chicago.[15]

The old-timers presented a challenge everywhere. There was no Social Security, and they had no pensions to rely on. Hiram Motherwell, head of the New England unit, sent a memo to Hallie Flanagan summing up the problem with brutal candor: "How much of a relief labor load of bona fide theatre people must we carry regardless of ability? . . . What is our responsibility to a) the rusty professional b) the old professional c) the unemployable professional (stage hands with hernia, actors without teeth, or with faulty memories; dancers with arthritis?) These people are going to be an increasing danger to the professional standards of the project . . . This menace is increased because an old actor never knows when he is old."[16]

Motherwell described an actor who embodied the problem: "A tall, imposing man of nearly seventy, white hair, with the dignity of a Roman Senator. He played almost-important parts all his life . . . His voice is tender like a woman's, and it quivers and hesitates ever so little, with the fear that becomes endemic after years of destitution. There is no dramatic part for him in any company this side of Paradise. I gave him—Heaven forgive me—the runaround."[17]

Hallie Flanagan acknowledged the challenge in her address to regional directors that fall, while continuing to urge bold experiment: "If we have 6000 theatre people on relief we all know that probably 4000 of them are not of the caliber to experiment. However, we must keep steadily in mind that we do not work with the 6000 alone. We work also with the 600 [the 10 percent of nonrelief personnel permitted under WPA regulations] whom we may choose to work with them."

It was tempting, Hallie warned, to return to the forms familiar to many of the older theatre workers: to standard vaudeville acts, minstrel shows, and plays like *Lord and Lady Algy* that used to bring in audiences in small towns all over America. But movies and radio had made the road show obsolete. "That the decline of the stage is not entirely due to the economic depression is one of the basic facts which we must consider. For if we attempt to put people back to work in theatre enterprises which are defunct, we are engaged in temporarily reviving a corpse which will never be alive again." The emphasis, she insisted, had to be on "rethinking rather than on remembering."[18]

All kinds of creative solutions were found by unit directors around the country. In Seattle, Esther Porter Lane discovered a way to use a skilled lasso artist who had worked only in burlesque houses and came with a routine that used one filthy joke after another. She cast him in a children's show based on Mother Goose rhymes. "We taught him one nursery rhyme: 'One misty, moisty morning when cloudy was the weather.' And he would rope for a while, which would fascinate kids, and then he'd say one line and he'd rope some more. He never was allowed to go on the stage in front of children and do anything but that nursery rhyme."[19]

The "theatre" in the Federal Theatre Project was defined broadly, so that entertainers of all kinds could qualify. Seventeen-year-old Virginia Wren was partnering in a dance act when she auditioned for a job in Boston. "There was a place called Filene's Basement where I got a black satin top that cost forty-seven cents and white flannel trousers that cost a dollar and that was my outfit. We really looked quite elegant." She was hired, for the salary of $16 a week, to tour CCC camps and hospitals.

"That sixteen dollars meant a great deal to me at the time—I gave my mother ten dollars a week and kept six dollars for myself."[20]

There was only one absolute requirement for a job with the Federal Theatre Project. "Before you got on the Project," aspiring young playwright Bud Fishel recalled, "you had to get on Home Relief." This required proof that you had no means of support and were therefore eligible for the minimal state handout. "It was a horrible experience," Fishel remembered. "You had to stay in a room that had no cooking facilities until . . . someone from the Home Relief called on you. You got no money, you got scrip, you got $3.50 a week for food which was redeemable at the various chain stores." For his trouble, Fishel was hired on to the playwriting division.[21]

Another young playwright, Arthur Miller, had no job but didn't qualify for relief because he was living at home and relying on family to support him. "A friend of mine had a room over on Forty-something and Eighth Avenue. I moved in there. I had a pair of shoes there and a hat, and the inspector came to see whether I really lived there. He decided I did. So that's how I qualified for the Project."[22]

By the end of 1935, Hallie Flanagan was able to report that the Federal Theatre Project had auditioned and hired 9,234 theatre professionals at centers all over the United States, "with many being added daily." The bulk of theatre unemployment, she reported, was in the large cities: New York, Los Angeles, Boston, Chicago, and San Francisco, with smaller numbers clustered in cities like Seattle, New Orleans, Philadelphia, Buffalo, Kansas City, Cleveland, St. Louis, Omaha, Dallas, and Minneapolis. Regional directors were developing plans tailored to the communities: In some, like San Francisco, everything would be housed under one roof. In Los Angeles, where there were fifteen hundred theatre workers, there would be several resident companies.[23] "We are living and making theatre history in America," Hallie wrote Phil on one of her better days. Even the skeptical Elmer Rice was hooked. "I never thought I could feel this way,"[24] he confessed at a meeting of regional directors.

Rice described plans for the thirty-five hundred theatre workers now on the rolls in New York City in a lengthy *New York Times* piece early in January 1936. "The Federal Theatre Project," he wrote, "has been variously characterized as a super-boondoggle, a sinecure for the faithful, an attempt to supplant the professional theatre by the amateur and a plot to overthrow the government of the United States." The truth, according to Rice, was "at once, simpler and more complex." The project grew out of the need to provide meaningful work to theatre people. But Rice also viewed it as an opportunity to supplant the theatre of the past, which radio and movies had rendered "as dead as Queen Victoria," with a new theatre "vested with a public interest" that can have importance as "a social institution and a cultural force."

Rice ended his article with a detailed explanation of the ambitious plans he and Hallie had developed for the New York division. There were to be five large units: Both the Popular Price Theatre and the Experimental Theatre would present premieres of new works, while the Tryout Theatre placed the stress on plays with a track record. Then there was the Negro Theatre: "Except for a few technicians and stage directors, the entire personnel of the theatre is Negro," Rice explained. Finally, there was the Living Newspaper unit.

The Living Newspaper had been Rice's pet project from the beginning and was moving quickly toward an opening night. The material, he explained, was being gathered "by a staff of newspapermen and playwrights," with "considerable emphasis . . . laid upon sound and lighting effects." The first production, dealing with the "Italo-Ethiopian situation, both in Africa and in Europe," was scheduled to open at the Biltmore on West Forty-seventh Street[25] in less than three weeks. "The performance will last about an hour and there will be three shows each evening. The admission price will be 25 cents."[26]

At the time, there was no reason to doubt Rice's confident announcement about *Ethiopia*: Rehearsals were going well; lights, sound, costumes, and minimal set were coming together. And journalist Morris Watson, along with an aspiring writer with borscht belt experience named Arthur Arent, had managed to make some pretty good theatre out of the news.

One of the inspirations for doing *Ethiopia* in the first place had been the need to find roles for an African troupe stranded in New York.[27] Asadata Dafora Horton, a native of Sierra Leone, had brought his dancers to the United States to perform his own dance drama, *Kykundor*, and they were looking for more work.[28] It was decided that they could be used to create atmosphere in Haile Selassie's court. Dressed as warriors carrying guns and spears, as tribal chiefs with headdresses of lion manes, and as musicians carrying drums and biblical harps (*herars*), they provided drumbeats, song, and dance, lending color and excitement to the entrances of Emperor Haile Selassie.

The actual words of Haile Selassie and Mussolini provided dramatic, dueling calls to arms. "It is far better to die in the field of battle, a free man," says the emperor of Ethiopia, "than to live as a slave!"

"The blackest injustice is being attempted against us," protests Mussolini, "that of taking from us our place in the sun." Surely France and Britain will not want "to spill blood and send Europe to its catastrophe for the sake of a barbarian country unworthy of ranking among civilized nations!"[29]

By the time Rice made his announcement in the *Times*, *Ethiopia* had been in rehearsal for nearly six weeks. The company, including actors, writers, and backstage personnel, numbered three hundred—confirming Hallie's idea that Living Newspapers could employ more people than the usual stage play. Nothing seemed to stand in the way of the opening.

Then Morris Watson, the Living Newspaper's head writer, made the mistake of sending off a letter to Stephen Early, FDR's press secretary, asking for a recording of the speech Roosevelt had given criticizing "aggressor nations."

Watson's letter set off alarm bells in the corridors of power. "What is the 'Living Newspaper'?" Early wanted to know. "Extreme care should be used in presenting a dramatization of the Ital-Ethiopia [*sic*] war . . . if this is a Government production . . . we are skating on thin ice." Early ended his letter by recommending a "thorough study."[30]

At this point, Hallie Flanagan entered the fray. Knowing full well that "a thorough study" was the kiss of death, especially since *Ethiopia* was scheduled to open in a mere two weeks, she wrote to Harry Hopkins, explaining the Living Newspaper concept and the "enormous amount of research" that had gone into preparing the script. "All the famous people," she assured Hopkins, "are characterized with great respect and with no attempt at cartooning. This is particularly true of Mussolini, who is presented sympathetically and with power."

Hallie concluded with a reminder to Hopkins of his commitment, made first in Iowa, to "produce strong plays of contemporary material," and evoked the all-powerful name of the first lady, pointing out that *Ethiopia* "fulfills many of the desires stated by Mrs. Roosevelt at a recent press conference." She included a script of the play with her letter.[31]

Perhaps things would have turned out differently if Harry Hopkins had been in town to receive her letter. But as it turned out, the letter and script came to his assistant, Hallie's nemesis Jake Baker, who had little sympathy for the troublesome arts projects. Baker, in turn, sent it back to FDR's press secretary, Stephen Early, who had raised the alarm in the first place and who repeated it, without reading *Ethiopia*. "He still feels," an assistant wrote, "that any such program dealing with foreign relations or the foreign angle in any way is dangerous and lays us open to the comment that the U.S. is financing anti-foreign policy."[32]

At that point, Hallie decided, as she had during the September impasse, to go directly to Eleanor Roosevelt.

On January 17, with less than a week left before the opening of *Ethiopia*, Hallie met with the first lady to make her case. The Living Newspaper, she told Mrs. Roosevelt, is "the most powerful project in New York." She described the opening, in which "the beat of tom-toms in Ethiopia changes to the bang of a gavel and lights come up on the peace table in Geneva.

"There is no attempt to take sides," she insisted, "simply to present the facts." Hallie listed all the participants in the project, including the New York schools and universities, and pointed out that shutting down the production, after all the publicity, was going to cause "a storm of newspaper publicity claiming censorship for political reasons."

The first lady called Stephen Early on the spot. After she hung up, she conveyed the message: "Mr. Early says he is very busy and this is all right this time, but next time he suggests you be careful about foreign powers." After instructing Hallie to "personally see the rehearsals and make sure nothing offensive goes in," Eleanor Roosevelt concluded the meeting, assuming the matter was settled.[33]

But the next day, Hallie got a letter from Jake Baker ordering that no Living Newspaper "shall contain any representation of a foreign state" without approval of the State Department—an order that made the production virtually impossible.[34] Once again, Hallie appealed to the first lady, this time over the phone. Eleanor reassured her. She said she'd taken up the matter with the president, who "thinks it would be deplorable to drop *Ethiopia*." But she added that FDR felt that "famous people, such as heads of nations and statesmen," should not be shown in person; perhaps the news could be communicated "through a secondary person."[35] Though well-intentioned, Eleanor Roosevelt didn't seem to understand that putting dialogue into the mouths of "secondary persons" would drain the life out of any theatre production.

It was becoming obvious to both Hallie Flanagan and Elmer Rice that *Ethiopia* was in extreme peril unless Harry Hopkins could intervene. On January 21, the day before the planned opening, Rice sent Hopkins a telegram reminding him that he had been promised "a free hand" and "no censorship," adding that "if you support Baker's decision there is nothing for me to do except regretfully tender my resignation." The same day, Hallie sent a telegram to Jake Baker warning of "highly unfavorable publicity" if the show was stopped and asking him to "allow *Ethiopia* to go on with slight changes at my discretion."

There was no response from Hopkins, but at this point he undoubtedly was aware of the confrontation. Baker, who did reply, changed his position too slightly to matter.

On January 23, the day after *Ethiopia* was supposed to open on Broadway, Elmer Rice, with Hallie at his side, marched into Baker's office in Washington to make a final plea for *Ethiopia*. But Baker refused to budge, and Rice therefore tendered his resignation. Baker was ready for him: He reached in his drawer and pulled out an acceptance letter: "When difficulties have arisen in the past . . . you have proposed either to resign or to take the difficulties to the press. Now that a problem has arisen in connection with a dramatization that may affect our international relations, you renew your proposal of resignation in a telegram to Mr. Hopkins. This time I accept it, effective upon receipt of this letter."[36]

"Mr. Baker," Hallie remembered later, "took out his pen, signed the letter, and rose. We rose also. It was one of several occasions on the project when homicide would not have surprised me."[37]

Hallie herself came very close to resigning along with Elmer Rice. After the set-to in Baker's office, she decided not to go back to her hotel, where she would be faced with a barrage of reporters. Instead, she hid out in the hotel room of her assistant, former Vassar student Esther Porter, and debated her future with several co-workers on the project. Should she stay, or should she preserve her integrity and quit? The colleagues pointed out that the censorship, if it happened once, was going to happen again "no matter what Hopkins says."[38] Hallie knew this, of course. She worried, as she wrote Phil, that the Federal Theatre Project "would never be able to do anything except pap for babes and octogenarians."[39] Yet she decided to stay on. Perhaps it was because resignation would have been an admission of failure, and, as she told Phil, "I despise failure."[40]

A final dress rehearsal of *Ethiopia* was scheduled for the next day at the Biltmore Theatre. In what he described as a "final blow against censorship," Rice invited all the New York drama critics to attend. "They all came," he wrote, "and, because of the circumstances, gave the production much more attention that it would otherwise have received." He added: "It was a fine show and the notices were very positive."[41]

It is true that some critics praised what they saw. Brooks Atkinson of the *New York Times* called it a "sobering and impressive—even frightening" account of a "breach of peace that is happening under our nose" and concluded that "the result amply justifies the hard work that has gone into it." But Atkinson's overall assessment of the situation was gloomier. "What we all know now is that a free theatre cannot be a government enterprise."[42]

The hostile press had a field day. HOW THE ALPHABET GOVERNMENT LAID A MILLION-DOLLAR BROADWAY EGG, crowed the anti–New Deal *Sunday Mirror*. A color spread included tantalizing pictures of the African performers in full regalia—"all decked out," sneered the *Mirror*, "in Ethiopian finery . . . Rehearsed for Weeks to Emote in the 'Living Newspaper' without Presenting a Single Performance . . .

"The New York City Federal Theatre project . . . has turned out to be a fiasco," the article claimed, concluding that "the salaries and rehearsals go on and on but few regular public performances, other than the vaudeville-circuses, have come out of the Government Federal Theatre Project."[43]

Columnist Drew Pearson wrote in the *Washington Herald* that *Ethiopia* was really a victim of domestic politics and particularly the sensitive issue of the plight of southern sharecroppers, who were beginning to organize for the first time not only against the oppression of their landlords, but also against the unintended but adverse consequences of New Deal programs on poor blacks and whites in the South. The Roosevelt administration, needing the support of powerful southern senators, didn't want to stir that particular pot. "Italian complaints to the State Department could have been ignored. But the sharecroppers offered a greater problem."

Pearson's inside sources seemed to have gotten it right. On January 25, Aubrey Williams, Harry Hopkins's assistant, wrote to Eleanor Roosevelt claiming that *Ethiopia* was just the tip of the iceberg. "It has developed that with the presentation of *Ethiopia*, they have in mind producing Soviet Russia, the Scottsboro case, Sharecroppers, etc. . . . Mr. Hopkins has decided that in view of this, it is not wise to go ahead with this project and instructed Mr. Baker to so inform Mr. Rice through Miss Flanagan."[44] (Williams was stretching the truth: A Living Newspaper about the plight of the farmers was percolating, but neither Soviet Russia nor the Scottsboro boys were part of future plans.)

Hallie Flanagan was discovering that the support of her powerful allies at the top had limits. Eleanor Roosevelt spoke out loud and clear to Hopkins and to the president, but they didn't always do as she requested. And Harry Hopkins wanted the Federal Theatre Project to be "free, adult, and uncensored," but only as long as it didn't stir up political trouble for his boss on sensitive issues abroad and, more important, close to home.

chapter six

TRIPLE-A PLOWED UNDER

One day in May 1934, the dust storms that had crippled the Great Plains paid a call on New York City. A huge cloud carrying three tons of dust for every American alive formed over the Midwest and expanded eastward until it covered Manhattan, forcing cars to turn on their lights at midday and coating the Statue of Liberty with a layer of gray topsoil. For five hours, until the eighteen-hundred-mile-wide cloud moved out to sea, New Yorkers got a taste of the devastating conditions that were driving farmers off their land and contributing to the worst farm crisis in the history of the nation.

In Washington, a leftover dusting descended on the National Mall and the White House, providing a gritty reminder that the plight of the farmers constituted a national emergency. No group, with the possible exception of African American workers, had been harder hit by the Depression than the farmers. In the three years after the Crash, farm prices fell more than 50 percent and farm foreclosures went through the roof. As in England, Arkansas, farmers around the country were taking the law into their own hands, blocking milk trucks along highways and showing up in large numbers to thwart foreclosure proceedings. In April 1933, five hundred farmers turned up in a courtroom in Le Mars, Iowa, to protest a foreclosure and were scolded by the judge for smoking and wearing hats in the halls of justice. The crowd reacted by dragging the judge from the bench, slapping and mauling him, blindfolding him, and transporting him out of the city in a pickup truck. They left him by the side of the road, trouserless, smeared with grease, with a rope around his neck and a hubcap on his head, but still breathing and still refusing to recant and suspend foreclosures on their farms. It was one incident among many that caused Edward A. O'Neal,

"Dust!" A scene from *Triple-A Plowed Under* (National Archives and Records Administration)

head of the Farm Bureau Federation, to warn a Senate committee that "unless something is done for the American farmer, we will have a revolution in the countryside within less than twelve months."

Roosevelt understood. Soon after taking office, he sent a bill off to the special session of Congress, proposing drastic measures that could be undertaken in time for spring planting. FDR knew the plan was so bold that it risked shocking many of the members. He wrote his defense in longhand: "I tell you frankly," he warned, "that it is a new and untrod path, but I tell you with equal frankness that an unprecedented condition calls for the trial of new means."

The "new means" he proposed was a multifaceted bill entitled the Agricultural Adjustment Act (AAA), meant to address a legacy of excess planting that had caused both drought and oversupply. The idea was to reward farmers—using money raised from a tax on food processors—for *not* planting and even for destroying some crops and livestock. The bill provoked immediate indignation from conservatives in Congress: Representative Fred Britten of Illinois declared the bill "more Bolshevistic than any law or regulation existing in Soviet Russia," and Representative Joseph W. Martin of Massachusetts declared, "We are on our way to Moscow."

Even among supporters of the New Deal who understood the plight of the farmers, AAA went against the grain. "You don't mean," asked Senator "Cotton Ed" Smith of South Carolina, "to advocate, in order to maintain prices, the destruction of crops that are already produced, do you?" That was exactly what the Roosevelt administration had in mind. And not only crops, but thousands of gallons of milk and—in what turned out to be the most unpopular and probably unwise of measures— baby pigs. The unnaturalness of the program was shocking even to the mules, who resisted walking over and plowing under rows of cotton. Henry Wallace, Roosevelt's visionary secretary of agriculture, felt the insanity of it as much as anyone. "The plowing under of 10 million acres of cotton in August, 1933, and the slaughter of 6 million little pigs in September, 1933," he wrote afterward, "were not acts of idealism in any sane society."

Iowa-born Henry Wallace lacked the sophistication and small talk of the other experts who surrounded Roosevelt, but he had thought deeply about the cultivation of the land. In his view, no civilization could survive without a balance between the country and the city—a balance that had been upset by the collapse of agriculture.[1]

But the crisis on the land that worried Henry Wallace was remote from the daily lives of city folk, unless a dust storm blew in and interfered with their breathing. So it was a surprise to some who were following the early struggles of the Federal Theatre Project to read in the *New York Times* on January 28, 1936, that a Living Newspaper on "the farm problem" was being "rushed into production." Philip Barber, who had succeeded Elmer Rice as director in New York, told the *Times* that he fully expected the new production to proceed without the interference that had doomed *Ethiopia*. And if there was a repeat of Washington censorship? Barber told the *Times* he was "not borrowing trouble." In the end, trouble came anyway. But it came from different sources.

Triple-A Plowed Under opened at the Biltmore Theatre, on the northern edge of the Broadway theatre district, on March 14, 1936. From beginning to end, it was an attempt to explain why country folk and city folk needed each other if they wanted to climb out of the Depression.

The action of *Triple-A Plowed Under* begins in 1917 with what would become a signature of the Living Newspaper: a chorus of crescendoing voices, one after the other. "The boys in the trenches need the men in the fields," says a voice. A trumpet sounds. "Every bushel of barley is a barrel of bullets," echoes another. "Every head of cattle can win a battle," shouts a third.

The blackout, a technique borrowed from vaudeville routines, punctuates a series of swift scenes, in which we learn of the buildup of production during the Great War and of the deflation that followed as a result of oversupply after the war ended, resulting in an economic chain reaction— no more exports, no more farm loans, farmers going bust, and manufacturers suffering the consequences. The whole vicious cycle is summed up in a staccato interchange: "I can't buy that auto," says the farmer to the car dealer. "I can't take that shipment," says the car dealer to the manufacturer. "I can't use you anymore," says the manufacturer to the worker. "I can't eat," says the worker. Blackout.

The most admired scene involved another Living Newspaper innovation: the disembodied "Voice of the Living Newspaper" coming over a loudspeaker. "Drought sears the Midwest, Southwest, West," says the Voice. Lights go up on a tableau of a farmer examining the soil. Two other voices come over the loudspeaker with the weather report: "May first, Midwest weather report," says the first. "Fair and warmer," says the second. "May second, Midwest weather report," says the first. "Fair and warmer," says the second. The voices repeat the same forecast as the music grows in intensity. "Fair and warmer. Fair and warmer. Fair and warmer," the second voice chants. The farmer scoops up a handful of dirt from the ground and rises, sifting it slowly through his fingers. He speaks a single word: "Dust!"

The Living Newspaper had to be nimble to keep up with events. It was necessary, for instance, to explain not only the farm crisis, but the effects of New Deal policies on the crisis. Between enactment of the AAA in 1933 and early 1936, when the play opened, there had been a dramatic turn-around. AAA programs—production control, benefits to farmers, loans, and other measures in the omnibus bill—had worked. Farm income had increased by 50 percent. "Corn is 70 cents on the farms in Iowa," Senator Louis Murphy wrote to Roosevelt. "Two years ago it was 10 cents. Top hogs sold at Iowa plants yesterday at $4.50 or $5.00 better than a year ago. Farmers are very happy and convinced of the virtue of planning . . . Sec-retary Wallace can have whatever he wants from Iowa farmers."[2] Paradox-ically, the terrible drought and dust storms had contributed to the improvement. Though individual farmers suffered, the net result of the bad weather was decreased yield and increased prices.

But there were other unintended consequences as well: The same AAA policies that helped farmers increased prices for consumers—a conflict that threatened to divide farmers from consumers in the cities and towns. The quick rise in prices also made some market speculators rich. This effect was illustrated in *Triple-A* by a scene in a swank restaurant. A couple in evening clothes order caviar and Château d'Yquem 1926. "Wheat's up and I've been saving a lot of it to unload," says the commodities trader to his date. "So what will it be, a new car or a sable coat?"

At the same time, AAA policies were doing almost nothing to reach the poorest of the poor: tenant farmers and sharecroppers in the South. By the early 1930s, there were a million whites and seven hundred thousand blacks in the South trapped in a tenant system that reduced them to terri-ble penury, working from dawn to dusk for next to nothing, living in ram-shackle cabins, subsisting on sowbelly, meal, and molasses, and falling prey to all the diseases of contaminated creeks and poor sanitation. Henry Wal-lace, after touring the South in 1936, declared that "one third of the farm-ers of the United States live under conditions which are so much worse than the peasantry of Europe that the city people of the United States should be thoroughly ashamed."

A scene in *Triple-A* features a black tenant farmer named Sam, singing about his new mule, which he has named "Guv'ment" because it was sup-plied to him in exchange for not planting cotton. Soon enough, the sher-iff appears on the scene and takes the mule as compensation for back taxes he claims Sam owes. "Giddap, Guv'ment," says the sheriff as he drives off the mule. The next scene shows sharecroppers talking among themselves about forming a union. This scene, too, is based on real events: Angered by the New Deal's neglect, tenant farmers did begin to organize in parts of the South, with the encouragement of fiery speeches from Socialist Norman Thomas, among others. The landowning classes, used to submission, were alarmed. "We have had a pretty serious situation here," reported a leading citizen of Arkansas, "what with the mistering of the niggers and stirring them up to think the Government was going to give them forty acres."[3] In fact, AAA payments rarely reached these tenant farmers, and their plight became a rallying point for critics on the left, including the Communists as well as Norman Thomas.

The most important development, however, was the one that gave the play its title. On January 6, the Supreme Court took up residence in its newly built Greek Revival edifice on Capitol Hill. It was, as a *New Yorker* writer quipped, "a magnificent structure with fine big windows to throw the New Deal out of."[4] That same day, the Supreme Court declared the AAA unconstitutional by a vote of 6–3. According to the majority, the bill encroached upon powers that should be reserved to states and unlawfully expropriated money from one group (the food processors) to benefit another (the farmers). Justice Owen Roberts, a former corporation lawyer, concluded that the United States would, if the AAA was allowed to stand, be "converted into a central government exercising uncontrolled police power in every state of the Union, superseding all local control or regulation of the affairs or concerns of the states."[5] The federal government was ordered to turn back $200 million to food processors who had been taxed under the AAA.

In the penultimate scene of *Triple-A Plowed Under*, a facsimile of the Constitution is projected on a glass curtain. Various figures appear in black silhouette against the projection and voice the arguments for and against the AAA. Justice Roberts, standing with the five other justices in the majority, speaks first, defending the limits of power set out in the Constitution. Justice Harlan Fiske Stone speaks for the minority, arguing that judicial power can be abused. The several defenders of the Supreme Court decision appear and speak, followed by Earl Browder, general secretary of the U.S. Communist Party, and finally by Thomas Jefferson, who declares, rather inconclusively, that "the ultimate arbiter is the people of the Union."[6] All the words of all speakers were taken from the record, of course, and carefully documented, but the inclusion of Earl Browder, the face of the Communist Party in the 1930s, was a literal red flag.

The composer Virgil Thomson complained, after working on a Living Newspaper production, that the entire enterprise was "up to its ears in commies,"[7] and that was probably only a slight exaggeration. The prevalence of left-wing idealogues within the New York Federal Theatre, and especially within the 10 percent of productions that addressed social issues, reflected a similar phenomenon in the larger intellectual community.

Many intellectuals, like Hallie Flanagan, had made the pilgrimage to Russia in the twenties and early thirties and come home impressed. Between 1929 and 1931, some fifteen thousand Americans visited the Soviet Union. Among the most enthusiastic returning visitors was the psychiatrist Harry Hopkins consulted about his marital problems, Dr. Frankwood Williams, who reported that "Russia is a place where all problems of human relationships have been solved."[8] Many shared Dr. Williams's conviction that Russia was a better place to live than the United States. In 1931, at the height of the Depression, the Soviet trading corporation in New York was receiving 350 applications a day from Americans looking for jobs in the Soviet Union. And in 1933, some fifty thousand people marched in the May Day parade, a pro-Communist exercise, in New York City.

Among those who marched that day was Malcolm Cowley, then a writer for the *New Republic* and a true believer. "In the beginning," Cowley explained in his memoir, *The Dream of the Golden Mountains,* "the dream had been composed of several elements, all fitting together. There was the notion that capitalism and its culture were in violent decay and on the point of being self-destroyed. There was the idealization of 'the workers' as the vital class, the only one fated to survive . . . All of us joined in brotherhood, our right fists raised in the Red Front salute . . . The Soviet Union had shown us the way."[9]

Communism presented itself as the alternative to fascism, rising ominously in Europe, and to the racism and anti-Semitism that accompanied it, all of which added to its special appeal, particularly for American blacks and for Jews. And the Communist strategy in the 1930s was to form a "popular front" with other organizations on the left. For all of those reasons, communism enjoyed more support between 1935 and 1939 than at any other time in American history.[10]

There were times when Hallie Flanagan sounded like a true believer herself. At the first staff meeting of the Federal Theatre Project in the McLean mansion in Washington, D.C., she made a point of distancing herself from the "bourgeois" trappings of the place, formerly the preserve of Hope diamond heiress Evalyn Walsh McLean. "Irrespective of the merit of its art treasures," she told the group, "the McLean mansion represents the conception of art as a commodity to be purchased by the rich, possessed by the rich, and shared on occasional Wednesday evenings with the populace." The mansion, she told the group, reminded her of her visit to Russia, where the "golden palaces" of the czars had become the preserve of the proletariat. There in "the great Hall of Mirrors in Leningrad . . . which once gave back the image of the Empress . . . I saw the faces of Stalin, Litvinov . . . and other leaders of political, educational and theatrical life" as they "met to discuss . . . how the theatre could serve in educating the people and in enriching their lives."[11] If Gordon Craig had been around to comment, he might have told Hallie that such romantic notions of Stalin and his gang in 1935 were "silly"— or worse.

Clearly, Hallie's naive infatuation with Russia remained intact, as did her ability to sanitize a regime that by that time had shown its tyrannical face to the world. But some of this talk merely reflected the fashion of the times. The thoughtful critic John Gassner noted that, for many artists in the thirties, "Marxist theory was just one more attractive piece of driftwood afloat in the current of fashionable intellectualism, along with amateur Freudianism and hazy, antibourgeois romanticism."

Over time, Hallie came to resent the Communists, who made noise and trouble for the Federal Theatre Project, and for Federal One, far in excess of their numbers, especially in New York. They were the force behind the Workers Alliance, a union of WPA employees without other union affiliation that turned out flyers, organized petitions, and manned picket lines whenever firings and budget cuts threatened. And they were probably behind the provocative use of Earl Browder in *Triple-A Plowed Under*, as well as the play's "conversion ending," a standard device of left-wing agitprop theatre. In the last scene, workers and farmers pledge to work together in support of the radical (but non-Communist) Farmer-Labor Party.

The left-wingers on *Triple-A Plowed Under* succeeded in provoking controversy. On the day the play was to open in New York, a small group calling themselves the Federal Theatre Veterans League held a protest meeting at an auditorium a block from the theatre. The stage manager for the production, one Willis Browne, accused Morris Watson, president of the newspaper guild and supervisor of the Living Newspaper, of being a Communist and favoring all his Communist friends with tickets. There was talk of storming the stage that night, pulling down the lights, and disrupting the opening with a rendition of "The Star-Spangled Banner."[12]

Meanwhile, Hallie Flanagan learned that the Veterans League was itself the creation of powerful reactionary forces, "allied with—and probably

fostered by—the American Legion, the D.A.R.—and the Hearst Press."
The Hearst press had been hammering away at the Federal Theatre Project
for months and now seized on the occasion of the *Triple-A* opening to run
screaming headlines about communism in the Roosevelt administration.
The *New York American*, for instance, ran a front-page story with a huge
headline: U.S. CONTRIBUTES TO REDS THROUGH THEATRE PROJECT.[13]

That same day, it was discovered that the Hearst organization, always
willing to go to great lengths to pursue a target, had been paying spies to
undermine the project. The *Sun*, one of Hearst's papers, had been buying
scripts from two Federal Theatre insiders for large sums of money. "We
fired the two men on whom we have the goods," Hallie reported to her
husband. What's more, she wrote, a secretary named Hazel Huffman,
whom Hallie had personally hired to sort through her correspondence in
the mailroom, was informing to the Hearst organization. Others had suspected Hazel Huffman earlier, and Hallie had defended her. But now there
was proof positive: One of Hallie's staff showed her an affidavit, given by
Hazel Huffman to the Hearst press, saying that she had opened Hallie's
mail for three months and found it "incendiary, revolutionary, and seditious." Hazel Huffman was rumored to have been paid $1,000 for the affi-
davit.[14] Clearly, the Federal Theatre Project had become the locus for a
larger struggle between New Deal and anti–New Deal forces.

The most unscrupulous opposition tactics were those employed by the
Hearst press and orchestrated by William Randolph Hearst himself. Heir to
millions from his father's silver mines and other acquisitions in the West,
Hearst had multiplied his initial fortune many times over in the newspaper
business. He had begun in California, but his ambitions were national—in
fact, he tried at various times to become a senator (like his father), a mayor,
and president of the United States. He managed only one term in the
House of Representatives. When his political career disappointed, Hearst
turned his attention to promoting his agenda through his newspapers. He
was an early and successful practitioner of character assassination and other
practices that would later be put to use by congressional committees going
after alleged Communists in and out of government.

In the early years, Hearst used his papers to drum up support for over-
seas adventures—the Spanish-American War was brought about partly by
hysterical and largely untrue correspondents' reports on his front pages. By
the time of the New Deal, the Hearst chain had become a behemoth:
twenty-nine newspapers in eighteen cities, with a circulation of over five
million. All the newspapers were the personal instruments of Hearst, by

then in his seventies and hell-bent on his "anti-Communist" mission; his troops either did his bidding or lost their jobs.

The words *Fascist* and *Communist* were thrown around with abandon in the charged atmosphere of the 1930s. But in the case of William Randolph Hearst, the Fascist label was earned. In 1934, Hearst paid a visit to Adolf Hitler in Berlin and came away impressed with what he saw. To his mind, the capitalist system had been endangered in Germany until Hitler came along and saved it, and similar measures needed to be taken to save capitalism in the United States. Hearst even tried to defend Hitler after news of persecutions of Jews and minorities began to surface. In an editorial in the *Los Angeles Examiner*, he explained that Hitler's ministers had "got out of hand" and were proceeding without Hitler's authorization.

Hearst wisely dropped his public defense of Hitler at that point, but he continued his pursuit of right-wing goals. His first step was an attempt to "purge" the universities of so-called Communists, a large category in his lexicon. On the basis of very little, he began to run stories in his papers about universities that were infected with communism. Interviews with professors were arranged and their contents mangled to prove "Red" sympathies. Professors at Harvard, Columbia, and NYU were named. Anyone who had attacked the Nazi regime was fair game: Hallie Flanagan made one of his lists even before she gained visibility as head of the Federal Theatre Project.

After the Hazel Huffman subterfuge came to light, Hallie wrote to Phil: "I begin to see my incredible naivete as to the political embroglio back of all this . . .

"She was purely a stool pigeon," Hallie wrote, "and no wonder I have been saying the NY office made me feel queer." It was not the last time Hallie's naïveté, about both the Left and the Right, would get her into trouble. Nor was it to be her last encounter with Hearst, the Veterans League, or the devious Hazel Huffman. But the whole episode left her, as she wrote Phil, with "a fierce and burning determination to win this fight."[15]

The first major victory came on the night of March 14, 1936. As curtain time approached, the threat to *Triple-A Plowed Under* dissipated, and the whole situation descended rapidly into farce. The Veterans League decided, in the words of one of their leaders, that "going in singing 'The Star Spangled Banner' in a group is nothing more than communism," and they did not want to place themselves "in the same category as them [that is, the Communists]."[16]

The captain of a police detail, hired to keep the peace, assured regional director Phil Barber that he had absolutely nothing to worry about. "We won't let this play open," he told Barber. "We'll shut it right down." The captain had to be told that this time his assignment was to keep the play *open*, not shut it down.[17]

As it turned out, police services were scarcely needed. At one point, during a scene in which housewives are assailing a butcher over his high prices, a man in the back of the house rose and said, "Come on, friends, let's sing 'The Star-Spangled Banner.'" Police escorted him out as he began to sing.

Later on, when Earl Browder—or, more accurately, the actor who was impersonating Earl Browder—began to speak, there was a loud reaction from the audience of booing and cheering. But according to a report in the *New York Times* the next day, the cheers seemed to outnumber the boos.[18]

Triple-A Plowed Under turned out to be a triumph—and a desperately needed one after many false fits and starts. The major papers reviewed it favorably the next day. It had an extended run of eighty-five performances in New York and was later produced, in ever evolving forms, in Chicago, Cleveland, Milwaukee, and Los Angeles.

"We played to a crowded house both shows," Hallie reported to Phil when she got back from the two shows given opening night. "Never saw such excitement, boos, hisses—cries of shut up etc. It was a swell show . . . They clapped for eight minutes at the end." Perhaps most critical of all, Bruce McClure, Baker's assistant and frequent nemesis, had rushed up from Washington, in a panic about the Veterans League threats, and stayed to become a convert. He is "absolutely sold on it," Hallie wrote Phil. McClure told Hallie to call Eleanor Roosevelt first thing in the morning and invite her up to New York to see it.[19]

entr'acte one

THE CCC MURDER MYSTERY

We are going to make a country in which no one is left out.

—FDR to Frances Perkins[1]

The Civilian Conservation Corps was one of Roosevelt's pet projects, established with remarkable speed in the early days of the New Deal to provide temporary employment to the thousands of young men who were desperate for work and sustenance. It was, as FDR explained to Congress, to be "used in simple work, not interfering with normal employment, and confining itself to forestry, the prevention of soil erosion, flood control and similar projects." The original plan was to recruit 250,000 unemployed and unmarried men between the ages of eighteen and twenty-three. But the program grew at its height to half a million. Some "experienced men" and veterans joined the ranks, but they were in the minority.

To the "boys" who joined up, FDR offered his congratulations and best wishes for "a pleasant, wholesome and constructively helpful stay in the woods." Roosevelt himself had spent happy hours in the woods as a boy, hunting birds for his collection. But his exposure to nature as a privileged youth was a far cry from that of the CCC boys, who acquired the nickname "peavies" because of their frequent use of a log-hooking spear called by that name. The peavies hand-built lodges stone by stone, wrestled stumps out of the ground to clear roads, dug millions of holes for new trees, attacked mosquito infestations, rescued flood victims, and risked their lives fighting forest fires. Many were sent far from home, into remote areas of the West. City boys from New Jersey who had never been off the pavement struggled to keep up with country boys, who at least knew how to

CCCers felling a tree, 1933 (Franklin D. Roosevelt Presidential Library)

wield an ax and pull one end of a crosscut saw. A good number of enrollees got fed up or homesick and left without official permission.

Yet most of those who signed up for the CCC viewed it as the best chance of their young lives. The pay was $30 a month: $25 for the family back home and $5 for the CCCer. "The money my parents received was Gold Money," one recruit remembered. "It was survival. I can't describe it." Many, like Elias Covington, a young black fifteen-year-old from North Carolina, inflated their age to get in. Others fretted because they were too thin to meet the weight requirement. John Chepetz, a young Ukrainian American from a coal-mining town in Pennsylvania, weighed only ninety-seven pounds when he signed up—ten pounds under the CCC requirement. But his mother begged and pleaded on his behalf, and he got in. Chepetz then walked and hitchhiked twenty-two miles to catch the train to the camp. When he left the CCC a year later, he was fit and 150 pounds—"strong enough to start working in the mines."[2] Another recruit, from Alabama, was six feet tall and weighed 122 pounds on arrival at Camp Icicle in Washington State: Six months later, he weighed a muscular 214.

For many enrollees, joining the CCC meant having enough to eat for the first time ever: The average CCC enrollee gained eight pounds in the first six months. "The only difference between you and me," FDR told the recruits on one occasion, "is that you're gaining weight, whereas I am trying to take some off." In truth, a chasm separated FDR from the CCC boys. Yet many enrollees believed they had a special connection to the president. A CCC recruit who marched in the 1937 inaugural parade imagined FDR's emotions as he watched "the crooked, olive drab lines of 400 CCC marchers straggle by . . . Maybe . . . they did march the best of all that day, if you look for spirit deep inside and not for outward show. Where military outfits carried the trappings of war, they carried nothing. Their hands swung—those were their tools of trade. When the man who had conceived this army of peace looked down at them, he must have felt proud."[3]

But even Roosevelt, who argued that the CCC could create "future national wealth," could not have imagined how vast would be the permanent legacy of the CCC, in creating wilderness areas and parks, rescuing forests, and reshaping watersheds all over the United States. Certainly it was one of the New Deal's most successful undertakings, both as a conservation measure and as an alternative, for many young men, to joblessness and despair.

Hallie Flanagan first saw a CCC camp on a trip through the South and painted a bleak picture in a letter to Phil: "gray unpainted buildings against a gray unpainted sky—no trees—not one beautiful or clean thing as far as you could see . . . It makes me wild and it makes me afraid. I would like to take the funniest and most beautiful and gayest plays we have and tour them through the camps, distributing cans of paint after the show."[4]

Before the Federal Theatre Project started, traveling companies had toured the CCC camps under sponsorship of the WPA's predecessor, FERA, which subsidized state efforts with federal money. But actors who went on those early tours urged Federal Theatre leaders to give up on the whole idea. "CCC camp theatre," one actor wrote, "has done more to hurt our project than benefit it." The actors wrote of "playing in badly cast and hastily organized companies, where constant replacements are made by officials who haven't even read the play and wouldn't know how to cast it if they had," of "playing on improvised stages, with little or no lighting and with scenery that would put a medicine show to shame," of "playing under the direction of a Supervisor who has been selected because he is 'somebody's friend' and with the mental equipment of a moron."

The pre-WPA companies had to ride rough and muddy roads in the backs of army trucks, exposed to the elements, in weather that went down to thirty-eight below. "The human liver and the human spine," one actress wrote, "were never designed for army trucks." Once they reached the camps, the actors often lived in rougher conditions than the CCC boys. "When we have to sleep in the recreation hall," one actor reported, "we cannot rest our travel-beaten bodies until after the play, then an orderly places the beds in a windrow on the stage." Another time, this actor was forced to sleep in an unheated garage, "through the wall-boards of which the snow fell on my face and the blankets all night . . . "

"In my wildest days of Repertoire," another actor complained, "all over Canada, Newfoundland, and the NE States in the dead of winter, the actor ALWAYS HAD A ROOM and a little privacy."[5]

The terrible conditions on the CCC tours, along with the mediocrity of the productions, convinced Elmer Rice and Hallie Flanagan to shut them down, against the wishes of CCC officials, until they could make changes. But Hallie was determined to find a way to turn the CCC debacle around.

Her first step, in the spring of 1936, was to appoint a military man, Major Earl L. House, to be coordinator of the CCC tours. In general, she was averse to military oversight of the theatre programs, but the CCC camps were different: They were run in military style—a fact that caused some early critics on the left to warn of fascism—and headed by reserve military officers. House himself had been a CCC camp commander and knew how to enlist the camp officers' support. And even though he believed in doing everything strictly by the book, he seemed to have some sympathy for the artistic enterprise.

House swung into action. He arranged a $2 per diem for the actors to give them some independence while on the road[6] and replaced the army trucks with Chevy Carryalls that had FEDERAL THEATRE emblazoned on their doors.

The next challenge was finding the right material. In the past, the standard CCC fare had been variety: "snappy music, songs, laughter, group singing, novelty, and dancing," in the words of the PR department. The climactic final act in one touring show featured "Huston, Illusionist extraordinary," breaking a rock slab in two over the chest of a woman suspended in the air. Another CCC show featured "Chief Eagle Feather," known in vaudeville as "America's foremost Indian entertainer." One actor blamed the audience for the mediocrity of the productions: "The show was of a low calibre on account of the type of boy that we played to," he wrote. "We had to carry the idea to them in a broad manner or they would not get it."

But Hallie Flanagan argued that "three hundred thousand boys in CCC camps throughout the United States want dramatic entertainment. They are being educated by the movies and they do not want from us pallid productions of the classics or lukewarm imitations of Broadway. The camps deserve and should have the best that we can send out." Hallie appealed to her directors around the country: "Recognizing the limited stage facilities of the camps, can't some of you evolve a technique whereby a company acts in the center of the mess hall, drawing the audience into the show, catching in dramatic form the spirit which makes *Happy Days*, the camp newspaper, so exciting?"[7]

Hallie Flanagan's instincts about the CCC camps turned out to be right. *Happy Days*, the semiofficial newspaper of the camps, was an exercise in participatory journalism: It solicited poems from CCCers for a column called "Brother Can You Spare a Rhyme"[8] and paid a dollar to anyone who sent in a useful invention, such as a method for peeling potatoes with one hand or finding your way in the woods in the dark. It also spawned and encouraged local camp papers: Some five thousand were published during the CCC years, mostly on mimeograph machines. The papers were christened with humorous names like *By a Dam Site* and *Upandatem* and were filled with very local news about the goings-on in camp, along with poems and jokes.[9]

Clearly, the young men in the CCC camps excelled at amusing one another. And this fact, along with extensive interviews with CCCers, led a Hollywood screenwriter named Grace Hayward to write an unusual play, exclusively for the camps, called *The CCC Murder Mystery*.

The plot of *The CCC Murder Mystery* was right out of a Hollywood movie: A young CCCer is brought before judge and jury in handcuffs. He is accused of murdering his rival from town, in a fit of jealousy over a woman. According to the prosecutor, this young CCCer invited his rival to his mother's cottage, knocked him out, and then burned down the cottage with him in it. As the parade of witnesses comes before the court, we gradually come to understand that no murder has actually taken place. The whole thing turns out to have been a sting operation, designed to trap an evil butler who is scheming to inherit the wealth of the family from town.

The story of a scheming and evil butler would hardly seem relevant to a CCC audience. But the success of the production had little to do with the convoluted plot: It was based instead on an elaborate scheme to involve the CCC boys themselves in the show. Several days before the players got there, a packet arrived at the camp, addressed to the camp educational director, providing him with a brief description of the play along with instructions for selecting men to participate. CCCers would be asked to play the twelve jurors and to come up with a verdict at the end of the play. In addition, there were about a dozen speaking parts for the CCC men. According to the instructions, the accused should be played by one of the most popular men in the camp, and there were parts as well for the "camp Casanova" and someone so loyal to the accused that he refuses to sit on the jury. The CCC men got their parts a few days before the show and rehearsed with the coordinator. "Each boy becomes an actor," the advance packet explained, "and the character he portrays is himself." All the boys in the cast were sworn to secrecy. The show's success depended on surprise.

The CCC Murder Mystery almost didn't get off the ground. At the first tryout, in a camp near Peekskill, New York, there was so much noise from the beer-drinking boys at the back of the hall that it was hard to hear the play. Since there were no chairs, and the boys were exhausted from a long day's work in the woods, some sat on a Ping-Pong table and it collapsed, causing bruises and minor injuries. The professionals didn't have a good grasp of their lines. And, most important, the script was way too complicated and involved too many CCC actors. The audience, once they heard their friends' joking lines, joined in with wisecracks of their own. In short, it was a disaster.

After Grace Hayward simplified the script, there was a second trial, at a camp near Syracuse, New York. This time, it clicked. The twelve professionals of the Federal Theatre company got the audience going with exchanges right out of a Marx Brothers movie.

The District Attorney, played by a touring actor, asks the CCC boy, "What is your full name?" The CCC boy answers: "I don't know; I ain't never been full." The DA asks another witness: "What do you earn here in the camp?" The CCC boy answers, "A hundred dollars a month."

"I understood you only got thirty," says the DA.

"That's what I get," answers the CCC boy. "I earn more."

One of the favorite bits involved a "Gracie Allen" type named Mugs Murphy, who tweaks the judge by calling him "Judgie" and confesses to having dated several boys in the camp, whom she mentions by name— causing uproarious laughter in the hall.

Judge to Mugsie: What did he say when he left you?

Mugsie: Shall I leave out the profanity?

Judge: Of course.

Mugsie: Then he didn't say anything.

Mugsie's irreverence especially appealed to the CCCers, who dealt every day with the hierarchy of the camp.

The CCC boys played their parts with gusto. "Even the late Will Rogers, an ad lib expert himself, would have laughed if he had heard the CCC amateur actors add pungency to their lines," reported the *Syracuse Herald*.[10] There were surprises for the CCC actors as well as the audience. "The whole thing is so arranged," the *Syracuse American* noted, "that the patchwork pieces of the witnesses fit together to make the story, and the subsequent thrill the boys get by finding out what happened is a generous reward for their own efforts as performers."[11]

By the time Hallie Flanagan saw *The CCC Murder Mystery* in Virginia, the opening had acquired new polish: "It was very warm and the small hall was crowded with boys, sitting on the floor, on tables, on windowsills. I wondered how any actors could hold this high-spirited, restless audience. Suddenly an automobile drove up, a man jumped out and, displaying a sheriff's badge, drew the commander aside for whispered consultation. Everyone grew silent. The sheriff pounded on the table, 'Men, I'm sorry to break in on your meeting this way but on account of the fact that so many witnesses in this case are CCC workers, and that the camp is so far from the county courthouse, His Honor has decided to hold court right here.'"

At that point, the rec hall doors swung open again: A judge in robes, followed by two men in suits, the defense and prosecuting attorneys, entered and took their places on the makeshift stage. "The eight actors," Hallie wrote, "who, with no scenery and only a few hand props, carried the weight of the play, acted with a contagious intensity which communicated itself to the twenty impromptu actors from the camp and to the audience."[12]

The CCC Murder Mystery was a hit. Nine Federal Theatre companies picked up the play and toured with it over the next two years. Eventually, it was performed in 258 camps all along the Atlantic coast and would have toured the entire country were it not for cuts in the budget.

"It would be difficult to decide who enjoyed the play more," one coordinator reported, "the fellows who actually had a part or those who were spectators merely . . . In the productions staged here in the past I always had the impression there were some things lacking . . . *CCC Murder Mystery* went over big."[13]

chapter seven

THE SIMPLE AND THE DIFFICULT

Of all the triumphs of the Federal Theatre Project, the first two—*Triple-A Plowed Under* and *Murder in the Cathedral*, which opened a week later—may have been the sweetest for Hallie Flanagan. It was she, after all, who had championed the Living Newspaper, only to see it threatened with extinction. And it was she whose history with T. S. Eliot made *Murder in the Cathedral* seem a natural choice for the Federal Theatre. Hallie had met and gotten to know T. S. Eliot during her Guggenheim tour, and she subsequently produced an early verse work of his, entitled *Sweeney*, at Vassar. Eliot visited Vassar at the time of the production and stayed long enough to answer some questions from the Vassar undergraduates.

"Was the production what you expected?" asked a Vassar student.

"The moment expected may be unforeseen when it arrives," Eliot answered.

He used that same tantalizing line three years later in *Murder in the Cathedral*.[1]

After Eliot left Vassar, he wrote Hallie from Cambridge that "the whole experience was very memorable for me; and if I ever do succeed in producing a complete play—whether you like it or not—I shall attribute its completion to the stimulus which I received at Vassar."[2] The "complete play," Hallie Flanagan believed, was *Murder in the Cathedral*.

Murder in the Cathedral was the production that forced critics to take the Federal Theatre Project seriously. Before the opening, many viewed the Project as a rescue effort. Wrote Bosley Crowther in the *New York Times*: "Whatever view one takes toward it—that of a Liberty Leaguer[3] or that of an otherwise unemployed actor—one vital point remains: a lot of theatre people have lived through the Winter because of it."[4]

Murder in the Cathedral (National Archives and Records Administration)

After *Murder in the Cathedral* opened, it was no longer possible for critics to view the Federal Theatre Project as a purely charitable undertaking. Eliot's verse play, which takes place in the hours after Thomas à Becket's return to England from seven years in exile, surprised and delighted the critics. Stark Young, the thoughtful reviewer for the *New Republic*, called the production "an astonishing combination of the simple and the difficult, almost the impossible," and concluded that it was "one of the distinguished moments in the year's theatre."[5] *Billboard*, one of the professional organs that, along with *Variety*, viewed the Federal Theatre Project as a threat to standards, concluded that the production should "completely smother the old cries of incompetence directed against the project."[6]

Robert Benchley, humorist and sophisticate, wrote in the *New Yorker* that *Murder in the Cathedral* was "the most ambitious, and also the best, of the Federal Theatre offerings so far." Benchley's praise was interlarded with complaints about the atmosphere surrounding Federal Theatre productions. Benchley longed for the good old days of decorous theatregoing: "An unfortunate feature of governmental control of one of the arts," he wrote, "seems to be a tendency to factional snarlings and bad-blood spilling. Heads may be in the clouds, but chips are on every shoulder. The lobby of the Biltmore Theatre during the run of *Triple-A Plowed Under* has the tense atmosphere of a high-school foyer on the eve of an inter-sorority debate, and resignations, criminations, and recriminations fly through the air with each production."

Benchley's sharpest barbs were aimed at left-wing ideologues, who were incapable of understanding Eliot's satirical thrust in *Murder in the Cathedral*. After Becket is murdered because of his refusal to condone the king's heresy, the four knights who have done the deed deliver a series of speeches in which they try to justify their violent acts. One knight explains: We knights had nothing to gain by the murder, and we did it only in service of the people and of the greater good: Order needed to be restored. Besides, concludes another of the assassins, the archbishop provoked us to it: He *wanted* a death by martyrdom, in order to enhance his cause. "I think, with these facts before you," concludes another of the knights, "you will unhesitatingly render a verdict of 'Suicide while of Unsound Mind.'"

The knights' speeches at the conclusion of *Murder in the Cathedral* were Eliot's oblique references to Hitler and Mussolini, whose threats of violence were casting an ominous shadow over Europe by the spring of 1936. Robert Benchley praised them as "first-class modern satire."

But according to Benchley, Eliot's satire was lost on some members of the audience. "A little nest of ardent proletarians," he reported, "all set to applaud any reference to the Cause, heard one of the speakers say that 'under certain circumstances, violence is permissible,' and, forgetting that it was *Fascist* violence that was being excused . . . burst into ecstatic hand-clapping . . .

"We must all be very careful," Benchley scolded, "to listen to just what cause is being advocated before we applaud a phrase which might apply to several. In fact, these little groups of applauders constitute one of the main nuisances of the Federal Theatre Project."

Despite his grousing, Benchley agreed with the growing consensus. "All over town," he wrote, "from Harlem down to Macdougal Street, little groups of hitherto unemployed actors, musicians, and technicians are putting on shows of their own, under the auspices of the federal government, and darned good shows, too, some of them."

Benchley even admitted there were some things the Federal Theatre Project could do that profit-making theatre couldn't. *Murder in the Cathedral*, he wrote, "is a production of which any commercial manager would be proud, although probably no commercial manager would undertake it. You can't blame the commercial managers, but you can be glad that the Federal Theatre has come along to give us plays that otherwise we might not see."[7]

As Benchley might have expected, the Communist *Daily Worker* disliked *Murder in the Cathedral* intensely because it dealt with religion, the opiate of the people. The *Daily Worker* declared it to be a tract "based entirely on medieval philosophy and superstitions" and "almost as dull as a sermon and about as effective as an encyclical." It consisted, complained the Communist organ, of "long, long tedious declamations, interspersed with frequent chants by a chorus of women who wail in dark brown costumes."[8]

The *Daily Worker* notwithstanding, *Murder in the Cathedral* was a credit to the ingenuity of its director, Halstead Welles, a twenty-something disciple of the revolutionary theatre of Meyerhold. "No production of recent memory," wrote John Mason Brown in the *Post*, "stands more in debt of its director . . . In his handling of crowds, in the lovely fluidity of his choral groupings and in the high visual excitement of those moments when his stage swarms with ominous lancers and red-robed assassins, Mr. Welles shows himself to be as resourceful as he is inventive."[9]

A paradox underlay Welles's triumph. His actors were, by and large, old stock players and vaudevillians for whom the highly intellectual, poetic drama of T. S. Eliot, played on an avant-garde set that consisted of unadorned risers, ramps, and stairways, was an entirely new and alien experience.

Norman Lloyd, a young actor who knew and liked many of the old-timers, recalls being up on a ramp on one of these stripped-down sets with an accomplished old pro named Fuller Mellish. Suddenly, Mellish shouted out toward the director: "I say, old boy, how do I get home to my wife?" Mellish had never been on such a set in his entire acting career, and he didn't know how to get down.[10]

Social Security hadn't yet gone into effect in 1936. Particularly for the old actors on the project, the weekly $23.86 paycheck was crucial, and plays like *Murder in the Cathedral*, with its large choruses, were welcome, even if they required new learning. Halstead Welles recalled that many old women in the chorus "had been out of work for so long, they glowed to be working. They were so thankful to have a line of poetry to say that their voices quivered and they wrapped their words in tinsel." Welles told them, "Don't quiver for beauty, give me simplicity and whiskey voices."[11]

The lead role in *Murder in the Cathedral* was played by a longtime Shake-spearean actor named Harry Irvine, who had been out of work for almost ten years when he arrived at the WPA offices. An old theatre friend recognized him and convinced him to go on relief—the prerequisite for getting a job. Irvine's pride was wounded, but he went along. By the time casting got under way for *Murder in the Cathedral*, he was official. He auditioned and got the part of Thomas à Becket.

The Becket role is a challenge to any actor: forty pages of dense verse to memorize and bring to life. Irvine proved equal to the task. Nearly all the critics took note of Irvine's noble performance. "Harry Irvine," wrote Joseph Wood Krutch in the *Nation*, "gives Thomas fine dignity and fire."[12]

"It is certainly one of the glories of the much-abused Federal project that it has provided him [Mr. Irvine] with his long-overdue opportunity," wrote Richard Watts in the *Tribune*.[13]

Murder in the Cathedral played at the Manhattan Theatre for six weeks. Toward the end of the run, Eleanor Roosevelt came to see it. When she entered the theatre, accompanied by her son and his wife, the audience rose and applauded. As they neared their seats in the front of the house, the orchestra members rose, too, and bowed. According to Hallie, who accompanied her, Eleanor Roosevelt was so impressed that she asked to go backstage and visit with the cast. "The hush that fell over the company of some two hundred actors, stagehands and staff as she spoke to them and told them that she was deeply moved by the production and that she was very grateful to the Federal Theatre for producing this play, is something to be remembered." Harry Irvine, the old actor playing Becket, expressed his gratitude by kissing the first lady's hand.[14]

Three days after the triumphant opening of *Murder in the Cathedral*, Hallie left on a tour of the South in a mood of high optimism. "Leaving Washington by car in the morning," she wrote Phil, "on a perfect day with blue mist over the Capitol and the markets along the river front spectacular with piles of orange carrots, sacks of new potatoes and great clumps of bananas, cabbages, broccoli and daffodils all mixed up in a fine confusion."[15] The date was March 24, 1936. Another Federal Theatre production of even greater historic significance was just three weeks away.

chapter eight

DO YOU VOODOO?

In late 1934, a year before the Federal Theatre Project began, two electric encounters in New York theatres profoundly influenced its fate. The first occurred downtown in Union Square, a vortex of soapbox oratory and left-wing agitation, following the performance of a play about New Orleans dockworkers called *Stevedore*. *Stevedore* may well have been the most radical play of its time. Like Clifford Odets's *Waiting for Lefty*, the call to action that has been called "the birth cry of the thirties,"[1] *Stevedore* whipped its audience into a frenzy and sometimes propelled them onto the stage to join the final battle on the barricades. But what made *Stevedore* more daring than *Lefty* was its head-on attack on the issues of race that most theatre of the time, whether written by whites or blacks, avoided or sugar-coated.

Stevedore tells the story of a New Orleans white woman who is brutally beaten by her illicit lover, then tries to protect herself from scandal by claiming she was raped by a black man. In the police lineup that results, she identifies her assailant as one Lonnie Thompson, a black stevedore and leader in the fight for union rights on the levees. Lonnie manages to escape arrest and go into hiding, but the incident stirs up a white mob, who riot in the streets. It takes the solidarity of union men, black and white, to drive them off.

Stevedore's content alone—the rape, the framing of a black man, the overarching message of union solidarity between blacks and whites—was enough to create controversy in many circles. What's more, *Stevedore* mirrored the ongoing case of the Scottsboro boys, nine young black men who had been falsely accused of and arrested for rape after a racial incident in Alabama in 1931. The Scottsboro boys' case was a *cause célèbre* in

Voodoo *Macbeth* (National Archives and Records Administration)

leftist circles. *Stevedore* was provocative enough to get the attention of some members of Congress during its five-month run in Union Square. Later, as a Federal Theatre production, it got their attention a second time.

Written by a Kentuckian named Paul Peters and reworked by a young Baker workshop graduate named George Sklar, *Stevedore* was greeted enthusiastically by most of the New York critics and even more enthusiastically by its mixed-race audiences. Blacks and whites together lustily stamped their feet and cheered on the stevedores. And according to a *Times* reviewer, "The final scene on the barricade, in which . . . struggle is visualized in gunfire, gathering mobs and flying bricks, remains a climactic triumph."[2] The tap-dancer Bill "Bojangles" Robinson reportedly was so stirred that he jumped out of his seat and ran up onto the stage, where he joined the stevedores in fighting off the white racist mob.

Some nights, shouting matches and fistfights kept going even after the curtain came down. And it was on such a night that Canada Lee, a member of the *Stevedore* cast, came to the rescue of a very tall young man with a little-boy face and violent dark eyes who was rising to the bait of some dangerous toughs in the audience. "One guy came at him with a big blade," Canada Lee recalled. "I jumped up and told the guy to get the hell out of there."[3] The young man Canada Lee rescued that night was Orson Welles.

The contrast between Orson Welles and Canada Lee was striking: Welles was a pale, pudgy giant, awkward on his feet and supremely unathletic. He had traveled the world with his father and liked to think of himself as a sophisticate. But Welles was more book-smart than street-smart, which made his tendency to court danger all the more alarming. Canada Lee, on the other hand, was compact, graceful, and supremely street-smart. Before he became an actor, Lee had made a national reputation as a prize-fighter. In more prosperous times, Canada Lee had cut a stylish figure in Harlem nightspots, drinking moderate numbers of Shandy Gaffs and surveying the crowd from beneath a snap-brim hat.

Before that night in Union Square, Canada Lee had viewed acting as a lark and a temporary means of support. But all that changed after his encounter with Orson Welles.

The second fateful moment came not long after the first, on the Broadway opening night of one of the most highly touted productions of the year: a star-studded *Romeo and Juliet* that the *New York Times* elevated to "a high place of modern magnificence—another jewel on the cheek of the theatre's nights." In attendance that night at the gilded neo-Byzantine Martin Beck Theatre[4] was a young producer and director named John

Houseman. The evening was "glossy and successful," Houseman remembered, and included a "fervent Juliet" performed by the renowned Katharine Cornell and a "polite, middle-aged Romeo" played by the great Basil Rathbone. But what stood out for Houseman was the "excitement of two brief moments when the furious Tybalt appeared suddenly in that sunlit Verona square: death, in scarlet and black, in the form of a monstrous boy—flat-footed and graceless, yet swift and agile . . . What made this figure so obscene and terrible was the pale, shiny child's face under the unnatural growth of dark beard, from which there issued a voice of such clarity and power that it tore like a high wind through the genteel, modulated voices of the well-trained professionals around him. 'Peace! I hate the word as Hell!' cried the sick boy, as he shuffled along, driven by some irresistible interior violence to kill and soon himself, inevitably, to die."[5] The "monstrous boy" playing Tybalt was Orson Welles. John Houseman's fascination with Welles, which began that night, was about to lead to one of the most important artistic alliances in theatre history.

A successful international grain merchant until he lost everything in the Depression, Houseman had a commanding presence that made him seem older than his thirty-two years. He had begun to build a reputation for himself as a sort of maverick highbrow producer. His first success had been an opera called *Four Saints in Three Acts*, with music by Virgil Thomson, based on a text by Gertrude Stein. The opera, performed to critical acclaim on Broadway with an all-black cast, resulted in ties to the Harlem community and made Houseman a palatable choice when Hallie Flanagan and her assistants were casting about for someone to head up the Harlem Negro theatre unit.

Right from the start, Hallie Flanagan had committed the Federal Theatre Project to an enlightened race policy: Black performers would receive equal pay for equal work, and audiences for all Federal Theatre performances would be integrated. This was unusual at the time. Only two other New York companies insisted on integrated audiences: the Group Theatre (producer of *Waiting for Lefty*) and the Theatre Union (producer of *Stevedore*). Surprisingly, even shows that claimed to glorify the black experience didn't necessarily give equal pay or insist on integrated audiences: Marc Connelly's Pulitzer Prize–winning *Green Pastures* paid its black actors below scale and was performed in a theatre in Washington, D.C., that did not admit blacks.

Under Hallie Flanagan's watch, the Federal Theatre Project did not tolerate such discrimination. If a theatre refused to seat blacks and whites together, the Federal Theatre canceled the performance. Racist employees were not tolerated, either. When a white project manager tried to segregate black actors and white technicians traveling to Dallas on a private railroad car, the actors protested and the manager was fired. A white assistant director of the vaudeville and circus program was removed because he was unable to work well with blacks. In fact, the Federal Theatre Project was probably the least discriminatory of all the WPA programs.[6] Certainly it was years ahead of that other branch of the federal government, the United States military, which remained segregated until well after World War II.

Although some Federal Theatre productions mixed whites and blacks, the plan from the beginning had been to establish Negro units all around the nation, with the hope of fulfilling W. E. B. Du Bois's dream of a theatre of the people, for the people, by the people, and *near* the people.[7] To this end, Hallie Flanagan had called on Rose McClendon, a majestic actress who had starred in *Porgy* and Langston Hughes's *Mulatto* and founded the Negro People's Theatre, to advise her. Hallie remembers that at a first meeting of Harlem theatre people, at Rose McClendon's house, she asked if the Negro unit in Harlem should be headed by "members of their own race."[8] McClendon maintained that a white director would be better able to lead the company. Apparently, her opinion was shared by other experienced professionals in Harlem. "You [had] to have somebody," explained Carlton Moss, who became Houseman's African American assistant, "who the community felt could go downtown and not be thrown off the elevator or not be insulted before he got into the building."[9]

So even though there were blacks with much more theatre experience, John Houseman was asked to co-direct the Negro unit in Harlem. His partner was to be Rose McClendon. But by late 1935, when the Negro unit got under way, McClendon was fatally ill with cancer. Thus the white man, John Houseman, stood alone, charged with the task of breathing life back into the Lafayette Theatre at 132nd Street and Seventh Avenue, once the home of a respected black company, and, more important, restoring hope to Harlem's large and destitute community of performing artists.

To rich visitors from downtown, Harlem during the Depression looked like a carefree place. "From midnight until dawn," reported *Variety* in 1929, "it is a seething cauldron of Nubian mirth and hilarity." There were fashionable nightclubs like the Cotton Club and Small's Paradise, Connies' Inn and the Nest, where white clientele flocked to see girls with fans and feathers dance to whirling renditions by Duke Ellington of tunes like "When My Sugar Walks Down the Street" or to marvel at the virtuoso tap-dancing of Bill "Bojangles" Robinson and Kid Chocolate. There were also, until FDR put an end to Prohibition, untold numbers of speakeasies. Every other cigar store and beauty parlor in Harlem, it seemed, sold gin on the side. Harlem was a playground after dark, for white and black gentry alike.[10]

But in truth, Harlem had never been as gay and carefree as the readers of *Variety* were led to believe. There was a black social life in Harlem, but it took place at smaller speakeasies and rent parties, not the highly visible clubs frequented by Emily Vanderbilt and others on the *Social Register*. Those were "white trade" nightclubs, 90 percent white owned, which barred "mixed race" couples and all but a very few blacks with some claim to fame. At the Cotton Club, writes David Levering Lewis, "very light Afro-Americans were given the green light by the manager, George 'Big Frenchy' Demange. Otherwise, the only Harlemites seen by seven hundred white revelers each night were high-stepping, high-yellow chorines ('Tall, Tan and Terrific') and tuxedoed musicians."[11]

In fact, Harlem was a community of poor people who worked when they could. Fifty percent of the 350,000 blacks in Harlem were on relief. Without the protection of the growing union movement, which denied them membership for the most part, African American men were last hired and first fired. African American women, who could often find work only as domestics, were equally hard hit and worked for lower and lower wages as the Depression deepened. It was, as *Ebony* magazine described it, "a time of appalling suffering and privation, of grown men crying, and women wringing their hands in empty kitchens," of "battered furniture standing on concrete curbs, of crowds protesting and Communists organizing the discontent, of big government trucks cruising through Negro neighborhoods and dropping off navy beans and powdered milk."[12]

Not long before Houseman began to set up the Federal Theatre Negro unit, a false rumor that police had brutally beaten, and perhaps even murdered, a Puerto Rican boy for shoplifting had set off a riot in Harlem. Thousands of angry Harlemites had filled the streets, breaking store windows and looting, yelling at police and merchants. The white store owners asked for help from the governor. Mayor Fiorello LaGuardia, urging calm, appointed a commission. The Puerto Rican boy, as it turned out, was unharmed, but one suspected looter was killed and more than a hundred were wounded. Predictably, some accused "Reds" of stirring up the crowd.

Yet in the weeks that followed, it became obvious that the real cause of the rioting was the desperate situation of Harlem residents. "It was not a riot," a young Adam Clayton Powell Jr. wrote a week after the disturbance, "it was an open unorganized protest against empty stomachs, overcrowded

tenements, filthy sanitation, rotten foodstuffs, chiseling landlords and merchants, discrimination on relief, disfranchisement and against a disinter-
ested administration. It was not caused by Communists."[13]

"A great majority" of the participants, according to Powell, "were men
and women who have worked and held decent jobs in the past, but who
have no reason or self-discipline when their bellies are rubbing their back-
bones."[14]

Outside the Lafayette, where the Federal Theatre was preparing to take
over, there was an elm tree some called "the tree of hope," which entertainers rubbed for good luck. But in recent times, the tree hadn't been
much help. Even in the federal relief programs that preceded the WPA,
blacks believed they had been discriminated against. "What about Federal
Relief jobs?" wrote Powell. "In the field of drama . . . the Civil Works
Administration refuses to hire Negroes. Out of thirty or more productions
under the CWA only one employs Negroes, and that is exuberantly entitled *Meek Mose.*" Powell added: "I forgot, one Negro has a stellar role in
the production of 'Julius Caesar'—the part of the slave."[15]

All that was about to change. Recruiting for the Harlem unit began on
a large scale in late fall of 1935, in a temporary space on lower Madison
Avenue—a vast empty hall with concrete floors and hastily assembled par-
titions containing secondhand desks and benches. The rush for admission
to the Negro unit, John Houseman remembered, "was such that guards had
to be summoned to control the flow of milling applicants, many of whom
arrived downtown in a state of bewildered and angry hysteria."[16] Rumors
of job opportunities brought established relief cases and new applicants, all
of whose skills were difficult or impossible to verify. In the beginning, the
Negro unit accepted all comers who had authentic relief documents. But
the real challenge came in finding experienced performers who might *not*
have relief credentials but were needed to make the project work. To this
end, the Negro unit under Houseman took unusual liberties.

Leonard de Paur, a young choral director, remembered being "rushed
onto relief" in three days, when the process usually took weeks.[17] Other
professionals were hired, like Houseman, as part of the nonrelief 10 percent. By the time it was all over, the Negro unit had hired about 750 people to work onstage and backstage, doing everything from carpentry to
clerical work to costume making, from ushering to timekeeping, almost all
at the going government rate of about $23 a week. The Negro unit of the
Federal Theatre Project became, in a matter of weeks, the largest single
employer in Harlem. Of the 750 on the payroll, according to Houseman's
calculations, between 400 and 500 were officially classified as actors,

singers, or dancers. And of these, about one third had never been onstage in their lives, while half of the rest had been part of a chorus as singers or dancers or played an extra in a film. That left perhaps 150 with professional experience.

"Late in October 1935," Houseman recalled, "about the time Mussolini was invading Ethiopia, the Negro Theatre Project, with its more than seven hundred and fifty men and women and its battered desks, chairs and filing cabinets, began its move from lower Madison Avenue to Harlem." Then came the task of renovating the Lafayette, a turn-of-the-century theatre that had once housed a Negro stock company but which had become, in Houseman's words, "a sordid icy cavern . . . with peeling plaster, a thick accumulation of grime, burst bulbs, rotting carpets and broken seats in the hairy recesses of which lurked rats, lice and other horrors."[18]

Within a month, the house of the Lafayette had been decently restored, and miracles had begun to happen on the stage itself. Carpenters and electricians who had been denied membership, because of color, in the stagehands union were working again in their profession. "The miles of new rope that Feder [lighting director Abe Feder] had requisitioned, the scores of up-to-date electrical units hanging overhead and the six portable dimmer boards with their dozens of multicolored switches and levers were a source of excitement and pride" to the stage crew, Houseman reported, making them "the most consistently enthusiastic department of the project."

Early on, members of the all-white stagehands union had come to Houseman to protest the nonunion shop building the sets and running the show. When Houseman told them he'd be glad to hire union labor if they would admit blacks, the union members threatened to picket. He responded: "If you seriously think you can picket a theatre in Harlem for hiring Negroes, go right ahead." Needless to say, they didn't picket.

Houseman's next daunting challenge, as a white man directing an almost exclusively Negro project, was to decide on repertoire: Whatever he chose must take into account the wildly varying levels of ability and experience in his very large company. Also, most important, it must be acceptable to the Harlem community, which was already predisposed to distrust the federal relief effort. Relying on the advice of Carlton Moss, a Harlem theatre man with his ear to the ground, Houseman quickly ruled out the options that were most likely to offend. There had been a whole group of successes on Broadway that involved Negro casts, including Eugene O'Neill's *Emperor Jones* and the play *Porgy*, as well as "folk" dramas written in a black idiom by white men, like Marc Connelly's *Green Pastures*, a fantasy about an all-black heaven presided over by De Lawd. These had been popular on Broadway, but Harlem audiences would have resented white-authored interpretations of black experience on their own stage. Various reviews and musicals, which had long been a source of employment for blacks downtown, were also ruled out as "handkerchief head."

Finally, Houseman hit on a two-part solution: One half of the Negro unit would perform plays by and for Negroes, in Negro locales and addressing contemporary issues. The other half of the Negro unit would focus on the classical repertoire, "without concession or reference to color."

Houseman settled on Frank Wilson's *Walk Together, Chillun!* a drama laced with spirituals, as the first production of what he called the "indigenous" unit. Then, convinced that success depended on "exceptionally high" quality in the classical productions, Houseman paid a visit to the "monstrous boy," Orson Welles, in the basement apartment on West Fourteenth Street where he was living with his new wife, Virginia. By that time, Welles and Houseman had spent a good deal of time together, fantasizing about producing classic repertoire. "I suggested that our dream of staging a whirling Elizabethan drama might now be realized under unusual but attractive conditions—with Uncle Sam as our angel."

Welles said yes immediately. And at two A.M. the next morning, he placed a follow-up phone call to Houseman to relay an inspired idea from Virginia. The first production of the classical Negro unit should be *Macbeth*, relocated to the island of Haiti in the early nineteenth century, a time of turmoil that would parallel the violent events of the Scottish play. The witches in this *Macbeth* would use voodoo to conjure up their "double, double toil and trouble." Thus was born one of the most important and sensational of the Federal Theatre productions, universally described as "voodoo *Macbeth*."

Within a week, Welles had constructed a plasticene model of the set on an ironing board in his apartment. It consisted of a series of ramps and parapets anchored by two squat, fat pillars and a multistoried tower suggesting Macbeth's castle. His design was based loosely on the grand residence built by the courageous but tyrannical Henri Christophe, Haitian ruler in the early 1800s. Welles also began working with designer Nat Karson, an out-of-work graduate of the Chicago Art Institute who would provide the production with the eye-popping Directoire costumes and eerie jungle backdrops Welles envisioned.

To cast what was, as Houseman noted, "the first full-scale professional Negro Shakespearean production in theatrical history," he and Welles sought out black actors with experience in contemporary theatre. Jack Carter, who was cast as Macbeth, had made a reputation playing Crown in the original *Porgy*, as well as the lead role in *Stevedore*. Edna Thomas, cast as Lady Macbeth, had also played in *Stevedore*, as well as a popular black-authored folk play, Hall Johnson's *Run, Little Chillun*. Probably the least experienced of the principals was Canada Lee, who had first encountered Welles the year before when he rescued him from the marauders in Union Square. Welles cast Lee as the worthy but doomed Banquo, who carries knowledge he dares not reveal. The role of Banquo promised to be the biggest challenge by far in Canada Lee's fledgling career.

When it came to casting the "witches," Welles got lucky. The same African troupe, led by Asadata Dafora Horton, that had inspired Hallie Flanagan and Elmer Rice to attempt *Ethiopia* found the perfect fit in voodoo *Macbeth*. To this core of African performers, Welles added two dozen male and female voodoo celebrants, thus enlarging the circle, and the importance, of the three weird sisters in Shakespeare's original.

Anyone in the Negro unit who wanted to could try out for a role in *Macbeth*, and Houseman and Welles spent the better part of a week in the large recreation hall belonging to the Ancient Order of Monarch Elks, auditioning hundreds of aspirants. "Old and young," Houseman recalled, "male and female, singers, dancers, semiliterates and intellectuals—some in deadly earnest, some giggling in self-conscious embarrassment; still others who came suspiciously, regarding the whole thing as an elaborate joke." The cast, in the end, numbered over one hundred.[19]

Orson Welles had been reworking the Shakespeare plays since adolescence and had even put on a compilation of Shakespeare's history plays, which he called *The Winter of Our Discontent*, when he attended the Todd School for Boys in Woodstock, Illinois. So it is not surprising that he took great liberties with *Macbeth*, eliminating some minor characters and building up others, all in service of the voodoo idea. Even Lady Macbeth, so often seen as the malevolent schemer who spurs her husband on to murder, had stiff competition, in voodoo *Macbeth*, from the witches. In particular, Welles gave unprecedented importance to chief witch Hecate. In Welles's version of *Macbeth*, the role of Hecate is played not by a woman, but by a man, and a scary one at that—peering out with black-socket eyes from beneath a hooded robe and wielding an enormous bullwhip.

Hecate has one scene in Shakespeare's original. In Welles's voodoo version, Hecate appears in the opening scene with Macbeth, urges him to kill Macduff's family, joins in the murder of Banquo, and has the last word before the final curtain. It is but one example of the way in which Welles was willing to manipulate the text to serve his vision and to defy the Shake-spearean traditions he found so stifling.

What Welles especially liked about working with a black cast, as he ex-plained to a *New York Times* reporter who visited rehearsals, was that "these Negroes have never had the misfortune of hearing Elizabethan verse spouted by actors strongly flavoring of well-cured Smithfield. They read their lines just as they would any others. On the whole, they're no better and no worse than the average white actor before he discovered the 'red plush curtain' style."[20]

Orson Welles was only twenty when he made these pronouncements. The fancy references to "Smithfield" ham and " 'red plush curtain' style" were obviously meant to impress the *Times* reporter with his theatrical savoir faire. He also managed to obscure his age (the *Times* report men-tions the twenty-year-old Orson is "not yet 25") and to pad his résumé, citing experience at four different theatres in London and Dublin, even though he had worked at only one theatre in Ireland, playing a bit part and painting scenery.

Orson Welles's tendency to inflate his credentials and to claim all the credit offended many who were older and wiser. "Welles," noted Phil Bar-ber, the new head of the New York division, "has all the gall that you can possibly conceive of any human being ever having."[21]

But even those who resented Orson Welles were impressed by the clar-ity of his vision. "He was extremely professional," recalled Virgil Thom-son, who was in charge of music for the production, "and he knew exactly what he wanted. He knew it so well and so thoroughly that I, as an older musician with a certain amount of pride . . . would not humiliate myself to write so precisely on demand."[22]

It was Orson Welles's knowledge of Shakespeare and his vision of the production that allowed him to get by with his sometimes outrageous be-havior during the twelve weeks of strenuous rehearsals, in which he endlessly worked and reworked scenes. Even when he was absent, as he often was be-cause he was earning a good living with his consummate radio voice during the day, Welles left behind precise instructions for stage manager Tommy An-derson. Crowd scenes were choreographed: On beat one, actors moved up-stage, on beat two they moved right, and so on.[23] When Welles arrived, around midnight, he would have new, sometimes contradictory, ideas and in-structions. Rehearsals often kept going until two or three in the morning.

A sampling from Welles's notes, dictated to his wife, Virginia, eleven days before the opening, provides evidence of his vituperative directing style:

Fix Canada's turn.

Jack [Carter, playing Macbeth] should look more into the air.

JACK FOR GOD'S SAKE LEARN YOUR LINES, AND TAKE
THE WEARINESS OUT OF YOUR BODY WHEN YOU GO
UP STAIRS.
JESUS CHRIST.

PACE, pace, pace, pace . . .

Christ—first half of scene needs ENORMOUS amount of work.

Jack too casual.

"Stay there till we call"—get that move right, for Christ's sake.[24]

Somehow, despite showing up late, drinking on the job, and demanding the impossible, Welles managed to stay in the good graces of the company. "He would rave and rant like a bull," remembers assistant stage manager Edward Dudley, "but people gave him the recognition . . . he was due because no one in the whole outfit knew half as much as he did. He was accepted as a strange kind of man who knew what he was doing."[25]

Once in a while, however, even this long-suffering company had more than they could take. One time not long before the opening, at around four in the morning, after the cast had been rehearsing for almost ten hours in heavy uniforms, the actors simply refused to continue. First Project adviser Eddie Perry and then Orson pleaded with them, explaining that there were certain movements that needed to be fixed that night or not at all, for technical reasons. But no one budged.

Finally, a tall and imperious figure, magnificent in his Napoleonic regalia, appeared on the battlements and began to harangue the mutinous crowd below. It was Macbeth himself, in the person of Jack Carter. Carter, a man who was famously temperamental and inclined to drunken rages, had forged a powerful bond with Orson Welles, introducing him in their few free hours to his Harlem underworld connections and pleasures. Now he came to Orson's rescue, pointing out to the mutineers that he was exhausted, too, and had a bigger part than they did. They might have been working for over nine hours, but he had been working for thirteen. And what was a little fatigue when the whole future of the Negro theatre was at stake? What right had they to squander an opportunity afforded them by Harry Hopkins and the president of the United States?

When Carter finished, the actors, slowly and reluctantly, began to pick up their props and return to their positions. But then Carter added a final insult: "So get back to work! You no-acting sons of bitches."

That did it. The rehearsal deteriorated into a brawl, resulting in some smashed scenery and a slightly injured court lady. No more work was done that night.[26]

The work with the actors was only one part of the overall vision Welles had for *Macbeth*. He wanted the production to be a total theatrical experience, an electrifying and unforgettable assault on all the senses that would make Shakespeare live as he had for Elizabethan audiences. Lighting, costumes, sets, music—all were part of his vision, and he worked tirelessly, and sometimes discordantly, with his talented team to pull it off.

From the start, Welles got into furious battles with the lighting designer, Abe Feder, who had plenty of opinions of his own. Houseman believed that Welles's public yelling at Feder may even have been calculated, since it allowed the Negro cast to see that Welles screamed at whites as well as blacks. Whether because of Welles's attacks or in spite of them, Feder ended up by introducing important innovations into the lighting of *Macbeth*. In the past, Tommy Anderson noted, the rule had been that Negroes should be lit in amber, which had a darkening and deadening effect. Feder devised light-friendly makeups for the cast and found a way to use pinks, blues, and greens in the same frame. "He called it his chocolate color," Anderson recalled.[27]

Sound was as important as light in Welles's conception. The overture was a piece called "Yamekraw," which its composer, the stride pianist James P. Johnson, described as a rhapsody combining spiritual, syncopated, and blues melodies. It was performed by a "first class" orchestra, according to music director Virgil Thomson. "Harlem in the thirties," he noted, "was full of black musicians. The Philharmonic wouldn't engage them. Or any other symphony orchestra."

After the curtain rose, the atmospheric noises began: a trumpet boom, a low roll of thunder, then rain. Then, before long, the beat of the drums, provided by Asadata Dafora Horton and his troupe. "We simply slotted them into the production," Thomson recalled. "I had nothing to do with rehearsing them, because he [Asadata] could do that better than I could."[28]

Yet Thomson did intervene at one point, because he felt the troupe's voodoo didn't seem ominous enough. "Are you giving me the real voodoo?" Thomson asked Asadata suspiciously. Oh yes, Asadata insisted, this was real voodoo. But then it turned out that it was the kind of voodoo that was designed to *ward off* illnesses like beriberi rather than *bring on* illnesses. Houseman claimed that the voodoo chants got darker after that and may even have included the phrases *Meesta Houseman* and *Meesta Welles*. "I never told Orson," Houseman wrote later, "for he was ridiculously superstitious."[29]

Even though Welles had provided the architectural frame, it was Nat Karson who designed painted screens, filled with oversize jungle plants or enormous bones to create an "eerie, luminescent" quality. And it was Karson who created the spectacular costumes. He claimed to have exaggerated only the ensemble costumes, for fear that the entire production would "look like a musical comedy." But in truth, all the costumes were highly exaggerated. In the men, he achieved "almost an architectural form," with huge epaulets that created the impression of "a Greek column with its attendant decoration and tapering to a waistline."[30] Boots were high, often up over the knees, and the soldiers' cylindrical hats were enormous, as were the blunderbusses over their shoulders. The women were swathed in bright satin gowns with Empire waists and huge puffy sleeves. Crisscross patterns of gold ribbon and contrasting colors gave an art deco effect to many of the men's jackets and women's flowing skirts. The colors, as Welles and Karson planned them, were in subdued reds and greens in the beginning and crescendoed to brightest colors in the climactic scene at the center of the play: the banquet scene, which Welles turned into a ball, in which Macbeth sees Banquo's ghost.

As opening night grew near, the huge company and accompanying props and costumes of *Macbeth* began to encroach more and more on the backstage space of the "indigenous company," which had moved on by then from *Walk Together, Chillun* to a popular play by a local physician called *Conjur Man Dies*. Outside the Lafayette, the large company and the elaborate preparations of sets and costumes, along with the voodoo rhythms that went on until all hours of the morning, had aroused the curiosity of the Harlem community. Not all the rumors were friendly; some suspected the production was designed to burlesque Shakespeare and degrade blacks. Others reported that Houseman and Welles were boyfriends who had exhausted the Negro unit's budget on a folly.

But Carlton Moss, assistant director, found ways to build support for the production. Three days before the opening, Harlem residents woke to find "*Macbeth*" stenciled in luminous paint on every corner from 125th to 140th Street and from Lexington Avenue to Broadway. The "tree of hope" in front of the Lafayette was decorated with ribbons and garlands for good luck, and there was a free preview showing for a select local audience. Well before the opening, every ticket had been sold and every first-string critic in town had reserved a seat.

Hallie Flanagan remembered opening night, April 14, 1936, as a series of "lightning flashes: flash of ten thousand people clogging the streets, following the scarlet and gold bands of the Negro Elks, marching with flying banners bearing the strange device: *Macbeth by Wm. Shakespeare*—flash of police holding back the crowds, of newsreel men grinding their cameras on sound-trucks—flash of jewels, silk hats, and ermine. Inside, African drums beat, Lady Macbeth walked on the edge of a jungle throbbing with sinister life, Hecate with his bull-whip lashed out at the witches, Macbeth, pierced by a bullet, took his terrific headlong plunge from the balustrade."[31]

When the curtain rang down on voodoo *Macbeth*, the applause was thunderous and kept going for fifteen minutes, during which time an exuberant Orson Welles joined the cast onstage. The next morning, *Times* critic Brooks Atkinson dropped by Hallie Flanagan's office. Ordinarily, he explained, he wouldn't be up so early in the morning. But he had been so excited about *Macbeth* the night before that he couldn't sleep.[32]

Like most critics, Atkinson had reservations. In particular, critics didn't share Welles's wish to get away from well-spoken and refined Shakespeare, and he worried that the Bard's language didn't get the respect it deserved in the Harlem production. Arthur Pollack of the *Brooklyn Daily Eagle* wrote that the actors "play Shakespeare as if they were apt children who had just discovered the Bard"[33]—a condescending observation that Welles surely took as a compliment.

Yet no one denied that *Macbeth* made a memorable evening in the theatre or that the voodoo elements cast a powerful spell. "The witches scenes from 'Macbeth,' " wrote Atkinson, "have always worried the life out of the polite tragic stage . . . But ship the witches down into the rank and fever-stricken jungles of Haiti, dress them in fantastic costumes, crowd the stage with mad and gabbling throngs of evil worshipers, beat the voodoo drums, raise the voices until the jungle echoes . . . there you have a witches' scene that is logical and a stunning triumph of theatre art."[34]

In the black community, *Macbeth* meant more. "The Negro has become weary of carrying the White Man's blackface burden in the theatre," Roi Ottley wrote in the *Amsterdam News*. "In *Macbeth* he has been given an opportunity to discard the bandanna and burnt-cork casting to play a universal character."[35]

The success of the production had important implications backstage as well. Until the Federal Theatre Project came along, as assistant stage manager

Edward Dudley noted, there had "never been a [black] technician south of 125th street."[36] As a result of *Macbeth* and other productions of the Negro unit, black stagehands were admitted to the union for the first time.

Macbeth was a huge success with Harlem audiences and visitors from downtown. It played at the Lafayette for ten weeks, then traveled south for a brief Broadway run before embarking on a triumphant nationwide tour. Sadly, touring in America presented the black cast and crew with constant evidence of Jim Crow. Because hotels refused to accommodate them, cast members often had to stay at the local Negro Y or be put up in churches, schools, boardinghouses, and private homes.

Yet despite these humiliations, there was satisfaction in knowing that voodoo *Macbeth* was challenging racist practices. In Cincinnati, when management refused to allow blacks out of the segregated balcony seats, performances were canceled. In Bridgeport, Hartford, and Chicago, in Indianapolis, Detroit, Cleveland, and Dallas, a total of 150,000 people of all races sat together to watch an unprecedented all-black Shakespeare production.

The 168 members of the voodoo *Macbeth* company returned to Harlem in triumph in October 1936 aboard a six-car special train. They had traveled four thousand miles. Several hundred friends and relatives were on hand to greet them, accompanied by the swing melodies of the Harlem Elks band. According to the *Herald Tribune*, the actors and actresses were led off the train by Canada Lee, wearing a ten-gallon sombrero he had acquired while the troupe was performing at the Dallas fair.

For Canada Lee, voodoo *Macbeth* was a life-transforming event. Watching Orson Welles in action, he realized he had "found something," a way to make a lasting impact as a serious actor playing genuine, nonstereotyped roles. During rehearsals, "I wanted to stay there all the time, watching and listening. I was so excited I couldn't sleep when I went home." Once he encountered Orson Welles and Shakespeare, "I knew it was the theatre for me, for good."[37]

chapter nine

IT CAN'T HAPPEN HERE

These are not normal times; the people are jumpy and very ready to run after strange gods.

—Franklin Delano Roosevelt, 1935

On May 13, 1935, the bullet-riddled body of a young father named Charles Poole was discovered in a ditch on a lonely road outside Dearborn, Michigan. The timing of his murder added to its cruelty: His wife was in the hospital when he died, giving birth to the couple's second child. Police were puzzled at first: The Poole murder looked like a gangster killing. But Poole was a family man without vices or known enemies. Like millions of others, he had lost his job, then found work on a WPA project after FDR took office. What could have provoked such violent retribution against a seeming innocent?

Charles Poole was murdered because he broke ranks with an organization called the Black Legion, active in the industrial cities of Ohio, Michigan, and Indiana and claiming the allegiance of 135,000 in Michigan alone. According to their creed, the enemies of the Black Legion were "all aliens, Negroes, Jews and cults and creeds believing in racial equality or owing allegiance to any foreign potentates. These we will fight without fear or favor as long as one foe of American liberty is left alive."[1] The Black Legionnaires claimed to be heirs to the Minutemen, freeing the country of foreign domination.

The Black Legion's leverage came from its ability to provide jobs to desperate men. With the aid of industry leaders opposed to union activity, the legion controlled hiring in certain pockets of the steel and auto industry as well as certain New Deal welfare jobs. Leaders boasted that they ran

Scene from the Yiddish production of *It Can't Happen Here*: Doremus Jessup (played by Julius Adler) at left, taking orders from Corpo Shad Ladue (Maurice Krohner) (National Archives and Records Administration)

the entire Federal Emergency Relief Administration in Allen County, Indiana. Indeed, at a time when many were still without work, Black Legion members, even when they came from out of state, all seemed to have jobs. As the investigation proceeded, it became increasingly clear that the Depression was the Black Legion's most powerful recruiting tool.

Around the time the Black Legion arrests were shocking the country, Senator Huey Long of Louisiana reached out to the nation with his "Share Our Wealth" campaign. Huey Long, aka "Kingfish," argued that wealth in America should be taken out of the hands of the few and distributed to the many. He proposed new laws that would use millionaires' incomes to provide every household in America with a "homestead allowance" of $5,000. In the first three months of 1935, Long went on national radio six times. After each broadcast, his office received as many as sixty thousand letters from converts to his cause. Few doubted that Long's timing was linked to presidential ambitions.

The red-nosed, potbellied Huey Long did good things for the poorest people in his state. When Hallie Flanagan visited New Orleans on an inspection tour of Federal Theatre Project units in 1935, she was impressed. "Huey, like Benito [Mussolini]," she wrote in her notebook, "thought in epic sweep. He thought in terms of roads, sea walls, park systems, trade schools, all for his own glory possibly, but also for the people who had never had roads, parks, schools."[2]

Huey Long was famous for getting what he wanted: When he was elected governor, he tore down the governor's mansion, which he considered a hopeless antique, and made his mistress secretary of state. But these were minor infractions compared with his assault on the democratic institutions of the state: He introduced a bill that established a separate police force, answerable only to him, and he required all state workers to contribute 20 percent of their salaries to his coffers. He even kidnapped critics who threatened to expose him.

Long had been an effective campaigner for FDR in 1932, but not long after that the two had parted ways, following a visit in which the Kingfish tried to collect favors from "Frank" for his allegiance. By the time of the 1936 campaign, Roosevelt had come to dislike Huey Long immensely and insisted that no one in his administration have anything to do with him.

On the other hand, FDR tried to stay on the good side of another influential demagogue, the radio priest Father Charles Coughlin. Father Coughlin was the first preacher to make use of mass media as a persuasive tool, and he did it with stunning success. By 1935, he had become one of the most popular men in America, receiving eighty thousand admiring letters a day from those who listened with rapt attention to his *Hour of Power* on the radio.

While Long named the names of his enemies, Coughlin preferred to ascribe all problems to a shadowy conspiracy. Coughlin blamed Jewish international financiers for the Depression and the Communists for everything else. When possible, he combined the two enemies: As a star witness for a congressional committee investigating the Communist threat in 1930, Coughlin explained that "the Hebrew Karl Marx" had invented communism and predicted that the Communists were likely to take over America "by 1933, unless something is done." By the time the 1936 presidential campaign got into full swing, Coughlin was calling FDR the "anti-God." "As I was instrumental in removing Herbert Hoover from the White House," he intoned, "so help me God, I will be instrumental in taking a Communist foe from the chair once occupied by Washington."[3]

Both Long and Coughlin appealed to people for whom the New Deal seemed remote and complicated. According to them, the enemy was centralized power in the hands of a few—in the hands of greedy millionaires, according to Long, or alien money changers, according to Father Coughlin. Ironically, both derived their power from radio, a centralizing force if ever there was one. Like Roosevelt, they were masters of the medium.

Father Coughlin's radio voice was his greatest asset, a "beautiful baritone," according to novelist Wallace Stegner, which "always began in a low rich pitch, speaking slowly, gradually increasing in tempo and vehemence, then soaring to high and passionate tones.[4] Although born in Canada and broadcasting out of Detroit, Coughlin enhanced his appeal with the rolled r's and old-country pronunciations of his Irish ancestors. He was especially popular in states like Massachusetts, which had large Irish Catholic populations.

Long, too, was a gifted radio speaker—some said even better than FDR, whose "fireside chats" had captivated the nation. The question in the Roosevelt camp, as the 1936 election approached, was whether FDR's substance could triumph over the paranoia and anger stirred up by the radio demagogues. Their rise, paralleling the rise of Mussolini and Hitler in Europe and Stalin in the Soviet Union, made many fear that the country might be veering toward totalitarianism.

That summer, while Father Coughlin was packing them in at Madison Square Garden and Huey Long was recruiting for Share Our Wealth over the radio, the novelist Sinclair Lewis put the finishing touches on *It Can't*

Happen Here, his fictional account of a 1936 Fascist takeover of America. Leading the charge, in Sinclair Lewis's novel, was a character named Buzz Windrip, a country boy who boasted in his campaign biography that he was not an educated man but had "read the Bible through from kiver to kiver . . . some eleven times." Buzz Windrip was, like Huey Long, a "Professional Common Man" with "a luminous, ungrudging smile which . . . he turned on and off deliberately like an electric light."

In the Lewis novel, a character named Bishop Prang is a stand-in for Father Coughlin. The bishop's organization of millions operates under the banner of the "League of Forgotten Men" (echoing Roosevelt, who had famously spoken of "the forgotten man"). Bishop comes out foursquare in support of Windrip for president. "And may the Lord guide him and us," the bishop prays on the radio, "across the desert of iniquitous politics and swinishly grasping finance into the golden glory of the Promised Land!"[5]

Up until that juncture, there is more talk than action. But once Windrip, with the endorsement of the bishop, becomes president, the novel takes a frightening turn into the territory of the Black Legion. The soldiers of Windrip's army of Corpos (named for Windrip's ruling Corporative Party) are backed up by a terrorizing militia who claim, like the Black Legionnaires, to be heirs to the original Minutemen.

No doubt Sinclair Lewis, who was famous for accumulating detail from real life, relied heavily on newspaper reports in his creation of the Corpos, the Minute Men, Bishop Prang, and Buzz Windrip. But the most important source for his tale of Fascist horror was the firsthand knowledge his wife, Dorothy Thompson, had acquired as a journalist in Adolf Hitler's Germany.

Dorothy Thompson was among the first to interview Adolf Hitler and to alert the world to the Nazi menace. Within a week of the Nazi takeover, she was writing home to her husband, Sinclair Lewis, about "the chancellor's private army, the S.A. troops, and their picked division, the black-breeched S.S. men" who "broke up opposition meetings, terrorized the streets, staged rows, beat up Social Democratic deputies, and even assaulted leading Catholics."

"You must believe it," she wrote a friend, "because I saw victims with my own eyes . . . They beat them with steel rods, knock their teeth out with revolver butts, break their arms—a favorite trick—give them a liter of castor oil; bring them out of unconsciousness by throwing water in their faces, or mustard in their eyes, urinate on them, make them kneel and kiss the Hakenkreuz [the swastika]." She added: "Not a single newspaper dares to bring out anything of true events."[6]

Because of her bold and early truth telling, Dorothy Thompson was expelled from Germany in 1934. When she returned home, she was besieged by requests for interviews and speeches. Sinclair Lewis was, by that time, a renowned American novelist who had won the Nobel Prize. A brilliant wit and mimic who liked parlor games, Lewis found the constant discussion of Hitler and the Nazis around his house to be oppressive. On more than one occasion, he told friends that if he ever were to divorce Dorothy Thompson, he would name Adolf Hitler as corespondent.[7]

Lewis obviously resented his wife's success, which had stolen the limelight from him. He also had a distaste for abstract discussion of political affairs. His great gift, in chronicling life in Middle America in such novels as *Babbitt*, was his eye for the specific and his ability to build up detail until he had captured a world. At times, Lewis was known to split a party at his home into two groups: those who wanted to talk about "It" with Dorothy and others who wanted to talk with him about "something useless." If he arrived late to one of Dorothy's soirees, he would ask with trepidation, "Is she talking about *It*?" If "It" was the subject, he was likely to slip out again.[8]

Yet had it not been for Dorothy Thompson, Sinclair Lewis would never have written *It Can't Happen Here*. Her detailed knowledge of events in Germany turned up everywhere in his American version of fascism: His torturers used the same methods, right down to the castor oil, his MMs were clearly an American version of the Nazi SS. And the overarching message of the book came from Thompson, who held that Hitler came to power in Germany "because so-called civilized people did not believe that he could."[9]

Thompson provided the protection Lewis needed to write the book as well. During the summer of 1935, the two of them holed up at their home in Barnard, Vermont, where Thompson fended off visitors. Lewis was "working nine hours a day," she explained to a friend, "on a novel which he is writing all in one flood with great enthusiasm and to the exclusion of everything else."[10]

The long novel, begun in May, was finished by mid–August and published in October. *It Can't Happen Here* became an immediate success. Ironically, since Lewis disliked political argument, the novel was hailed by reviewers everywhere as a political act rather than an artistic achievement.

Not long after Sinclair Lewis created the character of Buzz Windrip, his real-life inspiration ceased to be. On September 8, 1935, a young man dressed in a white linen suit suddenly broke through the phalanx of bodyguards surrounding Senator Huey Long as he left a session of the Louisiana

Legislature in Baton Rouge. The man in white withdrew a pistol from his pocket and fired it into Long's abdomen at close range. Within thirty hours, the Kingfish was no more.

Sinclair Lewis's story interested Hollywood nonetheless. MGM hired the well-known writer Sidney Howard to adapt *It Can't Happen Here* for the screen. But after spending $200,000 on the script, the studio dropped the project: Executives in the foreign department feared it might lead to a ban on all MGM pictures in Fascist countries. The MGM decision, which so clearly reinforced the point of Lewis's novel, resulted in a doubling of sales of the book, from twenty-five hundred to five thousand a week.[11] It also caught the attention of Hallie Flanagan and her play bureau director, Francis Bosworth. Very soon, they were talking about the possibility of a Federal Theatre production of *It Can't Happen Here*. Then Bosworth made a highly unusual proposal: Instead of mounting one production of *It Can't Happen Here* in New York, why not open the play simultaneously in theatres all around the country?[12]

Hallie Flanagan immediately loved the idea. Perhaps it reminded her of her conversation a decade earlier with Luigi Pirandello, who had a dream of simultaneous productions in three Italian cities.[13] But there was practical appeal as well. For one thing, it would force Federal Theatre Project managers around the country, many of whom relied too much on safe old material, to try something new. Furthermore, it would show off the Federal Theatre organization, one year on, by demonstrating its ability to raise multiple curtains simultaneously on a given date. "A year ago," she wrote in the *Federal Theatre Bulletin*, "our problems of requisition, of procurement, of working under government regulations were so great that it was difficult to state that any curtain anywhere would go up on a definite date. If we can now raise fifteen curtains simultaneously on a given date we shall have a least one measure of efficiency in the local and national control of our medium."

The plan could also demonstrate that the Federal Theatre Project was alive and well outside the big cities. Hallie Flanagan was well aware that Harry Hopkins, in particular, wanted the Federal Theatre to do more for small-town America. "Mr. Harry Hopkins," she wrote in her message to Federal Theatre workers, "has lived in Iowa; he knows the Midwest, the Northeast, and the South, as well as the East. Perhaps that is one reason why he conceived the Federal Theatre Project not exclusively as a New York City project . . . It was his belief . . . that wherever there was a group of theatre professionals out of work it might be possible to organize a theatre company and thus benefit thousands of other people unable to afford entertainment."[14]

Hallie knew that the views of "Mr. Harry Hopkins" were critical in 1936, a presidential election year. Privately, Harry told Hallie that the Federal Theatre Project was the "best thing in the WPA." But the WPA in general and the Federal Theatre in particular were under bombardment from critics as the presidential campaign heated up.

The Federal Theatre Project had made itself vulnerable earlier that summer with a Living Newspaper production called *Injunction Granted*. The subject of *Injunction Granted* was the struggle between the courts and the labor unions—certainly a timely and legitimate topic. But the project's treatment struck most who saw it as blatant and not very artful left-wing propaganda. "The Moscow stylization of writing and staging," wrote Brooks Atkinson in the *New York Times*, "reduces the long struggle to adolescent gibberish . . . You can recognize the workers by their honest virility. The capitalists you can recognize by their morning coats and cunning demeanor . . . It bludgeons capital and the courts as if the revolution were already accomplished. If it wants to give the Federal Theatre a bad name for political insurgence it has found the most effective method."[15]

When Hallie saw *Injunction Granted* in rehearsal, she insisted on changes. "To show the history of labor in the courts is appropriate," she wrote. "To load that history with insinuation . . . is not appropriate."[16] But director Joe Losey, who was himself a Communist Party member, and Morris Watson, head of the Living Newspaper unit, didn't make the changes Hallie asked for. When *Injunction Granted* opened, Hallie was furious. "The production seems to me special pleading, biased, an editorial . . . ," she told them.[17] Even the *Federal Theatre Bulletin*'s editor, Pierre de Rohan, criticized the production as "violently partisan" and pointed out that "we must anger our listeners, not display our own anger."[18]

Irving Kolodin, an admirer of the Federal Theatre Project, noted in *Harper's Monthly* that "this laudable intention to relate its activities to the world of actualities has saddled the Federal Theatre in New York with one of its most vexatious burdens—all those adherents of the Cause, from parlor-pinks to cafeteria-reds . . . *Injunction Granted* is neither dramatic nor bitter nor just."[19]

"As I have repeatedly said, I will not have the Federal Theatre Project used politically," Hallie wrote Morris Watson. "I took your word and Joe Losey's word that it would not be so used and I think you both let me down. As you very well know the avalanche of unfavorable publicity on it is all ammunition against the project, to say nothing of being added ammunition against me personally." Hallie was especially upset to hear that left-wing literature was "being hawked in the lobby"[20] and ordered that it be stopped at once. Joe Losey left the project, with a push from Hallie Flanagan. Morris Watson stayed on.

After *Injunction Granted*, the anti–New Deal forces had a field day. The *New York Journal* accused the government of "supporting a Communist-infested national theatre . . . and Hopkins only knows what other seditious or freakish or fantastic enterprises."[21]

The widely read *Saturday Evening Post* weighed in with a scathing attack on Hallie Flanagan and the Federal Theatre Project in early August. "The Federal Theatre's hair is full of Communists," wrote Harrison Grey Fiske. "They found inspiration in the fact that Mrs. Flanagan cherished the ambition to Russianize our theatre. Mrs. Flanagan has openly stated that she is not interested in the American theatre or its methods, advocating the Russian stylized performances." Fiske claimed that all the Federal Theatre productions had been failures. Moreover, Communist propaganda was distributed regularly at rehearsals, and Communist meetings were being held on government time.[22]

Hallie Flanagan moved quickly to refute the *Post* charges one by one. Others pointed out that the author of the attack, Harrison Grey Fiske, was a creature of the commercial theatre, husband of the popular actress Minnie Maddern Fiske and producer of lightweight theatrical fare. But the *Saturday Evening Post* charges hung in the air and were reused by congressional critics. The Federal Theatre needed a big public victory and needed it soon.

Opening *It Can't Happen Here* around the country would take the focus off New York City, the seat of almost all the radical elements in the Federal Theatre Project. It helped, too, that Sinclair Lewis, both in his novel and in public appearances, made it clear that he had no more sympathy for Communists on the left than he did for Fascists on the right. Everyone called Lewis "Red" because of his once red hair, not his political persuasion. He summed up his views succinctly for the *Federal Theatre Bulletin*: "The struggle today is not one between communism and fascism; it is the struggle between tolerance and bigotry—bigotry preached equally by communism and fascism."[23]

Furthermore, as Hallie Flanagan put it in a message to Federal Theatre employees, the plan provided theatres with a chance to do innovative, *American* theatre. "We are committed to the belief that we will not find material for plays or methods of production by imitating the past or by borrowing from abroad," she wrote. "We want to do *It Can't Happen Here* because it is a play by one of our most distinguished American writers. We want to do it because it is a play about American life today, based on the

passionate belief in American democracy. The play says that when dictatorship comes to threaten such a democracy it comes in an apparently
harmless guise, with parades and promises; but that when such dictatorship
arrives the promises are not kept and the parade grounds become encamp-
ments. We want to do *It Can't Happen Here* because, like Doremus Jessup
[the novel's newspaperman and hero] and his creator Sinclair Lewis, we, as
American citizens and as workers in a theatre sponsored by the government of the United States, should like to do what we can to keep alive the
'free, enquiring, critical spirit' which is the center and core of a democracy."[24] Hallie Flanagan's repeated use of the word *American* was clearly
aimed at critics like Harrison Grey Fiske, who claimed she was out to
"Russianize" the Federal Theatre Project.

Within days of coming up with the idea, Francis Bosworth made the
trip to Vermont to see if Sinclair Lewis would agree to multiple productions. And on August 21, 1936, the *New York Times* reported on the front
page that the Federal Theatre was planning to produce *It Can't Happen
Here* in fifteen theatres all around the United States. "In spite of commercial offers for the dramatization . . . ," Sinclair Lewis told the *Motion Picture
Herald*, "I prefer to give to [*sic*] the Federal theatre for two reasons; first, because of my tremendous enthusiasm for its work; and second, because I
know I can depend on the Federal Theatre for a non-partisan point of
view."[25]

After all the attacks, Sinclair Lewis's ringing endorsement, and especially
his use of the word *nonpartisan*, must have been music to Hallie Flanagan's
ears. Ten days later, she sent off a note to Harry Hopkins and enclosed a
clipping from a Detroit newspaper, announcing the upcoming local production of *It Can't Happen Here*. "Dear Harry," she wrote. "I hope you are
pleased with the avalanche of favorable publicity, even from anti-
administration press, on the Lewis play. Sinclair Lewis is coming to Poughkeepsie next week and we're working on the dramatization."[26]

Hallie Flanagan had a tendency to jump into enormous projects without
fully considering the potential complications. In the case of *It Can't Happen Here*, there were many.

In the first place, there was the challenge of working with Sinclair Lewis,
an unpredictable alcoholic, charming in the early stages of a drunk but vit-
riolic as he descended deeper into a stupor. He was famous for making public scenes. At a banquet honoring Nobel Prize winners, he made a row that
prompted the *New York Times* to comment: "Sinclair Lewis paid tribute to
the memory of the inventor of dynamite by exploding in his honor."[27]

After *It Can't Happen Here* was published, a left-wing group called the League of American Writers invited Sinclair Lewis to yet another banquet, thinking to claim him as one of their own. Author Malcolm Cowley recalled that "I wasn't enthusiastic about the proposal, knowing Red [Lewis] as I did, but still . . . I signed the letter of invitation." The dinner didn't turn out well for the hosts. Lewis started out by saying that *It Can't Happen Here* "isn't a very good book" and adding, "Furthermore I don't believe any of you have *read* the book; if you had, you would have seen I was telling you all to go to hell." He ended by proposing that everyone rise, link arms, and sing "Stand Up, Stand Up, for Jesus."[28] It was yet another display of Lewis's unpredictable behavior under the influence.

It was well known, however, that Lewis never drank anything but coffee when he was working: Francis Bosworth remembered that he always had a cup in his hand, which shook so badly that the cup would dance in the saucer. What's more, Lewis had collaborated successfully in the past, helping to turn his novel *Dodsworth* into a successful Broadway play, starring Walter Huston, two years earlier.

The greater problem may well have been the book itself. Clifton Fadiman, writing in the *New Yorker*, called *It Can't Happen Here* "one of the most important books ever produced in this country."[29] But the book was difficult to adapt for the stage. It had been written in haste and was overcrowded with people and events. The choice of a rookie Hollywood writer named Jack Moffitt added to the recipe for trouble. And trouble came early to the collaboration.

Between mid-September, when Lewis came down from Vermont to New York with a secretary, a typewriter, some paper, and a first draft,[30] and early October, the deadline for the final script, the adaptation turned into torture for all involved. Lewis and Moffitt were no longer speaking to each other: Lewis was holed up in a suite on the twenty-second floor of the Essex House on Central Park South and Moffitt was up on the thirty-eighth floor. Hallie herself had the job of ferrying notes back and forth between the two suites, "since by that time I was the only acceptable medium of communication between the embattled collaborators."[31] Hallie carried not only messages to the collaborators, but generous supplies of black coffee, ice water, and Fannie Farmer candy.

Finally, the collaboration blew apart entirely. Moffitt fled to the West Coast, and Lewis, after threatening for a week to pull out altogether, agreed to work with another writer. According to a report in the *New Yorker*, the new collaborator, Vincent Sherman, who was directing the Broadway version of the play, went to visit Sinclair Lewis with trepidation. "Mr. Sherman addressed Mr. Lewis for forty minutes in ambassadorial language," the *New Yorker* reported, "suggesting in a certain scene Buzz Windrip, the dictator, should talk less. When he finished, Mr. Lewis said, 'Christ, I never liked that scene anyway.' After that they were friendly throughout."[32]

Hallie wrote to Phil, back in Poughkeepsie: "We are rewriting the whole play and Lewis says 'magnificent.' It is getting damn good."[33]

The final version of the play called *It Can't Happen Here* opens in Mt. Beulah, a small Vermont town that strongly resembles Sinclair Lewis's own Barnard. A homespun ignoramus named Berzelius "Buzz" Windrip has just been elected president, on the Corporative Party ticket, and the inhabitants of Mt. Beulah are reacting with varying degrees of excitement and skepticism. Doremus Jessup, the sensible editor of the town's newspaper, is thinking this Buzz Windrip might not be so bad: The youth are jobless and unruly, and Windrip is providing them with a new mission, recruiting them to march in his "Corpo" militia. Editor Jessup, a widower, has a woman friend named Lorinda Pike, who writes for the society pages of the paper. Lorinda, like the real-life Dorothy Parker, senses trouble from the start. She doesn't want Jessup to have anything to do with President Buzz Windrip or his Vermont deputies. "Get enough people in uniform and any fool knows what happens next," she declares.

Lorinda's worst fears are realized. When a spirited local grocer confronts and jeers at the "Corpos" parading past his store, he's beaten up and killed. When Jessup's son-in-law decries the murder, he, too, is murdered. Jessup, though terrified at first, realizes he must join the opposition, and he and Lorinda, along with his widowed daughter and a few sensible townspeople, begin a furious underground effort to distribute anti-Corpo literature. Jessup is discovered, arrested, and beaten with a metal fishing rod (offstage), then sent to a concentration camp. The final scene takes place at the Canadian border, as the anti-Corpo conspirators attempt to escape the country and join the opposition government in exile. The editor Jessup and his companion, Lorinda, make it through, as does his grandson, but Jessup's daughter is discovered.

There were several different versions of what would happen next, during the frenetic writing and rewriting. But in the final version, Jessup's daughter, Mary, avenges her slain husband by shooting the corporal who murdered him. A border guard then shoots and kills Mary. The curtain goes down on Mary saying final words of farewell to her son and to her father, Doremus, who lives on to fight the Corpos another day.[34]

The final version of *It Can't Happen Here* was turned out at the very last minute, much to the consternation of directors all over the country who were trying to stage it. The number of theatres planning to open the play simultaneously had ballooned from fifteen to twenty-three and included productions in Spanish and Yiddish as well as English. Each revision meant new work for all the companies. Actors had to learn new lines, directors had to stage new scenes. In some cases, translation was required as well. Opening night was looming.

But Hallie was determined to make the simultaneous openings work, "even if," as she told *Variety*, "the actors have to walk around the stage reading their parts off a script in their hands and wearing signs identifying themselves."[35] And as opening night grew closer, it looked as though all the productions *would* raise curtains on October 27—all, that is, except the flagship production Sinclair Lewis was overseeing at the Adelphi Theatre on Broadway.

On Sunday morning, October 25, Hallie's telephone in Poughkeepsie rang. It was Sinclair Lewis, in despair about the sets for the Adelphi production:

> I haven't slept all night—for the matter of that as you know I haven't slept for weeks. Nobody can say I haven't given everything to the Federal Theatre . . . Now it is all terrible—everybody has gone into a coma . . . I want you to get right on the train and come to New York and postpone the play a week and get new people to do everything, or do it yourself. Why, the living room they have got up there on the stage looks like a cheap boarding house on Second Avenue. It doesn't look any more like the house of Doremus Jessup than I look like Jack Moffitt. It is all terrible. It is all a failure.

Hallie did come to New York and learned from cooler heads that the production at the Adelphi could still be salvaged. She persuaded Sinclair Lewis, Vincent Sherman, and set designer Adrian Cracraft to go home to bed.

> With the assistance of a few devoted stagehands we set up, scene by scene, Mr. Cracraft's realistic sets which somehow had been bungled in the execution. We started in to re-arrange, re-paint, and re-dress the sets. Somehow we got into our warehouses and secured different furniture and draperies and lamps and pictures. Considering the fact that I had spent ten years previous to the Federal Theatre fighting interior decoration on the stage . . . the activities of this Sunday were not without their irony.[36]

On opening night, Hallie watched the first act of *It Can't Happen Here* at the Adelphi on Broadway, then took a taxi over to the Biltmore to see the second act in Yiddish. The Yiddish production included a scene in which Jessup, the newspaper editor, is imprisoned in a concentration camp, which had been cut from the Adelphi version. "We were beginning to get all the refugees from Austria and Germany—the Jewish refugees—at this time," another audience member recalled. "At the Yiddish theatre opening, there were two or three people that fainted. They were identifying."[37]

By the time Hallie returned to the Adelphi, the third act was under way. She watched from the back of the theatre, along with Sinclair Lewis and Vincent Sherman, who had helped to rewrite the play in the final weeks. Sinclair Lewis was too nervous to stay through the whole show. He went out to a drugstore midway to get a cup of coffee and some doughnuts and was astonished to discover that the people in the drugstore were going on about their business as usual and didn't "care a damn" about the momentous opening that was taking place nearby.[38] But Lewis returned in time for the final scenes, eager—like Hallie and Vincent Sherman—to see how their last-minute rewrite of the ending would go over.

The audience at the Adelphi that night responded with thunderous applause, and the cast took one curtain call after another. Sinclair Lewis was discovered in the back of the theatre and hauled onto the stage. "Speech, speech!" came the cries from the audience. Lewis, in response, looked at his watch and said simply, "I have been making a speech since eight forty-five."

The New York critics were less enthusiastic than the opening night audience. Some, like John Anderson of the *New York Evening Journal*, were appalled by the adaptation. "Mr. Lewis as dramatist has been so cruel to his own novel," he wrote, "that you'd almost think . . . that he hadn't read it."[39] Others found that the particular brand of fascism in the play was so extreme as to strain credulity. "There are no doubt many versions of the term 'fascism,'" Stark Young wrote, "but to make it mean only demagoguery, brute force and rapacity is to bring the discussion down to the sophomoric, and the play to mere melodrama."[40] Brooks Atkinson delivered the cruelest blow of all when he wrote that "like most Federal Theatre productions . . . *It Can't Happen Here* is not well done; it is careless, slipshod theatre work, according to Broadway standards."[41]

The opinion of the New York critics, however, didn't matter nearly as much in this instance as the astonishing fact that *It Can't Happen Here* opened simultaneously that night on twenty-one different stages in twenty-one different versions, each reflecting local sensibilities and capabilities. On that night and subsequent nights, one thousand theatre people all around the country were working onstage and backstage, and twenty thousand were in the audience, watching a play that raised timely questions about totalitarianism. "Through a subtle twist in emphasis in a time of emergency," Brooks Atkinson wrote, "the code of political morals which is popularly looked upon as American might prepare the ground for a Fascist dictatorship. Many of our bullying jingoes are Fascist when they believe that they are defending the faith of the Founding Fathers. The American who hates foreigners and screams 'Red' whenever he encounters a difference of opinion could join in a Fascist dictatorship under the pious impression that he were saving American democracy . . . Americans are easily stampeded into righteousness; they dote on evangelism—for a year or two. And a sincere man with a magnetic personality might make a Fascist dictatorship sound holy . . .

"Thousands of Americans who do not know what a Fascist dictatorship would mean," Brooks Atkinson concluded, "now have an opportunity to find out, thanks to Mr. Lewis' energetic public spirit and the Federal Theatre's wide facilities."[42]

Every production had its own backstage stories to tell. In Chicago, an old actor named Oscar O'Shea, who had made a million dollars performing comic roles before the Depression and then lost it all, was acting in a serious drama for the first time in his life. O'Shea, observed Claudia Cassidy in the *Chicago Journal of Commerce*, "turns in a genuinely moving performance as Jessup, something beyond the amiable character work for which he is known. He has the feel of helpless tragedy, of fear stirred to fury."[43] Afterward, O'Shea left the federal payroll: Gummo Marx, who saw O'Shea onstage, signed him to a long-term contract at MGM.

In Seattle, the role of the dictator Buzz Windrip was played by a vaudevillian named Toby Leitch, who "bellowed with uncomfortable realism."[44] Leitch had to play much of his part sitting down, because his legs had been crushed in a barrel-diving act years before.

In Birmingham, President Buzz Windrip's speech was delivered in the manner of a southern political rally from a rococo box, draped in red, white, and blue bunting, in the elegant old Jefferson Theatre. To bring the threat of fascism closer to home, Mt. Beulah, Vermont, became Salida, Colorado, in the Denver production and Plattsville, Nebraska, in the Omaha production.

In Omaha, flyers advertised the production as "Omaha's only stage show with a professional cast." Tickets were twenty-five cents.[45] In Denver, the opening night audience braved a snowstorm to make their way to the Baker Theatre, newly acquired by the project following the exodus of a group of zealots who had been camping out there awaiting the end of the world. When the world didn't end in mid-August as anticipated, the group dispersed and *It Can't Happen Here* moved in.

Productions by minority companies found ways to make *It Can't Happen Here* relevant to their audiences. The only Spanish-language production, in Tampa, cast Buzz Windrip, Bishop Prang, and the Corpo overlord as non-Spanish types, while the rest of the cast were recent Cuban immigrants. In Seattle, the Negro theatre company took a similar tack: Three white actors were cast in the parts of the Fascist leaders, and the rest of the cast, including the courageous Doremus Jessup and his cohorts, were African Americans. The locale was changed to the black section of Seattle.

The one thing directors all across the country seemed to agree on was that the production requirements were unrealistic: The original script called for nine sets and fifteen changes of scene. Some companies were undone by the scene changes: In Los Angeles on opening night, the second act finished at eleven P.M., and the audience sat impatiently in the dark, waiting for the third. But in San Francisco, the scene changes were all accomplished in under a minute, and intervals between scenes were filled with the sounds of radio broadcasts and air raids. "*It Can't Happen Here*," wrote *San Francisco Chronicle* critic John Hobart, "is probably the most 'important' production the Federalites have yet put on. It also happens to be one of the best."[46]

The Suitcase Theatre, which was scheduled to tour the boroughs and then travel to CCC camps, faced the greatest production challenge. The company needed a set that could fold into a thirty-foot-long, eight-foot-wide truck trailer. The trailer opened on one side to become a dressed stage and on the other to form dressing rooms for the actors. The solution for *It Can't Happen Here* was a collapsible frame covered in black velour, with painted drops for various scenes. Set pieces were covered in white velveteen, which gave a sculptural effect, and then painted. The illusion of crowd scenes and parades was created by the giant shadows of cardboard cutouts moving across a diorama.

It Can't Happen Here wound up playing a total of 260 weeks, or five years, in theatres all around the country. It was seen by more than 316,000 people. "No one agreed on the play," Hallie Flanagan told an audience some months later, "but everyone had to see it. It was called good, bad, savage, mild, American, un-American, Fascist, communist, too far left, too far right, a work of genius, a work of the devil." There was, she conceded, "some mystic connection with the coming election, though whether the play was designed to elect Mr. Roosevelt or to defeat him was a moot question."[47]

Some claimed that the entire undertaking had been aimed at bolstering support for FDR and the New Deal. Harold Lord Varney, writing in the Hearst-controlled *New York American*, complained that *It Can't Happen Here* was "a venomed libel upon the D.A.R., the American Legion, Rotary International, and all of the other non-radical movements" and went on to attack Hallie Flanagan as "a pathetic misfit as director of the Federal Theatre project. In any other administration except the present one it would quickly sound the gong upon her career of government financed leftism."

But a few others saw *It Can't Happen Here* differently. It was, after all, the Republican opposition that had been warning of FDR's dictatorial ways. *It Can't Happen Here*, wrote a Seattle critic, "might be called propaganda against the very government which was the 'angel' for the production of the play." To this critic of the Roosevelt regime, the title of the play could have been changed to *It Is Happening Here*.[48]

The death of Huey Long didn't end the grassroots uprising he had begun. On June 19, Representative William Lemke, a Republican from North Dakota, announced that he was running for president on the Union Party ticket. The issue before the nation, he said, was "economic slavery." Lemke was an obscure congressman from a sparsely populated state, and his announcement wouldn't have made a ripple, were it not for the endorsement of the man who had invented the Union Party, the Reverend Charles Coughlin.

Lemke's announcement was timed to coincide with Father Coughlin's *Hour of Power*, and the radio priest used his sermon to endorse Lemke and rally his followers to the Union Party cause. Lemke, he said, was "a poor man who has worked with his hands against the hostile forces of nature and with his soul against the destructive forces of private money control."

Two days later, as expected, the Union Party received the endorsement of Gerald L. K. Smith, Huey Long's former lieutenant, and Dr. Francis E. Townsend, a septuagenarian who had attracted a huge following to his old age pension movement. Smith and Townsend made a highly unlikely couple. Townsend was a frail, earnest physician whose speeches put people to sleep but whose visionary idea of providing old people with government support (an idea the Roosevelt administration was in the process of implementing in a more sophisticated form) had made him a hero to millions across the country. Smith, on the other hand, was a large, restless man looking for trouble, "the only man," Huey Long once said, "who is a better rabble-rouser than I am."

Smith promised to "personally impeach" Roosevelt if he was reelected. The man, he said indignantly, "would do anything to reelect himself."

In the ensuing months, however, that charge seemed to apply best to Smith, Coughlin, and their Union Party, who held one convention after another to rally their troops. In July, the followers of Francis Townsend came to Cleveland in record numbers; there were more voting delegates to the Townsend convention than to either the Democratic or the Republican one. The aging delegates had come to hear their leader, Francis Townsend, but it was Gerald L. K. Smith who stole the show. The choice, he told his audience, was either "the Russian primer or the Holy Bible. It is the red flag or the Stars and Stripes. It is Lenin or Lincoln—Stalin or Jefferson."

"His speech," wrote H. L. Mencken, "was a magnificent amalgam of each and every American species of rabble-rousing, with embellishments borrowed from the Algonquin Indians and the Cossacks of the Don. It ran the keyboard from the softest sobs and gurgles to the most-ear-splitting whoops and howls, and when it was over the 9000 delegates simply lay back in their pews and yelled."[49]

Roosevelt's campaign strategists took the threat from the Union Party seriously right from the start, knowing that its supporters might combine with Republican voters to defeat the president. They discussed modifications of the platform that might draw off some of the Union Party vote, and they moved to block the Union Party from state ballots wherever possible. But FDR, the perceptive politician, observed early on that "when it comes to a Show-down, these fellows cannot all lie in the same bed and will fight among themselves with almost absolute certainty."

In the end, the same prediction turned out to apply to the Republicans. There was a fanatical right-wing branch of the party who had their own *It Can't Happen Here* scenario. They saw FDR as a dictator in the making, a man of wealth and breeding who had betrayed his own and gone over to the Communists. There was also a moderate branch, who viewed the New Deal as democratic but spendthrift.

The Republican convention in Cleveland that June reflected the divide within the party: The most rousing speech came from ex-president Herbert Hoover, who told the delegates that Roosevelt's second term would result in the "violence and outrage by which European despotisms have crushed all liberalism and all freedom." The Hoover speech, reported the *Times* the next day, produced "wild and uncontrollable bursts of frenzy" in the partisan audience.

But the Republican nominee, Governor Alfred M. Landon of Kansas, did not share Hoover's apocalyptic vision or his ability to whip up the crowd. Alf Landon, a forty-eight-year-old oilman who had built his reputation on fiscal austerity, was the only Republican governor to win election in the West in 1932, and he repeated the feat two years later. He planned to attack the Roosevelt administration for overspending. But Landon was a bland candidate in every respect: a man of medium height with gray eyes behind rimless glasses. Although he was privately charming, his speech was flat and drawling and he had no gift for oratory. Father Coughlin, who should know, once described Landon as "a most honest man but the most colorless candidate in the history of the United States."

Nothing could have demonstrated the contrast between the Landon and Roosevelt candidacies better than their nominations. Landon, not wanting to look as if he were emulating Roosevelt, accepted the Republican nomination *in absentia* on June 11. Sixteen days later, Roosevelt arrived at the Democratic convention in Philadelphia to once again accept his party's nomination in person.

"There is a mysterious cycle in human events," Roosevelt told the delegates. "To some generations much is given. Of others much is expected. This generation of Americans has a rendezvous with destiny."

Roosevelt spoke of critics within the country, "economic royalists" who "complain that we seek to overthrow the institutions of America" but who are really complaining "that we seek to take away their power." He spoke, too, of people "in other lands" who "have sold their heritage of freedom for the illusion of a living . . .

"I believe in my heart that only our success can stir their ancient hope. They begin to know that here in America we are waging a great war. It is not alone a war against want . . . It is a war for the survival of democracy . . .

"I accept the commission you have tendered me," Roosevelt concluded, "I join with you. I am enlisted for the duration of the war."

The roar of the crowd drowned out the words that followed "I accept" and continued for ten minutes. Then, as the president stood surrounded by his family, the orchestra struck up "Auld Lang Syne." When they had finished, Roosevelt asked them to play it again. He began to sing, and the huge audience in the open stadium joined in.

The song set the perfect tone for the campaign Roosevelt intended to wage. Old friends should not be forgot. And in FDR's view, everyone in the country was a potential old friend, not only Democrats, but members of other progressive parties, as well as labor leaders, women, and blacks. Right from the start, the president insisted on a "gentle and happy" approach to campaigning.[50]

FDR let others do the attacking. Harold Ickes proved an eloquent critic of the Republican Party. And Harry Hopkins defended New Deal programs in his usual blunt style. "The last Republican administration," Hopkins told a Pennsylvania audience, "had soup lines and Hoovervilles. We abolished them. We provided jobs. They had riots and we have order, because we have given the jobless man a chance."[51]As for Landon's claims that he had balanced the budget in Kansas, Hopkins retorted that "the Governor of Kansas has never put up a thin dime for the unemployed in Kansas . . . The last thing I knew about the Governor he was trying to get money out of me to keep his schools open." If the governor had balanced the budget, said Hopkins, he had "taken it out of the hides of the people."[52] Hopkins's harsh style worried campaign manager Jim Farley, who asked him to stop making public statements. "The boss," however, told Hopkins that he had a right to defend his programs.

But FDR took a different path, simply reminding people everywhere he went of how much better things were in their particular town or city. And the response was rapturous. Huge crowds gathered, shouting out as the presidential car went by, "Thank you, Mr. President!" and, "God bless you!" and "You saved my home!" When he arrived in Chicago on October 14, the police could barely keep a corridor open for his car to enter the stadium, and the explosion of sound from the crowd when he came to the platform seemed to astound even Roosevelt.

At the end of September, Roosevelt finally began to take on his critics. In Syracuse, he addressed the increasingly strident accusations from the Hearst papers and from Republican right-wingers that he was allied with the Communists. "I have not sought, I do not seek, I repudiate the support of any advocate of Communism or of any other alien 'ism' which would by fair means or foul change our American democracy . . . The most serious threat to our institutions," he told the Syracuse audience, "comes from those who refuse to face the need for change."

Despite the enthusiasm for FDR everywhere, except in a few pockets of privilege, there were still some who doubted he could win. The *Literary Digest* poll, which had never been wrong in the past, continued throughout October to predict a victory for Alf Landon.

Yet there were all kinds of signs that the opposition was unraveling. Alf

Landon's rhetoric was becoming increasingly strident, as he responded to pressure from his subordinates to take a tougher line. He now said things like "We have a choice to make between the American system of government and one that is alien to everything this country has ever known." But Landon was issuing warnings he didn't really believe himself. And his delivery was as flat as ever.

Nor did the extremists, on the right or the left, look nearly as powerful in October as they had in July. As FDR had predicted, the Union Party coalition collapsed. On October 20, Gerald L. K. Smith announced a plan to go out on his own and "seize the government of the United States." Townsend then renounced Smith, and Union Party candidate Lemke did the same. Father Coughlin ignored everyone but himself. In his last New York rally, he didn't even mention Lemke's name. On the left, neither the thoughtful Norman Thomas nor the Communist Party candidate, Earl Browder, stood a ghost of a chance.

In the eyes of some critics, the one viable candidate who seemed to exhibit dangerous dictatorial tendencies was Roosevelt himself. Even some Democrats had left the fold because they feared the concentration of power in the hands of "a small group of men in Washington."[53] Dorothy Thompson, who had witnessed fascism firsthand, worried publicly about "the move away from an *informed* public to a *persuaded* public."[54]

On October 31, with just five days to go before the vote, FDR made a speech at Madison Square Garden that seemed to reinforce Thompson's misgivings. Roosevelt had been enraged, in the weeks leading up to the election, by a Republican scare campaign that suggested that the new payroll tax workers were contributing toward Social Security might be diverted to other uses. Worse yet, they warned, the payroll tax would provide an opportunity for government snooping and labeling. A page one feature in the Hearst papers read, "Do You Want a Tag and a Number in the Name of False Security?"

Roosevelt, infuriated by the misleading campaign, vowed to take off the gloves at his wind-up speech in Madison Square Garden, before a wildly enthusiastic audience. "Never before in all our history have these forces been so united against one candidate," he told the crowd. "They are unanimous in their hate for me—and I welcome their hatred." The president moved to his climax: "I should like to have it said of my first Administration that in it the forces of selfishness and of lust for power met their match. I should like to have it said of my second Administration that in it these forces met their master."

The roar of the crowd was deafening. But afterward, many among his advisers wished that he had not put it quite that way. Not only was Roosevelt a member of what some might consider the ruling or master class in America, but he was using a word that in 1936 was familiar from the hate-filled rhetoric of Adolf Hitler, who was making claims for a "master race."

But whatever damage might have been done was invisible on election night—a night that gave the lie to all predictions. Even Roosevelt—ever confident of a substantial win—had underestimated the size of his victory. Early in the evening, a bulletin came through that New Haven had gone for Roosevelt by fifteen thousand votes. FDR didn't believe the margin could be that high and asked that the figures be checked. When he learned that they were accurate, he leaned back, blew a smoke ring into the air, and said, "Wow."[55]

In the end, FDR won by the largest plurality in United States history and by the largest proportion of electoral votes since 1820. He lost only two states: One was Maine, and the other was Vermont, the home state of sensible moderates like Doremus Jessup.

Alf Landon was gracious and amusing in defeat. He told the story of the Kansas farmer who watched a tornado demolish his barn, his outbuildings, and finally his house. When it was all over, the farmer simply stood there looking and laughing.

"What are you laughing at, you darned old fool?" his wife asked.

The farmer replied: "The completeness of it."

The completeness of it was so great that even Roosevelt's enemies, including Hearst, rushed to get on the bandwagon. Dorothy Thompson, one of the doubters, recalled being at a party that night with a group of Landon supporters and, of all people, Harry Hopkins. Almost everyone there, except Hopkins, was wearing a Landon sunflower button. A screen had been set up to flash election returns, but as the evening wore on, the guests stopped looking at it. Finally, as it became obvious that FDR was winning by a huge margin, Thompson suggested to Harry Hopkins that he propose a toast to the victor.

"Here?" Harry responded. "Are you crazy? We'd probably be lynched."

Finally, Dorothy Thompson herself got up and toasted FDR. The room responded with sullen silence.

"We drank our toasts," Thompson wrote afterward, and "Harry choked on his, he was so amused, and spurted champagne just past my nose . . . Still, I thought Harry's own feeling a little hilariously vindictive. Whereas I was perturbed by the attitude of the crowd, he was delighted with imagining the further chagrins they would feel before the next administration was over."[56]

Unlike Harry, Hallie Flanagan worried that the sheer size of the victory might cloud Roosevelt's judgment. "I wish Roosevelt hadn't gone in with such a big [majority]," she wrote Phil from Washington. She was uneasy about Hearst and the *Herald Tribune*, both vicious foes of the Federal Theatre, getting on the Roosevelt bandwagon. "And I don't like [Roosevelt's] rush back here with the rapturous upturned grin and the remark about 'balancing the budget.' I hope he won't forget that he was elected by the workers."[57]

AFTER THE FLOOD

On January 13, 1937, just one week before Roosevelt's inauguration to a second term, a heavy and relentless rain began to pour down on cities and towns in the Ohio River valley. By the time it stopped ten days later, the river had risen an unprecedented twenty feet and crashed through levees and flood walls with the force of Niagara. The great flood of 1937, one of the most devastating in the nation's history, drove a million residents of the cities and towns along the Ohio and its tributaries out of their homes. One hundred and thirty people died. But the death toll would have been much higher had it not been for the speedy intervention of the federal government: By the second day of flooding, eighteen thousand WPA workers were on the job, rescuing thousands and ferrying them to safety in rowboats.

Hallie Flanagan got a firsthand report on the devastation in early February from two WPA officials who had just returned from the disaster area, where they spent three days in little boats rowing around the streets of lost towns. The officials suggested that the refugees, cooped up and dispirited, would enjoy a visit from a Federal Theatre vaudeville troupe. So Hallie went about getting the necessary permissions from the War Department. "It is right," she wrote to Phil at the time, "that the theatre should be at the heart of the government this way."[1]

On February 17, the twelve-member Mobile Variety Unit loaded their costumes, piano, accordion, set, and lighting equipment onto a one-ton truck and left New York City for the refugee camps in Tennessee and Kentucky, where thousands were waiting out the flood in improvised shelters. One of the company comedians drove the truck. The rest of the troupe followed along in a Chevrolet Carryall, a long car seating eight, "expertly

Children watching a Federal Theatre Production, 1935 (Franklin D. Roosevelt Presidential Library)

handled," according to company coordinator Herbert Price, by the piano player. Two days later, they arrived at their first booking, in Knoxville, Tennessee.

In the segregated South, blacks and whites were housed separately: An old brick shirt factory sheltered 750 blacks, with the men on one floor and the women and children on another. Next door, 150 whites were housed in another shelter. But when the variety unit put on their show, on a stage they built quickly from lumber provided by the WPA construction project, both black and white refugees formed the audience.

For the next three weeks, the company traveled from camp to camp, stopping in Chattanooga in Tennessee, in Mayfield and Hickman in Kentucky, and across the Mississippi in Cairo, Illinois. Everywhere, they performed to large crowds. On several occasions, they got help from the choruses of the WPA sewing rooms, where women worked to make clothes for those in need. Everywhere, they ended their performances with a community sing.

The high point of the tour, according to Price, came on one cold and rainy night in Tullahoma, Tennessee, where the troupe performed for two hundred black refugees housed in a cavernous military garage. They folded up all the cots in the garage to make enough space and put tables together to make a stage. There wasn't much room for the audience to sit down, so some climbed onto the building's crossbeams, providing the company with an instant gallery. "This was truly a grand show," Price reported, "refugees, Red Cross nurses, officers and National Guardsmen all entering into the spirit. Our community sing was led by a colored preacher and when 'Goin' Home' was sung, many eyes were wet with tears."

By early March, refugees were beginning to leave the shelters and return home, and the traveling players decided to head back to New York City. It had been three weeks since they left, and in that time they had performed for perhaps five thousand refugees. "We felt," Herbert Price wrote in his report, "that for at least an hour and a half we had taken their minds away from the horrors of the flood and given them a lift."[2]

chapter ten

UNDER A POWERFUL STAR

On inauguration day, Hallie Flanagan joined the throng heading up to Capitol Hill to hear President Roosevelt lay out his agenda for his second term in office. Some of what he said that day may have reassured Hallie that he hadn't forgotten the people who elected him. As the rain poured down on the audience and swept into the inaugural pavilion, Roosevelt spoke eloquently, in his penetrating tenor, of those "who at this very moment are denied the greater part of what the very lowest standards of today call the necessities of life . . . I see one-third of a nation ill-housed, ill-clad, ill-nourished," he told the audience. ". . . The test of our progress is not whether we add more to the abundance of those who have much; it is whether we provide enough for those who have too little."

What the president said that day became the basis for a Federal Theatre production called *One-Third of a Nation,* an indictment of slum housing that some thought the very best of the project's Living Newspapers. But what the president *didn't* say turned out to be even more important to the future of the Federal Theatre Project.

Seven of the nine justices of the Supreme Court were sitting in the pavilion with Roosevelt on that momentous occasion. Yet the president chose to make only veiled references to his frustration with their anti–New Deal rulings. His true feelings he expressed only to himself, during the swearing-in. "When the Chief Justice read me the oath," he later told an adviser, "and came to the words 'support the Constitution of the United States' I felt like saying: 'Yes, but it's the Constitution as *I* understand it, flexible enough to meet any new problem of democracy—not the kind of Constitution your Court has raised up as a barrier to progress and democracy.'"[1]

Orson Welles as Faust (National Archives and Records Administration)

Nor did the inaugural dwell on another of FDR's preoccupations: achieving a balanced budget. Contrary to the claims of his critics on the right, FDR had always been, like his Dutch ancestors, a believer in economy. Back in 1933, he had proposed drastic cuts in salaries, pensions, and spending as one part of the recovery program. Now that the Depression seemed to be abating, he was hell-bent on balancing the budget again. "I have said fifty times," Roosevelt told his vice president, "that the budget will be balanced . . . If you want me to say it again, I will say it either once or fifty times more."[2]

Within the year, Roosevelt's determination to challenge the Supreme Court and to balance the budget would threaten the very survival of the Federal Theatre Project. But for the first five months of Roosevelt's second term, the project blossomed as never before. Perhaps this was because, according to Momodu Johnson, the medicine man from voodoo *Macbeth*, Hallie Flanagan was protected by a powerful star.

Momodu had acquired a formidable reputation in Federal Theatre circles: People said he was responsible for casting a spell over the *New York Herald Tribune* critic Percy Hammond, after he dared to call *Macbeth* "an exhibition of de-luxe boondoggling." The day Hammond's review came out, Johnson and the Nigerian troupe talked it over with John Houseman, who agreed with them that it was "the work of an enemy." And that night, the stage manager at the Lafayette Theatre reported hearing unusual drumming and hair-raising chants coming from the basement. The next day, a brief item in the paper announced the sudden illness of the distinguished theatre critic Percy Hammond. He died some days later—perhaps of pneumonia. Or perhaps, as some believed, from the curse put on him by Momodu Johnson and company.[3]

Thus Hallie Flanagan had good reason to take the medicine man seriously when he warned that "many of your so-called friends are in reality your enemies." Even in her own office, Momodu warned, a certain party was bearing a grudge. But there was good news along with the bad. "Don't be afraid," Momodu told Hallie. "You are being protected by a very powerful star." As long as she killed and ate a black-feathered chicken on this star's birthday and performed certain rituals with a protective charm he was providing, her star would continue to protect her.[4]

It did seem, during the early months of FDR's second term, that Hallie and the Federal Theatre Project were basking in the glow of a benevolent star. Everyone knew that painful cuts and layoffs were coming, but for a time they were kept at bay. Hallie was able to report, in the *Federal Theatre Bulletin* early that year, that twelve thousand people were working in 158 theatres in twenty-eight states, playing to weekly audiences totaling five hundred thousand.[5] A reorganization plan would soon provide greater freedom, at least for a while. Major publications, including the *Daily News* and *Fortune* magazine, published extensive reports on the Federal Theatre's impressive accomplishments. "From any point of view save that of the old-line box-office critics to whom nothing is theatre unless it has Broadway stars and Broadway varnish, the Federal Theatre Project is a roaring success," wrote *Fortune*.[6]

Even critics from the generally hostile trade press grudgingly gave Hallie Flanagan credit. *Variety*, reporting on a party thrown by WPA employees, noted that every mention of Hallie Flanagan from the speakers' table was "cue to rumble the rafters with palm-pounding."[7] And *Billboard*, while continuing to refer to the project as "show-biz make-work,"[8] admitted that "there is not the slightest doubt . . . in the minds of all of those who have felt the magic of her personality that Mrs. Flanagan is eminently well fitted to carry on this gigantic work."[9]

Most gratifying, for Hallie, was the increasingly high quality of the work itself. "The people of the Federal Theatre," she told her national staff proudly when they gathered that March in Washington, "have put across against tremendous odds, working within a governmental machine (the inflexibility of which can scarcely be imagined), working against a tide of public opinion which in the beginning was almost universally scornful, snobbish, contemptuous—these people have put across a program unparalleled in its audacity, originality and scope."[10]

Perhaps Hallie was thinking in particular of the classical theatre unit in New York, established several months earlier by Orson Welles and John Houseman. It was Houseman who initiated the idea of a classical unit, mainly as a way of continuing his partnership with Welles. Welles, he knew, had no particular interest in continuing to work with the Negro theatre company, and Houseman believed the company could continue to thrive without him. So he turned the leadership over to a triumvirate of black directors and approached Hallie with his idea for a classical unit. She quickly agreed.

Some of the most successful Federal Theatre undertakings, Hallie observed at that same March meeting, had been done "out of the fever of excitement and adventure."[11] The Houseman/Welles classical unit was one of them. Since they found the "classical" label confining, Houseman and Welles decided to adopt the language of the bureaucracy and call their undertaking Project #891. And in the summer of 1936, Project #891 took over the Maxine Elliott Theatre, recently rented from the Shuberts by the WPA.

The Maxine Elliott was a nine-hundred-seat jewel box of a house on the southern edge of the Broadway theatre district.[12] Financed by J. P. Morgan for his favorite actress and named after her, the 1908 theatre was perfect in every detail: gold silk on the walls, veined marble in the lobby, and modern plumbing in the actors' dressing rooms. Under the aegis of Welles and Houseman, the elegant Elliott became the scene of inspired but decidedly inelegant mayhem.

Project #891's first production, *Horse Eats Hat*, was a drastically altered version of a nineteenth-century French farce by Eugène Labiche,[13] chosen in large part to accommodate the available performers left over from numerous other productions in the city. "It was a bizarre collection of aging character actors, comics and eccentrics that delighted Orson's heart," Houseman remembered.[14] Welles proceeded to use their talents, along with those of younger recruits including Joseph Cotten, Paula Laurence, and Arlene Francis, to turn *Horse Eats Hat* into an orgy of pratfalls, wild chases, collapsing scenery, and general insanity. The original plot, which concerned a bridegroom who was trying to get to his wedding but was waylaid by his horse's ingestion of a telltale hat, became a mere scaffolding on which to hang an increasingly elaborate series of absurdities.

"I can still see Joe Cotten [the bridegroom]," recalled Houseman, "wearing his bright yellow leather gloves, with the coveted straw hat grasped firmly between his teeth, caught between the Countess' indignant guests and the vengeful pursuit of the wedding party, leaping from sofa to table to piano top to chandelier which, at that instant, started to rise like a great golden bird, carrying him upward in a wild, forty-foot flight till he vanished into the fly-loft, while a three-tiered fountain flung a giant jet upward at the seat of his pants and Cotten himself, clinging to the rising chandelier with one hand and grasping a siphon in the other, squirted streams of soda water over the madly whirling crowd below."[15]

It was Welles who pushed the actors to wilder and wilder heights, while Houseman watched with alarm. Bil Baird, a young puppeteer who had been recruited to construct a horse out of brown plush and build several breakaway chairs—"so Joe Cotten could fall on his butt"—remembered the day he got recruited for some of the stunts. Welles was trying to get one of the actors to fall into the orchestra pit. When the actor refused, Baird, a former gymnast, volunteered. "So I went, 'Whoop' . . . and did a flop and landed on my back in the orchestra pit and everybody applauded and Orson said, 'Mr. Baird, you're hired.' "[16]

Baird wound up doing padded falls throughout the show, including one designed to shock the audience during what was supposed to be the intermission. First, a woman trumpeter appeared in the right mezzanine box, wearing a white satin hussar's uniform trimmed in gold, and played a loud and brilliant version of "Carnival of Venice."[17] Then, suddenly, a player piano in the upper stage box broke in with a frenzied version of "Rosy O'Grady." And at that point, Bil Baird, apparently a drunken refugee from earlier festivities onstage, emerged from behind the player piano, climbed up with great effort over the edge of the box, slipped and fell, got one foot caught in the railing, and dangled there upside down just above the heads of the audience, while the player piano played on furiously.

It was but one example of the radical way in which *Horse* extended the sense of danger out past the proscenium. In this mad, irrational world, where whole backdrops crashed to the stage and stagehands turned up in the middle of scenes, it was often hard for the audience to tell whether the stunts were intentional or accidental. During one scene, when the curtain closed and then came crashing to the stage floor, a woman in the audience was heard to remark, "It's wonderful! They should keep this in the show."[18]

The reaction of preview audiences, many of them earnest left-wingers, was something less than the company had hoped for. "They laughed but they were uneasy," Houseman recalled, "and as the evening advanced and the antics of the corrupt bourgeoisie became ever more frantic, their uneasiness grew."[19] When the show opened, critics also had mixed feelings, citing "corking good moments"[20] but faulting the excesses. Hearst papers, predictably, found the play vulgar. "Dozens of young men and women," wrote the *New York American* critic, "are compelled by stress of circumstances to participate in this offensive play, that represents a new low in the tide of drama."[21]

But among those who got it, *Horse Eats Hat* turned into a destination. Playwright Marc Connelly described sitting in the audience and laughing so hard that the tears were running down his cheeks, then coming out at intermission and encountering the novelist John Dos Passos, who was equally beside himself. In the second half, they sat together and screamed with laughter in the midst of silence.[22] As time went on, the true believers filled the audience more and more, many returning (at a top price of fifty-five cents) twice, three times, even twenty times. *Horse Eats Hat* played to good houses, increasingly full of repeaters, for three months. On closing night, only those who had seen it before were allowed in.

Hallie wasn't entirely comfortable herself with *Horse Eats Hat*: There were, she wrote rather primly, "occasional too physiological moments."[23] Perhaps she was influenced in part by the anxiety emanating from Washington. Composer Virgil Thomson, the man who inspired *Horse Eats Hat* and collaborated with Paul Bowles on the music, complained that Washington inspectors kept "combing its language for indelicacies. Every day or two another telegram arrived, ordering that such and such a line be cut."[24]

Despite some uncomfortable moments, however, Hallie insisted that she liked the show. "I feel sorry for people who did not see *Horse Eats Hat* and even sorrier for those who didn't like it," she wrote later. Her amusement was heightened, on opening night, by the sight of Harrison Grey Fiske, who had slammed the Federal Theatre in the *Saturday Evening Post*, sitting in the audience "rigid with horror making notes in a little book."[25]

About Project #891's next production, Christopher Marlowe's *The Tragical History of Doctor Faustus*, Hallie had no reservations. In fact, the night she attended *Faustus*, after a celebratory dinner with Phil, was surely one of the happiest of her tenure as director of the Federal Theatre Project. "I loved the gay dinner," she wrote Phil afterward, "and I loved *Faustus*, and I would rather dine and theatre with you than anything in the world." And later in the same letter: "I like the production inordinately and love remembering it, don't you?"[26]

Project #891's *Faustus* was everything Hallie had argued that the Federal Theatre should be: innovative, inclusive, and memorable. Right from the start, Welles decided on an unconventional approach to the material. There would be no sets and very few props. Light would provide the excitement, along with a bag of magic tricks that included colorful explosions, Bil Baird's ghoulish and terrifying puppets (playing the Seven Deadly Sins), invisible black hands that made objects appear and disappear, and so many trapdoors that the stage required reinforcement. Because he wanted to approximate the playgoing experience of Elizabethan times, Welles had two dozen seats removed from orchestra center and replaced them with a prowlike apron that placed the actors right on top of the audience. It may have been the first such breach of the proscenium in the history of Broadway theatre.[27]

Orson Welles not only designed the stage, oversaw the magical effects, and designed the costumes, he also played the role of Faustus, the philosopher who sells his soul to the Devil in exchange for knowledge and power. It was a role, according to John Houseman, with which he felt a deep personal connection. Welles himself was a driven man who almost never slept and who "in his most creative, manic moments, in his wildest transports of love or on the topmost peak of his precocious victories . . . was rarely free from a sense of sin and fear of retribution."

Welles chose the tightly wound Jack Carter, the African American actor who had played Macbeth in Harlem and become a frequent late night companion, to play the role of Mephistopheles. It was a risky choice: Carter was a drinker who had stormed off during the *Macbeth* road tour, leaving the company in the lurch. But Welles viewed Carter as a kindred spirit—the perfect partner for his crazed Faustus. Welles and Carter, Houseman recalls, made a special intimate connection. "Their presence on the stage," wrote Houseman, "was unforgettable: both were around six foot four, both men of abnormal strength capable of sudden, furious violence. Yet their scenes together were played with restraint, verging on tenderness, in which temptation and damnation were treated as acts of love. Welles was brightly garbed, bearded, medieval, ravenous, sweating and human; Carter was in black—a cold, ascetic monk, his face and gleaming bald head moon-white and ageless against the surrounding night . . . he had the beauty, the pride and sadness of a fallen angel."[28] Later, theatre historians would cite the Welles/Carter duo as one of the earliest instances of integrated casting on Broadway.

The other starring role in *The Tragical History of Doctor Faustus* was played by Abe Feder's lighting. Even though Welles and Feder battled constantly, their collaboration brought astonishing results. "The lighting effects by Feder," wrote Robert Benchley in the *New Yorker*, "are among the finest this side of the borealis."

"Feder," wrote *New Republic* critic Stark Young, "seems one of the attendant spirits or demons of the piece."[29]

"At times Feder applies a dim, solitary shaft of light to Dr. Faustus in the rear of the stage," noted the *Herald Tribune*. "As Faustus speaks he walks into darkness and then emerges into another cone of light far down stage. The effect is startling: the technique is that of the films for the figure has appeared from the distance into a close-up."[30]

"That a starkly bare stage could, by intelligent handling of electricity, be more eloquent than the most elaborate setting ever devised," wrote another observer, "should come as a shock to the average Broadway producer."[31]

Such comments undoubtedly pleased Gordon Craig disciple Hallie Flanagan, who had consistently argued that more could be achieved with fewer props and sets. She would have been pleased, too, with the ingenious use Orson Welles made in *Faustus* of the old vaudeville actors. "Too often," Hallie had written her national staff the year before, "vaudeville is a dreary succession of outworn acts. I think it is our job, as directors, playwrights, and designers, since at least one-third of all the people on our project are vaudevillians, to . . . work out new and exciting ways to use vaudeville technique."[32]

In *Faustus*, Welles reused the vaudevillians' expertise in his staging of the Elizabethan clown scenes. One very old bald actor named Harry McKee came up with a variation on his old act, including an imaginary game of golf. McKee died that spring, but not before receiving his first review ever from an erudite dramatic critic. "Mr. Harry McKee," wrote Stark Young in the *New Republic*, "was the best clown I have ever seen in Elizabethan revivals."

Stark Young was also taken with the way Welles staged the most famous moment in Marlowe's tragedy: Faust's doomed encounter with the most beautiful of women, Helen of Troy. "At the back of the stage is Helen, not stupidly classic but looking like Diane de Poitiers on a tapestry in the silver moonlight, the long open bodice, the high breasts, the coif, the stiff folds. Presently, Faustus will go to her and she will give him her hand, for we are not to think his enjoyment of her is ghostly or unreal. But for the moment Mr. Welles by a very brilliant invention has Faustus there at the front right looking out away from Helen, to recite those incredible lines:
'Was this the face that launched a thousand ships,
And burnt the topless towers of Ilium?
Sweet Helen, make me immortal with a kiss.' "[33]

Stark Young was one of the many thoughtful critics who had high praise for *Faustus*. "Everyone interested in the imaginative power of the theatre," wrote Brooks Atkinson in the *New York Times*, "will want to see how ably Orson Welles and John Houseman have cleared away all the imposing impedimenta that make most classics forbidding and how skillfully they have left 'Dr. Faustus,' grim and terrible, on the stage." Welles and Houseman, he wrote, "have gone a long way toward revolutionizing the staging of Elizabethan plays." And in conclusion: "This is a simple experiment that has succeeded on its merits as frank and sensible theatre, and a good many people will now pay their taxes in a more charitable frame of mind."[34]

The only dissenting voices came from the Left. Groups from the City Projects Council, the radical union of government workers, canceled blocks of tickets because *Faustus* had no social value. Hallie, paraphrasing Marlowe's description of the hour of damnation, when "Christ's blood streams in the firmament," noted acidly: "I suppose they wanted Lenin's blood streaming from the firmament."[35]

To the astonishment of those who thought Marlowe's tragedy irrelevant in troubled times, *Faustus* played to full houses for four months, accommodating a total of eighty thousand paying customers, including thirty-six hundred standees.

One night in February, about halfway through the run, a gaunt, unassuming gentleman slipped quietly into a back row. No one had recognized him at the ticket counter. But then an usher figured it out: Harry Hopkins, the man responsible for the Works Progress Administration in general, and their jobs in particular, had come to see the show. By the time Faustus sank howling into the flames, everyone in the company had heard the news. John Houseman came out to greet the big boss and take him backstage.

Houseman "led the head of the New Deal's Works Progress Administration between gaping stage traps, through sulphurous fumes, backstage, to where Welles lay—huge and half-conscious on a broken sofa—gasping and sweating from his descent into hell."[36] Hopkins had only one question for the dynamic duo: Were they having a good time working for the Federal Theatre? They both told him they were.

Hallie Flanagan had invited Hopkins to New York not only to show off *Faustus*, but also to attend the opening night of *Power*, a new Living Newspaper about public versus private ownership of utilities. It was a hot topic at the time. FDR, whose commitment to public ownership went back to his days as governor of New York, had undertaken an enormous public works project, called the Tennessee Valley Authority (TVA), which would transform the Tennessee River Valley, a locus of flooding and soil erosion, and would generate cheap electric power and provide jobs and hope to the impoverished farmers of the area. Private electric companies objected to the government's becoming a provider of electricity and had taken their case all the way to the Supreme Court. Neither side had yet won a clear-cut victory when Harry arrived in New York to attend the opening, with Hallie on his arm.

Hallie had been involved enough in the preparation of *Power* to know that its arguments came down squarely on FDR's side. She also knew that the writers had fortified their arguments by sending an annotated script, with extensive documentation, to all the critics likely to attend opening night. Nonetheless, as she walked into the Ritz Theatre with Harry on opening night, she had reasons to worry. The last Living Newspaper, *Injunction Granted*, had been so blatantly left-wing as to place the future of the innovative form in doubt. Friends and top staff members had argued, after it opened, against any continuation of the Living Newspaper.[37] If *Power* didn't succeed, it would spell the end of the experiment.

What's more, when she attended a rehearsal just seven days before the opening, she was shocked and outraged by the ways in which *Power* had

strayed from the original plan. "On January 15," Hallie wrote in an indignant memo, "I saw a run-through on a bare stage at the Ritz, and found
the whole thing clean-cut and exciting. Immediately after the reading of
the script . . . we spent three hours in a very detailed discussion of how this
play was to be done. We decided to use nothing except projections [slides
and film projected onto gauze and screens] in an attempt to make a real
contribution to experimentation in stagecraft." At rehearsal a month later,
she protested, "we start with a stage completely jammed with realistic
properties. A real switchboard, several sewing machines, a real operating
scene, an old man and a lady by the radio, etc." The memo went on and on
about all the problems: The timing wasn't crisp, and the acting had "lost all
zest" and was "colorless and meaningless." There did not seem to be any
"enveloping concept" for the show. All in all, she viewed *Power*, just seven
days before the fateful opening, as "the most bungling and inept piece of
work the Federal Theatre has yet produced."[38]

It is impossible to know what happened between that rehearsal and
opening night. Maybe her critique transformed the show. Or perhaps she
was just reacting angrily to the departures from *her* concept of the show;
she had already had the unpleasant experience, with *Injunction Granted*, of
seeing a show slip out of her control. In any case, *Power* turned out to be an
enormous success with audiences and critics. The "new theatrical form has
grown up," wrote a *Newsweek* critic. "Three preceding newsreels sputtered
like the histrionics of inarticulate youngsters. Now drama, information,
and acting pour through the mold of adroit production." Even Hearst paper critic John Anderson admitted to liking it: "Its "arguments have lost
most of the sullen snarl that could be heard in other editions of the Living
Newspaper."[39]

Unlike previous Living Newspapers, the final version of *Power* was the
work of a single writer, Arthur Arent, who had begun his career as a *tumm-
ler*, writing and acting in comedy skits for the amusement of the guests at a
resort hotel in the borscht belt. Those borscht belt skills were evident
throughout.

"If a lecture on the history, business methods and politics of electric
light seems to you like a dull subject," wrote Brooks Atkinson, "you have
only to see what the aggressive and versatile lads of the Living Newspaper
can do when they have a regiment of actors on their hands and a battalion
of theatre technicians. They have turned *Power* into one of the most exuberant shows in town. Minsky has nothing quite so hot to offer."[40]

Over and over, Arent combined education and comic shtick, and the actors played the comedy to the hilt. A scene explaining interlocking directorates has a single actor moving back and forth between spotlights of flesh pink and steel blue, talking to himself. Says blue Mr. Carmichael, "I've got a couple of propositions for you, good propositions. I've decided to merge your company with National Electric." Says pink Mr. Carmichael, "National Electric! Why, they've been losing money for years!" Says blue Mr. Carmichael, "I know it. That's why I'm doing it." Back and forth go the Mr. Carmichaels, "But, Mr. Carmichael?" "Yes, Mr. Carmichael?" "Oh, never mind . . . Where do I sign?" The dialogue goes faster and faster as blue Carmichael urges pink Carmichael to sign and sign and sign until he's sweating and exhausted.

Power's leading man was the Consumer, one Angus Buttonkooper, a hapless victim of high electricity rates, played in Chaplinesque style by the clowning comedian Norman Lloyd.

In one scene, Buttonkooper encounters the utility mogul Samuel J. Insull, whose midwestern empire of interlocking directorates collapsed in 1932 and cost many small investors their savings.

Insull: Now, son, just sit still and watch me and I'm going to show you how to make a lot of money.

Consumer: What do I have to do?

Insull: Just keep quiet and when I need you I'll let you know.

Insull lures the Consumer with promises of riches to come—a sixteen-cylinder Cadillac, a chauffeur, a home on Long Island with 160 rooms and a string of polo ponies. The grin on the Consumer's face grows wider and wider. He hands Insull his money, which goes into various pockets, and Insull hands him stock certificates.

Consumer: How much is the dividend going to be, Sam?

Insull: Well, that depends on how much we make.

Consumer: How do we know how much we make?

Insull: Why, I write it down in the books.

Consumer: Can anybody look at the books?

Insull: Oh, no. This is a holding company. We don't have to show our books to anybody . . .

Consumer: Well, how much have you got invested in it?

Insull: *Not one red cent!*

Blackout

Will Rogers had already provided the public with a definition of a holding company. "A holding company," he'd said, "is where you hand an accomplice the goods while the policeman searches you."[41] But *Power* went into greater detail. To explain, Arent introduces the Consumer's opposite number, the Man Who Knows. The Man Who Knows calls on stage-hands to bring out two blue blocks (operating electric companies), then to link them by placing a larger block of yellow on top of the two. The yellow block is the top holding company. Then he orders the stagehands to make another such pyramid of blue blocks joined by a yellow block. Then he calls on them to bring out an even larger orange block that links the two blue and yellow pyramids. That orange box is now the top hold-ing company.

"But what does it *do*?" asks the Loudspeaker.

The Man Who Knows has no answer.

At least one member of the audience made a personal connection to this skit: "That's where I lost my Insull stock," he told his neighbors, "in that yellow box over there."[42]

The hero of *Power* was the real-life senator George Norris of Nebraska, whose arguments in favor of public ownership are quoted at some length in the show. "When electricity becomes common in every house," Norris argues, "and as necessary as water to drink, if we are subjected to the will of a great monopoly that reaches from the Canadian boundary to the gulf of Mexico, and from ocean to ocean, we will become in reality, slaves." Norris was in his seventies when FDR was elected and stayed in office only because he hoped the new president would be able to realize his dream of public ownership, especially in the Tennessee Valley. And in 1933, the Senate took the first step by creating and funding the Tennessee Valley Authority.

Norris's dream is brought to life in the final scene of the first act. Mul-tiple projections of roaring waterfalls coming over the Norris Dam pour across three layers of scrim. A parade of men and women, many of them carrying lanterns, begin to move slowly through the rushing waterfalls, singing a Kentucky folk tune:

> *My name is William Edwards*
> *I live down Cove Creek way*
> *I'm working on a project*
> *They call the T.V.A.*
>
> *Oh, see them boys a-comin',*
> *Their Government they trust;*
> *Just hear their hammers ringing*
> *They'll build that dam or bust*

And in conclusion:

> *The Government employs us,*
> *Short hours and certain pay;*
> *Oh things are up and comin',*
> *God bless the T.V.A.*

Nowadays, a New York audience would scoff at such naive sentiments, and sophisticates would doubt the authenticity of the folk song as well.[43] But on opening night in 1937, the spectacle brought down the house.

Act 2, everyone agreed, didn't measure up to act 1, probably because the evil of the power brokers made more interesting theatre than the meetings of small farmers and businessmen banding together in cooperatives to oppose them. Also the show ended, necessarily, on an indecisive note.

Private utility companies, led by Wendell Willkie, president of the Commonwealth & Southern Corporation, had challenged the right of the TVA, a government entity, to distribute power, claiming it would destroy private competition in the area. For once, the Supreme Court, which had so often stymied New Deal programs, ruled on the side of the government.

In the final scene of *Power*, the Supreme Court justices appear as a striking abstraction: Nine scowling masks line up in a row on top of a giant podium. Chief Justice Charles Evans Hughes speaks the majority opinion: "Water power, the right to convert it into electric energy, and the electric energy thus produced constitute property belonging to the United States."

As the judge issues his pronouncement, the entire cast of *Power* mills about the stage, taking it in. When the news sinks in that the TVA has won, an impromptu parade begins. People throw confetti into the air and cheer and shout. Then more news arrives. The private power companies have procured an injunction, and a judge has signed a restraining order. The TVA won't be able to construct transmission lines after all.

Once more, the final decision rests with the Supreme Court.

The entire ensemble asks in unison: *"What will the Supreme Court do?"*

A huge question mark appears on a screen. The curtain falls. But after the curtain comes down and the house lights come up, the giant question mark reappears on the curtain. It will be another ten months before a transformed Supreme Court[44] makes a final ruling, in favor of the TVA, and provides the play with a more satisfying ending.

On opening night, the inconclusive ending didn't seem to matter. "As propaganda it is one-sided but effective," concluded *Life* magazine. "As theatre it is exciting and unique."[45]

Harry Hopkins agreed. Ushered backstage by Hallie afterward, he congratulated the company on a "great show." "It's fast and funny, it makes you laugh and it makes you cry and it makes you think—I don't know what more anyone can ask of a show. I want this play and plays like it done from one end of the country to the other . . . you will take a lot of criticism on this play. People will say it's propaganda. Well, I say what of it? It's propaganda to educate the consumer who's paying for power. It's about time someone had some propaganda for him. The big power companies have spent millions on propaganda for the utilities. It's about time the consumer had a mouthpiece. I say more plays like *Power* and more power on you."[46]

Power ran for five and a half months in New York and reappeared, in varying forms, in several Federal Theatre productions on the West Coast. The San Francisco show was, in the view of one critic, "a propaganda play minus the excitement." But in Seattle, where the private utility, Puget Power, and the public one, City Light, were doing battle, *Power* became a civic event. Florence James, who had previously directed the Negro unit in a successful production of *It Can't Happen Here*, took on the challenge of integrating the more successful black company with the struggling white one in the largest production the Seattle project had ever undertaken. The production had 162 light cues and required black technicians at times to give orders to white personnel. After some early tensions, "mixing the races" went well. But casting the two hundred speaking parts in the play, especially the white men, taxed James's ingenuity. An old vaudevillian wanted to know which of forty-six "mugs" he should use in performing his part. "I explained to him that he should memorize his lines and say them, and the mug he wore every day would be just fine," James recalled in an unpublished memoir. Another time, she asked a WPA worker who was mopping the floor if he would be willing to take a part. After he agreed and was transferred to the theatre project, he turned out to be illiterate. His lines had to be read to him so that he could memorize them. "He played the part of Wendell Willkie, and looked every inch the man when he was costumed in an elegant cutaway."[47]

The week of *Power*'s opening in Seattle was declared "Power Week" by the mayor, who issued a special proclamation celebrating Washington State, supplier of one fifth of the nation's electric energy. Huge spotlights, provided by City Light, were placed outside the theatre to light up the sky. Opening night was dubbed "City Light Night." "No night of Puget Sound Power and Light has been set as yet," commented an acerbic critic.[48] "That Old Debbil, the Power Trust," wrote another, "is the villain and the TVA is the hero in as fine a piece of overdone propaganda as ever trod the boards."[49] But audiences were enthusiastic, once they caught on. "About three scenes in, the audience would catch the rhythm and we never failed to close with at least four curtain calls," reported one of the directors.

The success of *Power* rescued the Living Newspaper from oblivion. After the opening night performance in New York, Harry Hopkins and Hallie Flanagan went out to supper and proceeded, according to Hallie, to plan the next Living Newspaper—this time about housing. There can be little doubt, however, that Hallie also used the opportunity to voice her frustration to Hopkins about Federal Theatre bureaucracy.

The constant reorganization of the Federal Theatre, during its brief life, had been a source of unending frustration for everyone on the project. Some found ways to laugh about it. Hiram Motherwell, perhaps the wittiest of Hallie's deputies, reported from his New England territory: "I expect to go to Leavenworth. I needed some of those XYZ forms, with lavender or amber colored duplicates. I asked Washington for them, and Washington in its majesty ignored me. All the same, Washington insisted on getting the forms in, and everything in its proper color. So I had the forms mimeographed here on white paper, and on the second white sheet I had typed: THIS IS LAVENDER PAPER or THIS IS AMBER PAPER . . . There hasn't been a squawk from Washington yet."[50]

Others wound up resigning in frustration over the endless battle with bureaucracy. "Every time a play is produced by the Federal Theatre," wrote Walter Hart, director of the Production Service Department, in his resignation letter, "a minor miracle has been passed. Only ceaseless, sleepless vigilance has saved the Federal Theatre from becoming a shambles under the barrage of constantly changing WPA rules and regulations and procedures in septuplicate."[51]

Some things had changed for the better. The previous summer, Hopkins had replaced Jacob Baker, who had never had much sympathy for Federal One, with a friend of Eleanor Roosevelt's named Ellen Woodward. Mrs. Woodward had seemed a natural choice to head up the women's division of the WPA, which oversaw work relief in traditionally female jobs, including sewing, nursing, museum and library research, nursery schools, and school lunchrooms. Now Hopkins added Federal One to her territory.

Hallie's opinion of the women's division, and Woodward's place in it, was summed up uncharitably in a letter she wrote to Phil describing Woodward's office, which was "full of silk doilies painted in oil and pussy willow gilded and fancy waste baskets and pictures of Mrs R. in white fur boa saying 'affectionately to Ellen,' etc." She added, "Aren't you glad I'm not in [WPA] women's work?"[52] Ellen Woodward, however, was at least sympathetic to the arts programs.

The problem in February 1937, when Harry Hopkins came to visit, had to do with the New York operation, which many described as "the artists versus the army." Harry Hopkins, with FDR's encouragement, liked to use the military to run WPA projects. Military officers got things done and were less likely to be corrupted by the many temptations bricks-and-mortar projects offered. But they proved to be woefully mismatched when it came to overseeing Federal One.

During the run-up to the election, in the summer of 1936, Lieutenant Colonel Brehon B. Somervell was assigned to take over the WPA arts programs in New York. Somervell was a capable enough officer from the Army Corps of Engineers, who would distinguish himself during World War II. But he had little or no sympathy, as Hallie's assistant Bill Farnsworth explained, with "the business of giving money to a bunch of artists to paint things and musicians to play stuff and . . . actors to act. It just rubbed him the wrong way."[53] Somervell believed people should be put to work building dams and bridges, and he had little patience with volatile artists who staged a demonstration whenever cuts were threatened. The artists in Federal One, for their part, viewed Somervell as an insensitive and uncomprehending martinet.

Eight days after the successful opening of *Power* in New York, it was announced in the papers that the reign of the army over the New York arts projects had ended. Lieutenant Colonel Somervell and his team were to be transferred elsewhere. Henceforth, the New York theatre project would be under the direct supervision of Hallie Flanagan, assisted administratively by Bill Farnsworth. There is no way of knowing what changed Hopkins's mind. Probably the New York radicals in the Federal Theatre Project worried him less after FDR's huge election victory. But it seems likely that he was also influenced by the excellence of *Faustus* and *Power,* along with the persuasive powers of his old Grinnell friend Hallie Flanagan.

A week after the announcement, Hallie wrote to Harry, giving him all the credit. "The reorganization is coming along splendidly in every respect. The morale on the project is high, and I am sure that you made, as usual, the right decision." In parentheses, she added a stage direction: "*(the last sentence to be spoken in a tone of combined humility and fierce determination!)*"[54] What she did not mention was that Hopkins had been responsible for the Somervell problem in the first place.

During this same period, Hallie signed the lease on a new space in the

Chanin Building at Forty-second Street and Lexington Avenue, which would allow everything except scenery-building shops to operate under one roof. "It will build morale, which has already gone up 50%, to the top," she wrote Phil. And soon after, she reported that "everyone is moved in and at work and I am so impressed with it all that I felt excited all day . . . It all seems too good to be true."[55]

Maybe the witch doctor had been right: Hallie did seem to be protected by a lucky star. Two more events, one small and one large, added to her satisfaction. Not long after the move to the new building, the procurement division was able to provide her, quite miraculously, with office furniture. Hallie wrote a grateful letter to the man responsible, Mr. R. H. Scott. "I am not sure how many lines of authority I am crossing in sending a letter direct to anyone in Procurement," she wrote, "but I shall have to run that risk in order to tell you how deeply appreciative I am of the effort you made to get the furniture for my office in the Federal Theatre Project. Mr. Connolly told me that you sacrificed your Saturday morning in order to assure delivery of this furniture Monday. After a year of WPA, I know something of what this must have meant. The furniture is beautiful, and I hope sometime when you are in the Chanin Building you will come in and look at it."[56]

The larger miracle was announced in the papers the following week: George Bernard Shaw had agreed to hand over the rights to all his plays to the Federal Theatre Project.[57] This permission did not, of course, drop from the sky. For some time, Hallie had been trying to figure out a way to get permissions from leading playwrights, despite the Federal Theatre's rock-bottom royalty rates of $50 a week.

Shaw's response to Hallie's plea was a delightful mixture of Shavian wit and idealism. "I know quite well what you are up against in this undertaking," he wrote Hallie. "It is useless to hope that you can find groups with a high degree of skill in acting and direction everywhere. You may not be able to find them anywhere. The plays will be murdered more or less barbarically all the time. That happens on Broadway too; and you must take what you can get in the way of casting and direction just as if you were a fashionable manager. So far from avoiding negro casts you will be very lucky if you can get them; for negroes act with a delicacy and sweetness that make white actors look like a gang of roughnecks in comparison."

Shaw's only concern was the possibility of getting entangled in bureaucracy. "They tell me that your theatre, being a Federal institution, is unable to move without miles of red tape being consumed, and that money can be extracted from it only after signing nine receipts. They also seem to think that every production will be a separate transaction involving a special license and weekly payments and acknowledgements. That will never do for me. As long as you stick to your fifty cent maximum for admission, and send me the accounts and payments quarterly, or half yearly if you prefer it, so that I shall have to sign only four or two receipts a year, and forget all about you in the meantime, you can play anything of mine you like."

He concluded: "Any author of serious plays who does not follow my example does not know what is good for him. I am not making a public spirited sacrifice; I am jumping at an unprecedentedly good offer. Faithfully, G. Bernard Shaw."[58]

No one could have been more pleased than Hallie at that point to dispense with unnecessary paperwork. Shaw's letter and payment scheme were accepted without further ado. Then, seven days after the announcement of Shaw's agreement, a second announcement came out in the papers: Eugene O'Neill had agreed to give the project rights to all his plays. According to Hallie, the Federal Theatre would produce them in varying and appropriate locations: *The Fountain* in Florida, *Anna Christie* in New England, and *Marco Millions* on the West Coast.

The O'Neill announcement came out in the papers on May 28, 1937, punctuating what had been five months of Federal Theatre Project triumphs. But the Federal Theatre's fate was ultimately in the hands of the Congress. And the Congress, by that time, was unhappy with Roosevelt because of his plan to restructure the Supreme Court. Some in Congress wanted to retaliate by cutting WPA funds even more sharply than FDR had proposed. It looked very much as though luck had run out for Hallie and the Federal Theatre.

Roosevelt devised his plan to remake the Supreme Court in early May, one day before addressing the Congress. Uncharacteristically, he consulted no one in advance: Even his inner circle were taken by surprise. Then, the day before addressing the Congress, he laid out the plan for the cabinet and congressional leaders: Every Supreme Court justice who stayed on the bench for six months after his seventieth birthday would be paired with a new justice, appointed by FDR. The proposal was couched in fancy legal language, but the crux of it was clear: It would give Roosevelt the power to add six justices of his choosing to the aging nine-man court, thus creating a Supreme Court that would go along with his program.

The congressional leadership was stunned. The opposition reacted with outrage, but so, more critically, did many among the progressive majority, which had until then been a rubber stamp for his programs. FDR's deviousness offended many of his allies. And the proposal itself, at a time when menacing dictatorships were gaining power in Europe, struck many as dangerously undemocratic. "If the American people accept this last audacity of the President without letting out a yell to high heaven," warned Dorothy Thompson, "they have ceased to be jealous of their liberties and are ripe for ruin."[59]

Senate hearings in March provided a forum for national indignation and dragged on for months. And Roosevelt refused to compromise, even when the Supreme Court began to issue rulings favorable to the New Deal. The president held out until July, when he finally had to admit defeat. But in the meantime, he had spent precious political capital. It was as though, observed FDR speechwriter Tommy Corcoran, one had a million dollars in the bank and suddenly got an overdraft notice. "Long-forgotten was the election," Marquis Childs wrote, "that parade of forty-six states. The opposition did a gleeful war dance on the floor of the Senate every day."[60]

In the midst of this struggle, Congress took up the WPA appropriation bill. Hopkins and FDR had decided to ask for $1.5 billion for the coming fiscal year—an amount that would require deep cuts but could keep programs, including the arts programs, going. But members of Congress, in a resistant mood because of the Court plan, decided it was time to reassert their authority. "It is the duty of Congress to balance the budget," announced one senator, "and this duty should not be shifted by the Congress to the President."[61]

Roosevelt's economy drive, reported the *New York Times* on May 6, had been "taken up with unexpected enthusiasm" by House leaders, who proposed cutting the relief budget by an additional half billion dollars. It was the first time in several years that Congress had dared to defy the enormously popular president.

Congressmen argued that the New Deal's success lessened the need for such a large relief appropriation. "There are many more opportunities now for people to find private employment than there were two years ago," claimed Representative John R. Mitchell of Tennessee.[62] "The emergency has passed," declared Senator James F. Byrnes of South Carolina.[63]

The fact that FDR was out of town made it easier for Congress to stage its rebellion. On the day the House announced its plan to slash the WPA, the papers carried a photo of FDR out in a boat in the Texas Gulf, smiling up at a huge tarpon he had caught. It was up to Harry Hopkins to stand in for his boss and defend the program.

On May 5, Hopkins went up to the Hill and warned a House subcommittee that the huge reduction they proposed would take four hundred thousand off federal rolls, at a time when the need was still great. Despite improvements in every sector of the economy, 11 percent of the workforce was still unemployed. And there were no good alternatives to federal relief, unless you believed that the Republican plan for "home responsibility and neighborhood opinion" could do the job.

Harry Hopkins's high spirits, so evident on the night of FDR's great victory, had been dampened since by private sorrow. He had learned that his wife, Barbara, was fatally ill with cancer. And he hadn't been entirely well himself. Still, Hopkins proved to be an eloquent defender of his programs.

But Congress, rather like a spurned lover, was accepting no substitutes. "House leaders proposed to advise Mr. Roosevelt upon his return from his vacation that unless he is prepared to use strong personal influence with many of their followers he might as well expect a substantial reduction."[64]

Meanwhile, back in New York, the excitable arts community viewed the congressional cuts as a near fatal blow to the Federal Theatre Project. "With the shekels no longer forthcoming," crowed *Billboard*, "the FTP seems destined to pass out of the federal relief picture, probably by easy steps . . . Indications are that directors in key cities will receive some form of bad news within two weeks."[65]

Brooks Atkinson wrote a Sunday piece in the *Times* that sounded like a valedictory, praising the "superhuman" work of Hallie Flanagan. "Although she has been violently criticized by both conservatives and radicals, she has never been criticized by anyone who understood the problems as thoroughly as she does or who is her equal for hard work, intellectual honesty and vision."[66]

Congress was in a state of suspended animation. CONGRESS PUZZLED, AWAITS ROOSEVELT, read a headline in the *Times* on May 9. "Congress members are wondering chiefly whether the President will hold firm against any compromise on the court reorganization issue and just what his attitude will be on the growing opposition in both chambers to his proposal to spend $1.5 billion for relief next year."

"Everything here is focused on Congress," Hallie wrote to Phil from Washington on May 13. "Hopkins is taking a terrible drubbing every day with all forces of reaction within and without the party hard upon him. Between attacks he lies down and drinks hot milk.

"In the face of all that," she continued, "I felt pretty mad listening to the luncheon speakers of the National Art Federation talk about Art. 'I do not worry about hunger,' said one large paunched gent. 'Artists have always been hungry—the greatest art has been created in garrets' . . . There was a lot of sneering at those of us who feel 'an apostolic zeal' about this 'wholesale robbery' of the everlasting taxpayer."

At last, on May 14, the *Times* reported that FDR was "speeding north-ward" on his special train, en route to Washington. Harry Hopkins pressed his advantage with the House Appropriations Committee. "Hopkins . . . testified that the full $1,500,000,000 was necessary and that even with it private industry would have to absorb 525,000 workers now on relief jobs." After that, the committee reversed itself, "partly on Mr. Hopkins ad-vice but perhaps quite as much on the consideration that President Roose-velt had demanded it."[67] The next day, the *Times* banner headline read, ROOSEVELT, BACK, DEMANDS PASSAGE OF HIS COURT PLAN AND $1,500,000,000 RELIEF FUND.[68]

Fortunately for WPA workers, Congress chose to decouple the two is-sues. The battle against Roosevelt's Court-packing plan droned on, but the $1.5 billion relief bill was now certain to get through relatively unscathed. Hopkins and WPA executives in Washington viewed this as a tremendous victory.

But no one working on the Federal Theatre Project was celebrating. Everyone feared deep and possibly debilitating cuts. Letters went out to Harry Hopkins from the project's National Policy Board, from Actors' Eq-uity, and from other unions affected, demanding an exemption for the Fed-eral Theatre. Hallie made repeated efforts to reach Harry Hopkins and Eleanor Roosevelt, but neither was responding to her calls.

"This place is in a fever of anxiety," Hallie reported to Bill Farnsworth, who was down in Washington trying to advocate. Hopkins, she argued, "should take a firm stand to keep the arts. They are going to stage terrific demonstrations. All the arts are together. It's much more vigorous than ever before. Mr. Hopkins and President Roosevelt should realize what's going on. Mrs. Roosevelt certainly should know about it. All of us should be on the side of the workers."[69]

The Workers Alliance was eager to propel the WPA artists into action, even if it required alarmist tactics. Way back in January, the alliance had passed out flyers headlined OBITUARY NOTICE, warning that 8,000 artists and 3.2 million WPA workers were at risk of losing their jobs and calling for a demonstration in Times Square.[70] As it became clear that job losses were likely no matter what happened in Congress, the Workers Alliance began to beat the drum for some kind of shutdown of operations.

Harry Hopkins's attitude toward the Workers Alliance was aptly de-scribed by *Collier's* writer Walter Davenport as "benign tolerance." The Workers Alliance existed because of the WPA—it had been formed to

represent all those on the government payroll who had no other union affiliation. Like other unions, the Workers Alliance had the right, under the
Wagner Act, to organize workers. But the Workers Alliance was less disci-
plined and rational than other unions. It was led by a Socialist, and much
of its leadership was Communist. Its meetings were wild and unruly. "It
lacks the business intelligence of the regular trade union," Davenport
wrote. "Its organizers, whoopers-up, shills, spellbinders and lobbyists spend
too much of their energy howling calamity, crying havoc and exhorting to
political action to give the necessary attention to humdrum details."[71]
Even though their membership was entirely reliant on the goodwill of
Congress, and ultimately of the people, the Workers Alliance leadership
gave little or no consideration to the possibility that they might, through
their actions, antagonize those on whom they depended for survival.

Hopkins and his aides, however, had just been through a bruising battle
to save WPA jobs for millions. Even at that moment, he was fighting a
rearguard maneuver in Congress to dilute the relief program by adding pet
pork barrel projects. The noisy protests of the Workers Alliance were the
last thing he needed.

Undoubtedly, under the circumstances, Hopkins was also annoyed
about Hallie's decision to produce a children's show called *The Revolt of
the Beavers*, which opened in New York just as he was trying to lock up
the relief appropriation. *Revolt* was a fairy tale with a message: It told the
story of a cruel beaver chief who keeps the underling beavers busy turning bark into products but shares none of the proceeds from their labor. A
hero beaver named Oakleaf organizes the beavers and leads them in a revolt. They shoot down the boss's company police, using revolvers and machine guns concealed in their lunch boxes, then gleefully send their
oppressors into exile. Children who saw the play reacted to the comic antics of the beavers, who glided around on roller skates. One member of
the audience recalled that "kids rushed to the stage, literally rushed it to
take sides." For them it was a tale of good and evil rather than a call to
revolution.

Hallie understood when she decided to produce it that *The Revolt of the
Beavers* was, as she wrote Phil, "very human and amusing and tragic and
very class conscious." Whether blinded by her own leftist sympathies or by
her inveterate optimism, Hallie didn't anticipate the problems the play
would cause with adult critics. Shortly after it opened, the Police Athletic
League canceled its block of fourteen hundred free tickets, claiming that
the show was designed to turn children into little revolutionaries. The *Saturday Evening Post* charged that the Federal Theatre Project was teaching

poor children to murder rich children. Worst of all, Brooks Atkinson scorned the play as "Marxism à la Mother Goose."

"Many children unschooled in the technique of revolution," he wrote, "now have an opportunity, at Government expense, to improve their tender minds." Very soon, copies of Atkinson's review appeared on the desk of every congressman in Washington.[72]

As if that weren't trouble enough, the Federal Theatre was making Hopkins and his WPA administrators in Washington nervous for another reason. Since March, Project #891 had been rehearsing a new musical work by a young composer named Marc Blitzstein. *The Cradle Will Rock*, a pro-labor call to action set in "Steeltown USA," was set to preview at the Maxine Elliott on June 16.

After *The Revolt of the Beavers*, Hopkins and his aides were keeping a close eye on Federal Theatre productions, especially if they dealt with the red hot topic of union strikes and company crackdowns. An advance scout came up to New York to attend rehearsal of the production with Hallie Flanagan. He pronounced it "magnificent."[73] But others in Washington continued to worry that this latest Welles/Houseman production might be dangerous for the Federal Theatre Project. *The Cradle Will Rock* turned out to be both.

chapter eleven

THE CRADLE WILL ROCK

By the time Hallie Flanagan heard Marc Blitzstein play and sing his one-man version of *The Cradle Will Rock*, he had performed it so often for wealthy prospects in exclusive New York apartments that he'd taken to calling it "my Essex House run." Many were intrigued, and some were even temporarily committed to producing *Cradle*. The Group Theatre, the Theatre Union, and the American Repertory Theatre all expressed an interest. But in the end, none of them came through. "I've apparently turned out a firebrand that nobody wants to touch," the thirty-one-year-old Blitzstein reported to his family.[1] The only person who remained committed to the script from early on was Orson Welles, who met Blitzstein during the run of *Horse Eats Hat* and was immediately fascinated by the intense composer and his music.

Marc Blitzstein, Welles wrote later, "was an engine, a rocket, directed in one direction which was his opera—which he almost believed had only to be performed to start the Revolution."[2] And yet, Welles noted, he had "the attentive stillness of some birds: one of the predators—a gyrfalcon. Serious rather than solemn, he brightens a room when he enters it. His political beliefs are . . . held with the most perfect serenity. In the Church he would be called saintly . . . If he sounds a little too good to be true, he is, almost, just that. It never occurs to him that his mere presence is a kind of rebuke to the rest of us."[3]

Hallie Flanagan first heard *The Cradle Will Rock* in the apartment John Houseman and Virgil Thomson shared on East Fifty-fifth Street, following what Houseman called a "well-planned dinner." Since Houseman and Thomson were aesthetes who spoke only French at breakfast, the meal and the wine were surely good enough to put everyone in a mellow mood.[4]

Memorial Day Massacre, Chicago, May 30, 1937 (AP Images)

Afterward, Marc Blitzstein sat down at the piano and pounded out his "proletarian" opera.

"It took no wizardry to see," Hallie wrote afterward, "that this was not just a play set to music, nor music illustrated by actors, but music + play equaling something new and better than either. This was in its percussive as well as its verbal beat Steeltown, U.S.A.—America 1937."[5]

Cradle was and remains impossible to categorize. It is part opera, part musical comedy, at times seething with revolutionary ardor, at other times farcical, and at other times sentimental. Blitzstein's principal inspiration was *The Threepenny Opera*, Bertolt Brecht and Kurt Weill's defiant, jazzy reinterpretation of *The Beggar's Opera*, but he admitted to throwing in "whatever was indicated and at hand. There were recitatives, arias, revue patterns, tap dances, suites, chorales, silly symphony, continuous incidental commentary music, lullaby music—all pitchforked into it without a great deal of initiative from me."[6]

Marc Blitzstein was part of the Composers' Collective, a Marxist-inspired group committed to writing "relevant" music that would stir the masses. "Music is one of the greatest education forces we know," Blitzstein wrote in one essay. "It can train, not only our minds, but our blood. Composers must come out into the open; they must fight the battle with other workers." Blitzstein shared this essay, along with everything else he wrote and composed, with his wife, Eva Goldbeck, a writer and translator. Theirs was an unconventional marriage: Marc Blitzstein was gay, but he was deeply attached to Eva. Eva was seriously anorexic. By the time she was finally hospitalized for her illness, it was too late. She died of the complications of anorexia in 1936.

Blitzstein was devastated by his wife's death. Most of his early works were dedicated to her, and the two shared a passionate commitment to creating revolutionary art. For a time after Eva Goldbeck died, Marc Blitzstein lost his fighting spirit.

It was during this period that a wealthy patron ran into Blitzstein on a street corner. Shocked by his appearance, she invited him to her Connecticut home, where he and Eva had spent a few weeks the year before, to recuperate. And there, in a large room in a renovated stable on his benefactor's property, Blitzstein took a kernel from past work, a song called "Nickel Under the Foot," and grew it into a ten-scene "play in music" called *The Cradle Will Rock*.

"Nickel Under the Foot" is the aching lament of a reluctant prostitute, Moll, who works at a regular job two days out of seven. "So I'm just searchin' along the street," she sings, "for on those five days it's nice to eat."

She tells the story of one night when she had no hope of a meal, then saw what looked like a nickel on the ground. "I tell you, Mister," she says, "you don't know what it felt like thinking that was a nickel under my foot." Having that nickel makes all the difference between happiness and despair, good and evil. "Every dream and scheme's depending on whether you've kept it warm, the nickel under your foot."

When Bertolt Brecht, during a visit to America, heard Blitzstein play "Nickel Under the Foot," he suggested that the composer write a larger piece about "all kinds of prostitution—the press, the courts, the arts, the whole system."[7] And that suggestion became the organizing idea of Blitzstein's allegorical opera, set in Steeltown, USA, on a night when the workers are gathering in the streets and threatening to strike. True to Brecht's suggestion, Blitzstein presents a rogue's gallery of middle-class hypocrites, all under the control of Mister Mister, the man who owns everything and everybody in Steeltown. Mister Mister has formed a Liberty Committee to fight the union. But on this night, the members of the Liberty Committee, who came to observe the union rally, have gotten hauled into lockup by an overzealous cop. And there in night court, with Moll looking on, we learn through flashbacks of all the ways they have prostituted themselves.

It was natural for Marc Blitzstein to focus on the class of people who might join the Liberty Committee. His own parents, although sympathetic to Socialist causes, were well-off, and he himself had trained at the renowned Curtis Institute before traveling to Europe to study with both Arnold Schoenberg and Nadia Boulanger. So even though his sympathies lay with the workers, most of the scenes in his opera focus on the class he knew better, the complacent bourgeoisie.

Even while he was enjoying the comfort of his benefactor's Connecticut retreat, Blitzstein invented two artist sycophants, a painter named Dauber and a violinist named Yasha, to mock the hypocrisy of artists who attach themselves to the rich. "Oh there's something so lowdown about the rich," sing Dauber and Yasha, noting that artists are allowed to be "rude, and insulting and lewd" around art-infatuated rich people. Yet when Mrs. Mister appears in her Pierce-Arrow, with a horn that plays the opening theme of Beethoven's "Egmont" overture, Dauber and Yasha clamor to be asked out to her place for weekends. "Ask us again, dear Mrs. Mister, Ask us again," they sing in graceful fox-trot rhythm. Even though the guests are "disgusting," and the "food is too heavy," they love the chance to live in luxury from Friday to Sunday. Blitzstein's own situation was not far from that of the effete artists he mocked, and his hosts, the

Eitingons, must have felt a shiver of recognition when they viewed the scene he had written at their home. But Blitzstein had allied himself with what the critic Alfred Kazin called "the toughness of the times . . . the militant new wind . . . the anger which was always in the air." Neither he nor his hosts could be spared.

There are no good middle-class people in the inflamed atmosphere of *The Cradle Will Rock*. Instead there is the Reverend Salvation, a member of the Liberty Committee who takes his cues from Mister Mister's loyal spouse, Mrs. Mister. One scene between Mrs. Mister and the Reverend recalls the events in Steeltown that led America into World War I. In 1915, the Reverend preached the commandment "Thou shalt not kill" and decried all wars. Then in 1916, Mrs. Mister told him, "Don't be quite so downright," since "it seems that peace can be a little expensive." So Reverend Salvation sang instead that "peace is a wonderful thing . . . but when I say peace I'm referring to inner peace." Then in 1917, Mrs. Mister comes to the Reverend with the news that war has broken out. So Reverend Salvation preaches, "This is the war to end all war" and "Make the world safe for democracy." "Kill all the dirty Huns!" screams Mrs. Mister. "Steel's going to go sky high!"

There is plenty of degradation to go around. The newspaperman, Editor Daily, joins Mister Mister in a Gilbert & Sullivan–style romp: "Oh the press, the press, the freedom of the press / They'll never take away the freedom of the press / With a hey-diddle-dee and a ho-nonny-no / for whichever side will pay the best." Then there's the slothful Junior Mister, who's sent off to Honolulu, on the wings of an undulating Hawaiian melody, to stay out of trouble, and there's Dr. Specialist, who lies about a worker's injury in order to keep his position as head of the Liberty Committee. There's also the college president, who answers the call to recruit college boys for Mister Mister's private militia.

The saddest tale of all is told by Harry Druggist, who, in order to keep his store, went along with a company plot to bomb union headquarters and wound up losing his son in the explosion. He comes to night court often now, because he's taken to drink.

The "people" in this people's opera are few and far between until the late scenes. But their presence is felt even before they appear. The Liberty Committee spends part of its time clamoring for Mister Mister to come and bail them out and the rest of its time asking the cops to produce the labor agitator who started all the trouble. At last Larry Foreman does appear, full of jokes and high spirits. The presence of the Liberty Committee, whose slogan is "America, cradle of liberty / Steeltown, cradle of the

Liberty Committee," inspires him to sing the ominous title song, a marching anthem addressed to the "this crowd here / Hidin' up there in the cradle of the liberty committee": "The lords and their lackeys and wives / A swingin' 'Rockabye Baby' in a nice big cradle." But, he warns, the thunder and lightning are "gonna surround you." "Well, you can't climb down, and you can't say 'No' / You can't stop the weather, not with all your dough / for when the wind blows / Oh, when the wind blows / The cradle will rock!"

The pounding accompaniment in a relentless march rhythm foreshadows the coming of the unions, united under one banner and gathering in large numbers out in Steeltown square with their trumpets, fifes, and drums.

Finally, Mister Mister appears in night court, frees all the members of the Liberty Committee, and confronts Larry Foreman. "I know a lot about you," says Mister Mister, "you used to be in my employ." Mister Mister urges Larry Foreman to join him in "one big united organization" since, after all, "we're both for the same thing." He promises the workers a swimming pool, a library, and a private park for their children, and he offers Larry Foreman a tidy sum to stop his troublemaking. But Larry Foreman tells him that all the workers really want is a union.

At this moment, Blitzstein introduces new musical complexity. Moll begins a reprise of "Nickel Under the Foot" in the background, while Mister Mister and Larry Foreman discuss the bribe. Simultaneously, members of the Liberty Committee urge Foreman to accept the money and Harry Druggist urges him to turn it down. Then we begin to hear the distant sound of fifes and drums coming from the square.

"That's the boilermakers!" shouts Foreman. "That's the roughers!" "That's the rollers!" "That's Steel, your steel! They've done it!" The strike is on.

The voices of the workers crescendo in a reprise of the marching song, "The Cradle Will Rock." The piano bangs a series of dissonant chords, à la Mussorgsky, and the chorus of workers shout out one last time, *"The cradle will rock!"*

By March, when Hallie Flanagan was trying to decide whether to allow the Federal Theatre to produce *The Cradle Will Rock*, strikes were breaking out all over the country: There were more strikes during 1937 than in any previous year in American history. It was a year of industrial warfare, not only between unions and industry, but also between the old established trade unions and the brash new Congress of Industrial Organizations, known universally as the CIO. And it was a year in which class warfare, as prophesied in Marxist theory, seemed a real possibility, even to the sober editorial writers of the *New York Times*. "The orderly process of American industry," worried the *Times*, "has been interrupted by a series of destructive strikes. Laws have been broken. Violence has been widespread. Feelings have run high and bitterness has mounted. There has been an unfortunate tendency to play straight into the hands of the enemies of the whole democratic system by encouraging public opinion to stratify along 'class' lines."[8]

Under the circumstances, there were some who thought Hallie would be foolish to endorse such an incendiary piece as *Cradle*, especially at the very moment that Congress was deciding the fate of the Federal Theatre Project. But John Houseman claimed in retrospect that Hallie "sensed, better than her more timid colleagues, that in the storm into which the Arts Projects were headed, there was no safety in prudence and no virtue in caution."[9] Certainly, that was Hallie's deeply held and oft repeated conviction. "It is the very essence of art," she told a group gathered in Washington around this time, "that it exceed bounds, often including those of tradition, decorum, and that mysterious thing called taste. It is the essence of art that it shatter accepted patterns, advance into unknown territory, challenge the existing order. Art is highly explosive. To be worth its salt it must have in that salt a fair sprinkling of gunpowder."[10] The day after she heard Blitzstein perform *Cradle* for her on the piano, the announcement went out that *The Cradle Will Rock* would be Project #891's next Federal Theatre production.

Surprisingly, since Marc Blitzstein's knowledge of labor and unions came in large part from reading Communist propaganda, *The Cradle Will Rock* managed to touch on many of the festering conditions that angered working people in the early 1930s. Moll the prostitute, for instance, who worked only two days because "the other time my services ain't required," was in the situation of many workers whose pay was low and whose hours were unpredictable.

Nearly half of autoworkers earned only $1,000 a year, and many never knew from one day to the next whether they would work at all. "When we went to work in the morning," remembers a metal finisher in the auto industry, "we never knew how many hours we would work. The metal finishers on repair were working as much as twenty hours per day. Workers in other departments . . . were often sent home without earning their carfare."

Sometimes the workers were promised a certain hourly rate, then found a much lower amount in their paychecks. But when that happened they were afraid to speak up. The foreman's answer when they did complain was, "There are a lot of people outside waiting to take your jobs."[11] There were no laws to protect workers who protested. And factory owners, evoking the threat of communism, had gotten more and more belligerent toward any hint of rebellion, quickly firing anyone they suspected of being an "agitator."

The Liberty Committee of *The Cradle Will Rock* was replicated in industrial cities all over the Midwest. There was a Law and Order League in Canton, Ohio, a John Q Public League in Warren, and a Mahoning Valley Citizens' Committee in Youngstown, all pledged to protecting "the American way of living" and keeping out "the advance guard of Communism."[12] There were also company unions, operating on Mister Mister's idea that "we're both for the same things."

Company towns like Steeltown were common. In Harlan, Kentucky, miners lived in company houses, received their pay in scrip, and were obliged to shop at the company store. The sheriff and his deputies, many of whom had criminal records, declared "open war on organizers" and, in some cases, carried out death threats. Sometimes control was exerted by inserting spies into every aspect of community life. In Aliquippa, Pennsylvania, espionage extended into schools, churches, and homes, and company police were used as "escorts" for union organizers. So when Mister Mister tells Larry Foreman, "I know a lot about you," it is art imitating life.

In his opera, Blitzstein has Mister Mister recruiting college boys for his private militia. Hiring enforcers and strikebreakers was common industrial practice at the time, but they tended to be unsavory characters with nicknames like "Snake-Eyes Kid Steinie" and "Stinkfoot McVey" and "Bennie the Fink," many of whom had done jail time. There was hardly a major American industry that didn't have a budget for spies, hired to keep union organizing in check. Many large companies also had large stockpiles of munitions on hand, in case trouble should break out.[13]

Given management's mastery of all the tactics of intimidation, it is not surprising that the labor movement grew weaker and weaker in the years after World War I, when unions had briefly flexed their muscles. Even before the Crash of 1929, the labor movement had fallen on very hard times. Union membership dropped from over four million in 1920 to not much over two million in the early 1930s.

Then in 1935, the new progressive majority in Congress passed the National Labor Relations Act, a bill that has sometimes been called "labor's Magna Carta." The bill, championed by Senator Robert Wagner of New York, protected the right of workers to organize and to bargain collectively with their employers. The act also allowed a majority vote to commit all workers in a plant to one union, a controversial provision that meant a minority might be forced to join and pay dues against its will. Although FDR was generally pro-labor, he was troubled by this "closed shop" idea, which he and many others viewed as undemocratic. But in the end, he reluctantly signed the Wagner bill, and it became the law of the land.

Then, very quickly, the labor movement caught fire. Recruiters fanned out over the country. Flyers were thrust into the blackened hands of miners as they emerged at the end of their shifts. There was even a flyer claiming to have FDR's approval. "The President," it read, "says you must join a union." Grimy union halls that had fallen into disuse bristled with new excitement. Within three weeks of the bill's signing, the International Ladies' Garment Workers Union tripled its membership to 200,000, and the United Mine Workers of America claimed 135,000 new members.

The head of the United Mine Workers was a burly giant of a man named John L. Lewis, who had begun work in the mines at twelve and now saw the chance to organize on a vast scale. He envisioned a union not just of coal miners, but of workers in all the huge industries of mass production in the industrial heartland: rubber, steel, automobiles. The Wagner Act gave John L. Lewis, a man who could bring a union meeting to its feet with his fiery rhetoric, an unprecedented opportunity.

Most who still belonged to unions when the Depression hit were members of the American Federation of Labor (AF of L), the Railway Brotherhood, and a handful of other independent unions, organized according to specific skills and trades. But these trade categories didn't apply to the vast new group of semiskilled workers engaged in mass production of steel and automobiles. These workers, who numbered in the hundreds of thousands, were often recent immigrants from Eastern Europe—Hungarians, Poles, Czechs, and Lithuanians—and were looked down on by the older trade unionists. Lewis was impatient with the AF of L's halfhearted efforts to organize them. And not long after the Wagner Act passed, he split with the AF of L and formed the CIO.

The first target of the CIO organizers was the steel industry, a bastion of resistance to unions. In steel, company unions were the rule, and workers were divided by their areas of expertise and often by ethnicity as well. As in *The Cradle Will Rock*, the boilermakers, the roughers, and the rollers had tended in the past to go their separate ways. But the CIO, with a $500,000 war chest and the protection of the Wagner Act, drew the workers together under the banner of the Steel Workers Organizing Committee (SWOC). And on March 8, 1937, to the surprise of many, the president of United States Steel signed a historic contract, granting recognition to SWOC in all its plants and providing a wage increase, an eight-hour day, a forty-hour week, paid vacations, and seniority rights. It was a great victory and a bloodless one. It was in this moment that Orson Welles began casting *The Cradle Will Rock*.

Howard Da Silva had all the right credentials for the role of Larry Foreman. Born Howard Silverblatt in Cleveland, Da Silva was the son of Yiddish-speaking Russian immigrants and worked his way through Carnegie Tech in Pittsburgh with a job in a local steel mill. Back in Cleveland, he had been "in the thick of it," playing the union organizer in a people's theatre production of *Waiting for Lefty* just at the moment that the CIO was organizing White Auto Body. So when Marc Blitzstein invited him over to Houseman's apartment for yet another "Essex House run," he found himself singing along. "Half an hour later we all agreed that I was Larry Foreman," Da Silva recalled.[14]

Others in the cast had varying degrees of experience. Will Geer, who took the role of Mister Mister, had real-life credentials as an activist: He had once been beaten up and hospitalized after an encounter with thugs from an organization called Friends of Germany. Although he would have to add years to play Mister Mister, he already had an impressive résumé as a stage and screen actor. Others in the cast had very little to recommend them besides the fact that they came from the relief rolls. Olive Stanton had never performed on Broadway, but her clear, thin voice and her own history of struggle made her perfect for the part of Moll. Not everyone took to the opera's political message: John Adair, cast as Harry Druggist, was heard to say that *Cradle* would make a wonderful Shubert musical if they would just get rid of the unpleasant lyrics.

In the first few weeks, according to Lehman Engel, who came on as music director, *Cradle* rehearsals were desultory. "A sunny day would send [Orson] out of the theatre for a long lunch. An interesting group of friends were sufficient excuse for canceling his evening schedule." Later, he went to the opposite extreme—starting at ten in the morning and often not leaving the theatre. "He might dismiss his cast at four the next morning, but when we would return at noon, we would find Orson sleeping in a theatre seat."[15]

Marc Blitzstein's apostolic zeal acted as a goad to Welles, who found various ways to challenge it. "He had been converted," Welles remembered later, "and he was like one of those little gray friars hopping around after Saint Francis had spoken." Welles took to inviting Blitzstein to share his lavish lifestyle of chauffeured cars and dinners at the 21 Club. "Do you think you'll have this after the revolution?" he asked his friend.

"*Everybody* will have it," Blitzstein replied.

Hallie Flanagan didn't see why they needed *any* scenery to perform *The Cradle Will Rock*. But Orson had a subversive plan to turn Blitzstein's revolutionary *Cradle* into a Broadway-style musical. He envisioned a lavish set, "full of metal and glass and the horror of Steeltown."[16] There were to be glass-bottomed wagons and moving platforms, and in the final scene, the entire stage, which was a sort of giant glass-bottomed boat, was supposed to rock like a cradle, while blinding lights shot up at the actors from below and loudspeakers positioned all over the house blared out the sound of the steelworkers' trumpets, fifes, and drums.

The musical accompaniments were to be equally extravagant. Conductor Lehman Engel was busy rehearsing a twenty-four-piece orchestra and a forty-four-member chorus of black and white singers, while Clarence Yates, a dancer from the Negro theatre project, oversaw the singers' choreography.

For musicians, Blitzstein's score held special delights and challenges. Even though he claimed to be composing for the masses, Blitzstein's works were replete with polyrhythms and dissonances that made them difficult for the singers, not to mention a large orchestra. They also contained all kinds of inside musical jokes. The Reverend Salvation's sermons, for instance, are set to variations on a Bach chorale, and the college president's scene includes quotes from the Yale song "Boola, Boola." There is an evocation of sentimental Yiddish love songs in an exquisite duet between a Polish steelworker and his wife. Later, a hard-driving number by Joe Worker's sister creates the dark mood of "Pirate Jenny" in *Threepenny Opera*. "How many frame-ups," sings Joe Worker's sister, "How many shakedowns, lockouts, sellouts / How many times machine guns tell the same old story, Brother, does it take to make you wise."

Music director Engel was a great admirer of Blitzstein's work, but he had the feeling that the composer was leery of success. "Often," Engel observed later, "[Blitzstein's] music was brilliant, but when it became too promising, Marc seemed to need to prevent its successful conclusion: he would do just about anything to frustrate a desirable resolution." It was part of a larger pattern Engel sensed about Blitzstein, with whom he continued to work on many occasions. "He was nervous, full of laughs (often derisive), somehow 'tight,' impatient, and—it was always my feeling—bent on self-destruction or failure."[17] But the original ideas Blitzstein introduced rather diffidently into *The Cradle Will Rock* were admired and expanded by composers who came after him, most notably his protégé Leonard Bernstein.

Hallie Flanagan knew from the start that *Cradle* was going to be controversial and that she needed to find a way to bring WPA bureaucrats on board. Her initial plan, after she first heard the opera, was to send Blitzstein, Welles, and Houseman down to Washington to perform it for Harry Hopkins. But that didn't happen, perhaps because Hopkins was too busy trying to save the whole WPA from the congressional hatchet. Then in early May, Blitzstein reported that "Mrs. Flanagan is getting scared all over again." To allay her fears, Hallie invited Lawrence Morris, Ellen Woodward's assistant, up from Washington to get a look at the production thus far. Morris pronounced it "magnificent." Virgil Thomson visited rehearsals and wrote up his impressions in the May–June issue of *Modern Music.* "The opera has passion and elegance," he wrote. "I predict a genuine success."

Then in mid-May 1937, Congress passed the $1.5 billion WPA appropriation. It was a victory for Hopkins and the Roosevelt administration, but even with that appropriation there wasn't going to be enough to fund the arts projects at the same level. Hopkins informed Hallie that the Federal Theatre Project was going to have to drop thousands of people from the payroll to meet budget requirements. In response to the news of cuts, the artists of Federal One, in the spirit of the times, laid plans to protest with picket lines, sit-down strikes, and a work stoppage on May 27.

In the beginning, when it looked as though the left-wing Workers Alliance alone was planning to stage the walkout, Hopkins aide David Niles told Hallie to fight back. "Are you going to abdicate and let the Workers' Alliance tell you how you can run your performances?" Niles asked. "Are you letting them tell you whether you can open or close your theatres?" Niles insisted to Hallie: "Mr. Hopkins does not want riots or disturbance mentioned in the papers."

On May 26, the day before the Federal One work stoppage was scheduled to take place, violence erupted at a Ford plant in Dearborn, Michigan. Autoworkers, who had scored spectacular successes at GM and Chrysler using the method of the sit-down strike, came up against the hard-nosed resistance of Henry Ford. FORD MEN BEAT AND ROUT LEWIS UNION ORGANIZERS, read the headline in the *Times.* Sixteen were injured, including seven women.

The next day, the artists of Federal One staged their work stoppage. Although the Workers Alliance had led the way, the strike spread to the WPA units of the Teachers Union, the Newspaper Guild, the Artists Union, and the American Federation of Musicians. In the end, seven thousand of the nine thousand Federal One employees in New York joined in the protest.

All of the project's theatres were dark that night, and patrons got their money refunded. Hallie spent the evening in a chauffeured car, traveling from theatre to theatre. There were policemen out in front, but there was no violence—nothing to make the strike the big story Harry Hopkins had warned against.

Yet because of Hallie, the strike got extra attention in the papers. On the day of the work stoppage, she addressed a meeting of the newly formed American Theatre Council and spoke out in defense of the strikers. Mrs. Flanagan declared, according to the *Times*, that "whatever we think of their method, we must inquire into the reasons for the protest. They find their jobs in jeopardy just as they are proving of some degree of usefulness to 20,000,000 people who have never gone to the theatre. They realize that if they are dropped from the rolls they must go back to destitution . . . It is against this perspective that I ask you to view this strike. If you object to that method, I feel that some word should come from the gathering as to a better method."[18]

Hallie had hoped her speech might help her cause with Hopkins and the administration, but it had the opposite effect. Word got back to her that Hopkins was unhappy. Immediately, she drafted an abject letter to Hopkins's deputy David Niles. "I am terribly upset," she wrote Niles, "that anything I said yesterday caused any embarrassment to Mr. Hopkins. I enclose a copy of the speech which received only the most favorable comment as an extremely objective treatment of the strike. You understand that everyone in the convention was criticizing the WPA for the strike and that I could not avoid answering the question as to why people were striking. I am now going into complete retirement until next Tuesday when I shall come to Washington. No one there will speak to the press under any condition."

On the day of the strike, the cast of *The Cradle Will Rock* was out on the streets with the rest of Federal One—living in real time the story they had been rehearsing onstage. Howard Da Silva surprised passersby with his Larry Foreman speech as he handed out leaflets: "Aint you ever seen my act? Well, I'm creepin' along in the dark; my eyes is crafty, my pockets is bulging! I'm loaded, armed to the teeth—with leaflets. And am I quick on the draw! I come up to you . . . very slow . . . very snaky; and with one fell gesture I tuck a leaflet in your hand. And then one two three— There's a riot."

Two days later, on Memorial Day 1937, outside the Republic Steel plant in South Chicago, there was a real riot—and a deadly one. But the victims were the strikers, and the aggressors, as it turned out, were the Chicago police.

The stage for the confrontation had been set three days earlier, when seventy-five thousand employees of "Little Steel" in Ohio, Illinois, Indiana, Pennsylvania, and New York walked off the job, demanding that management sign a contract with the Steel Workers Organizing Committee. But the management of Little Steel, inspired by the outspoken opposition of Tom Girdler of Republic Steel, adamantly refused to sign anything. Tom Girdler was a real-life Mister Mister, a veteran of thirty-five years in the steel industry who once said, famously, "With free water and cheap soap who, other than poorly trained children, really is obliged to live in filth?"[19] According to Girdler, there was not "a happier, better satisfied set of steel employees in the United States than the Republic employees working under the employee-representation plan [that is, the company union]." He wasn't about to let "Republic and its men submit to the communistic dictates and terrorism of the CIO."[20] Just to make sure this didn't happen, Republic Steel possessed an arsenal of gas guns, shells, and projectiles many times larger than that of the Chicago Police Department, along with hundreds and hundreds of revolvers, rifles, and shotguns, in order to be, in the words of one executive, "in proper shape to repel an invasion."[21]

Memorial Day 1937 was warm and sunny in South Chicago. At three P.M., two thousand strikers, along with their families and sympathizers, gathered six blocks from the Republic Steel factory gate and listened to SWOC organizers decry the restrictions on picketing. Then, with flags unfurled, the marchers walked up the dirt road to the factory gate, intending to establish a picket line. There they encountered hundreds of Chicago police.

A photographer from Paramount News captured the entire incident on film. The film shows the union leaders asking the police captain for permission to establish a picket line. Then, while they are talking, someone in the back of the crowd hurls a large branch at the police. Then the police retaliate with a vengeance, first firing shots into the air, then charging the marchers, swinging riot sticks, throwing tear-gas, and firing into the crowd. The crowd turns around en masse and begins to run, but the police keep firing, clubbing anyone they can grab and shooting others in the back.

"I could see the cops there shooting away with their guns," remembered Jesse Reese, a black steelworker who had become a union organizer. "At first I thought they were blanks—I really did. I could smell the gunpowder—I'll never forget it—and then I began to see people fall. I saw a boy run by, and his foot was bleeding. Then it dawned on me. They were shooting real bullets![22] There was a Mexican on my side, and he fell; and there was a black man on my side and he fell. Down I went. I crawled around in the grass and saw that people were getting beat. I'd never seen police beat women, not white women. I'd seen them beat black women, but this was the first time in my life I'd seen them beat white women—with sticks."[23] By the time it was all over, ten strikers were dead. Over one hundred were injured, some seriously. The police sustained only minor injuries.

Yet newspapers treated the incident at first as an example of union violence. STEEL MOB HALTED, read the headline in the *New York Times*. The strikers, according to the story, had attacked the police with an arsenal of dangerous weapons: "clubs, slingshots, cranks and gear shift levers from cars, bricks, steel bolts and other missiles." The *Chicago Tribune* characterized the incident as an invasion by "a trained military body."

Had it not been for the Wagner Act, that version of events might have prevailed. But the need to enforce the provisions of the Wagner Act, which protected the right of workers to organize, led to the formation of a congressional committee, under the leadership of the progressive senator from Wisconsin, Robert La Follette, and the incident came under the committee's scrutiny. The Paramount News film, along with extensive eyewitness testimony, led the committee inexorably to the conclusion that the police were responsible for the tragic incident. "The nature of the police injuries," the committee declared, "does not argue that the marchers put up marked resistance to the police; the medical testimony of the nature of the marchers' wounds indicates that they were shot in flight." The incident came to be known as "the Memorial Day Massacre."[24]

Despite the revelations of the La Follette committee, many Americans were troubled by the new union activism: It was rude and confrontational, and parts of it seemed undemocratic, if not illegal. The sit-ins, for instance, involved unlawful occupation of company property. And the "closed shop," which forced everyone to join the union and pay its dues, didn't seem fair. FDR, who was often held responsible for all of this, did his best to stay on the sidelines. He disapproved of the sit-ins, but he disapproved more of what would be required to end them.

"Well, it is illegal," he noted, "but what law are they breaking? The law of trespass . . . And what do you do when a man trespasses on your property? Sure you can order him off . . . But shooting is out and killing a lot of people because they have violated the law of trespass somehow offends me." In the case of the Republic Steel massacre, Roosevelt had competing loyalties to worry about. He didn't want to alienate his union constituency. But Mayor Ed Kelly of Chicago was also an important ally who had played a major role in his recent election victory. So he left the indictment of the Chicago police to the La Follette committee. Afterward, when John L. Lewis and Tom Girdler continued their war of words, Roosevelt said he thought most Americans were by then feeling "a plague on both your houses."

In the midst of this titanic struggle between management and labor, *The Cradle Will Rock*, an unrestrained pro-CIO polemic, moved into full technical rehearsals at the Maxine Elliott. The illuminated glass-bottomed floats Welles had envisioned were, according to Houseman, "cruising across the stage, pursued by panting players, trailing yards of black, writhing cable in their wake."[25] The actors generally hated the set. And when the full orchestra replaced Blitzstein's piano, they had trouble hearing and being heard. Nonetheless, the company was lurching toward the first public preview of the show, scheduled for June 16.

On June 10, orders came from Washington to cut the New York Federal Theatre Project budget by 30 percent: That meant laying off 1,701 workers. Hallie and her staff dutifully undertook the painful task. They decided to eliminate as many people as they could in the nonrelief category and to be guided, in laying off relief workers, by the person's usefulness to the project, professional training, achievement, and aptitude. It was a proper choice, since the project's mission was to provide work for theatre professionals. But it was also painful to execute, since it meant laying off nonrelief people who provided critical expertise and the least accomplished of the relief personnel, who had the fewest possibilities of finding paying work elsewhere.

After the cuts were announced, Hallie and Bill Farnsworth kept their doors open to a steady stream of protesters and grievance committees. Personnel director Charles Ryan stayed in his office all night, listening to the protests of people who had been discharged. Hallie was proud of the fact that there was "less disorder on the Federal Theatre than on the other [arts] projects."[26] But, Bill Farnsworth remembered, "she was terribly upset, because she was a very sympathetic person and wasn't quite as much of a realist as I was . . . It was a great blow to her."[27]

A reporter from the *New Republic* described a few of the supplicants who passed through the Federal Theatre offices. Some came from small units around the city that were now being shut down for lack of funds, including a white-haired man, dressed carefully in black, who had been a successful Broadway director for thirty-five years. Actors who had been out of work for over a year before the WPA rescued them were now forced to go back to "partial employment," often a recipe for starvation. A fifty-year-old actor named Herbert Winfield, with thirty-three years of experience in stock and on Broadway, had been forced to leave the Living Newspaper cast because of tuberculosis. His wife, an actress of

Austrian birth, had taken a Federal Theatre job in his place. But now she was given a pink slip because her slight Austrian accent made her harder to cast. "I have been saving our money to send my husband to Colorado for his health," she wrote in her petition. "Now I am unable even to buy him milk he needs in New York City."[28] If Hallie read this, it must have stirred up painful memories of her late husband Murray's struggle with tuberculosis.

The cast of *Cradle* was safe from the cuts, since they were involved in an ongoing production. But they were not immune to the directive that came from Washington a day later. "This is to inform you," it read, "that, effective immediately, no openings of new productions shall take place until after the beginning of the coming fiscal year, that is July 1, 1937."[29] The first public performance of *Cradle* was scheduled for Wednesday, June 16.

Immediately, John Houseman asked Hallie to intervene. She called Washington and argued for an exception. She cited the quality of the show, the vast cost in man-hours and materials, the size of the advance sale, which was impressive, and the adverse publicity that would accompany a delay—all to no avail. So Houseman and his team got on the telephone and began inviting every influential person they could think of to the show's final run-through, telling them, dramatically, that it might be their last chance to see *The Cradle Will Rock*. Several hundred people showed up, including such theatrical luminaries as George S. Kaufman and Moss Hart. Howard Bay, a Federal Theatre designer who was also in the audience that night, remembered that the show hovered on the brink of disaster, not because of the content, but because of Orson Welles's elaborate sets. "It was awful, just awful," he recalled. "They had all these mechanical things, these wagons with glass floors and lights coming up and the swings coming down. And the whole thing got out of hand."[30] There were those who believed that the ensuing events allowed Orson Welles to dodge a bullet.

The next day, June 15, a dozen uniformed guards sent by the WPA occupied the Maxine Elliott Theatre. When company members arrived, they found the theatre sealed and dark, along with the front of the house and the box office. Scenery, props, and costumes were off limits, too, and when Howard Da Silva attempted to retrieve his toupee, he had it snatched off his head by a guard at the stage door.

But down in the basement, the *Cradle* insurgency was in full swing. For the next thirty-six hours, Houseman, Welles, Blitzstein, Engel, and a handful of others stayed in the pink powder room that had become production headquarters, plotting a way around the ban. The authorities had informed ticket holders that the show was canceled, but these ticket holders were, as Houseman noted, the new left-wing audience that had sprung up during the Depression. "Fifty per cent of our public came from organized theatre parties, mostly of the left—prejudiced and semi-educated but young and generous and eager to participate in the excitement which the stage alone seemed to offer them in those uncertain times."[31] It was easy enough to convince this audience to defy the authority of the cruel WPA and show up at the theatre.

But the question was, what theatre? With the Maxine Elliott locked up by the "Cossacks," as the insurgents took to calling the guards, another theatre needed to be found that was empty and not too expensive. For this purpose a theatre broker, a small, seedy man in a black felt hat, was brought on board and began dialing up a long list of houses. Five hours later, he was still looking—it was hard to find someone in the middle of June who was willing to reopen a dark house.

Ironically enough, the second major obstacle to an unauthorized opening came from the unions. Actors' Equity and the American Federation of Musicians were both members of the old, trade-based AF of L and had no special enthusiasm for an opera that celebrated the CIO. Both issued rulings that made it essentially impossible for their members to participate: The musicians union said its twenty-four members would have to be paid union rates if they weren't working for the WPA. And Actors' Equity ruled that its actors could not appear on the stage, since they would be violating the agreement Equity had reached with the WPA.

The solution to the first problem was obvious: Marc Blitzstein, who knew not only the piano part but all the roles, could replace the twenty-four-piece orchestra. But what about the actors? The ruling from Equity seemed for a time insurmountable.

"Marc's despair at this point was ghastly to behold," Houseman wrote. "We could give a show without scenery and without an orchestra—but not without actors."[32]

Meanwhile, the press, hearing rumors of the showdown, had gathered at the Maxine Elliott, where Welles, radiating confidence, assured them that there would be a performance that night. The little man in the felt hat still hadn't located a theatre. But a plan for getting around the Equity prohibition had, according to Houseman, "evolved in the Ladies' toilet." Houseman told the actors that although they were forbidden by their union from appearing onstage, "there's nothing to prevent you from entering whatever theatre we find, then getting up from your seats, as U.S. citizens, and speaking or singing your piece when your cue comes."[33]

The reaction, Houseman recalled, was mixed. Some of the activists, like Will Geer and Howard Da Silva, were enthusiastic. But others—especially older members and members of the chorus—had more to lose and were understandably nervous about the plan.

Curtain time was two hours away, and members of the Downtown Music School, who had bought a large block of tickets, were already standing outside the locked doors of the Maxine Elliott. By seven, a sizable crowd had developed. "They formed little indignant knots," Houseman remembered, "between which members of the City Projects Council [a branch of the Workers Alliance] circulated, distributing handbills" about the cuts on Federal One. Two actors from the show, Geer and Da Silva,[34] came out and entertained the restless crowd with *Cradle* excerpts.

Howard Da Silva remembered doing Larry Foreman's speech about open and closed shop: "Open shop is when a boilermaker can be kicked around, demoted, fired, like that—he's all alone, he's free—free to be wiped out. Closed shop he's got 50,000 other boilermakers behind him, ready to back him up, every one of them, to the last lunch pail." Finally, at seven-forty, with less than an hour to go before curtain, the little man in the black felt hat got up and headed for the stairs, saying he didn't see what the objection was to the Venice Theatre. It seemed he had been trying to tell everyone for three hours that the Venice was available but couldn't get anyone to listen. Immediately, the theatre broker was plied with $20 bills and instructed to rent the theatre, a run-down cavern much larger than the Elliott and infinitely less elegant. Curtain time was moved to nine P.M., and everyone headed uptown to the Venice, twenty-one blocks north at Fifty-eighth Street, to make preparations.

Abe Feder installed a follow spot in the balcony. Even though it was a warm June night, Lehman Engel fetched an overcoat from home and used it to smuggle the score of *Cradle* out of the Maxine Elliott and into the Venice so that he could conduct the show from the orchestra seats. Someone found an upright piano for Marc Blitzstein, who insisted that the front be taken off to reveal the guts and increase the volume.[35] The house crew of the Venice was rounded up, the front curtain was lowered, and the doors were opened to the growing crowd that had arrived, on foot, by cab, and by bus, to join in the excitement. There were no ticket takers that night, so people just filed in and took any seat, except in the first two rows, which were hopefully reserved for the cast. By curtain time, there were no empty seats, and standees were beginning to accumulate along the back and sides of the big house.

After a curtain speech by John Houseman, expressing gratitude to "Mrs.

Flanagan" and the Federal Theatre Project for supporting the preparation of *Cradle*, and a second speech by Orson Welles, whose mention of the "cossacks of the WPA" was greeted with boos and laughter, the worn curtain rose to reveal Marc Blitzstein, seated center stage at the piano, looking pale and worried. The Venice Theatre was home to occasional performances by a part-time Italian stock company, and there was a washed-out view behind him of the Bay of Naples, with Vesuvius erupting in the distance. It was a far cry from the lavish sets now languishing under lock and key twenty-one blocks south at the Maxine Elliott.

"And there I was," Blitzstein recalled, "alone on a bare stage, perched before the naked piano in my shirtsleeves (it was a hot night): myself, produced by Houseman, directed by Welles, lit by Feder and conducted by Lehman Engel." Blitzstein didn't know how many actors had chosen to come or where they were in the audience, but he began "ready to do the whole work myself. I started singing the Moll's first song and heard the words taken from my mouth by the Moll herself, seated in the right loge; clever Feder instantly switched the spot to her."[36]

"So I'm just searchin' along the street," Moll sang, "for on those five days, it's nice to eat."

Years later, Hiram Sherman, who played Junior Mister, wrote to John Houseman about that moment: "If Olive Stanton [Moll] had not risen on cue in the box, I doubt if the rest of us would have had the courage to stand up and carry on. But once that thin, incredibly clear voice came out, we all fell in line."[37]

Marc Blitzstein takes up the story: "Then occurs a dialogue between the Moll and the Gent; again I heard an actor take over from me, this time from mid-center in the downstairs hall. Flashbulbs began to pop. The audience seethed with excitement; as the play progressed, it turned as at a tennis match from one actor to another, while Feder caught as many performers as he could with his spotlight, and musical conversations took place across the house. The cast had studied the work so thoroughly that they could have done it in their sleep . . . [It] held up astonishingly under this brutal manhandling."[38]

There were a few actors who stayed away. John Adair, who played the critical role of Harry Druggist but objected to the lyrics, didn't show, and neither did the actor who played the Reverend Salvation. But Hiram Sherman proved to be word perfect on several other parts he had never rehearsed, and Blitzstein filled in the rest. And even though the musicians were forbidden to play, one lone accordion player joined in from somewhere high up in the balcony.

John Houseman was most surprised and touched by the appearance of African American members of the chorus. "Just before leaving 39th St.," Houseman recalled, "I had made a last round of the theatre, thanked the members of the chorus for their loyalty and urged them not to take any unnecessary chances. It was all the more startling, therefore, in Scene Three, to hear the Reverend Salvation's booming pieties answered by an 'Amen' reverently intoned by two-dozen rich Negro voices. On their own, without consulting anyone, they had traveled uptown and found their places behind their conductor. Now, as their first cue came up, without rising, taking their beat from Lehman Engel, they sang like angels."

When the final curtain went down on *The Cradle Will Rock* that night, "there was a second's silence—then all hell broke loose. It was past midnight before we could clear the theatre. We had rented it till eleven and had to pay twenty dollars extra, but it was worth it."[39]

The next morning, a huge headline in the *Times* announced that the mayor of Johnstown, Pennsylvania, was asking Roosevelt to intervene in the steel strike and "remove the murderous element." A third of the way down the front page, another headline announced: STEEL STRIKE OPERA IS PUT OFF BY WPA: MANY AMONG 600 GATHERED FOR PREVIEW CHARGE CENSORSHIP.[40]

Hallie Flanagan had not witnessed the dramatic events at the Venice, but she had hoped to be part of any overtures to Washington on *Cradle*'s behalf. That didn't happen. On the morning after the opening, Orson Welles took it upon himself, without informing Hallie, to fly down to Washington and meet with WPA officials. He was told that Hopkins wasn't available, so he had to settle for two of Hopkins's deputies, Ellen Woodward and David Niles. He pleaded with them to allow *The Cradle Will Rock* to go forward as a WPA production.

Everything might have ended differently had either Hallie Flanagan or John Houseman come along for the meeting, but Orson Welles, perhaps asserting a prior claim to the show, went alone. And however brilliant he might have been as a director, Welles was a hopeless negotiator—arrogant, entitled, and stubborn. He seemed to have only one argument: Why not call the production a dress rehearsal rather than a regular performance and thereby get around the prohibition? No matter what Woodward and Niles said, he repeated the same argument, without expressing any sympathy for the embattled WPA executives or for their struggle to keep the WPA alive. Furthermore, he threatened them, almost from the start, with the possibility of a commercial opening. And before long, he managed to remind them that *he* had no need of government theatre, since he had turned down high-paying jobs to do the show.

Niles and Woodward viewed Welles's "dress rehearsal" argument as word parsing and added, "There is no reason why you can't have all the dress rehearsals after July 1."

It looked to Welles and his partisans as though the bureaucratic freeze were aimed specifically at postponing, or shutting down, *The Cradle Will Rock*. And it is possible they were right. But the freeze, which affected companies all over the nation, was an extremely inefficient way to censor one production. In Seattle, for instance, all the elaborate preparations for opening *Power* had to be put on hold. And Niles and Woodward were being bombarded by frustrated and unhappy people from all over. "I have seen people out here aging in the last few weeks," Niles said. "We get letters in not from New York alone but from all over the country. We certainly have a right to expect that we will try to pull together through this terrible thing." Niles insisted that all the producers who got the freeze order, including Welles and Houseman, should have said, "'I know what Mrs. Woodward . . . Mr. Hopkins are up against—we want to do everything we can to make it easier for them.'"

Welles's tone-deaf reply was, "How are we making it harder?"

If Hallie had been there, she would have at least had some understanding of how difficult the situation was for Niles and Woodward, who were both committed New Dealers and cared deeply about WPA programs. She, after all, had had to make painful cuts herself. But by the end of the disastrous interview, no one felt like compromising. Niles and Woodward ruled that if *Cradle* were put on again in defiance of the WPA order, it would be dropped from the Federal Theatre repertoire.[41]

It was clear that Welles fully intended to continue *The Cradle Will Rock* at the Venice without WPA backing. For the next two weeks, the show went on in the same manner as on the first night, with Blitzstein alone onstage and the actors in the audience. The audience for the show continued to grow, right up to July 1, when *Cradle* closed. WPA actors, who had been given a leave of absence, then went back on the government payroll. The elaborate and expensive sets at the Maxine Elliott were hacked to pieces and discarded.

Many years later, in his book about the period, John Houseman admitted that he and Orson Welles usually didn't care much about sticking to schedules: "As producers, Orson and I were not noted for our punctuality." But with *The Cradle Will Rock*, "we became demons of dependability,

scrupulous to honor our public and artistic commitment . . ." Furthermore, Houseman admitted, "I think we realized that our own days with
the project were numbered: we had served it well and had, in the process,
made reputations such as we could not possibly have achieved elsewhere.
Having nothing further to gain, we might as well make our departure as
explosive and dramatic as possible."[42]

After a two-and-a-half-month hiatus, Houseman and Welles announced
a new undertaking, to be called the Mercury Theatre, with plans to produce a season of classics. Critics, in announcing the Mercury's plans,
praised the Federal Theatre Project for launching the talented
Welles/Houseman duo. "No commercial manager in his senses would
have backed Orson Welles and John Houseman in the last season production of the classical *The Tragical History of Dr. Faustus*," wrote Douglas
Gilbert in the *World Telegram*. "Through the medium of the FTP this remarkable play of Marlowe's . . . became one of the hit shows of the last
season, inspired several Broadway classical revivals and stimulated Mr.
Welles and Mr. Houseman to unite in a theatrical enterprise of potential
merit."[43]

Astonishingly, Welles and Houseman, writing in the *New York Times*
about their new undertaking, gave the Federal Theatre no credit. They
praised only the new "fresh" and "eager" audience, without mentioning
the Federal Theatre Project's important role in cultivating it.[44] This despite
the fact that two of the plays the Mercury planned to do—Shakespeare's
Julius Caesar and John Webster's *Duchess of Malfi*—had been planned for
Project #891. And the idea of doing *Julius Caesar* in modern dress, for
which Welles received much praise, had already been realized in a Federal
Theatre production in Delaware.[45]

At the time of the showdown over *The Cradle Will Rock*, Hallie seethed
with anger toward the WPA bureaucrats who had stood in the way. She
dashed off a letter to Harry Hopkins (which she never sent) about the
"experience of sitting in a theatre in New York and hearing the Federal
Theatre and myself made fun of as being too timid to produce any controversial play. The audience hisses and boos censorship on our Federal Theatre." The "censoring of *The Cradle Will Rock*," she wrote Harry, was "a
tragic mistake in the history of the Federal Theatre . . . We spent seven
months and thousands of dollars on it, and sold 25,000 seats in advance.
Then in spite of my protest, the whole thing was stopped. I pointed out
that if it was stopped we would lose Houseman and Welles, my two most
valuable assets . . . In spite of that the censorship went through."[46]

As time went by, however, Hallie came to see that Houseman and Welles had relished the confrontation with authority. She believed that the government had wanted to silence *Cradle* at a time of labor unrest in the country. But she also believed that Welles and Houseman used the opportunity to turn *The Cradle Will Rock* into a major event in American theatrical history. "Probably," she wrote in *Arena* with veiled sarcasm, "it was worth a case of censorship to launch a group of our most brilliant directors and actors with a play for which the cast and rehearsal time had been provided, as well as an audience and a springboard for publicity."[47]

Ten years later, Hallie wrote to Marc Blitzstein that "important as the issue raised by *The Cradle Will Rock* was, it was not the only issue facing us. The thing that people on the New York Project never cared about, never understood, and never took the trouble to find out, is that this is a big country. The Federal Theatre Project was bigger than any project in it. It included not only *The Cradle Will Rock*, but the theatre for the children of coal miners in Gary, Indiana, the enterprise for vaudevillians in Portland, Oregon, the Negro theatre in Chicago, the research being done in Oklahoma."[48] Welles didn't care about any of that, and Houseman cared only a little. They had a show ready to open—and not just any show, but one that crystallized the struggle that was reaching a historic climax at that very moment in American history. The workers were on the march against the Mister Misters of the nation. The fact that Harry Hopkins was not Mister Mister and the WPA was nothing like Big Steel or the pogrom-loving Cossacks got lost in the excitement.

I'D RATHER BE RIGHT

On November 2, 1937, a musical send-up of the New Deal called *I'd Rather Be Right* opened on Broadway, to the delight of audiences and critics alike. It was decidedly not a Federal Theatre production. The coauthors, George S. Kaufman and Moss Hart, were two of the nation's best-paid playwrights: Their Pulitzer Prize–winning comedy, *You Can't Take It with You*, was still packing them in at a theatre nearby. The new show's music and lyrics were composed by the up-and-coming duo of Richard Rodgers and Lorenz Hart. And the star of the show was none other than the famous song-and-dance man George M. Cohan, pulled out of a very comfortable retirement to play the leading role. Not surprisingly, the show opened with an advance ticket sale of a quarter million dollars.

I'd Rather Be Right was designed to please the audience who could afford to pay top dollar and who were increasingly enraged at FDR's rhetoric and policies. They were the sorts of people the *New Yorker* cartoonist Peter Arno sketched—all dressed up in evening clothes and inviting their affluent friends to come out and "hiss Roosevelt"[1] in the newsreels at the Trans-Lux. This time, instead of the real Roosevelt, they got a dancing and singing George M. Cohan, impersonating a sitting president for the first time in American theatre history. They also got a chance to join in the mockery of New Deal programs, especially the Federal Theatre Project.

The audience in the orchestra seats did hiss Roosevelt, according to a first-night report, but the crowd in the galleries countered with cheers. And everyone, by the time the evening was over, realized that *I'd Rather Be Right* was harmless fun. "If they intended to tear the President limb from

George M. Cohan as FDR in *I'd Rather Be Right* (AP Images)

limb," noted Heywood Broun, "they would hardly have chosen George M. Cohan to endow the role with infinite benevolence and charm."[2]

The plot was extremely simple: A young couple named Peggy and Phil are wandering in Central Park, dreaming about the possibility of getting married, but as they see it, marriage isn't affordable unless Phil gets a promotion. What's more, the boss can't afford to give him a promotion unless FDR balances the budget, thus curing the nation of all its fiscal woes. As Peggy and Phil ruminate on their problem, who should appear but FDR himself! The Prez wants to help the couple out by balancing the budget, but he can't figure out how to do it.

"The trouble with this country," says FDR, "is that I don't know what the trouble with the country *is*."

His lament is interrupted quite suddenly and for no apparent reason by a dozen beautiful girls in gay musical comedy costumes, followed by a seedy-looking character who is their director. It turns out they're from the Federal Theatre, "Unit No. 864."

Roosevelt tries to turn them away, but they insist on putting on a show: "Whenever we see three people together, we're supposed to give a show. We're the Federal Theatre."

Roosevelt gives in, since it's the law.

"Say, you've got quite an organization, haven't you?" he comments.

"Oh, this is only one unit," the Director answers. "It's pretty hard to go any place these days without tripping over the Federal Theatre. Went into my own bathroom the other day, and there they were!"

"What were they doing," Roosevelt asks, "taking a bath?"

"No," explains the Director, "my wife was in the tub and they were giving a performance of *She Stoops to Conquer*."

Unit No. 864 proceeds to perform a banal number called "Spring in Vienna," which the Director explains cost $675,000.

"Of course we did it on a shoestring," he adds.

After the chorus departs, FDR continues in his quest to balance the budget, for the sake of the young couple. He tries passing a law, but as soon as he says the word *law*, the Supreme Court judges appear from behind rocks and bushes and shout, "No!"

Then, just to show FDR that they don't accept his labeling them "nine old men" from "horse and buggy days," they whistle shrilly and produce nine gorgeous young girls, ready and willing to provide "a little constitutional fun."

"The way they always want to be lawful, is awful," sing the girls.

The Federal Theatre makes a second entrance in act 2, after FDR tells his assistant, McIntyre, he wants to examine certain provisions of the Wagner Act.

McIntyre shouts an order to offstage, "The Wagner Act!"

A voice offstage echoes, "The Wagner Act!"

A blast of music accompanies the entrance of two large German acrobats, carrying their gear. They proceed to lift, grunt, and shout in the style of circus strongmen.

FDR calls for them to cease and desist. "McIntyre," he shouts, "have you gone crazy? I asked to see the Wagner Act."

"This *is* the Wagner Act, sir," McIntyre replies. "Hans and Fritz Wagner—Federal Theatre Project No. 34268."

George S. Kaufman was a comic genius who cared little about politics and may even have been a liberal at heart, but at the time he and Moss Hart wrote *I'd Rather Be Right*, the Republican Party was on the ropes, and, as he explained, there was nothing funny about a dead elephant. The burgeoning New Deal and its Federal Theatre Project, on the other hand, were a natural target. The Federal Theatre style even influenced one scene in the Kaufman-Hart show: A balloon salesman explains to FDR that he's lost his furniture business because of all the New Deal taxes, which he names one by one. Each time he names a tax, he pops a balloon. It is the kind of didactic routine the Little Man might easily perform in a Living Newspaper.

I'd Rather Be Right ran in New York for the better part of a year and then toured extensively, offering nightly evidence that the Federal Theatre Project, once pitied and scorned, had become a force worthy of satire and imitation.

Yet successful as it was, *I'd Rather Be Right* was out of date by the time it opened in November 1937. The Federal Theatre, reeling from enormous cuts, was no longer ubiquitous. Smaller units everywhere—in Nebraska, in Texas, in Delaware, and in Rhode Island—were gone, as were almost all touring companies to remote towns and to CCC camps. Only the caravan shows traveling to New York's five boroughs survived.

In an attempt to put the best face on the situation, Eleanor Roosevelt was enlisted to open the caravan summer season with a nationwide broadcast. "Somehow," Mrs. Roosevelt told her radio audience, "we must build throughout this country a background of culture. No nation grows up until that has been accomplished, and I know of no way which will reach more of our people than the great plays of the past and of the present-day authors."[3]

But as was so often the case, Mrs. Roosevelt was swimming against the tide. Indeed, it began to seem to Hallie Flanagan that the New Deal bureaucracy itself was turning against the Federal Theatre. Around the same time as the fight over *The Cradle Will Rock*, Washington ordered the project to stop putting out the *Federal Theatre Bulletin*, an increasingly lively publication that had served to inform units around the country of one another's activities and was widely read in theatre circles. The real reason for this order was never clear, but it seemed to have something to do with suspicions that the bulletin was pushing a Marxist agenda: There were suggestions that the editor was a Communist (he wasn't),[4] that the publication was sold in Communist bookshops (it was sold there, but also in Brentano's), and that the content was Marxist (based on a quote from W. H. Auden)[5] and focused too much on shirtsleeved audiences in parks and squatters in Oklahoma. Hallie saw this order from the higher-ups as an especially ominous sign, believing that the magazine's "economic, racial, and social point of view, in line with administration and WPA policies in 1935, was considered inimical in 1937. Washington no longer wanted our plays or our magazine to be the mouthpiece of the people on the project."[6]

But the Federal Theatre's troubles paled in comparison with Roosevelt's. The premise of *I'd Rather Be Right*—that balancing the budget would help get the country back on its feet—had turned out to be woefully misguided. The federal budget was actually balanced for a time in the spring of 1937. But what looked in May like a wave of recovery turned out by the fall to be an alarming downward spiral. Unemployment was going through the roof. Henry Morgenthau, secretary of the treasury and principal advocate of the balanced budget solution, warned the president that "we are headed right into another Depression." By October, the market was dropping so precipitously that FDR and those around him concluded that fiscal orthodoxy was no longer possible. In fact, many believed that the new and distressing "Roosevelt recession" was brought on by just that policy. Roosevelt was in a quandary about what to do. The only line in *I'd Rather Be Right* that rang true by November 1937 was Roosevelt's statement that he didn't know *what* the trouble was with the country.[7]

Believing that reform was losing momentum, FDR decided to call Congress back into session on November 15 to pass a series of modest New Deal initiatives, but by the time they adjourned, Congress had passed one measure only: a ten-point "Conservative Manifesto," signed by a coalition of southern Democrats and Republicans, which condemned sit-down strikes and federal taxes and warned of the dangers of government encroachment and the creation of a welfare class. The future did not look promising for the programs of the New Deal.

Hallie Flanagan's boss Ellen Woodward, who taken over Federal One from Jacob Baker the year before, appeared to be "in an advanced state of jitters," fearing that the tide had turned against the WPA.[8] When Congress went into session a few weeks later, Woodward called together her WPAers and instructed them to be careful and to "be very conscious that they are in session."

"Whether this means that we should prostrate ourselves every time we pass a fat man in an elevator or what it does mean none of us know," Hallie wrote Phil. "But it bodes no good to anyone. I'm glad I'll be gone when they begin to rant around."[9]

chapter twelve

CHANTS OF THE PRAIRIES

Increasingly, as Washington turned to the right and New York City stagnated in the aftermath of the cuts in the WPA budget, Hallie took comfort in her travels. In the first couple of years, the Federal Theatre Project had been tentative and wrong-footed in many parts of the country. Units in Chicago and California had looked enviously at the successes in New York City. But by the fall of 1937, when Hallie set out on a lengthy inspection tour, Federal Theatre companies in Chicago, San Francisco, Portland, Seattle, and Los Angeles were all mounting high-quality productions of their own.

Whenever she traveled, Hallie returned to her old habit of diary keeping and letter writing. Always, in her letters to Phil, she insisted on how much she missed him, missed the children, and missed home. But her intense enjoyment of her travels was manifest in every sentence.

"I'm so glad to be on a train again," she wrote Phil on her inspection tour. "It is reaching the point where a train is the only place where I can be free from this terrific pounding of telephones, telegrams, conferences."[1]

But it wasn't just the peace and quiet she loved. It was also the new sense the trips gave her of America: "I am getting the most intense pleasure out of all this," she wrote Phil. "I love these walks in strange towns, always with a curious exultant feeling that this is America. America, too, all the plains in between these villages—such quantities and quantities of America—I don't know why I have never before realized anything about the extent of America."

The train trips convinced her that Walt Whitman "knew more about America than anyone else." She wrote out—from memory, it would seem—a passage from his *Leaves of Grass*:

O Say Can You Sing? with Buddy Rich, among others, Chicago, 1936–37 (National Archives and Records Administration)

Chants of the prairies,
Chants of the long-running Mississippi and down to the Mexican sea,
Chants of Ohio, Indiana, Illinois, Iowa, Wisconsin, and Minnesota,
Chants going forth from the centre, from Kansas, and thence equidistant,
Shooting in pulses of fire ceaseless to vivify all.[2]

The subject matter of the Federal Theatre Project, Hallie argued to all involved, must be as multifaceted as the America she saw from her train window. Like the *American Guide Series* produced by the Federal Writers' Project, the Federal Theatre should represent America, in all its variety, on the stage. "I look at the map of the United States these days," Hallie wrote in an early *Federal Theatre Bulletin*, "as I never looked at it before, for the Federal Theatre Project has geographic implications which we are only beginning to realize."

There was a difference, Hallie told her regional directors, between a federal and a national theatre. "The word 'national,' means a definite attempt at uniformity; an attempt to have one theatre expressive of one national point of view. The word 'federal' means . . . many theatres brought together not so much for purposes of control as for purposes of mutual benefit."[3]

Hallie used every opportunity to promote her federal idea. After a visit with Florida's directors, she wrote: "The excitement of the last conference with you two, as we discussed the possibility of a play about Florida, developed as I traveled through the State. The racial mixtures in Tampa, the little-known tribal life of the Seminoles, the wealth of material being uncovered by the Writers' Project, the strange juxtaposition of events in Florida life today, all strengthen my conviction that you could do a really superb play. How do you like the title, 'Who Made Florida?' "[4]

Hallie's exhortations produced a few early successes. *Altars of Steel*, a Living Newspaper about the new industrial South, was viewed by the *Atlanta Constitution* as "beyond question the most impressive stage offering ever seen in Atlanta."[5] A collaborative effort called *Lost Colony*, a recreation on Roanoke Island, North Carolina, of Sir Walter Raleigh's futile attempts to establish a colony there in the 1580s, attracted a growing audience and the visit of "critical outlander" Brooks Atkinson, who described it as "a pageant that has made an extraordinarily versatile use of spectacle, sound, pantomime and cadenced speech."[6]

Despite such distinguished exceptions, most Federal Theatre productions outside New York City in the early days of the project were retreads from the days of stock and vaudeville. Reports from the field told of variety shows with vaudeville acts that were more stunt than theatre. From Tampa, for instance, came news of Mystini the Magician, a member of the Federal Theatre troupe, who was planning to drive a car through the downtown wearing a blindfold tied on by the local police chief.[7] Worse yet were reports of productions continuing old racist practices. In a Federal Theatre production of *Uncle Tom's Cabin* in Jacksonville, Florida, whites played all the roles, using blackface whenever necessary, and a black choral group provided music in a "screened-off section" segregating them from the white cast.[8] This was not the version of "regionalism" Hallie had in mind.

Nowhere was the situation more frustrating than in the Midwest. Both Harry Hopkins and Hallie Flanagan had high hopes for their home territory, especially after E. C. Mabie, head of Iowa University's theatre program, agreed to take on the job of regional director. Even before the Federal Theatre began, Mabie had been working to develop a network of regional theatres around the country, and he signed on to the project enthusiastically. "All of us felt," Hallie later wrote, "that the plains and river towns, the forests and farms of the mid-continent had a proud history, a friendly way of living, a robust point of view that might be vividly expressed in dramatic terms."[9]

But neither Hallie nor E. C. Mabie was prepared for the resistance they encountered in the Midwest to the very idea of a federally funded theatre. Bureaucrats at the state level refused to cooperate across state lines, even though they needed to pool talent. Often they didn't see the point of a professional theatre program anyway and preferred to use the funds for recreation. What's more, anti–New Deal newspapers operated on the assumption that the whole Federal Theatre Project was a fraud.

The problems in the Midwest reached a climax in the very first year of the project, when the *Minneapolis Journal* ran a story it headlined FEDERAL FAN DANCER NUMBER ONE. The fan dancer in question was a young woman named Ruby Bae (née Burns) who had worked for a time at a Minneapolis nightclub called Coffee Dan's. There she had performed a dance in the style of Sally Rand, using two huge ostrich feather fans to reveal and conceal her scantily clad body. One day, Coffee Dan's was raided by the police and closed down for indecency, so Ruby Bae found herself out of a job. Since Ruby's mother, too, was out of work, she applied to the Federal Theatre Project, where she might be able to use her talents to support the family.

One day in December, before Ruby Bae had even been hired, a reporter and photographer from the *Minneapolis Journal* showed up at a rehearsal of a Federal Theatre vaudeville unit, Project #1762, while they were preparing

a show for the Minnesota CCC camps. The *Journal* photographer shot a
number of performers in action—the magician, the Scottish comedian,
and the male hula dancing team. Then he asked to take some pictures of
Ruby Bae, who was auditioning to sing a couple of numbers in the show.
Ruby Bae was well draped in the photos, according to witnesses, "reveal-
ing just one leg to the knee." The director was satisfied that the photos
were entirely proper and in keeping with the Federal Theatre Project's
strict standards of decency.

But then the photographer convinced Ruby Bae to walk fifty feet down
the hall so he could take some *other* pictures of her, posing with her ostrich
feather fans in a rubber dress, which gave the illusion that she was nude.
And those were the images that hit the paper the next day, under the headline FEDERAL FAN DANCER NUMBER ONE. Ruby Bae was smiling wanly in the
photo, holding a fan behind her and lifting a bare leg through a slit skirt.
The *Minneapolis Journal* claimed she was about to go out and "manipulate
her quiver quills before the boys of Minnesota's 87 CCC camps."[10]

It didn't seem to matter, in the ensuing uproar, that Ruby Bae wasn't
even on the federal payroll yet, would not have done her fan dance in the
show in any case, and was probably in cahoots with the *Journal* photographer.[11] The state administrator of the Federal Theatre resigned, after the
University of Minnesota threatened to fire him, and the decision was made
to drop all theatre projects in Minnesota, thus depriving 112 theatre professionals of the possibility of work in their field. Worse yet, E. C. Mabie
resigned, concluding that no worthy theatre could be done in the Midwest
as long as state administrators were unwilling to cooperate and anti–New
Deal newspapers were intent on sabotage. "There is nothing that I can
possibly say to tell you how sorry I am that my most valuable regional director should have been put in so unfruitful a territory," Hallie wrote in a
letter accepting his resignation.[12]

The midwest territory never really recovered from the Ruby Bae incident. Without a strong regional director, programs in Ohio, Michigan, Indiana, and Wisconsin struggled with small numbers and small budgets.
Only Chicago, with its long theatrical tradition and large number of theatre workers, had the potential to break new ground. And in the beginning, Chicago didn't look promising, either.

Chicago's press was dominated by two press barons—William Randolph Hearst and Colonel Robert McCormick—who were unrelenting in
their attacks on the New Deal. McCormick, owner of the *Chicago Tribune*,
was even harsher than Hearst, publishing repeated claims that Roosevelt
was a Communist stooge. But FDR and the New Deal had powerful allies

in Chicago as the Depression deepened—most notably Mayor Ed Kelly, who presided over a well-oiled Democratic machine that knew how to deliver votes. Mayor Kelly declared proudly that "Roosevelt is my religion." The Roosevelt administration rewarded him with large WPA and PWA projects. But the Kelly machine had other important allies as well—organized crime prominent among them. Before Hallie even visited Chicago to help in setting up the Federal Theatre Project, she was bombarded with letters providing "confidential" information about who to appoint and who not to.

Some letters were anonymous and warned her not to investigate certain local relief projects too closely. Once, shortly before her first visit, her telephone rang in the middle of the night.

"Are you going to Chicago?" asked a sinister voice.

"Who is this?" Hallie asked.

"A friend," answered the voice. "Listen. *Don't go.*"

The receiver dropped into the cradle.[13]

Hallie was never able to trace the call or find out exactly what the threats were about. When she defied the warning, she discovered that she loved Chicago's bright colors and high energy. "You can't write about Chicago," she told Phil, "without crimson lights and whirlwind trips and high-powered cars." The Palmer House, with its "large, ornate, great gold and onyx vahses [*sic*] bulging in the corners and bellhops in line like soldiers," became her favorite refuge, especially the cocktail lounge, "which turns different colors along its glass walls so that you do not know how many Manhattans you have had."[14]

The problem with the Federal Theatre in Chicago, she soon discovered, was not so much corruption or shady dealings as it was bureaucratic cowardice. Just as the Ruby Bae incident epitomized the region's puritanical strain, a controversy surrounding a play called *Model Tenement* turned out to be emblematic of the problems the Federal Theatre Project faced in Chicago.

Model Tenement was the work of a gifted young Chicago writer named Meyer Levin and was based in large part on his own experience as the son of a small landlord on Chicago's South Side. It told the story of Irish, Polish, and Jewish families who occupied the same building and who got together to resist the eviction of one of their neighbors. "My only thesis," Levin explained, "was to show them driven to united action in the breakdown of our economy, and underneath, in my portrait of the well-meaning landlord, I was trying to cry out that the Jews were not to blame, that people like my own father were destroyed just like their tenants."

Things were going pretty well for the young Meyer Levin in 1935, when the Chicago Federal Theatre agreed to make *Model Tenement* their opening production. He had two magazine jobs, was at work on an ambitious new novel, and had recently married. Now his play, which he had adapted from an earlier novel,[15] was going into rehearsal.

Model Tenement required a large cast and a three-story set that would have scared off commercial producers. But it was well suited to the Federal Theatre Project. "About sixty actors were reading for parts," Levin remembered, "everything from broken down ex-vaudevillians to adolescent little theatre girls. Oddly enough, they made an excellent element for *Model Tenement*, as they were an assortment of people themselves, rather than an even cut of Broadway actors. And one could feel in them a pleased surprise that they were not after all boondoggling, but engaged in a production that spoke of their own problems, their own world. One could feel the play take life."[16]

Then one day, as Levin entered the large basement room in the naval armory where rehearsals were taking place, he was surprised to hear the actors speaking unfamiliar lines from a different play. Instead of *Model Tenement*, the actors were rehearsing Ibsen's *An Enemy of the People*!

Meyer Levin's surprise quickly turned to outrage. When he asked for an explanation, he was told that the mayor's office had sent an emissary who found the play objectionable. Since the mayor's word was law, that criticism had triggered an order from the bureaucrats in Washington to stop the play.

Levin decided to go to the very top and wrote a letter to FDR. "My play was approved by all of the Federal Theatre Project officials here, and by Hallie Flanagan," he wrote. "It is a play dealing with the housing problem . . . pointing out the very dilemma which has won your approval, Mr. President, for Federal housing projects . . . I am writing you because my play has now become a political football."[17]

When Hallie investigated the incident on her second visit to Chicago, in the spring of 1936, she discovered that the banning of *Model Tenement* was a classic example of the behavior of nervous bureaucrats, acting on the basis of very little information. The most telling remarks about the whole incident came out in a conversation she had with the WPA administrator in Chicago. When asked what he thought dramatic entertainment should be in Chicago, he answered, "Anything which will keep out of the papers." As for *Model Tenement*, he hadn't read it but dismissed it as "stuff written by a communist agitator" and pointed out that the mayor himself had stopped the play.

But when Hallie met with the mayor and raised the question of *Model Tenement*, he seemed "completely astonished" that he was being held responsible for shutting it down. Ed Kelly was a fiercely loyal New Deal Democrat who had been a sanitary engineer before the machine elevated him to the top post. He didn't have much interest in the arts and relied on a Catholic priest named Father Giles, who was editor of the *Franciscan Herald*, to stay on top of issues of morality and decency. When Father Giles advised the mayor to shut down *Tobacco Road*, Mayor Kelly obliged. He explained to Hallie that *that* play was obscene and had caused a dangerous increase in attacks on women in the city. But the mayor was never told anything about *Model Tenement* and insisted he had no intention of banning it.

The whole incident resembled a game of telephone, in which the message is altered at each transmission. Apparently, an actor on the project had reported to Father Giles that *Model Tenement* had objectionable material in it, and word had gone up the chain of command, through the cautious WPA administrator to regional WPA head Howard Hunter, that the mayor objected to the play. Howard Hunter immediately sent a telegram to Jacob Baker in Washington, warning him that *Model Tenement* must be shut down *at once* or he would close the entire theatre project in Chicago. "It would be a serious mistake for Mr. Stevens [head of the Chicago Federal Theatre] to see the Mayor about a thing of this kind," Hunter warned. "It will also be a mistake if Miss Flanagan attempts to force this play on Chicago."[18]

When Hallie protested, Baker silenced her: "Listen, Hallie, can we help it if the Mayor of Chicago doesn't like *Model Tenement?* He has the right of censorship . . . There's just nothing we can do."[19]

"What I consider the most outrageous," Hallie wrote after investigating the affair, "is that this play was evidently stopped by someone who never read the script at all and who has no idea of what the play really is about."[20]

Weeks later, when Father Giles finally read the script of *Model Tenement*, he pronounced himself very well pleased and suggested only minor revisions in language, which Meyer Levin was happy to make.[21] But by that time, five months had passed and the Chicago units had moved on to other things. It no longer seemed wise to mount a new battle for *Model Tenement*.

Yet the *Model Tenement* incident set the tone for Chicago during the project's first two years. Hallie reported to Phil that "art and music have swell projects here," but "the theatre is the joke of Chicago."[22]

Fear of the mayor's office, it seemed, still contributed to the problem. A production of *Chalk Dust*, a play about school reform that had done well in New York, had been deprived of its central conflict in Chicago. "In order to avoid pressure from the Mayor's office," Hallie wrote in her report on that visit, "mention of the radicalism of the central character and his consequent situation in the city high school have been omitted, thus reducing the play to the level of a restroom joke. It seemed incredible to me that I could be in Chicago, the third largest city, seeing one of the worst productions I have witnessed anywhere on the Federal project."

The Negro unit was performing a play called *Did Adam Sin?* that Hallie found "perfectly awful." "I am not clear about Adam," she wrote in her report, "but I certainly had a sense of guilt myself as I thought of spending taxpayers' money on this awful drivel." The only bright spot was an import: The Chicago version of *Triple-A Plowed Under*, performed in the long-dark Civic Theatre, was, as Hallie reported, "gorgeous, hard hitting, fast, much more finished than the New York show."[23]

On that second visit, Hallie took major steps to improve the situation. She replaced Thomas Wood Stevens, a Shakespeare specialist who had clearly been "asleep on the job," with an experienced and politically canny theatre man named George Kondolf, who had worked as a commercial producer. "Kondolf has his fighting blood up," she confided "and will, I think, clean it up, fire a lot of people and do a good job."[24] Before she left, Hallie and Kondolf "planned our campaign with the following slogan: 'smash-hit for Chicago within six weeks or bust.' "[25]

It would take a little longer for Chicago to get its first smash hit—nine months, to be exact. *O Say Can You Sing* was an astonishing undertaking, involving 250 actors, singers, and dancers in a musical revue that satirized the Federal Theatre itself. The show had everything: serious modern dance performed by an esteemed Chicago team; juggling by Tripp and McNally, who had been doing their lid-spinning routines for decades; fancy tap by a young Buddy Rich, who later achieved fame as a drummer; and clowning stunts by two acrobats billed as the oldest on any stage anywhere.

In a scene that eerily anticipated future events, the director of the imaginary theatre project, Augustus Q. Hamfield, is hauled up before the Senate Investigating Committee and charged with being a Communist because some of his actors use the Moscow art method. The senators sing:

"We're the Senate Bold Committee / And we'll show no trace of pity / And from the Communists we must expect the worst / They will bomb us to surrender / Then they'll rape our female gender / That's according to Herr William Randolph Hearst."

After the committee's song, the scene descends into farce: The accusations against Hamfield prove to be false, and his accuser is revealed to be the true "Red" when Hamfield pulls off the man's breakaway clothes to expose his bright red flannels.

The showstopper in *O Say Can You Sing* was a song-and-dance number called "Grandma's Goin' to Town," which included the entire cast, both black and white, while playfully celebrating the many old-timers on the project. Grandma, according to the song, used to be a simple creature who sat and knitted by the fireplace all day and hummed a sweet song. "We thought that Grandma'd always stay that way," goes the verse, "But then one day she heard Cab Calloway." The chorus strikes up the refrain: "Grandma's goin t' town . . . yeah! Grandma's truckin' on down! / The cane that she wore is a thing of the past / Her aches are forgotten, she's hot and she's fast / She's doin' the Can-Can / And shoutin' out 'yeah-man!' Grandma's goin' to town."

A troupe of white dancers come on to dance along with Grandma; then a black child enters, accompanied by a black dance group, and they dance an even faster chorus, only to be followed by a troupe of black men dressed as mammies (!), who do a still faster chorus. Then everyone, white and black, winds up onstage for the finale.

"Grandma's joined the tribe / Who worship Great God—Jibe! / When things seem to go wrong and she starts to fret / We tune in on Armstrong and his hot cornet / She's no longer icy / When Louie hits high 'C'— Grandma's goin' to town."[26]

Critics had their reservations about *O Say Can You Sing*. The *Tribune*, predictably, allowed that the show "will serve fairly well for an evening's play going, whether one is a regulation customer or merely a stooge of the bureaucracy" but added that the authors "have not been nearly as funny as the WPA theatrical management itself in its most serious moments."[27] A highbrow critic found it to be "commonplace stage stuff definitely dated."[28]

But the public loved *O Say Can You Sing*. The show opened at the Great Northern in December 1936 and ran there for over eight months. Harry Hopkins, who took in the show when he visited Chicago, liked it so much that he wanted to send it to New York. "I tell you," Harry told Hallie, "it makes those New York musical shows look as if they had low blood pressure."[29] Hallie would never contradict praise from Harry, of course, but she must have known that *O Say Can You Sing*, which she called "as Chicago as Chicago," would never make it in New York.

Despite Harry's recommendation, *O Say Can You Sing* never left Chicago. But it became the most prominent example of one of the things Chicago did best: vaudeville. From December 1935 to June 1937, Chicago-based vaudeville units played to over two million people, indoors all during the year and outdoors in the parks in summertime. *Billboard* predicted a "flesh" revival. "The 18-month run of Federal Theatre vaude units . . . here has revived interest in flesh in neighborhoods and small towns to such an extent that theatre operators have been pressed for the return of vaude," *Billboard* reported. "Combo policies," combining movies and live vaudeville, grew in popularity. And, added *Billboard*, many acts were leaving the Federal Theatre for the private sector.[30]

O Say Can You Sing was the first of several triumphs overseen by George Kondolf, who had turned out to be very good at whipping Chicago into shape. One of his smartest moves, no doubt, was establishing a personal relationship with the mayor, whom he reported to be "very pleasant and gracious" and quite willing to cooperate.[31] The old chestnuts of early months were replaced with original productions, including a well-received play called *The Lonely Man* starring the young Walter Huston as Abraham Lincoln. *Variety* reported in September 1937 that "Chicago now regards the FTP highly after laughing at it less than two years ago."[32]

So when Hallie stopped off briefly in Chicago on her trip across the country, in the fall of 1937, there was a lot to feel good about. Both the Negro and Yiddish units of the Federal Theatre Project were engaged in interesting work: A biblical extravaganza in Yiddish called *Monesh* was drawing good crowds at the Great Northern Theatre. "A little too florid for my taste," Hallie commented after taking in the first two acts. "The big scene is in hell where the devil makes Lilith to tempt men and she does for a whole act, very seductive, in black tights . . . We get away with lust as well as murder on this project, especially if it's in Yiddish or Spanish or South African."[33] Chicago critics had no reservations about *Monesh*: "fascinating production . . . gorgeous pageantry . . . impossible for you to remain unmoved," wrote one. "A 'must' for Jew and non-Jew alike."[34]

The high point of the visit, for Hallie, was a beautifully staged production of an early Eugene O'Neill play called *The Straw* at the Blackstone Theatre. There were many reasons for her to feel good about it. In the first place, it was but one example of the mutual benefits, to playwright and project alike, of the Federal Theatre's countrywide revival of the works of O'Neill.

The Straw is a closely autobiographical work. It takes place in a TB sanitarium very similar to Gaylord Farm, where the young O'Neill went in 1913 for treatment of his disease. When the play premiered in Greenwich Village in 1921, critics were lukewarm, praising the writing but disliking the subject matter. "It was disgusting," the theatre manager said at the time, "everyone walking around with sputum cups." *The Straw* closed after twenty performances.[35]

The Federal Theatre production in Chicago gave a worthy play another chance. *The Straw* is, in fact, an exquisitely nuanced story of a relationship between a self-absorbed newspaper reporter, temporarily in the sanitarium, and a lovestruck young woman who is clearly dying of her disease. The final scene alone, a haunting O'Neillian combination of love and deception, would justify the revival.

For Hallie, of course, the sanitarium setting carried special poignancy, inevitably recalling the terrible final days of Murray Flanagan's life in the sanitarium in Colorado Springs. She sat in the audience, next to her friend Kay Ewing, now a director on the Chicago project, and wept. But she was not alone. "The usually gum chewing Chicago audience snuffled and sobbed in an unbelievable manner," Hallie reported. "Even our hardboiled critic Ashton Stevens [of the Hearst-owned *American*] wept and had the decency to say so in his column. We're sold out for weeks so evidently tears are a pleasure to lots of people."

The next day, Hallie barely made it to her train. As she traveled west on the *Olympian*, gazing out her window at the endless fields of wheat, she was still glowing about *The Straw*. "Even in the light of the next day in South Dakota," she wrote Phil, "I think it is probably the most finished thing we've done on the Project."[36]

chapter thirteen

THE WEST

On the train ride west from Chicago to Seattle, Hallie spent most of her waking hours out on the observation deck. She watched the Great Plains go by the first day, followed the next day by hills punctuated with cactus and sagebrush. Then came oil wells and oil fires, the cattle ranges, then rivers and the blazing yellow trees of Montana, interrupted by "strange little gray towns in the midst of brilliant colored rocks and mountain torrents." By late afternoon of the second day, the train was climbing the steep mountains of the Continental Divide. "The train is way up ahead and you can see it moving perilously up the mountains," she wrote Phil as dusk fell. "I've had such a day of looking, of quietness and looking."[1]

There was more to look at from the large bay window of her hotel room: the city of Seattle, spread out over seven hills, the mountains beyond, and in another direction the ships bobbing in the wind-tossed harbor. "If I could only draw what I see from my window, you would know why I sent the telegram saying we must live here," Hallie wrote Phil enthusiastically.[2]

She was soon reminded, however, of some of Seattle's limitations. An obligatory luncheon with Anna Roosevelt Boettiger, daughter of the president, turned into a lecture on Seattle's dislike of controversial subjects. Anna Boettiger was FDR's beloved daughter, but she was married to a conservative and shared some of his views. Her husband, John Boettiger, had been a reporter on the viciously anti–New Deal *Chicago Tribune* when they met and had since, out of deference to his father-in-law, taken over as publisher of the slightly milder Hearst paper the *Seattle Post Intelligencer*. Over lunch, Mrs. Boettiger suggested to Hallie that the Federal Theatre Project should stick to light comedy. She particularly objected to *Power*

Stevedore, Seattle, Washington (National Archives and Records Administration)

and *Stevedore*. Seattle, she told Hallie, was not interested in that sort of theatre.[3]

It wasn't true. *Stevedore*, a Negro unit production that boldly confronted racism, and *Power*, which touched on the locally charged issue of public versus private ownership, had both done well in Seattle. But it was true that Seattle, like Minneapolis, had a low tolerance for anything that might possibly be considered improper. The acting mayor of Seattle, for instance, held up funding for a municipal natatorium because he didn't think boys and girls should swim together. And that politician, as it turned out, played a role in a unique and memorable case of censorship, Seattle style, that had occurred a year earlier.

The play involved was Aristophanes' *Lysistrata*, performed in an updated version by Seattle's popular Negro unit. *Lysistrata* was one of a series of plays mounted by the unit that attempted, in the words of playwright Ted Brown, to "break away from the 'Old Black Joe' idea and present plays whose universal theme remains the same regardless of race or creed."[4] Brown had updated the two-thousand-year-old classic about women who withhold their affections from their husbands in order to bring an end to war. His modern version was set in Ebonia and made elaborate fun of the frustrations of the men, as the women used their wiles to lobby for peace. A typical scene featured the returning warrior Cinisias and his wife, Myrrhina, who kept postponing sex by running off to get pillows and perfume and blankets. "Don't go after anything else!" the husband begs. "All I need now is you."

"My, you're trembling all over! You're cold!" says Myrrhina.

"I'm trembling from excess heat . . . not cold!" protests Cinisias.[5]

No one who saw *Lysistrata* in rehearsal, including regional Federal Theatre director Howard J. Miller, saw anything to object to. Nor did the thousand-plus members of the opening night audience, who reacted with enthusiasm. But sitting somewhere in the crowd was the wife of the WPA's state administrator, Don Abel, along with Abel's deputy. Unfortunately, as Howard Miller later reported to Hallie, this deputy was a man unschooled in the humor of vaudeville, "a choir singer who would cut the word 'bed' out of a furniture ad." The deputy reported to his boss that the show was indecent.[6]

The next day, the reviews were positive. "These boys and girls from the federal theatre project," reported the *Seattle Star*, "made the comedy by Aristophanes modern . . . once ear-burning jokes are harmlessly, lightly amusing and brought a hearty, healthy laugh from the audience."[7] The show was sold out for the next two nights and promised to be a hit. But

WPA boss Abel, who had never seen the play, was nervous about rumors of indecency, as was the squeamish acting mayor.[8] Abel sent down an order to close the show immediately, "for the best interests of the WPA."[9] Eleven hundred ticket holders, who were milling about outside the closed doors of the Moore Theatre, had to be given their money back.

The newspapers had a field day. On the strength of objections from two people, reported one paper, "a play which the Greeks thought a mighty good comedy when it was written by Aristophanes more than 2000 years ago was too risqué for Seattle." Members of the Negro unit claimed that the ban was based on racial prejudice, "an attempt to stifle any artistic advancement made by the Negro players group."[10] And the *Seattle Star* ran an "interview" with Aristophanes himself, illustrated with a Greek statue of the playwright under the heading "The Cause of It All." Aristophanes, called out of deep sleep in Elysium, suggested to the *Star* reporter that "probably the ways of man have changed since my day." Perhaps there were no longer wars? Or professional jealousies? Or politics? Aristophanes then became sleepy. "Well, it does not worry me, my son," he told the reporter. "I have been known 2000 years . . . I think my success has been assured by now."[11]

Hallie and her assistant Bill Farnsworth were outraged. Farnsworth assured the state Federal Theatre director, Guy Williams, that "we're behind you 100% in this *Lysistrata* matter even if it comes to closing the Project and removing the money."[12] Harry Hopkins also weighed in on the side of reopening. But what was done turned out to be difficult to undo, as Howard J. Miller reported to Hallie after looking into the situation. State WPA boss Abel admitted he had made a mistake in closing the show: He had taken a terrible beating for it in the press. But Abel told Miller that he would resign immediately if it was reopened. He was new to the WPA post, and the reopening would weaken him irreparably. Abel also threatened to put pressure on the city council to have the vice squad close the show again if it did reopen. Reopening, Miller concluded, would create an open breach within WPA ranks at a time when the program was on the defensive. Dropping the issue, he wrote Hallie, was "for the best interests of the WPA in general and of the Federal Theatre Projects in particular."[13] Hallie wrote back that he had handled the situation "very diplomatically."

"Do you ever, by the way, read the Bible?" she asked Miller. "It is the only piece of literature I know remotely resembling for variety and excitement the Federal Theatre."[14]

The *Lysistrata* showdown had demonstrated once again, as had the *Model Tenement* conflict in Chicago, that cautious bureaucrats and good theatre don't mix. "State administrators," Hallie later observed, "wanted a safe program which no one would criticize; on the other hand they wanted their projects to be critically acclaimed . . . Any theatre producer knows that you cannot achieve both of these aims simultaneously."[15]

A year had passed since the *Lysistrata* incident by the time Hallie arrived in Seattle in November 1937. Administrator Abel, chastened by that experience, eagerly took Hallie on a tour of the city and promised support for various project activities. And in the Negro unit, Hallie reported "a sense of things happening, plays being written, a crowded schedule." Undeterred by the problems with *Lysistrata*, the unit was performing another sly comedy: Bernard Shaw's *Androcles and the Lion*.

Hallie liked the "full-bodied and full-voiced Negro acting" in *Androcles*, but she wished for more resources. "These actors," she reported, "most of them tough old professionals, trained in vaudeville and tab shows, need retraining in diction, voice, movement." The play, she reported, "needs better principals, better lighting, more money. The music in our pits as usual is a disgrace. Must we continue to take a few broken-down hacks from the Music Project?"

Hallie's distress was accentuated by the fact that the University of Washington's theatre program was thriving and was about to acquire the services of a showboat theatre, renovated by the WPA. It was hard for her to enjoy the party put on for her that night: "I felt too wretched about our company."

When she got home from the party, she wrote Phil. "Why can't these people do a job?" she pondered. "Or is it just that I've neglected this region?"[16]

Watching the "white" unit rehearse the next day, in an old movie house, discouraged her further. "It struck me as pretty pathetic, thinking of a million dollars being spent [on the Bonneville Dam] for a ladder for salmon to run up on and spawn, that here, in a shabby, bare old room, with a gigantic picture of President Roosevelt smiling down on them, were the actors we are trying to save. After two years of good work and good press, they still have no place to act—to say nothing of spawn! . . .

"The cuts have been disastrous," she concluded as she left Seattle, "and again I say I think WPA labor should build us a theatre in every place where our theatre work justifies it. WHY NOT?"[17]

On the train south to Portland, Hallie alternated between looking out the window and reading a new Living Newspaper script entitled *Timber*, which told the story of the exploitation of the forests of the Northwest. "I'm riding through alternate forests and lumber stacked on wharfs," she reported, "and I'm reading." She passed Mount Rainier, with forest fires streaking down its side, she passed a log jam on a river, where yellow timber swirled on black water. "I'll never know whether this script is as good as I now think it is," Hallie wrote, "because here is its own story unrolling before me."[18]

Hallie's wish for theatres intensified as she traveled south to San Francisco. "I want five theatres," she wrote Phil, "each taking on the color of the region. That is my present dream."[19] At her stop-off in Portland, she watched "fifty derelicts—clowns and northern stock people, all working so hard and so excitedly in a bare old hall" on a Living Newspaper about the multimillion-dollar Bonneville Dam. Then she visited another WPA megaproject, Timberline Lodge, six thousand feet above sea level on Mount Hood, built by hand by four hundred men of the CCC and furnished with rugs, rough-hewn furniture, and hand-wrought hardware by local craftsmen. Timberline Lodge was the government's first venture into the hotel business, and it was already thriving.

"If the WPA blew up tomorrow," Hallie wrote with her characteristic enthusiasm, "the Federal Theatre would be forgotten in a year, but Timberline will exist for centuries." Timberline included a beautiful outdoor amphitheatre, set against the sky, in view of the pine forest in the valley below and the snow-covered peak of Mount Jefferson in the distance. Hallie told Oregon's state administrator, W. E. Griffith, that she wanted to fill the amphitheatre with plays on regional subjects that would "say for the West dramatically what Timberline says for the West architecturally." Plans were laid to produce a historical pageant about Paul Bunyan.

By the time she arrived in San Francisco, Hallie was nearly ill with fatigue. But the theatre she saw that night revived her. Considering the way things looked on her first visit to San Francisco, when the project was "just a crowd of anxious, frightened insecure actors meeting in an old hall," the change was nearly miraculous. The show she saw that night was a comedy set in Greek times: *The Warrior's Husband* by Julian F. Thompson. It was not a play she particularly liked, but it was an entirely professional job with an excellent orchestra and an enthusiastic audience. Even the Federal Theatre ushers looked good in their sharp maroon suits and gold-lined capes.

Best of all, *The Warrior's Husband* was playing in the Federal Theatre Project's very own theatre. The Alcazar was an exquisitely decorated Moorish dream of a theatre built in 1917 and beautifully refurbished to accommodate every part of the San Francisco project except vaudeville. There were set-building and costume shops, a research library exploring local theatre history, including Chinese theatre history, a dance studio, and an orchestra rehearsal space, as well as offices. It was, as Hallie pointed out to the newspapers the next day, "the finest and most efficient Federal Theatre plant under one roof in the country."

The San Francisco project owed much of its early success to vaudeville—but vaudeville cleverly updated and ingeniously promoted. At the Columbia, which had been part of the Orpheum vaudeville circuit in the old days, the Federal Theatre's first show featured Willa Holt Wakefield, who performed monologues at the piano and had been a headliner at the triumphant reopening of the theatre in 1907, following the San Francisco earthquake. Old mixed with new:A patter singer got raves for combining the "technique of the past with the patter of the present." On the other hand, the Three Deuces, a Harlem strutting dance team, swung to the latest thirties rhythms. There was a "clear tingling Negro singer whose 'Last Rose of Summer' was a high spot," a contortionist, a juggler, and, to close the show, a dog act, "seven smart pups whose canine capers tickled the audience and pleased (as they always have and always will) more than anything in the show."[20]

The project's publicity department found clever ways to connect current productions to the city's past: Cable cars used to stop directly in front of the Orpheum to drop off and take on passengers. When Uncle Sam returned vaudeville to the Orpheum (now the Columbia), the cable cars began stopping there again. A sympathetic press ran feature stories. Joseph Muller, an assistant manager in the employ of the Federal Theatre Project, reminisced for the *San Francisco News* about the days when he was "the swaggering, derby-hatted diamond-ringed manager of the Pacific Coast Orpheum circuit."

The result of these efforts was that vaudeville became fashionable again in San Francisco. "*Swing Parade*," reported one local paper, "has excited the interest of the dwellers of Nob Hill, Pacific Heights . . . and other districts in which the well known bay district conservative society element dwells. Friday and Saturday nights . . . are taking on the tone of a night at the opera, what with the white ties and tails of the men and the fur and furbelows of the women, the swank, long-bodied machines that whiz up to the curb and discharge their cargoes . . . And do they seem to enjoy the show, and how!"[21]

By the time Hallie visited in November 1937, the San Francisco project had established a reputation that went beyond vaudeville. While she was there, she watched a "very exciting" rehearsal of John Galsworthy's *Justice*, an exploration of the issue of harsh justice versus compassion in the trial of a forger. The *San Francisco Chronicle* deemed the 1910 play a "masterpiece in its own right" and a worthy companion to Galsworthy's monumental *Forsyte Saga*. "The Government," concluded reviewer John Hobart, "is doing us all a service in putting it back where it belongs."[22]

John Galsworthy was the fourth major writer to release his plays to the Federal Theatre Project for a nominal royalty, joining Shaw, O'Neill, and Elmer Rice. His signing on was a source of particular satisfaction to Hallie, who remembered her tea with him in London in 1926 as one of the high points of her Guggenheim year.

It was during this San Francisco visit, too, that Hallie had the satisfaction of telling Eugene O'Neill in person about the Federal Theatre's progress in producing his plays all around the country. Carlotta and Eugene O'Neill had been moving restlessly from place to place for years, trying to find the perfect climate and the right degree of isolation from the world to enhance the playwright's work. Late in the previous year, they had landed in California, where O'Neill was hospitalized with appendicitis and then had to stay on for months because of serious complications.

Afterward, the O'Neills decided to settle in the San Francisco area. They built a house into the side of a mountain some thirty-five miles outside the city, with a view of Mount Diablo. There, with Carlotta hovering, O'Neill grew strong enough to return to work on his cycle of nine plays tracing the continuity of one family, with deep connections to his own, over 150 years. The history plays, among them *Mourning Becomes Electra, A Moon for the Misbegotten*, and *Long Day's Journey into Night*, were to become his crowning achievement. But in November 1937, O'Neill was still keeping the plays under wraps.

After a ride through wild and remote mountain passes, with Carlotta at the wheel, Hallie arrived at the retreat of the great playwright, only recently the recipient of the Nobel Prize. "Mr. O'Neill, dark and quiet, came forward to me," she wrote later. "He asked with deep interest all about the project and went over the pictures and reviews I brought him." The project was in the midst of a nationwide cycle of his plays: Fourteen plays were to be produced in twenty-two cities of varying size around the country, and *Ah, Wilderness!* which had opened the month before in Des Moines, Iowa, was embarking on a twenty-nine-city tour.

O'Neill was full of praise for the Federal Theatre Project. "It has a tonic effect on me to think of my own plays being done in places where, without Federal Theatre, they would most certainly never have been produced."[23] But the greatest compliment came in the form of a request. He was working on a cycle of nine plays about an American family, he told Hallie, and was hoping to turn them over to a company for prolonged study and production, perhaps at the rate of two a year. Would the Federal Theatre be interested?

★   ★   ★

Months before her trip, Hallie had received a long, rolled-up scroll from California. Fearing an angry petition, she unrolled it slowly from the bottom up, taking in the six pages of names, signed in pen and pencil in a great range of styles—some scrawled, others writ large in calligraphy. The message at the top came as a pleasant surprise: "To all of us—both to those of us oldsters who have been in and out of the theatre of the past and have seen that old theatre languish and all but perish . . . and likewise to those younger ones among us who have striven to equip and train themselves . . . to all of us, the energy and vision, the imagination and devotion you have brought to your task as administrator of the National Federal Theatre Project have been an inspiration."[24]

Not surprisingly, the message came from San Francisco, where a feeling of goodwill prevailed despite budget stringencies. No such unanimous praise was ever likely to come from Los Angeles. Despite the fact that many of the fifteen hundred project workers were grateful for their jobs, there were pockets of ill will toward the project in Los Angeles that never entirely went away.

It started right at the beginning, when Hallie named Gilmor Brown, the renowned director of the Pasadena Community Playhouse, as head of the Los Angeles project. Some professionals in Los Angeles objected, because Brown came from community theatre and worked with amateurs. They maintained that this fact made him a "little theatre" devotee, interested only in highbrow plays. Hallie vigorously defended her choice, pointing out that Brown was the only producer in Los Angeles who had kept his theatre running through the Depression. "Irrespective of the caliber of professionals that might have been available for the post in Hollywood," she told the press on her first visit, "I think I would have chosen Mr. Brown on the basis of his worldwide reputation and his broad knowledge and proven ability in the theatre world."[25]

But the "amateur" charge stuck. It was pointed out by critics that Hallie Flanagan was herself an academic who, according to Los Angeles *Variety*, viewed the Federal Theatre Project as "more of an arty undertaking."[26] Eight months into the project, Brown stepped down, though he continued to advise Hallie informally. Then the project's foes found another reason to complain: The new director, the young, handsome, and energetic Howard Miller, was a recent college graduate with too little real-world experience.

In Los Angeles, everything tended to be personal. Asked at her first L.A.

press conference back in 1935 if she would allow a Communist play on the Federal Theatre, Hallie had responded, "If it was a good play, we would produce one written by a Republican."[27] But after that, politics rarely came up. Unfairness was more likely to be the charge, and usually the complaints were vague. *Variety* in particular printed unattributed accusations in passive voice: "Alleged czaristic tendencies of project are complained of bitterly . . . complaint is made that entire project is run by a clique,"[28] "Complaint is advanced . . . that personal vanity governs all actions"[29]—these were typical *Variety* rumblings.

Paradoxically, all of this resistance was taking place in a city where the theatre was in desperate straits: In late 1935, practically every commercial theatre in Los Angeles and Hollywood was dark, and the outlook for the future was dismal. Yet even as the project began to take hold and succeed, the accusations continued and escalated. Charges of fraud were added to the list, and telegrams were sent by the complainants to FDR and his top aides. The newspapers augmented and magnified the complaints with a barrage of stories: KICKBACK TACTICS IN LA, NEW DISCORD HITS FEDERAL DRAMA RANKS, THEATRE PROJECT STRIFE INCREASES, CASTING ILLS CHARGED AGAINST FTP IN LA.[30]

At one point, there were four separate investigations of the Los Angeles project under way: two by the WPA, one by Actors' Equity, and one by the Workers' Council, the leftist union. Finally, in March 1937, Ellen Woodward, Federal One head, sent out a long letter summarizing the findings of all the investigations. It turned out that the charges of favoritism and corruption and irregularities amounted to next to nothing. For example, it was charged that Howard Miller had a doghouse built by WPA workers on government time: The doghouse turned out to be a few pieces of plywood and broken wire, now holding timber instead of a dog. Other charges turned out to be about as insubstantial as the doghouse. Some young amateurs *were* hired on to the Federal Theatre Project, the letter explained, because young people were needed to fill out casts. "During the six-year period of the Depression," Woodward explained, "when thousands of theatres in America were dark or given over to the movies, these young people had found a precarious footing in Little Theatre Groups or Schools of the Drama."

Buried deep in the report was an explanation for the persistence of the attacks on the Los Angeles project. "The complaints," the letter stated tactfully, "come from a very small group of workers who feel that they possess outstanding abilities or professional qualifications which are not properly recognized. Complaints of this kind, which are of frequent occurrence in the world of the commercial theatre, are difficult to settle, since questions of opinion are involved."[31] One WPA investigator, Calvin Triggs, was more blunt in speaking with the press: The complaints were coming from a small group of "temperamental individuals with persecution complexes," most of whom had complained at least five times.[32] In particular, there was a spurned playwright named William J. Perlman who had turned attacking the Los Angeles project into a full-time job. In a town where movies reigned and gossip was king, the accusations had tremendous staying power.

But so, too, as it turned out, had Howard Miller, with the strong support of Hallie Flanagan. "I like my job and want to keep it," Miller announced in March 1937 when the investigations were finally over.[33] And it turned out he was very good at it.

"If a year ago anyone had told you that Los Angeles would have five legitimate theatres running full blast to nearly capacity audiences, you would have put that particular prophet down as a total loss, mentally," David Weissman wrote in the *Los Angeles Times* in April 1937. But the Federal Theatre had made it happen. "A year ago the Mayan, the Mason and the Musart were almost continuously dark. Tonight the footlights glare, and Thespia struts the boards not only in these three houses but at the Greek Theatre, the Hollywood Playhouse and the Beaux Arts Theatre."[34]

As in San Francisco, early successes in Los Angeles came from clever presentation of old vaudeville acts. "The biggest 50 cents worth of entertainment ever doled out in these precincts," raved *Variety* about a revue called *Follow the Parade*. It was "a revue, a miniature circus, a dash of the classics (musically) and a potpourri of what else comes under the head of entertainment." The big names from the old days were there, "still doing the old turn . . . but on and off so fast their brief interlude is a refreshing peek into the past."

Much of the credit went to Eda Edson, who conceived and directed the shows. Edson seems to have had sympathy for the old troupers: She once wrote a lengthy memo to the central office explaining why she couldn't hire one performer who came to an audition falling-down drunk. At the same time, she was attuned to the modern audience's expectations. "Everything is speeded up to double time," *Variety* reported, "and it is her direction that leavens the sags. After getting the show under way she drops into the pit to baton the ork the entire distance." *Variety*, not usually a fan of the Federal Theatre, concluded its review with Hollywood's highest praise: The show was better than a movie. "If picture house managers are looking for a good excuse for bad grosses here's one that's the McCoy. Let the cinematics try and match it for fifty cents."[35]

As in San Francisco, clever ploys were used to get the attention of the press and public. A musical melodrama called *The Black Crook* had created a sensation back in the Gay Nineties because the ladies of the ensemble cavorted in black tights. Frankie Bailey, as the star of the show, had become famous as "the girl with the million dollar legs." In the Federal Theatre revival of *The Black Crook*, Frankie Bailey, age seventy-seven, reappeared in a cameo role and of course made all the papers. In side-by-side photographs, her seventy-seven-year-old legs still looked good.

But the Los Angeles project wasn't all vaudeville: There was Shakespeare, political theatre, comedy, a strong Negro unit doing original works by black playwrights, and a lively Yiddish unit. And increasingly, word got out that the Federal Theatre Project was not to be scoffed at. "Don't get quoted as saying you'll never get caught playing in the WPA shows," wrote Hollywood gossip columnist Walter Winchell. "A lot of actors said that and were taken at their word, and now they're hamburger salesmen—that is, the lucky ones are."[36]

Local papers reported that movie scouts were coming to Federal Theatre productions looking for talent. "A lot of players—young ones getting experience, and old ones earning subsistence money—now have a chance to show their abilities to the people who really need talent and are willing to pay for it," wrote one Hollywood columnist.[37] Universal Studios, in particular, was said to be looking for fresh faces. There was even a charge, unsubstantiated as usual, that amateur actors were paying to get parts in Federal Theatre plays to showcase their talents for the movies. Confirming the rumors, a young Federal Theatre actress from Pocatello, Idaho, was signed to a long-term movie contract, and a twenty-five-year-old project actor was signed by Paramount.

By the time Hallie visited in November 1937, the Los Angeles project was the most successful in the country. *Ready, Aim, Fire!*—a musical satire on dictatorship written on the project—was, she reported to Phil, "very funny and expertly done" and was breaking all box office records. A ballet called *American Exodus*, a dance drama about the frontier that was also playing to packed houses, moved her to tears. What's more, the regional office, which operated as the hub of the West Coast project, was "simply marvelous, wonderfully organized, efficient, running like clockwork."[38]

A production of *Hansel and Gretel*, conceived by a highly original artist named Yasha Frank, turned out, she wrote Phil, to be "one of the most exciting shows of my life." Frank was deeply interested in the psychology of children and shared Hallie's view that much of children's theatre was embarrassingly overdone. "Adults acting for children seemed to try too hard,"

Hallie observed, "seemed not to realize that here was an audience, ready to believe without external nonsense."

Frank believed that "children are by nature dramatists and actors. They intuitively prepare themselves for their impending conflict with society by dramatizing their problems . . . Children love to learn but hate to be taught." The result was that his plays "achieved the rare distinction of being childlike without being childish,"[39] according to Hallie. "The cast expanded to include the audience, and fifteen hundred children clapped and laughed and sang."[40] Later in her visit, Hallie saw Frank's *Pinocchio*, which she liked even better than his *Hansel and Gretel*. *Pinocchio*, which was an obscure Italian folk tale before he rediscovered it, became a box office favorite with adults and children, first in Los Angeles and later in New York City.[41] "This man Yasha Frank is a genius," Hallie wrote Phil after seeing his *Pinocchio*.[42]

Rehearsals were also under way for Gerhart Hauptmann's *The Weavers*, "the most exciting and probably the most revolutionary play we have yet done." It was part of a planned cycle of international plays, including August Strindberg's *The Father*. The Federal Theatre Project in Los Angeles was successful enough to be "arty," in defiance of its critics.

But the project's enemies were still trying to stir up trouble. On the day Hallie arrived in town, the *Examiner* ran a story with the headline U.S. THEATRE HEAD PLEDGES GRAFT INQUIRY. According to the *Examiner*, a Hearst paper hostile to the WPA, Hallie had announced that she was ordering a "full investigation . . . into charges that graft exists in the project's Los Angeles unit."[43] The story was accompanied by a photo of Hallie, looking imperious in a Robin Hood–style feathered hat and pointing her finger as though issuing an order.

Hallie immediately denied the story, which had no basis in fact. FTP DIRECTOR ASTOUNDED AT REPORTS OF INQUIRY INTO CHARGES, read a headline later that day in the *Hollywood Citizen News*. "It is amazing that such a thing should be published," she declared. "I have not heard of any graft charges. I am not making any investigation of graft charges. I don't believe there is any graft in the Los Angeles Project."[44]

Four days later, all the employees of the Federal Theatre Project in Los Angeles, numbering approximately twelve hundred, gathered at the Mayan Theatre to hear Hallie's farewell address. Hallie had told Phil the night before that she was "terrified at the idea of speaking to them." But she wound up talking for an hour, without notes, linking what she had seen in Los Angeles to the national picture. She praised the workers' accomplishments and encouraged them to air legitimate grievances. But, she added, "you must stamp out poison in your midst before it stamps you out."[45]

"Sincere criticism is the lifeblood of the theatre," she told the project workers, "but we will not tolerate loose unauthenticated rumors and malicious gossip."[46] When she finished, she was greeted with an ovation.

By the time Hallie returned to Washington, the Roosevelt recession had deepened. The number of unemployed increased by nearly two million between mid-September and mid-December, and it looked to WPA officials as though another million would lose their jobs after Christmas. Roosevelt was still trying to decide whether to continue on the budget-balancing course or reverse himself and initiate new government spending. As he and his advisers weighed the options, Congress was becoming more and more critical of New Deal programs: It wasn't clear FDR could prime the pump, even if he decided to do it.

In the meantime, the budget-cutting wheels kept turning. Hallie returned from her trip to discover that the arts projects in Washington, D.C., had been moved "from the decayed splendor of the McLean mansion to the shabby, down-at-heels lassitude of the Ouray Building . . . small dull offices with dull tan walls and dull brown woodwork and brown burlap screens chastely concealing corner hand basins."

Hallie had long been uncomfortable with the luxury of the McLean mansion, which was lavishly furnished with carved Italian buffets and enormous bathtubs with gold fixtures. But if the McLean mansion had been too much, the Ouray building offices were too little. "The arts projects," she later observed, "had mysteriously become the poor relations of WPA."[47] Furthermore, there was pressure on the arts projects to cut what were called "man/month costs," the average cost per WPA employee per month, because they were higher than those on other WPA projects. One solution was to lower supervisory wages—a move that Hallie adamantly opposed because it would result in the loss of talented nonrelief people. She had already lost many and feared losing more if the top pay levels were reduced.

Then, to further complicate the situation, word came down that the president had finally decided to deal with the growing unemployment situation by adding 350,000 people to the WPA payroll *without additional funds*!

On December 9, 1937, as Hallie sat in a conference with Ellen Woodward and others of her staff, trying to figure out a way to deal with this impossible demand, she was told that Harry Hopkins wanted to speak with her in his office.

As she entered the room, Harry stood facing the window, his back to her. When he turned around, she was shocked by his haggard appearance.

"Hallie," Harry said, "I have got something I want to get off my chest. Sit down."

Hallie sat.

"Nobody knows this, but by tonight they will. I have got some damn thing wrong inside me. I have got to go and have it cut out. I guess it is a cancer. Anyway I have got to go to Mayo Brothers [the Mayo Clinic in Rochester, Minnesota] tonight. It is the devil and all to go just now and leave you all up against this new order to add more people when we haven't got enough money to take care of what we've got."

Harry told Hallie that he had sent for her to say good-bye. "And to say I'm sorry about the mistake of not seeing you oftener. You've done a big job, nobody knows how big—and I'm grateful. I wanted you to know it. And if you possibly can stand it, I want you to keep on during the hard days coming. We can't lose what we've gained."[48]

chapter fourteen

PAST IS PRESENT

In the spring of 1937, there was yet another lynching in the South. Two black men, accused of robbing and killing a grocer, were confronted by an angry mob outside the courthouse in Winona, Mississippi, thrown into a school bus, and driven out into the woods. There they were chained to trees and seared with a blowtorch until they confessed. One of the two, Bootjack McDaniels, was then killed by a volley of bullets. The second, Roosevelt Townes, was burned to death in a brushfire, built around him and ignited with gasoline, as a crowd of five hundred townspeople looked on. A deputy sheriff approved, noting that "it was all done very quickly, quietly and orderly."[1]

Three days later, the House of Representatives, galvanized by the shocking cruelty of the double lynching, voted favorably on an antilynching bill sponsored by Senators Robert F. Wagner of New York and Edward P. Costigan of Colorado. But the House vote immediately put southern Democrats in the Senate on high alert: They viewed the antilynching legislation as a dangerous threat to the status quo in the segregated South—the first step in a replay of Reconstruction. In January 1938, when they returned from their Christmas holiday back home, the southern senators mounted a filibuster against the Wagner-Costigan antilynching bill.

On and on the senators droned, paralyzing the legislative process for weeks. Josiah Bailey of North Carolina voiced the southerners' fear that the Wagner-Costigan bill was "the forerunner of a policy studiously cultivated by agitators, not for the purpose of preventing lynching, but for the purpose of introducing the policy of Federal interference in local affairs. The lynching bill would promptly be followed by a civil rights bill . . . I

One-Third of a Nation (National Archives and Records Administration)

give you warning." Senator Pat Harrison of Mississippi warned of the looming dangers of "miscegenation," and Senator Allen Ellender of Louisiana vowed to "fight for white Supremacy" as long as he was in the Senate.

As the southern Democrats held forth on the floor of the Senate, Hallie Flanagan was called to testify before a House committee looking into the possibility of creating a federal Department of Science, Art and Literature, proposed by Representative William Sirovich of New York. Apparently, no one took Congressman Sirovich or his dream very seriously. Sirovich was a physician and aspiring playwright who had been touting his proposal on the arts for twelve years, and his bill was laden with impractical ideas. Among other things, he proposed a science, art, and literature edifice on Capitol Hill "to balance the new building of the Supreme Court." Nor did the House Committee on Patents, which Sirovich chaired, seem the best platform for an arts bill.

But Hallie welcomed the opportunity to testify before the Sirovich committee. Although the Sirovich bill was wordy and unrealistic, there was another stronger bill waiting in the wings. The Coffee-Pepper bill (sponsored by Congressman John Coffee [D] of Washington State and Senator Claude Pepper [D] of Florida), which proposed using the WPA arts programs as a foundation for a permanent federal Bureau of Fine Arts, just might put the Federal Theatre Project on a steadier course.

What's more, by the time Hallie arrived in Washington to testify in early February, she was contemplating using the Sirovich hearings for another purpose: to protest in public about drastic changes within the project.

The old battles between the artists and the bureaucrats were once again consuming the project in its two liveliest and largest locations, New York and Los Angeles. The situation in New York was complicated: George Kondolf, who had turned the Chicago project around, had been called in to take over the directorship in New York, where budget cuts had strengthened the hand of the militant Workers Alliance. Kondolf was taking a tough line against protesters, with strong support from regional WPA director Paul Edwards. Employees who picketed on government time were summarily fired, as were nonprofessionals on the rolls, especially if they seemed to be activists in the Workers Alliance. The activists retaliated with more protests and demands for the resignation of Edwards and Kondolf.

It had been Harry Hopkins's idea to call in Kondolf to take over New York from Phil Barber. Hallie may not have liked it, but she grudgingly accepted it. "He is a conservative appointment," she wrote Harry, "at a time when we are given to understand that such an appointment would be advisable."[2] Kondolf had little sympathy for the Workers Alliance, which he saw as a "direct arm of the local Communist party . . . the actors that were put on were picked by them whether they had experience or not . . . I felt very strongly . . . fire them and save the legitimate actors."[3]

What Hallie didn't know was that Hopkins had asked Kondolf to report directly to him, bypassing Hallie.[4] Apparently, he was starting to believe that Hallie had too much sympathy for the radicals. Hopkins, like his boss, FDR, avoided confrontation whenever possible. Certainly he remained friendly on the surface to Hallie, but his actions suggest that he believed she was becoming a liability at a time when reaction had set in in Washington.

The Kondolf/Edwards reign triggered the resignation of Edward Goodman, director of the Popular Price Theatre. Goodman criticized the WPA's "sometimes-veiled, sometimes-outspoken anti-union policy" and "the indefensible doing to death of one of the most forward achievements our government has ever made."[5] Worse yet, Brooks Atkinson, one of the Federal Theatre's best and most articulate friends, seemed to share Goodman's opinion of the situation.

"Although Mrs. Flanagan remains national chairman of the Federal Theatre," he wrote in the *New York Times*, "all the four arts projects are now actively administered in this city by Paul Edwards, who manages them in an eminently businesslike fashion as relief projects . . . Although he has reduced expenses considerably, the progressive theatre which Mrs. Flanagan was succeeding in developing is now falling apart—particularly in New York, which employs 4000 of the 8000 people on the national project. Many people believe that Mrs. Flanagan was gracefully pushed to one side because the Federal Theatre is unpopular in Washington. It is noisy all out of proportion to its size. Unlike the WPA labor projects, which employ people by the hundreds of thousands and are scarcely heard from, it meets millions of Americans across the footlights . . . it is conspicuous, builds up opposition when it treads on political toes and endangers the whole of WPA in Washington."[6]

Brooks Atkinson was right about the nervousness in Washington. Harry Hopkins was still recovering from cancer surgery, but it seems likely that he condoned the clampdown not only in New York, but also in Los Angeles. Hallie believed, however, that the new director in Los Angeles, Colonel Donald Connolly, had gone even further than Hopkins and the Washington bureaucrats intended.

"Things are pretty black," Hallie wrote Phil in early January. "Connolly has taken over the project in California, notified us that we are not to communicate with our people—except through him. He called them in and said, 'Henceforth I am boss. There is no Washington boss of the Federal Theatre. There is no Federal Theatre in Southern California. There is only a drama unit and I decide its plays.' "[7]

Not long after, she got word from an intermediary that Connolly had decided to cancel two plays that he claimed wouldn't do well at the box office. Connolly gave an order to "pass word on as we shall not contact Flanagan." Hallie wrote Phil, "That is just too bad for C[onnolly] because F[lanagan] has every intention of contacting him and in ways disrupting."[8]

As in the past, the battle was joined over censorship. The two plays Connolly wanted to cancel were *Judgment Day* by Elmer Rice and *Stevedore* by George Sklar and Paul Peters. The Rice play, a courtroom drama that takes place somewhere in middle Europe, evokes the issues surrounding the 1933 Reichstag fire trial in Germany, in which Hitler scapegoated the Communists in order to assume dictatorial powers. *Judgment Day* is an anti-Fascist screed, with sympathy for the Communist opposition in Germany. And no politically aware bureaucrat could fail to see the risks of putting on *Stevedore* while southern Democrats were filibustering in the Senate against an antilynching bill. Clearly Connolly decided to ban these two plays because he wanted to avoid controversy. It had nothing to do with box office.

There had been so many censorship fights, starting right at the beginning with *Ethiopia*. There had been the *Model Tenement* battle in Chicago, the flap over the Negro unit's *Lysistrata* in Seattle, the devastating incident in Minnesota with "Federal Fan Dancer Number One." Every time, the censors had won. But this time, Hallie decided she would either defeat Connolly or quit.

She began by writing a long letter to Connolly, laying out the difference between her responsibilities and his. "The Los Angeles Project," she wrote him, "has one of the most distinguished records of any Federal Theatre in the country" and is "a nerve center and supply station for all the Projects west of the Mississippi." She went on to explain in detail the various activities of the project, all of which "seem to me of profound importance . . . I hope very much that we can work together with complete harmony. I shall rely on you for administrative matters and I trust that you will realize that Mr. Hopkins entrusts me with all decisions as to theatre policy and program."[9]

As it became clear that Connolly was ignoring her, Hallie wrote to Harry, who was convalescing in the South, asking him to intervene. "Only you are powerful enough to end the censorship and intimidation now wrecking your Federal Arts Projects in southern California," she wrote. "Colonel Connelly had not been in office a week when he proceeded to violate every understanding which Mrs. Woodward had given us to understand would be observed . . .

"Harry," she concluded, "you know my devotion to you personally and you know that my very life is bound up with this project. I believe in you, in the project, and in the magnificent future of both. Please help me in carrying out your own order to create a 'free, adult American theatre.' "[10]

By the time of the Sirovich hearings in Washington, *Variety* and other California newspapers were running stories alleging censorship on the Los Angeles project, and prominent actors, including Burgess Meredith and Henry Fonda, were wiring protests to the WPA in Washington. Then, on February 7, Morris Watson, newspaperman and founding writer for the Living Newspapers, told the Sirovich panel that "censorship and suppression" had taken over the project in California. He named the plays at issue: *Judgment Day* and *Stevedore*. And he told the committee that the WPA should "keep the army out of art."[11]

That was the situation as Hallie sat in the offices of her WPA superiors in Washington discussing what she should and should not say when she appeared before the Sirovich committee. Her superiors wanted her to calm the waters—to tell the committee that there was no censorship on the California project and there had been no plan to produce those two plays in the first place. She refused to say this. Her superiors threatened to fire her. They also threatened to reveal "dark secrets" about the Los Angeles project, including charges against Howard Miller. At eight P.M., with everyone exhausted and hungry for dinner, a wire from Connolly was produced saying that he was not banning but only postponing the plays. Finally, after five hours of wrangling, the two sides reached a compromise. Hallie agreed to tell the committee that *Judgment Day* and *Stevedore* had not been suppressed, merely postponed. But in exchange for smoothing things over, she exacted a promise that the plays *would* be produced in Los Angeles during the spring season. "We have won a sort of victory," Hallie wrote Phil. "Is any victory ever clear cut in this thing?"[12]

On the witness stand, Hallie proved to be a consummate actress. Asked by Sirovich about the censorship on the Los Angeles project, she answered that the two plays were not "stopped" but merely "postponed." What was the WPA policy on censorship? asked Sirovich. "Our idea," she replied, "is to set up a free adult theatre. However, we have not been able to do exactly what we want in every city. We have difficult local situations, but I think we have the freest subsidized theatre in the history of the world."[13]

Hallie came away feeling pleased with her debut as a congressional witness. "The testimony was quite exciting," she wrote Phil. "The Congressmen, especially Connery [William P. Connery] from Boston, and a big bull like one from Minnesota, were wonderful. I got very tough cross questioning but I did know the answers."[14]

Hallie had been understated in her presentation, telling the congressmen that the Federal Theatre "has made a beginning . . . We realize more keenly than our severest critics the increasing strides in plan and execution we must make; for all Federal Theatres are theatres in the making, eager, ambitious, necessarily nervous, poised on the brink of uncertainty."[15]

Yet despite the tensions, the New York project was enjoying an unprecedented success as she spoke. *One-Third of a Nation*, a thoroughly documented exposé of slum housing, took its name from FDR's second inaugural, in which he asserted that "one-third of a nation is ill-housed, ill-clothed and ill-fed." When it opened at the Adelphi in New York on January 17, the critics were nearly unanimous in their praise: Most saw it as the most successful edition yet of the Living Newspaper, the Federal Theatre Project's "superb contribution to the contemporary theatre."[16]

"By the simple process of tearing a filthy old tenement out of its normal setting and putting it on a stage," the *New York Post* reported, "the Federal Theatre has succeeded, in its housing drama, *One-Third of a Nation*, in making us really *see* that horror as we have never bothered to see it before. Under the proscenium arch and behind the velvet curtain it gapes at us and we gape at it and we realize at last with what ghastliness the lives of up to 2,000,000 New Yorkers are surrounded."[17]

The set at the Adelphi, a multistoried cross section of a tenement building, was made into a central character in the story. Time passed, but the tenement, with its inadequate plumbing and dangerous fire escapes, endured. "Here are the narrow halls, the crowded rooms, the wabbling [*sic*] fire escapes, the piled-up refuse, the patched pipes, the unsanitary plumbing and the human misery the tenements have exposed to every investigating committee since the first one was built," wrote Burns Mantle in the *Daily News*.[18]

Every night, the tenement in *One-Third of a Nation* caught fire twice, once at the beginning of the show and once at the end, thus illustrating that things don't change for the better in the slums. In between, the Living Newspaper dug deep into causes, examining the land-grabbing of

Colonial forefathers, the venality of Victorian housing officials, and the inadequate response of current legislators and regulators to the problem. Even the Wagner-Steagall bill, which proposed new housing, was dismissed as a grossly inadequate solution to the problem.

The Little Man, aka Angus K. Buttonkooper, makes an appearance in *One-Third*, as in previous Living Newspapers. But in this one, his wife plays an important role, too. When she hears that the Wagner-Steagall appropriation has been cut from $1 billion to $500 million in order to balance the budget, she says, "Balance the budget? What with? Human lives? Misery? Disease? What was the appropriation for the army and navy for the last four years?"

"Three billion one hundred and twenty-five million," comes the answer.

"Well," she says, "there's one thing we can do right now. We can holler. And we can keep on hollering until they admit in Washington it's just as important to keep a man living as it is to kill him!"

"It is amazing to see how dramatic and absorbing they manage to make the frank message of *One-Third of a Nation*," wrote Richard Watts in the *New York Herald Tribune*.[19] "It possesses pace, force and poignancy," wrote the essayist John Gassner. "It possesses style—the style appropriate to its material."[20] And John Mason Brown, who was hard to please, wrote that it was "every good citizen's duty" to see it.[21]

Many citizens did. *One-Third of a Nation* played in New York to soldout houses for nine months, setting a Federal Theatre attendance record of over two hundred thousand, including many standees. Walter Winchell, on his radio program, called the show "Uncle Sam's first big footlight smash."[22] Paramount Pictures turned it into a movie, using the same name.

What's more, *One-Third of a Nation*, building on the tradition established by *It Can't Happen Here*, traveled to ten other cities, where it was altered to reflect local architecture and issues. When a slum apartment building collapsed in Philadelphia, *One-Third* was rewritten accordingly. Instead of opening with a fire, the Philadelphia show began with the crashing of a building, followed by screeching fire engines and victims being carried out on stretchers. Everywhere it went, *One-Third of a Nation* received high praise and ran for weeks and sometimes months.

The success of *One-Third of a Nation* was especially satisfying for Hallie, because the production had first taken shape during a six-week workshop she led at Vassar the previous summer. She had convinced the Rockefeller Foundation to underwrite the workshop, as a way of deepening and broadening the experience of forty of the best directors, actors, and designers on the Federal Theatre Project all around the country. In Poughkeepsie, the participants were involved in all aspects of production: building scenery, painting screens, running sewing machines, taking acting and dancing classes, and, finally, performing in the premiere production of *One-Third of a Nation*. No critics were allowed to come to the opening, but a reporter from *Variety* sneaked in and reported that the "show has been mounted with maximum effectiveness." There were even some who preferred the suggestive costuming and surreal set of the Vassar production to the more literal version that opened six months later in New York. The giant images of a rusty water tap, a cracked toilet seat, an "old law" fire escape, and a huge garbage can were, Hallie noted, "enlarged or distorted only as life in slum conditions distorts such objects."[23] Howard Bay, who designed both sets, believed Hallie was disappointed when he resorted to realism the second time around.[24] But in both versions, *One-Third of a Nation* was a lively and defiant rejoinder to the bureaucrats who wanted only bland productions.

One of the few places where *One-Third of a Nation* did not get a positive reception was on the floor of the United States Senate. Still filibustering against the antilynching bill and needing to fill time with talk, the southern senators fastened on a rumor that they were held up to ridicule in the course of the play because of their criticism of the housing bill. "It seems a bit unfair," Senator Charles Andrews of Florida noted, "to take funds we provided for relief in order to hold us up to derision . . . I don't think Americans are responsible for this kind of presentation," he added. "I think some foreign element must be behind this."[25]

Arthur Arent, head dramatist for *One-Third of a Nation*, issued a response in the press, encouraging the senators to see the play and insisting that all the words attributed to them were taken directly from the *Congressional Record*. Arent denied that the remarks of Andrews, and of his fellow senators Harry Byrd and Millard Tydings, were hissed by the audience. "There was no attempt to satirize any of these gentlemen,"[26] Arent insisted, noting that the speeches were so brief and rapid-fire that there was no time for audience reaction.

New York Post columnist Ernest Meyer suggested that it "might be illuminating to dramatize the filibuster against the anti-lynching bill . . . The scenes would include groups of undernourished and unemployed citizens staring vacantly into the night while the Senators uphold the merits of lynching Negroes, labor agitators and other undesirables without insolent Federal interference."

Meyer ended his column with a story provided by Representative

Maury Maverick of Texas, a man who lived up to the family name. Congressman Maverick, the only southerner in the House to vote in favor of the antilynching bill, noted that some of his southern colleagues held surprising views on slum conditions. "I talked to one Representative recently about the housing problem," Maverick said. "He said he couldn't get excited because there were no slums in his district."

"No slums?" exclaimed Maverick. "But I've seen your district and I've seen acres of miserable shacks, whole miles of them!"

"Oh, those aren't slums," Maverick's colleague responded. "That's where the Negroes live."[27]

On February 21, the filibuster against the antilynching bill finally ended, six weeks after it had begun. The segregationist South had won the day: The bill was withdrawn, in order to allow the Senate to get on with other pressing business.

The next day, the Senate began a debate on whether to increase relief expenditures in the face of growing unemployment. Senator Josiah Bailey of North Carolina, one of the leaders of the filibuster, argued that the current recession proved that New Deal policies had failed. "The whole theory under which we have proceeded these last six years has been exploded by the conditions which we see about us today," said Bailey. Then the senator, apparently in a jovial mood following the success of the filibuster, returned to the subject of *One-Third of a Nation*. For an hour and a half, Bailey read from the script, supplying gestures and lengthy asides for the amusement of the well-filled gallery, which had come to hear a debate on relief.

"We learn," said Senator Bailey, turning from his desk to address Senator Robert Wagner, who sat next to him, "the WPA has a theatre in New York and has put on a play in which my distinguished friend, the junior Senator from New York, Mr. Wagner, is the hero, and in which my friend, the junior Senator from Virginia, Senator Byrd, is the villain." Wagner, of course, was the sponsor not just of the housing bill, but also of the antilynching legislation.

Senator Bailey proceeded to read an exchange between Wagner and Senator Andrews of Florida, taken from the *Congressional Record*, included in the play, and now inserted into the *Congressional Record* a second time:

Andrews: I should like to ask the Senator from New York where the people who live in slums come from.

Wagner: What does the senator mean? . . . Whether they come from some other country?

Andrews: I think we ought not to offer any inducement to people to come in from our country or foreign countries or anywhere else and take advantage of our government in supplying them with homes. For instance, if we examine the birth records in New York, we will find that most of the people there in the slums were not born in New York, but the bright lights have attracted them from everywhere and that is one reason why there are so many millions in New York without homes."

Finished with script reading, Bailey concluded sarcastically, "It is a great thing to know that we have this great activity for which we may appropriate money, and which will make us all actors on the stage forever."

Senator Sherman Minton of Indiana finally rose to the defense of the Federal Theatre Project, but he managed to insult the whole undertaking in the process: "I heard the sneering and the sniggering and I say shame on the Senate . . . when it can take that kind of attitude toward any poor devil trying to make a living doing the thing he thinks he can do. I don't think the play is very hot myself, but somebody sweated to produce it. There are more than 8500 employees on the Theatre project of the WPA and I say don't sneer and laugh."[28]

Not surprisingly, displays like this one on the floor of the Senate alarmed true friends of the Federal Theatre like Burns Mantle of the *Daily News*, who warned that "the time is galloping toward us when something will have to be done about this relief project if any thing is to be saved of the foundations it has laid for a true national theatre . . .

"The time to take steps is now!" Mantle warned. Then, paraphrasing Shakespeare, he wrote, "Let the Roosevelts, the Hopkinses and the Flanagans look to't NOW!!"[29]

The closest thing to a rescue plan for the Federal Theatre Project was the Coffee-Pepper bill, which was scheduled to come up for a vote before the end of the session. Predictably, the Coffee-Pepper bill provoked right-wing newspapers to warn of the dangers of government interference in the lives of artists. It was "an importation," warned the *Journal American*, "from the totalitarian countries of Europe," and it would simply institutionalize mediocrity, producing "a vast trough of Federal largesse, at which the incompetents, hangers-on and pretenders would feed."[30]

Even among artists, there were those who deplored the idea of a government bureau involving itself in the arts. The eminent actor Cornelia Otis Skinner dismissed it as "a sop to the servants." "Good God!" protested Otis Skinner. "What has this Federal Theatre done? It is simply enabling a lot of unworthy people to make a livelihood in the theatre in which they could not exist otherwise."[31]

The playwright Channing Pollock produced a jeremiad against the bill, which he called "the first step toward the destruction of liberty . . .

"The true artist doesn't want to be encouraged," he told a society audience at the Biltmore. "He is an internal combustion engine. He wants to be free." If the WPA artists keep going, Pollock quipped, "we shall soon have to begin painting murals on ashcans, stone fences and outhouses—the only places left to paint." As for *One-Third of a Nation*, it was enough to give a person "apoplexy."[32]

But when hearings on the Coffee-Pepper bill began in early March before the Senate Committee on Labor and Education, an impressive array of artists came to testify in its favor. Burgess Meredith argued that art made the nation stronger, and Lillian Gish, first lady of the silent screen, praised the Federal Theatre Project and urged Congress to establish a permanent theatre based on competence rather than relief. The novelist Theodore Dreiser advocated for the bill before the committee, as did the painter Stuart Davis. The playwright and actress Jane Cowl, looking "demure and girlish, in spite of her long career on stage and screen," came to testify wearing a red-peaked hat and a scarf of silver fox. Miss Cowl argued that "we should have not one but many national theatres"[33] and noted rather melodramatically that it was the "strange fate of American artists that they give their abilities to everybody yet are given assistance by no one but themselves."[34] Perhaps most surprising of all was the appearance of Orson Welles, who noted that he had graduated from the WPA and was in favor of the bill, even though he had parted ways with the Federal Theatre Project over *The Cradle Will Rock*.

Unfortunately, however, the Coffee-Pepper bill was flawed in ways that even friends of Federal One viewed as insurmountable. It proposed a Bureau of Fine Arts that would carry over "all persons presently employed upon federal arts projects of the Works Progress Administration" without interruption of employment or salary.[35] A circle of seventeen major theatre critics came out against it because it essentially took a relief operation, developed in the desperate circumstances of the Depression, and turned it into a bureau of the arts for all time. A Ministry of Fine Arts, argued John Mason Brown in the *New York Post*, must begin life "unencumbered by the dead wood of any preceding organization" and have one goal of "bringing the best art and the best artists to the greatest number of people throughout the country."[36]

Even those who fervently wished for a permanent Federal Theatre, including Hallie Flanagan and Burns Mantle, did not disagree. Hallie later wrote that the importance of both the Sirovich and Coffee-Pepper bills was "in their spirit rather than in their content. Both saw government as related to the arts; both sought to enlarge the cultural base of American life by making art the enjoyment and the privilege of all the people. In specific detail, both plans were . . . somewhat unrealistic."[37]

In the increasingly conservative atmosphere of the Seventy-fifth Congress, and without the wholehearted endorsement of friends of the arts, the Coffee-Pepper bill didn't stand a chance, even after it was revised and conflated with the Sirovich bill. It died an undignified death in the House in June, during the closing hours of the session. Congressman Dewey Short, who hailed from the Ozarks, rose to ridicule the idea of a federal subsidy for the arts, zeroing in particularly on the dance. He stood on his tiptoes, spread out his arms, and executed a brief solo turn. "We are asked to teach people to do this," he told the assembly, "at a time when twelve millions go hungry and unemployed."[38] His colleagues laughed uproariously. Congressman Short went on to argue that Milton was blind when he wrote *Paradise Lost* and Beethoven was deaf when he composed his greatest works—proof, supposedly, that true artists didn't need any handouts, no matter what obstacles they faced.

"The strange ways of the Representatives," wrote Ernest Meyer in the *Post*, "are enough to confuse anybody, especially when they go in for vaudeville and terpsichore. Here we'd all of us been taking this thing pretty seriously, writing impassioned pieces for or against, making speeches, telegraphing Congressmen . . . And all it gets from Congress after all the sweating and fuming is a couple of quips and a horse laugh! There just don't seem to be room for Art down in Washington."[39]

Nonetheless, during the five months between the start of debate over the Coffee-Pepper bill and its demise, the Federal Theatre Project had managed to get a second wind in major cities around the country. The project had hits running in four theatres in Los Angeles that spring. And by Easter week of 1938, the New York project had three hits doing record business—not only *One-Third of a Nation*, but also a straight play, *Prologue to Glory*, downtown, and a historical swashbuckler called *Haiti* up in Harlem.

Prologue to Glory, an account of the young Abraham Lincoln's love affair with Ann Rutledge and its transformative effect on his life, was a hit with all the mainstream critics. Burns Mantle gave *Prologue to Glory* four stars and included it in his *Best Plays* anthology.

But a far more daring New York hit was the Negro unit's production of *Haiti,* by William DuBois, which opened in March at the Lafayette Theatre in Harlem. *Haiti* was a melodramatic recounting of the same uprising

Orson Welles had used as a basis for his voodoo *Macbeth*. But this time, the drama was based on the actual uprising of Toussaint Louverture and his successor, Henri Christophe, against the invading army of Napoleon.

The history itself, of the retreat into the mountains by Christophe and his men, the slow weakening of Napoleon's army as it succumbed to disease and debauchery, and the final stormy battle in which the former slaves, led by Christophe, drove Napoleon and his army into the sea, made for a rousing evening.

But it was the subplot, which touched on the issue of miscegenation, that promised to arouse controversy. In *Haiti*, a former slave and spy for Christophe named Jacques turns out to be the father of a mixed-race woman in Napoleon's retinue. New York critics and audiences found this relationship, between a black father and his "white" daughter, intriguing and deftly handled. But others would later point to this treatment of "miscegenation" as yet more evidence of the Federal Theatre Project's radical ways.[40]

Even more unusual and dangerous, in 1938, was the fact that *Haiti* involved substantial numbers of both white and black actors, performing together in a production on a Harlem stage.

Maurice Clark, the black director of *Haiti*, remembered the awkwardness of the first rehearsal of this mixed cast, with "the whites on one side of the stage and the blacks on the other, as though ne'er the twain would meet except in make-believe in the space between them." Clark plotted "an experiment in integration." He sought out a well-known nightclub that was willing to serve lunch to black cast members. "We would come back to rehearsal glowing with delight over the good food we had just had. Finally one of the white actors timidly asked me: 'Where can I find a good place to eat?'

" 'Your problem is solved,' I told him, 'just follow us.' Within five days the entire white cast had a unique experience of a night club in the daytime and eating with different colored actors. There was a kind of joyous relief about it, as though they had escaped from something which had troubled them and filled them with doubts for years."

Clark arranged the dressing rooms "with equal parts pepper and salt. When the actors would arrive for performances you would hear these greetings: 'Good evening, you big black bastard' and 'Good evening, you lily white son-of-a bitch,' but the tone was: only nit-wits take racism seriously."

William DuBois had stipulated that whites and blacks should not touch each other onstage during his play. But Maurice Clark remembered that "on the fifth curtain call, I had set up the bows with black and white alternating, hand in hand, a line reaching across the big stage. The audience nearly lifted the roof off the old Lafayette. They, too, got the cleansing message."[41]

Haiti seems to have been a happy experience for many of the participants. Leonard de Paur, who wrote the musical score, remembered it as the Federal Theatre production he enjoyed the most.[42] And Alvin Childress, who received critical praise for his portrayal of Jacques, the spy and father of the mixed-race woman in Napoleon's retinue, remembered that "everyone loved the loud noisy thing . . . I've had only two or three roles in my life that I have enjoyed and this was one." Later in his career, Childress made a living playing Amos in *Amos 'n Andy* on television.[43]

Haiti played to sold-out houses at the Lafayette for 103 nights before moving downtown to Daly's, where it continued to do well. In fact, it outlasted and outsold voodoo *Macbeth*. The role of Christophe, the hero of the piece, was played originally by Rex Ingram, a large and powerful actor who raced around the stage with infectious energy. After the show moved to Daly's, Ingram was replaced by Canada Lee, who reportedly gave a more nuanced interpretation of the part. It was Lee's first starring role and an important milestone in what was to be a successful career on the stage and in film.

Chicago, which had never been particularly daring in the past, was also enjoying new success with cutting-edge plays in the spring of 1938. One was a Living Newspaper called *Spirochete*. Spirochete is the name of the spiraling bacterium that causes syphilis, a venereal disease that reached epidemic proportions in the country during the 1930s. The spread of the disease was accelerated by taboos: Even the word *syphilis* rarely appeared in print. But in 1936, the surgeon general, responding to the mounting death toll from the disease, announced a "war on syphilis."[44] *Spirochete*, which used the Living Newspaper technique to tell the story of the spread of the disease and scientific discoveries that made it treatable, complemented the government crusade. On opening night, in the lobby of the Blackstone Theatre, doctors and nurses from the syphilis control program stood ready to test the blood of members of the audience. One reviewer was offended by the sight of a medical procedure in a theatre lobby, but many in the audience took the blood test, joining in a campaign that resulted in the discovery and treatment of fifty-six thousand cases of syphilis in Chicago alone. The play itself, by general agreement, was both "informative and sturdily entertaining."[45] "Chicago," observed one reviewer with a hint of pride, "dares to think candidly."[46]

Even more candid, and daring, was the Chicago Negro unit's production of a new play by Theodore Ward called *Big White Fog*. There had been tension in the Negro unit about what kinds of plays to do. Some radicals, including the writer Richard Wright, who was working in the publicity department of the Federal Theatre Project, wanted the unit to get away from the production of ordinary plays, "revamped," as he put it, "to 'Negro style,' with jungle scenes, spirituals and all." He suggested Paul Green's *Hymn to the Rising Sun*, a brutal portrait of life on a chain gang in the South, as an example of "adult Negro dramatics." But the actors rebelled, protesting to the director that the play was indecent and humiliating; they didn't care to play prisoners in leg chains, falling to the ground under the whip of a white prison guard.

Wright was outraged. "I could not believe my ears. I had assumed that the heart of the Negro actor was pining for adult expression in the American theatre, that he was ashamed of the stereotypes of clowns, mammies, razors, dice, watermelon, and cotton fields . . . Now they were protesting against dramatic realism! I tried to defend the play and I was heckled down." Wright attributed the objections to the fact that the actors had "spent their lives playing cheap vaudeville."[47] Not long after, at his request, he was transferred to the white experimental company.

But the kind of play Wright was advocating did eventually open at the Great Northern Theatre in downtown Chicago, even though it, too, troubled some members of the black community with its candor. That play was Ward's *Big White Fog*. Theodore Ward, like Richard Wright, was part of the great migration of blacks from the South to the North. He left Thibodaux, Louisiana, at age thirteen and traveled around the United States, working as a bootblack and hotel bellboy before entering the University of Utah and then continuing his studies on a scholarship at the University of Wisconsin. When he moved to Chicago after graduation, he met Richard Wright and became part of a group of aspiring black writers in the South Side Writers Club.

The idea for *Big White Fog* came to him when he was traveling west on the Great Northern railroad, at a moment when he, like Hallie Flanagan, was powerfully moved by the beauty outside his window.

"I was going to the Pacific coast," Ward explained, "and we happened to reach the Great Horseshoe Bend on the Great Northern. It's magnificent. If you've never seen it, you don't know what a tremendous spectacle it is. The trains have to . . . cross the canyon. God knows how deep it was . . . You see the fog is growing . . . across us all the way up. And so I saw this and I was very struck by the magnificence of America and all of a sudden it occurred to me, 'What the hell you lookin' at? This don't belong to you.' And that set me back and I began to dwell on the question of where do we stand in America . . . I began necessarily going back over what did I know about what was to be done about us. What could we do? It occurred to me that we just didn't have any point of view. We didn't have it and what we did know was only the idea of the white folks. So we were surrounded by this big white fog."[48]

Ward's central character in *Big White Fog* does have a point of view. Victor is an ardent follower of Marcus Garvey, the leader of the Back-to-Africa movement. He has come north to Chicago with his wife and family, looking for a better life. But his outrage at the racist treatment of those around him leads him to sacrifice his hard-earned laborer's wages to the Back-to-Africa cause. In the end, he bankrupts the family—alienating his wife and endangering his children's future—for the dream of a homeland.

Victor's arguments with his brother-in-law, Dan, who is investing in "kitchenette" apartments and turns up in a Cadillac, vividly lay out the conflicts between success in the white man's world and the Garveyite alternative:

Vic: (*defensively*) You don't understand the new spirit, Dan. We're out to wrest our heritage from the enemy.

Dan: (*challengingly*) What *our*? My heritage is right here in America!

Vic: (*quietly*) What? A lynch rope?

. . .

Dan: Like hell. If those chumps down South haven't got sense enough to get out from under Mr. George, they ought to be strung up.

Vic: You talk like an imbecile, Dan— Have you forgotten East St. Louis, Tulsa, and Washington?[49]

Big White Fog, which treated such uncomfortable issues as skin color distinctions within a black family, received a mixed reception when it was tried out in a reading in the black community, especially after Kay Ewing, a middle-class white Vassar colleague of Hallie's who directed the show, made the mistake of saying the play portrayed a "typical Negro family."[50] Shirley Graham, the only black director on the Chicago project, warned that the play's treatment of color difference "tears open old sores and leaves them uncovered and bleeding." The ending also worried some in authority in the WPA. Les, Vic's son, is attracted to communism's promise of uniting the working classes. In the final scene, just as the family is about to be evicted from their apartment, the son's "Comrades," black and white, come to their rescue.

Despite misgivings from several different quarters, *Big White Fog* opened at the Great Northern to positive, if often condescending, reviews and played there to substantial mixed audiences for seven weeks. Then something happened that has never been fully explained. Harry Minturn, director of the Chicago project, decided to move the show into a high school in a black neighborhood on the South Side, where it died after only a few days. Minturn claimed it was part of an effort bring theatre to the black community, but Theodore Ward was convinced that it was sabotage, committed by the local WPA administration, who resented Hallie's championing of the play.[51]

Whatever the cause, it was an unfortunate ending for an important original work: *Big White Fog* is probably the best play written on the Federal Theatre Project. "It is the greatest encompassing play on negro life that has ever been written," Langston Hughes wrote later. "If it isn't liked by people, it is because they are not ready for it, not because it isn't a great play."[52]

On May 19, Hallie and the other three Federal One directors met with Harry Hopkins in Washington. All had the same objective in mind: They wanted him to reaffirm to state WPA administrators that artistic decisions were in their hands. And they wanted him to agree that wage levels on the arts projects would not be altered because of pressure to place more people on relief. The arts projects, Hallie and the other national directors believed, could not survive if further cuts were made at supervisory levels.

Hallie had been worrying for some time that she was losing the strong support she had long enjoyed from Harry Hopkins. She suspected he was avoiding her when they both passed through Miami in March. "Harry was right there you know," she wrote Phil, "and it was in all the papers that I was there. But not a word from him." But then in April, Harry paid a visit to the New York production of *One-Third of a Nation*, in the company of FDR's son James Roosevelt, and told the press afterward that "of all the things I have done, that which I am proudest of is the development of the Federal Theatre," adding that the Federal Theatre Project would continue for "a long long time."[53]

When the four Federal One directors met with him that May, Hopkins, looking "brown and well and very happy,"[54] reaffirmed his support. He agreed there should be no change in wage levels and that artistic control should remain in the arts directors' hands. Later that day, at a luncheon for two hundred invited guests from the art, music, and literary worlds, Hopkins talked of his pride in the arts projects and insisted that as long as he was connected with them, they would remain under federal rather than state supervision.

The four arts directors knew that their most important ally, besides Hopkins, was Eleanor Roosevelt, and they planned to enlist her support that same day at a tea at the White House. But Hallie almost didn't make it. She had come rushing back from her previous meetings to the Hotel Powhatan, with only ten minutes to get dressed. When she got to her room, she discovered that the dress she planned to wear had not been delivered by housekeeping. She phoned the hotel clerk and told him "that I was entirely fed up with the Hotel Powhatan and all of its ways. Having delivered my ultimatum to the Hotel Powhatan, I went into the bathroom, banged the door and locked it. I took my solitary and furious bath, and while doing so I heard a terrorized flunkey deposit the dress on my bed. I was just thinking smugly to myself that the only way to get service in a hotel was to raise a row, when I tried the door and found that I could not get out. I twisted and turned, banged and rattled. The door would not budge. I tried to soap the lock. I held hot cloths against the door. I hit it with slippers . . . Thinking of Mrs. Woodward's chauffeur waiting below, I alternately cried and laughed. I shouted and banged, and finally in despair I appealed to the public. Chastely enveloped in a bath towel, I began to call and lean out of the seventh story window. My motions at first were delicate and tentative. However, all the activities of life went rushing past me. No one looked up. No one paid the slightest attention to my calls—'O, mister' 'Messenger boy' 'pardon me, sir.' My tactics grew bolder. I began waving another towel out of the window and shouted 'Murder.' At this point, I saw people in the building across the street laughing and this added to my fury. Two girls passing on the street saw me and giggled and went right on . . . I finally got the attention of a rather elderly and terrified looking gentleman. We conversed in dumb show, since the noise was terrific. I spelled out the number of my room. By this time a large group had collected in the street and its members were looking up with strange expressions of fear, amazement and indignation—but on the whole complete hostility. I know exactly how a sane person, who is accused of being insane, feels. A short time after this signal, people burst into my room and the Chief Clerk and two or three bellboys in frantic excitement, asked me what had happened; they tried the door and after much rattling and guttural cursing, called the engineer, who took the knob off."[55]

Hallie made it to the White House tea and was able to talk with Eleanor

Roosevelt, who was supportive as usual. But the incident at the hotel was like the dumb show preceding an Elizabethan tragedy. It comically foreshadowed the painful events of coming months. The forces pushing for change and the forces of reaction were about to engage in a battle for control of the Congress. During the battle, the Federal Theatre would become a whipping boy, and Hallie would be, maddeningly, unable to make herself heard above the fray. She would be like the crazy woman in the towel, shouting out the bathroom window at the Hotel Powhatan, trying to get her message across to an uncomprehending crowd below.

chapter fifteen

ENTER HUAC

The long and successful filibuster against the antilynching bill set the tone for the entire 1938 legislative session. Afterward, the southern Democrats managed to block nearly every New Deal initiative that came before them. The one piece of legislation FDR did succeed in passing that spring merely heightened his conflict with the southerners. The Fair Labor Standards Act was the very first federal law setting minimum wages and maximum hours. In the North, it had little immediate impact, since most workers earned more than the twenty-five-cent hourly minimum set by the bill. But in the South, the bill did have an effect. In southern sawmills, for instance, it raised the wages of 44 percent of the workforce.[1]

Lower wages were, in the southerners' view, one of the few advantages they could claim in competition with the North. Besides, as "Cotton Ed" Smith insisted, a man could support himself and his family in his state of South Carolina on fifty cents a day. "Southerners actually froth at the mouth," observed Attorney General Homer S. Cummings, "when the subject [of the minimum wage] is mentioned."[2] Once again, southerners feared the meddling of the federal government in their affairs. The unspoken, underlying fear was that blacks in the South would begin to assert themselves and that Eleanor Roosevelt and her kind would encourage them to challenge white supremacy and demand their rights.

For his part, Franklin Roosevelt came to feel, as the legislative session dragged on, that his entire program of reform was endangered by the reactionaries within his own party. He developed a plan to campaign in the South during the 1938 primary season and to endorse alternative Democratic candidates running against some of his most vehement Senate foes, including "Cotton Ed" Smith of South Carolina, Walter George of

Martin Dies (Library of Congress, Prints and Photographs Division)

Georgia, and Millard Tydings of Maryland. The press quickly labeled this plan a "purge."

Meanwhile, at about the same time the minimum wage bill passed, the House endorsed the formation of a new committee, to be called the House Committee on Un-American Activities. As chairman, they appointed a young congressman from East Texas named Martin Dies, who had been one of the leaders in the fight against the minimum wage bill.

Congressional committees proliferated during the Depression and were used by both sides as a means of promoting their causes. The Senate Banking and Currency Committee had investigated banks and the stock exchange in order to push through Roosevelt's reform measures. Another committee had gone after the utilities lobby. There had been a whole series of committees, starting in 1930 under chairman Hamilton Fish, charged with investigating fascism and communism on native soil. And of course there was the La Follette committee, which was continuing to investigate antiunion activity in corporations. Martin Dies had originally hoped to chair a committee that would counter the findings of La Follette and focus on the practices of the CIO, which he considered to be a Communist-infiltrated organization promoting outrageous illegal acts, including sit-down strikes.

But Dies was shrewd and ambitious enough to know that the chairmanship of any committee would be a boon to his career. The prerogatives of the chairman of a congressional committee are broad: The rules of the courtroom do not apply, and the tone of hearings is set by the chairman himself. As Representative Lindsay Warren of North Carolina observed, in the debate over establishing the House Un-American Activities Committee, "Investigations of this nature . . . are generally for the self-glorification and advertisement of those who conduct them and who have an itch and flair for publicity."[3]

At the time of the committee's formation that spring, Martin Dies presented himself as the most fair-minded of men, pledging to investigate the activities of the American Fascist and Communist movements with equal rigor. "I am not inclined to look under every bed for a Communist," he assured the Congress, insisting that there were "fundamental rights far more important than the objective we seek."[4] What's more, he agreed that the House Un-American Activities Committee, which came to be known as HUAC, should last only as long as the legislative session.

Even with all those reassurances, it was clear to the Roosevelt administration that the Dies committee was out to discredit the New Deal and its allies, at the very moment when FDR was setting out to defeat conservative candidates in the South. In the beginning, the New Dealers dismissed the committee as a minor annoyance. But eventually, FDR and those around him discovered that the public, and the press, had a taste for the kind of fearmongering that became Martin Dies's stock in trade. Instead of ending with the seventy-fifth session of Congress, HUAC lived on, with a pause during World War II, for thirty-seven years.

According to journalist Marquis Childs, Martin Dies was not only the youngest member of the House when he arrived at age thirty in 1931, he was also the most cynical. "I doubt whether I have ever encountered a more cynical man than this lank Texan with the sallow gray face," wrote Childs. "He was a leading member of the Demagogues Club, made up of younger members like himself who had pledged themselves to vote for any appropriation bill that came onto the floor of the House, no matter what it was for. It was a hell of a good joke and they made the most of it, these young *sans culottes*. You would see Dies standing at the back of the House, surrounded by two or three fellow members of the club, a good-natured grin on his face. When a roll call came, he would stalk onto the floor and roar out his yea in a lusty voice, usually drawing tolerant laughter."[5]

But when Dies became chairman of the House Un-American Activities Committee, he focused on his mission, which very much resembled that of his father, who had served in Congress before him. When Martin Dies Sr. arrived in Washington from Beaumont, Texas, in 1909, there were two hundred thousand people in his district, but only seventeen thousand were registered to vote; poll taxes and intimidation kept the rest, including a large population of blacks, away. At that time, the senior Dies announced that white supremacy in the South "is secure and unshakable as the eternal hills." And Martin Dies Jr. had no reason to doubt that this was still true when he was elected twenty years later. The population of the district had grown, owing in part to the discovery of oil, but the number of voters remained small, and the belief in white supremacy united them.

Campaigning among the whites in his district who could vote, Martin Dies Jr. praised the brave Confederate soldiers who had kept the South from being taken over and run by "ignorant niggers," and he promised that when he did get to Congress, he would knock down Oscar De Priest, a Republican from the South Side of Chicago who was the first black to serve in Congress in the twentieth century. According to Dies Jr., De Priest had brought dishonor on the South by "marching two buck Negroes down the aisles of the Congress and introducing them as gentlemen of his race."[6]

Once in Washington, Dies shifted his animus to foreigners, who he claimed were the root cause of the Depression. In this, as in his racism,

Dies was his father's son. The father had warned of the dangers of "illiterates from abroad," with their message of "Bolsheviki socialism." Martin Dies Jr., not long after his arrival in the House, introduced a bill that would stop immigration for five years and deport the "several million foreigners" who were in the country illegally. The foreigners, he argued, were the principal cause of unemployment, and things would not get better as long as America allowed itself to be the "dumping ground for Europe." The next year, he submitted a bill to expel alien Communists from the United States. He warned that the American Communist movement was controlled by Moscow (in this, at least, he was undoubtedly correct) and that it was, among other things, "promoting discontent among Negroes." In 1935, Martin Dies traveled to New York to observe the May Day festivities and concluded there was not one American in the crowd. "If I had my way I would deport every one of them," he wrote a constituent back in Orange County, Texas.[7]

Martin Dies's bill proposing the establishment of HUAC provided an especially broad mandate. The term *un-American*, which was coined in connection with HUAC's formation,[8] could mean just about anything the chairman wanted it to. Congressman Maury Maverick, who led the opposition to the Dies bill, pointed out that the resolution gave "blanket powers to investigate, humiliate, meddle with anything and everything" and that "un-American is simply something somebody else does not agree to."[9] Despite arguments like these, the Dies resolution forming the House Committee on Un-American Activities was approved by a vote of 191–41.

The resolution passed the House on May 26, 1938. On June 6, members were named. Martin Dies was to be chairman, and his committee would consist of two conservative Democrats, two right-wing Republicans, and two not very assertive New Dealers. The first hearings of the committee began in mid-August, some two months after it was formed, but even before the hearings opened, J. Parnell Thomas, a Republican committee member from New Jersey, announced to the press that he intended to conduct a "sweeping investigation" of the Federal Theatre Project.

Thomas told the *Times* and other papers that he had been conducting "informal hearings" in New York, just as other members of the committee were doing in other parts of the country. "It is apparent from the startling evidence received thus far," he said, "that the Federal Theatre Project not only is serving as a branch of the communistic organization [the Workers Alliance] but also is one more link in the vast and unparalleled New Deal propaganda machine." As for Hallie Flanagan, "important witnesses" had informed him that she wrote and produced a play in Russia called *Hear*

Their Voices and approved only plays that contained "communistic or New Deal theories." Among such plays, he cited *Prologue to Glory*, the play about the young Lincoln, as well as *Haiti* and *One-Third of a Nation*.[10]

A few weeks later, Thomas elaborated on his original charges. He claimed to have "sworn testimony" that the Federal Theatre Project was supplying jobs to Communists who had no previous theatrical experience. Thomas was even more adamant than before: He had "a mass of evidence" that the project "is now completely dominated by Communists. I will demand the resignation of Federal Theatre officials who are responsible," Thomas declared, "and I also will recommend that the entire project be closed until a thorough cleaning has been made."[11]

The committee opened its hearings in mid-August with a brief exploration of the activities of the German American Bund, a Fascist organization, then turned to a more lengthy examination of communism within the recently formed CIO. The principal witness was the president of the rival American Federation of Labor, John P. Frey, who told the committee that the labor movement had been free of Communists until the CIO came along. Frey had detailed knowledge, provided by an informant on the National Committee of the Communist Party. He named 284 organizers, among them Harry Bridges, the Australian-born head of the West Coast longshoremen.

Undoubtedly, Communists were numerous among early members of the CIO; they were often the workers who knew how to organize a meeting or speak in public. But the committee's undemocratic procedures severely compromised its revelations, in this and every subsequent case. No serious attempt was made to cross-examine the witness, who clearly had a vested interest in discrediting the rival CIO. Martin Dies sat back, smoking one of the eight cigars he allowed himself each day and watching the reporters take notes. The people Frey named were so numerous that there was not even the possibility that they could be called to defend themselves, even if it had occurred to the committee that they should.

The day after Frey's testimony, the *New York Times* headline read: COMMUNISTS RULE THE C.I.O. FREY OF A.F.L. TESTIFIES; HE NAMES 284 ORGANIZERS. It was the first of many uncritical headlines, and stories, that made the front pages of newspapers in the early months of the Dies committee hearings. The *Times* alone gave the committee's doings over five hundred column inches in its first six weeks of life, and other papers gave them even more. One reason was that it was August, and Roosevelt was on a fishing cruise in the Pacific and Caribbean. There wasn't a lot of news. Besides, the committee hearings, which were open only to the press, made for great theatre. "In the early days especially," wrote Marquis Childs, "the performance was made to order for a certain section of the press. The Chairman provided everything but the pink lemonade."[12]

The House Un-American Activities Committee was on a tight budget—Congress had granted them only $25,000 to do their work. What's more, the Roosevelt administration, which had provided investigators to the La Follette committee, had no intention of funding investigators for HUAC. FDR, when told of Dies's complaints about the situation, reportedly responded, "Ho-hum."[13] But because the committee didn't have funds or personnel to do its own investigating, it relied on volunteer witnesses. "The best people do not offer themselves for such work," noted historian Walter Goodman, "and the volunteers of 1938 turned out to be a gamy bunch."[14]

Nowhere was this truer than during the investigation of the Federal Theatre Project, which began on the eighth day of the new committee's life. The first volunteer witness was Hazel Huffman—the woman Hallie had hired in 1936 to work in the mailroom, who had turned out to be a paid spy for Hearst.

None of Huffman's past history came out during her testimony before the committee. She identified herself as the secretary of the Committee on Relief Status of Professional Employees, an organization that she claimed had nine hundred members, although there is no evidence that it had any besides herself and her husband, who testified after her. The *New York Post* described her as a "plump young woman with an obvious grudge" and noted that the southern congressmen were entirely pleased with her testimony but uncomfortable when photographers took picture after picture of her lighting cigarettes in unladylike fashion.

Speaking in a low voice, Hazel Huffman told the committee that Hallie Flanagan was either a Communist sympathizer or a Communist. She couldn't be sure she was a Communist, she added conscientiously, because she hadn't actually seen her membership card. But certainly she was an admirer of Russian theatre, which she had studied at first hand, and her Communist sympathies were "well-known as far back as 1927." Hallie Flanagan said she wanted to do "plays of social significance," said Huffman, adding that "in other words, they are Communist propaganda plays."

As for the Federal Theatre Project, it was dominated by the Communist Workers Alliance, and only actors who joined up were hired.

Here Martin Dies interjected, "Do you mean to tell me that the taxpayers' money—it is almost unbelievable to me—is being used to support the Communist Party?"

Hazel Huffman replied: "Yes. In my opinion, yes." As an example of the Communists' control, she cited the story of a hotel chambermaid who was given the lead in a Federal Theatre play even though she had no previous theatre experience. She was, however, a committed Communist.

Huffman wandered off-message at times, as when she noted that some of the Federal Theatre plays had "perfectly filthy themes." And there was a whiff of anti-Semitism in some of her testimony, as when she described Charles Rose, a longtime Yiddish theatre actor, as "a peddler of razor blades on the Bowery" who had been made a unit director, and a man named Solomon Goldstein who was retained on the project because he grew a "very luxuriant beard" and "grand sideburns" that supplied "atmosphere." (Goldstein was in fact an experienced actor and member of Actors' Equity.)

"I know that taxpayers will get consolation out of learning that they pay for the growing of sideburns," Dies responded.[15]

Hazel Huffman was later employed as a committee investigator.

J. Parnell Thomas punctuated Huffman's testimony with a speech of his own. "On the face of the record before us, there cannot be any doubt whatever about it," he declared. "Communists and their sympathizers, who polled 80,000 votes in the last presidential elections, today have more influence in Washington than has the Republican party with its 17,000,000 voters."[16]

The next day, the committee heard from half a dozen other witnesses, several of whom were no longer with the Federal Theatre Project, who complained of the domination and intimidation they had experienced at the hands of the Workers Alliance. Seymour Revzin, Hazel Huffman's husband, testified that Communist literature was sold on the project and funds were raised on government time for such causes as loyalist Spain. Furthermore, he said, there was constant talk among the actors about how much better conditions were in the USSR than here at home.

Several witnesses complained that nonprofessionals were favored over professionals because of their Workers Alliance affiliation. Frank Verdi, an older actor who had fought vociferously against admitting Federal Theatre actors into Actors' Equity, claimed that he had been demoted from direc-tor to actor on the project because he didn't belong to the Workers Al-liance. He also claimed to have conducted an investigation of project employees to determine how many were amateurs, a survey that Hallie Flanagan had requested and then refused to read. (In fact, Verdi's prelimi-nary report was so inaccurate that the president of Actors' Equity told the Federal Theatre Project administrator that he would not accept any report Verdi prepared.)

Charles Walton, a stage manager who tried and failed as a director on the project, reported on a conversation he had with George Kondolf in which the New York director said that the project was a "cesspool of un-Americanism" and that he could not purge the rolls of Communists because "his hands were tied" by Washington. Walton also reported on a party he went to at which black youths danced with white girls and speeches were made praising the Workers Alliance. "I became so disgusted I left right in the middle of the evening," he said. Race mixing and communism were viewed by the committee, and apparently by its witnesses, as two sides of the same coin.

The star witness on race mixing was a dainty blonde of Viennese origin named Sally Saunders, who had been rehearsing in *Sing for Your Supper* in New York when a black man in the company, a Mr. Van Cleve, reportedly asked her for a date. She was shocked. But when she confided in the director, Harold Hecht, he said, "Sally, I'm surprised at you. He has just as much right to life, liberty and pursuit of happiness as you have."

Sally Saunders then complained to several women on the project, who made fun of her scruples. Finally, she appealed, through a friend, to Senator Pat Harrison of Mississippi, who was more sympathetic. Saunders requested and was granted immediate transfer from *Sing for Your Supper*, where the incident took place. The day after her testimony before the Dies committee, the *Journal American* ran a large photo of Saunders, looking ladylike in a flowing summer dress, its V-neck punctuated with a brooch, with a dark saucer of a hat perched at an angle over her blond pin curls. Above the photo was the headline REDS URGED "MIXED" DATE, BLONDE TELLS DIES PROBERS.[17]

Sally Saunders stayed with the project for two months after giving her testimony, at which point she was fired for refusing to accept a work assignment with the touring company of *Haiti*. In an affidavit inquiring as to the cause of her firing, she explained that she told Maurice Clark, the director, that "I could not work with Negroes because of odor, which seems part of their race . . . if a Negress did my laundry, I had to air it out before I could wear it." Clark, she reported, "became very angry" and told her that Negroes didn't smell any different than anybody else.[18]

The issue of race was never far from the surface in the Dies committee's assault on the Federal Theatre Project. In fact, the success of many productions of the Negro units, and the visibility they brought to blacks—not to mention the integration the project sponsored in its casts and in its audiences—were all viewed by the committee as signs of Communist influence. In truth, for most on the committee, and certainly for Martin

Dies, its chairman, the racial policies of the Federal Theatre Project struck a deeper note of alarm than the alleged Communist infiltration. Dies, however, knew better than to flaunt his Texas racism in Washington. When Sally Saunders testified, he warned her that "we have to be very cautious about race feeling."[19] But his attitudes hadn't changed: The Federal Theatre was thumbing its nose at all he held dear. It was the idea of racial equality, more than the threat of communism, that made the Federal Theatre Project truly dangerous. As Missouri congressman Joseph B. Shannon observed, the Dies committee sought to "camouflage its racial prejudices and antilabor feelings by going 'hog wild' on the subject of Communism."[20]

It turned out that the American public was impressed by the activities of the House Committee on Un-American Activities. The day after Sally Saunders gave her testimony, Martin Dies told reporters that there had been an amazingly positive response, surprising even to committee members. "About 90 percent of the letters we receive are complimentary," he said.[21]

The first official response to the attacks on the Federal Theatre Project came from New York's WPA boss, Paul Edwards, who took a neutral bureaucratic stance, encouraging any and all members to testify if called upon and promising to look into the allegations. In early September, George Kondolf sent an affidavit to Harry Hopkins, denying that he ever said the project was "a cesspool of un-Americanism" or that he was limited by an unseen force in Washington. He also explained the WPA labor policy, which forbade union or political activity on the project but protected workers against discrimination on the basis of union or political affiliations off the project.[22]

At around the same time, Hallie wrote a letter to Chairman Dies:

"May I call to your attention," she wrote Dies, "to the fact that on August 5 . . . I wrote to your committee, saying that I would hold myself in readiness to testify. I further stated that the National Policy Board of the Federal Theatre Project would be in session [in Washington] during August and that directors of the Federal Theatre Projects all over the United States would be available to assist your committee. In the course of the month since I wrote to you, no person concerned with the direction of the Federal Theatre Project has been called to testify."[23] Two days later, in the Sunday *New York Times*, Hallie wrote about the Federal Theatre Project's ambitious national plans for the coming season. Along the way, she pointed out that "the largest number of plays done so far in the Federal Theatre, contrary to loose and inaccurate statements of the ill-informed, are by well established dramatists, from Clyde Fitch to Thornton Wilder. The second largest list consists of over a hundred new plays by American dramatists."[24]

Finally, on September 14, a protest letter was sent to the committee by Ellen Woodward, head of Federal One, pointing out that the right of a hearing was one of the "traditional safeguards of American justice" and that the directors of both the Federal Theatre and Federal Writers' Projects had volunteered to appear before the committee. "In insisting that these officials be heard," Woodward wrote, "we do so in the belief that a work of very great value is at stake."[25]

But Martin Dies, who had promised all along that the directors would be given a chance to testify, had no intention of allowing them to defend themselves before the November election. Instead, Parnell Thomas continued to hammer away at the project, claiming that Hallie Flanagan "has had some success as a dramatist in Soviet Russia" and insisting that he had "ample proof to back up everything." Meanwhile, Martin Dies won the Democratic primary in Texas in October, which meant, in the all Democratic South, that he had no need to go back to Texas to campaign for votes in the general election. Instead, he devoted himself, through the committee, to going after the New Deal.

Since the early days of the hearings, an accusation had been repeatedly leveled against Secretary of Labor Frances Perkins. Martin Dies accused her, in a series of public attacks, of refusing to enforce the law and deport Harry Bridges, whom Dies certified to be a Communist. Bridges may well have been a party member, and was certainly sympathetic to communism, but there was no proof; even if there had been, as Perkins had explained repeatedly to the committee, the courts had ruled that party membership was not grounds for deportation. However, Dies kept the charge against Secretary Perkins alive, as proof that the administration was soft on communism.

As the November election neared, Dies focused the committee's attention on New Deal candidates involved in close races. Two right-wing extremists testified that the Democratic candidates for governor, lieutenant governor, and senator in California were controlled by the Communist Party. Seven witnesses testified that the Minnesota Farmer-Labor Party of Governor Elmer Benson, who was running for reelection, had been taken over by Communists. And in Michigan, the committee took testimony against Governor Frank Murphy, who was caught up in a tough race. According to a Republican judge and the Flint city manager, Murphy had displayed a "treasonable attitude" in condoning the sit-down strikes against General Motors in 1937.[26]

While HUAC was holding its hearings, Franklin Roosevelt returned from his fishing cruise and began a tour through the sweltering South, in support of the candidates he hoped would replace reactionary southern Democrats in the primary elections. The president talked to southern voters about the deficiencies in wages, education, housing, and manufacturing in the South and urged them to repudiate politicians who condoned such conditions. He told a crowd in South Carolina that no man could live on fifty cents a day, notwithstanding the claims of "Cotton Ed" Smith, and he told an audience in Georgia, in a face-to-face encounter with Senator Walter George, that on "most public issues, he and I do not speak the same language."

Roosevelt's attempts to influence the southern primaries failed utterly. The incumbent senators attacked him as a meddlesome northern carpet-bagger, and the voters agreed. Nor did he have much better success in helping to reelect his allies elsewhere. Maury Maverick went down to defeat in Texas, as did Governor Frank Murphy in Michigan, no doubt with a push from the Dies committee. The Republicans scored their biggest gains since 1928, winning thirteen governorships, doubling their seats in the House, and gaining eight new seats in the Senate. The election was a rebuke to the president and something close to a knockout blow to the New Deal.

In December, with the elections over, Martin Dies sent word that his committee was prepared to take testimony from the directors of the Federal Theatre and Federal Writers' Projects. In late November, Hallie wrote Phil from Washington that she was spending her days preparing with lawyers for testifying. "Today a meeting in W[oodward]'s office and tomorrow another about the probable Dies call next week. They are in the panic they should have been in three months ago."[27]

chapter sixteen

MARLOWE'S GHOST

Man, proud man,
Drest in a little brief authority,
Most ignorant of what he's most assured

—Measure for Measure, II, ii

In December 1938, Hallie Flanagan's most important ally, Harry Hopkins, made two decisions with important consequences for the Federal Theatre Project. He decided to resign as head of the WPA in order to become secretary of commerce. And he decided that Hallie's immediate boss, Ellen Woodward, rather than Hallie herself, should defend the project before HUAC.

No New Deal program was attacked as frequently as the WPA. And no official was more often the butt of hostile cartoons and editorials than its boss, Harry Hopkins. Hopkins, his critics claimed, had boldly predicted before the last election that "we're going to tax and tax, and spend and spend and elect and elect." It turned out he had never actually said this. And even though there were local instances of misuse of WPA influence during the 1938 election, Hopkins had been remarkably effective in controlling waste and corruption in a huge spending program, a program that had provided jobs for millions and contributed, in lasting ways, to the improvement of cities and towns all across America. But none of this mattered to Hopkins's detractors, especially after the anti–New Deal victories of 1938. Hopkins understood that his political future, which might include a run for the presidency in 1940, depended on his separating himself from the WPA. So with the encouragement of FDR, he made the decision to leave and to turn the leadership over to a no-nonsense military man

Ellen Woodward (National Archives and Records Administration)

with little knowledge of the arts, Colonel Francis C. Harrington. "With the natural regret born of leaving a fascinating job," Hopkins wrote FDR, "but with gratitude for opportunity you have offered of service in another and perhaps larger field, I tender my resignation as Administrator of the Works Progress Administration."[1]

Just before he left the WPA, Hopkins oversaw the strategy for defending Federal One in front of the Dies committee. Everyone in the Roosevelt camp despised Martin Dies and his committee. "I christen him 'Bubble Dancer' Dies," Harold Ickes wrote in his diary, "who cavorts lumberingly on the Congressional stage with nothing but a toy balloon with which to hide his intellectual nudity."[2] Hopkins was as eager as anyone else to strike back at the committee, which had played a key role in the defeat of New Deal candidates in 1938 and impugned not only Federal One, but Eleanor Roosevelt, whom they accused of naive fellow traveling.

Under the circumstances, it is surprising that Hopkins insisted on sending Ellen Woodward, a southern woman of firm convictions but with a superficial knowledge of the federal arts projects, before the committee. Certainly he knew that Hallie would give the committee a tougher fight than Woodward. Perhaps he wanted to avoid a confrontation at a time when his own future position in the cabinet was going to require congressional approval. Hallie, for her part, was baffled and frustrated. She had been working for weeks on a two-inch-thick brief that repudiated, point by point, all the claims made by prior witnesses attacking the project, and she was eager to make her own case.

"It seems incredible to me," she wrote *Daily News* critic Burns Mantle, "that that committee has been allowed for four months to interrogate witnesses who know absolutely nothing about the project except from what might be regarded as a worm's eye view. I had hoped to be allowed to present this brief myself on next Monday. Now for some inscrutable reason Mr. Hopkins has ruled that my administrative superior, Mrs. Ellen S. Woodward, is to read the brief."[3]

Perhaps Hopkins was hoping Ellen Woodward's southern accent would play well with Dies. But in fact Woodward was a courageous progressive by the standards of her state. After she attended a Federal Writers' Project party in Washington that included blacks, she was castigated by her state's senator Theodore Bilbo on the Senate floor. Bilbo protested against this violation (the mixed-race party) of a "flower of Mississippi womanhood" and promised that "if this had happened in Mississippi, long before the sounds of revelry had died, the perpetrator of this crime would be hanging from the highest magnolia tree."[4]

When she appeared before the committee on December 5, 1938, Ellen Woodward proved to be more than a decorative flower. She turned the committee's own language around and called them "un-American." The committee, she charged, was "violating the American system of fair play . . . Your committee, instead of hearing all available witnesses, chose to limit the inquiry to the testimony of a few witnesses most of whom were disqualified by their background to testify on the subject matter under investigation."

Woodward called the charge that the Federal Writers' Project and Theatre Project were dominated by Communists an "absurdity." And when Martin Dies suggested that attendance at a Communist meeting was sufficient proof that a person was a Communist, Woodward countered that she had attended many Republican meetings, even though she was a Democrat.

But when it came to detailed questions about particular plays and publications, Woodward was at a disadvantage. She attempted to defend the twenty-six plays Hazel Huffman had claimed were "communistic," citing the praise of critics in each instance. When Congressman Joe Starnes, a Democrat from Alabama, asked if she had read the plays, she countered by asking if anyone on the committee had read the plays.

This prompted a stern reprimand from Congressman Starnes: "You are not going to ask this committee questions because we are going to ask the questions."

The truth was, however, that Ellen Woodward had *not* read the plays, and that made it very difficult to defend them. When Starnes brought up *The Revolt of the Beavers*, which Brooks Atkinson had famously attacked as a primer for children in the "technique of revolution," causing the police commissioner to cancel his block of tickets, Woodward could counter only that Atkinson was "not infallible."

And when Starnes confronted her with quotations from an essay by WPA writer Richard Wright, Woodward didn't know enough about the source to defend the Writers' Project. The quotations came from a collection called *American Stuff: WPA Writers' Anthology*.

Starnes warned that the passages required "a strong constitution," then proceeded to read several excerpts from Wright's essay "The Ethics of Jim Crow," including this one: "If yuh say yuh didn't I'll rip yo' gut-string loose with this f—kin' [*sic*] bar, you black granny dodger. Yuh can't call a white man a liar 'n git away with it, you black son of a bitch."

Dies commented that the passage was the "most filthy thing I've ever read." And Starnes pressed Woodward, "Do you see anything rehabilitating in that?"

Woodward answered, "No, I do not."

The confrontation was the first of many in which the committee put the witness on the defensive by quoting a specific, purportedly offensive passage. Several times, the quote was by or about the experience of a black man and was read to a white woman. It was also usual for the committee to bring in material from outside the project, which turned out to be the case with the Wright essay. After getting some coaching from her advisers, Woodward was able to assert that the collection *American Stuff* had been written by WPA authors on their own time and published privately by Viking Press.[5]

What no one on the committee pointed out was that Richard Wright, who came to be recognized as one of the most important American writers of the century, *was* an avowed Communist, although a restive one, and was working at the time as Harlem editor of the *Daily Worker*. Wright's Communist Party membership was not as shocking to the southern-dominated Dies committee as the rage of his words—further proof, if such were needed, that what truly alarmed the committee about communism was its role in empowering black Americans.

Ellen Woodward, pressed for greater detail about both the Federal Writers' Project and the Federal Theatre Project, finally agreed to allow Hallie Flanagan and her Writers' Project counterpart, Harry Alsberg, to testify. For Joe Starnes, who had been claiming from the start that Ellen Woodward wasn't qualified to testify, this concession looked like a victory. But Starnes would come to view it very differently the next day, after Hallie Flanagan took the stand.

Even before she entered the hearing room that fateful morning, Hallie had acquired a sense of the committee's modus operandi. Most of the committee members kept silent most of the time. There were three activists: Congressman Dies, Congressman Joe Starnes, the Democrat from Alabama, and Congressman J. Parnell Thomas, Republican from New Jersey. Thomas was a freshman but an enthusiastic opponent of the New Deal, eager to jump in whenever he could. Congressman Dies hung back much of the time, interrupting only occasionally when the questioning wandered too far astray. Yet Dies, when he did rouse himself, asked the most relevant questions and sometimes made convincing points. Congressman Starnes, who came from Guntersville, Alabama, was prickly: He took offense when he felt witnesses weren't answering his questions. He also had a strong belief in the incriminating power of the printed word: It was he who quoted the offending Richard Wright passages to Ellen Woodward, and he would use the same tactic with Hallie Flanagan.

Within minutes after the hearing started, Hallie, knowing she had a limited amount of time to get in her points, managed to surprise Dies by describing her job as "combating un-American inactivity."

Dies was caught up short. "Inactivity?"

"I refer to the inactivity of professional men and women," she answered. "It was my job to expend the appropriation laid aside by congressional vote for the relief of the unemployed as it related to the field of theatre."

It was one of the few times Hallie was able to control the focus of the interrogation. Joe Starnes, the first questioner, turned to Hallie's background and particularly to her relationship with Russia. Hallie explained that she had spent her Guggenheim year in Europe, in 1926–1927, studying the theatre in twelve European countries.

Starnes: You spent most of the time in what country?

Flanagan: In Russia . . .

Starnes: Did you or [did you] not make the statement that the theatres in Russia are more vital and important?

Flanagan: Yes, I did find that. And I think that opinion would be borne out by any dramatic critic that you cared to call to this chair.

Starnes: What is it about the Russian theatre that makes it more vital and important than the theatres of the continent and the theatres of the United States?

Flanagan: I would be glad to do that [i.e., answer the question], but before doing it I would like to say that this is the first time since the Federal Theatre started that I have had occasion to answer that question. I have maintained consistently that we are starting an American theatre, which must be founded on American principles, which has nothing to do with the Russian theatre.

Starnes: I know, but you are not answering the question, Mrs. Flanagan.

Hallie did go on to answer the question, describing the Russian theatre's long tradition and current mix of political and classical theatre, as well as the European theatre she saw and the book she produced about her experiences, *Shifting Scenes*. She offered to read reviews of the book, in which "not one critic picked out anything that was in that book that was subversive or un-American." But Starnes refused the offer, claiming once again that she wasn't answering his question.

When the committee finally turned to the Federal Theatre Project, Hallie was able to make strong rebuttals to a number of charges. When J. Parnell Thomas, for instance, asked her about *The Revolt of the Beavers*, she informed the committee that a survey of fifty children who had seen the show suggested that they had taken the piece much more lightly than Brooks Atkinson. One child said the play "teaches us never to be selfish," and another praised how well the beavers made their way around the stage on roller skates. A third said the play taught that "it would be more fun if everyone was nine years old" in "a land of talking beavers on roller skates."

"I was very sorry that Mr. Brooks Atkinson, whose skill as a critic and whose learning are valued very greatly, was disturbed by this play," Hallie told the committee, "and that the police commissioner was disturbed; but we did not write this play for dramatic critics nor did we write it for policemen. We wrote it for children . . . we found that the children, the audience for which it was planned, enjoyed it and found, as I have told you, nothing subversive in it; and we went right on giving it."

When Thomas asked her if the Workers Alliance dominated the New York project, she told the committee that that wouldn't be possible, since most of the actors and backstage personnel in the project belonged to other, older unions that forbade their membership in the Workers Alliance. As for proselytizing on the project, Hallie told the committee, "I spent about half of my time the first year in the New York project, it is half of our project, and I have never seen these activities carried on. I have never seen subversive literature or Communistic literature on the project bulletin boards, nor to my knowledge, have I ever known of a Communist meeting being held on Project property."

The problem with all such denials, of course, was that the denier never had perfect knowledge, and the committee rarely failed to point this out. This was the insidious and long-lived weapon of such investigations. For instance, Hallie told the committee that she had affidavits from all the supervisors accused in previous testimony. "We have every one of those cases listed here with accompanying affidavits," she explained.

"That they are not Communists?" asked the chairman.

"No; on the charges," she answered.

"Did you ever secure from any of the supervisors affidavits as to whether they were not Communists?" asked Dies.

"No," she answered.

"So you are not able to produce any evidence on the question as to whether they are not Communists."

"No," Hallie was forced to answer.

It did no good to repeat, as she and Ellen Woodward had, that it was against federal law to discriminate on the basis of political or religious affiliation and that the question Dies wanted answered could not be asked.

There was one long exchange between Martin Dies and Hallie Flanagan that actually raised important questions about the role of a federally funded theatre. Early in the hearing, Hallie defended the word *propaganda*, which has come in our time to be entirely pejorative. "I should like to say very truthfully that to the best of my knowledge we have never done a play which was propaganda for communism, but we have done plays which were propaganda for democracy, propaganda for better housing."

This led to a line of questioning from Martin Dies. He asked how Hallie and the other directors decided on which plays they would produce.

"I'm glad you asked that question," she replied, "because it is an important one . . . We have always believed . . . that any theatre supported by Federal funds should do no plays of a subversive, or cheap, or shoddy, or vulgar, or outworn, or imitative nature, but only such plays as the Government could stand behind in a program which is national in scope and regional in emphasis and democratic in attitude."

Was the primary purpose entertainment or instruction? Dies asked.

"A good play must always entertain the audience," Hallie answered.

"That is the primary purpose of it?" asked Dies.

She added, "It . . . can also often teach."

Dies: It can be used as a vehicle, in other words, to impart to an audience certain ideas either along moral lines or along social lines or economic lines; isn't that a fact?

Flanagan: Yes.

Dies asked her about the Living Newspaper *Power*: "What is the objective of the play, what impression is it designed to bring in the mind of the audience . . . that public ownership is a good thing?

Flanagan: I think the first thing the play does is to make you understand more about power, where it comes from, and how it is evolved, about its whole historical use.

Dies: All right.

Flanagan: I think it also does speak highly for the public ownership of power.

Dies: Let us take just that one instance. We will assume, for the sake of argument, that maybe the public ownership of power is a desirable thing, but do you not think it improper that the Federal Theatre, using taxpayers' money, should present a play to the audience which champions one side of a controversy?

Flanagan: No, Congressman Dies; I do not consider it improper. I have just said that I felt that in a small percentage of our plays and pointed out that it is 10 percent that do hold a brief for a certain cause in accord with general forward-looking tendencies, and I say—

Dies: Who is to determine what is a forward-looking tendency?

Flanagan: Why, our play policy board chooses these plays . . .

Dies: All right. Now, would the same thing be true with reference to the public ownership of railroads because the policy board— . . . The point I am trying to draw out is, having accepted . . . the principle that you have the right to exhibit a play championing the right of public ownership of utilities, how could you draw the line having established that as a precedent?

Flanagan: Each play draws its own line. It must draw its own line. Each play makes its own contribution and has its own question.

Later in the exchange, Hallie said, "Let me answer it this way: If someone came up with a very good play proving that private ownership of railroads was the best possible thing, and the play was a good play, we would do it."

But then Dies asked if she would also do a play "showing public ownership of all the property in the United States . . . you would also exhibit that, would you not?"

Hallie responded, "No. I would not. We would stop with that, because that would be recommending the overthrow of the United States government, and I do not want that, gentlemen, whatever some of the witnesses may have intimated."

But Dies had made his point. Hallie insisted that the Federal Theatre Project rested on "the widest, most American base that any theatre has ever built upon," but she operated within certain liberal parameters that excluded the point of view of taxpayers like Martin Dies. Not long after the hearing, Hallie wrote a letter to the chairman, inviting him to come to New York to see *Pinocchio*, no doubt hoping to prove that the Federal Theatre did plays even he could love. But Dies never responded to the invitation.

In the course of his questioning about the Federal Theatre's repertoire, Dies brought up *Stevedore*, the play about a black man falsely accused of raping a white woman. From the point of view of southern congressmen, this play, with its clear parallels to the case of the Scottsboro boys, was a red flag, and Hallie knew it.

Perhaps that was why she initially denied that the project had ever done *Stevedore*. It was true that the play had not yet been produced in Los Angeles, although Hallie had fought with Colonel Connolly over his attempts to censor it. But *Stevedore had* been produced by the Negro unit in Seattle early on, and it seems unlikely she had forgotten that.

Dies then insisted on reading into the record an excerpt from *Stevedore*, a line spoken by a black man named Lonnie: "God damn dem, anyhow.

What dey think I am? Do I look like some kind of animal? Do I look like somebody who'd jump over a back fence and rape a woman?"

Chairman Dies used this excerpt to launch a speech: "I am not going to read all of the things in here, but there are numerous examples of absolutely vulgar statements and the frequent use of the Lord's name in a profane way. Now, what I am asking you is this: Do you think it is proper that the taxpayers' money of America should be used to produce a play to an American audience that contains such vulgarity and such profanity as that? I am not undertaking to indict you or anything you have done; I am just getting your idea as to whether you think that is a proper thing to do?"

Hallie chose not to argue. "I have no defense for blasphemy," she told Dies. When he asked her if it was proper for the Federal Theatre Project to produce such a play, she answered, "I think we should look into the matter."

Later, Congressman Starnes, the document man, insisted on reading a longer passage from *Stevedore* into the record. He had pulled out twelve lines from different spots in the play in which whites and blacks swore and used racial and sexual insults against each other. The word *rape* appears eight times in the excerpts, the word *nigger* appears eight times. As with the excerpt from Richard Wright, no one on the committee mentioned anything about the play's portrayal of racism, which was the true source of the committee's outrage. It had very little to do with taking the Lord's name in vain.

Stevedore was proof, in the eyes of Joe Starnes, that the project was "communistic." But the document that he offered as proof of Hallie Flanagan's subversive ideas was a 1931 article she had written for *Theatre Arts Monthly* about workers' theatres. It was entitled "A Theatre Is Born." It is clear from the tone of the article that Hallie Flanagan admired the attempt to create theatre in factories and mines. But Starnes wanted her to admit that she was involved in promoting these grassroots theatres, with their strong Communist precedents.

Starnes quoted paragraph after paragraph of this article, offering it as proof of Hallie Flanagan's views. She responded over and over that she was *reporting* on the phenomenon of workers' theatres, not endorsing them. She used the words *report* and *reporting* thirteen times in her answers to Starnes. But he either didn't understand the distinction or refused to make it.

For instance, the John Reed clubs were mentioned in the article.

Starnes: Now, John Reed, of course, is a Communist?

Flanagan: I was reporting on a meeting. I must go back and back to that point.

Starnes: Please answer my question. John Reed was a Communist, wasn't he?

Flanagan: He was.

Starnes: He was a Communist all through?

Flanagan: He was.

Despite her insistence that "I had nothing whatsoever to do with setting up the workers' theatre, nor with their project; nor was I ever associated with one," Starnes kept returning to the article as evidence of Hallie's Communist sympathies.

Starnes finally came to the penultimate paragraph of Hallie Flanagan's article on the workers' theatre. "This is your language I am quoting," he told Hallie, and proceeded to read:

"The workers' theatres are neither infirm nor divided in purpose. Unlike any art form existing in America today, the workers' theatres intend to shape the life of this country, socially, politically, and industrially. They intend to remake a social structure without the help of money—and this ambition alone invests their undertaking with a certain Marlowesque madness."

Starnes: You are quoting from this Marlowe. Is he a Communist?

Flanagan: I am very sorry. I was quoting from Christopher Marlowe.

Starnes: Tell us who Marlowe is, so we can get the proper reference, because that is all that we want to do.

Flanagan: Put in the record that he was the greatest dramatist in the period of Shakespeare, immediately preceding Shakespeare.

The spectators at the hearing erupted in hoots of laughter. When the hilarity died down, Starnes made a futile attempt to recover his dignity by making a reference to the Greeks and Euripides, but the damage was done.[6]

The next day, there were lengthy reports in most newspapers on Hallie Flanagan's testimony before the committee. The *Tribune* chose to mimic the committee, quoting long excerpts from Hallie's writings and ignoring the Starnes gaffe. But the others reported the incident, and some made it the headline. SO HALLIE FLANAGAN LANDS A HAYMAKER IN HER BOUT WITH DIES COMMITTEE, read the headline in the *Washington Daily News*, followed by the subhead "Rep. Starnes Suspects an Elizabethan Poet of Being a Red."

Heywood Broun wrote a sly column lavishing praise on Joe Starnes, noting that "he can detect a radical at a distance of more than three centuries." Kit Marlowe was, Broun observed, a bold iconoclast with a leaning toward atheism, and it caused him no end of trouble with the authorities.

"Joe Starnes certainly should not be criticized by the press or by his colleagues on the Dies committee," Broun wrote, "for it seems to me that he has shown in a striking way the need for further appropriation. His chance shot question as to the heresy of 'this Communist Marlowe' has brought the searchers for subversive activity all the way down to the year 1593 . . . which leaves the committee one up and only 345 years to go."[7]

Congressman Starnes's Marlowe gaffe made a great story, but it left Hallie Flanagan with an uneasy feeling. She knew it was dangerous to humiliate a member of Congress, even unintentionally. What was worse, her long brief, painstakingly prepared, was dismissed with an offhand promise to include it in the record. "I presented a brief not only refuting every charge brought but presenting irrefutable testimony as to the incompetence of the five previous witnesses," she wrote her ally, Senator Claude Pepper, a few weeks later. "Eventually, I assume that the material presented at this hearing will be printed but how many people will ever read it or hear of it? In the eyes of the public at large, the project and its director still stand falsely accused."[8] She was especially disappointed that she didn't get a chance to make a final statement. Dies had told her, "We will see about it after lunch." But after lunch, the committee brought on the next witness.

chapter seventeen

AN ACT OF CONGRESS

The next witness was Henry Alsberg, director of the Federal Writers' Project, who made matters worse. Alsberg presented himself as a fervent anti-Communist who had had to "clean up" the Writers' Project and who had even threatened to shut it down when sit-down strikes were imminent. The right-wing *Chicago Tribune* deemed Alsberg a "much more satisfactory witness," and even the *New York Times* noted that Hallie Flanagan "did not fare as well" as Alsberg. But although the Alsberg testimony may have gone over well with the committee, it reinforced the impression that the arts projects were teeming with Reds.

Within Federal One, Hallie Flanagan's firm and articulate defense of her programs made her a hero and diminished the stature of Alsberg. Even *Variety*, ever fickle, judged "the diminutive Vassarite" a victor in her first-round skirmish with the committee. The problem was that the first round was to be the only round. And Hallie's triumph was a double-edged sword. On the one hand, it won her many admirers among artists and intellectuals. On the other hand, it made the Federal Theatre Project and its spunky director the most appealing targets for the New Deal haters. The result, as the old year ended and the new one began, was a heightening of everything: The attackers became more strident, and new champions sprang in ever growing numbers to the project's defense. Hallie herself, because she had made a splash in her appearance before the Dies committee, became fair game for those who were out to slay the Federal Theatre Project and thus strike a blow against the whole WPA.

The first bad news came within days of the hearings, and it came from within: The WPA administration announced that fifteen hundred people were to be dropped from the rolls of the Federal Theatre and Writers'

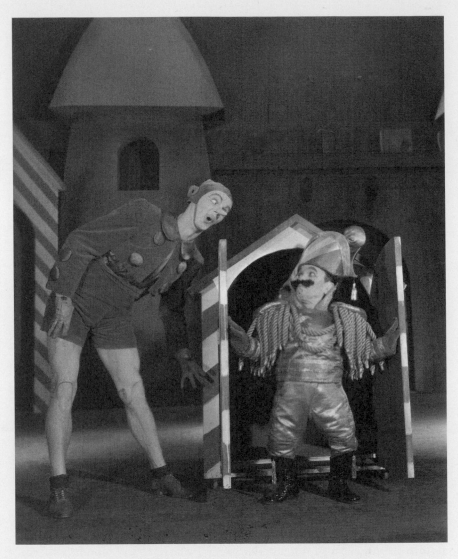

Pinocchio (National Archives and Records Administration)

Projects. The *Times* made a direct connection between the layoffs and the accusations in the Dies hearings, noting that the Federal Theatre and Writers' Projects "have been denounced as centers of Communist activity in testimony before the Dies committee." The *Times* offered no comment on the unfairness of either the hearings or the cuts, which hit writers and theatre people harder than anyone else.

Hallie received desperate letters. "I am sure you did not mean to cause me to lose my job," a circus performer wrote her. "I simply have to have my job! I support a psychopathic brother (veteran) and two children. I haven't a cent saved and haven't even a winter coat!"[1]

Ironically, the quality of Federal Theatre productions had never been higher. Right around the time that the cuts were announced, Bernard Shaw's *Androcles and the Lion* opened at the Lafayette Theatre in Harlem. Brooks Atkinson and John Mason Brown both judged it a much better show than the Theatre Guild's 1925 revival. "Androcles and the Lion do very well in Harlem," Atkinson wrote. "Shaw should give them his genial blessing."[2]

Soon after, *Pinocchio*, the Yasha Frank children's show that Hallie had seen and loved on the West Coast, opened at the Ritz in midtown Manhattan. *Pinocchio*, as commentator Willela Waldorf pointed out, was (unlike *The Revolt of the Beavers*) "a children's show without an agenda. Pinocchio is not a Communist nor yet a Fascist. Just a puppet who comes to life."[3] The production turned out to be a hit with adults as well as children. By the end of the month, *Pinocchio* was playing to standing room only and contributing to the best matinee business Broadway had enjoyed since 1929.[4]

In January, the slings and arrows continued. A group of Los Angeles clubwomen sent one hundred cables to FDR demanding the "immediate firing of Communist Hallie Flanagan wrecking the lives and morals of innocent people."[5] Even when Hallie left for a trip to the milder Midwest, she couldn't escape the enemy. In Detroit, a WPA assistant state administrator told her, "The Federal Theatre is Communistic." When she retorted that the Dies investigation was "no good," he said "with a sneer . . . 'Well, I notice Congress doesn't agree with you—they've just given them $100,000 more—and what's good enough for Congress is good enough for Detroit.'" Hallie wrote Phil: "There are times, my darling, when I really do have a chill of the blood at all this."

But then she watched a dress rehearsal of *The Merry Wives of Windsor* that was "fast and funny" and going out to Detroit schools. "I do love these people," she wrote Phil. "They have worked like slaves under terrible odds—they have no equipment and no theatre. Again—too cheap stuff in beautifully designed costumes—no proper lights. I grit my teeth seeing the unfairness of a lot of it."

In San Francisco, once again, she was greeted by cheers—and jeers. When she arrived at her hotel, there were fifty cards awaiting her from the Democratic Club of Los Angeles, her old nemesis, demanding her immediate removal on the grounds that she was a Communist. But there were also seven boxes of flowers. There was the Saint Francis, her favorite hotel, with its blue glass chandeliers, onyx pillars, and great lobby. And there was, above all, the Federal Theatre's coming role at the Golden Gate International Exposition—one of the main reasons for her trip.

The exposition was an extravaganza on a giant scale—a zany and impractical undertaking that made the Federal Theatre Project look restrained in comparison. It had begun, several years before, with the creation of a whole new island, to be called Treasure Island, in San Francisco Bay. This required the dredging of twenty million cubic yards of sea bottom and the hauling of thousands of square yards of sand and loam to create a new rectangular landmass, connected by causeway to the Bay Bridge.

So ambitious were the planners that they invented a new architectural style, "Pacifica," for the buildings on Treasure Island and erected structures in the art deco mode with names like Tower of the Sun and Court of the Moon and Stars, as well as exotic buildings for participating Pacific nations, with Cambodian, Mayan, and Incan motifs. The island's colors were said to represent "the first extensive application of chromotherapy." In the daytime, the effects were achieved with an abundance of flowering plants and tinted walls. At night, a vast $1.5 million network of electric lights produced the illusion of a magic city of light, floating on the waters of San Francisco Bay and visible from one hundred miles away. Those who needed something beyond chromotherapy could stroll over to the Gayway, a neon-lit cluster of carnival rides and strip clubs, including the Sally Rand Nude Ranch.

The exposition was a joint public and private undertaking, but it included a $1.5 million Federal Building. And within that building, sitting right along the water on one side of the rectangular island, was the very first theatre built by the Federal Theatre Project, using $65,000 in admission funds from Federal Theatre productions. It was actually three theatres in one: an outdoor theatre, with log seats and California trees; a children's theatre; and the main five-hundred-seat theatre, built of redwood, steel, and glass, with a clean sweep of a stage and a generous curve of steps leading down to the audience. The traditional curtain was nowhere in sight. And there was another experimental element: A lighting designer named George Izenour, who had come on to the Los Angeles project on the strength of a master's degree in physics, was given $26,000 to install his new system, which allowed him to orchestrate the lighting of a show from one "console." The Izenour console, first installed at the project's theatre on Treasure Island, changed stage lighting forever.

Hallie wrote about the exposition with the same enthusiasm she had lavished on the St. Louis World's Fair at age fifteen. San Francisco, she wrote Phil, "is a large, terrific, beautiful city and Treasure Island is the most beautiful Island you ever saw and our theatre is a dream and all three hit me simultaneously."[6] The Federal Building, she reported to Phil, was "the most superb building" in the entire fair, and the new theatre was "the most modern and beautiful in America."[7] She arrived on February 9 and discovered that expo commissioner George Creel was determined to open the Federal Theatre on February 18. But there were problems: The theatre was unfinished, and the architect had given expensive and terrible advice on color that was going to saddle them with blue rugs, rose walls, and seats in "the most horrible mottled orange leather—an eye splitting color which with the rose walls was so outrageous that everyone got really ill."[8] Lighting genius Izenour told her that the theatre couldn't possibly be ready before June. And the architect and engineer weren't on speaking terms, communicating in dumb show only.

This was exactly the kind of challenge Hallie relished. "We are working like hell," she reported, "to get something ready for Creel on the 18th . . . I'm spending my days in cold mud up to my knees (it is the rainy season) being idiotically happy."[9] Five days later, she wrote, "Darling, I haven't been so happy since the beginning of the project!"[10]

Hallie had planned a variety of shows for the expo: *Hansel and Gretel* for the children's theatre; Living Newspapers and dance for the outdoor space; and, in the large theatre, the second act of the Los Angeles Negro unit's production of *Run, Little Chillun*, a musical drama that had been one of the Federal Theatre Project's greatest successes.

Run, Little Chillun was created by the well-known black choral director Hall Johnson. He had thought at first that it would be a drama within one of his choral concerts, but the idea grew over time into a full-length piece, which combined traditional spirituals with his own compositions. The central character is a minister's son, torn between his loving and virtuous wife, a pillar of the Baptist Church, and a beautiful temptress from the wrong side of town, Sulamai, who lures him toward the New Day pilgrims and the practice of a religion of sensual joy and abandon. The final scene is a revival meeting at the Hope Baptist Church—"a scene that combines music and drama," in the words of one critic, "to electrifying effect."[11]

"It is the sort of show," wrote another critic, "that makes a spectator want to shake hands with perfect strangers sitting around him and congratulate them on being present."[12]

The Los Angeles production of *Run, Little Chillun*, which had opened in July 1938, was still selling out when Hallie visited the West Coast in February 1939, by which time a second all-black cast was performing the show in San Francisco to full audiences and rave reviews. Now it was to be the centerpiece of the Federal Theatre Project's opening day on Treasure Island.

The day before the opening was exhausting. Hallie and her team were "so tired we hated each other, Federal Theatre and even the thought of the Golden Gate International Exposition." Then came the day itself, "a day never to be forgotten, funny, wild, exciting, incredible, just as California is all of these things."

Everyone met in front of the Alcazar in San Francisco. The 150 members of the cast of *Run, Little Chillun* climbed onto trucks for the trip to Treasure Island, wearing cowboy hats, sombreros, and exposition scarves over their costumes. Hallie and others followed in the Federal Theatre station wagon. There were already two hundred thousand people on the island—fairgoers from all over the world—when they arrived.

"It was really a gorgeous affair," Hallie reported to Phil. "The great Tower of the Sun gleaming, the elephant Towers blazing, the avenues gay with bands and fountains . . . leaping into the air. There was the theatre clean and shining and everything ready and the showboat [where the actors were to live] gleaming in the bay and the pretty ushers very excited in their new uniforms . . . and we did five shows all on the day and hour scheduled three months ago."[13]

Hallie wrote a defiant memo to her regional and state directors: "I know that some of you have accused me of wishful thinking when I said that we were building a Federal Theatre on the grounds of the Golden Gate International Exposition. However, I can now report that it is built, it is beautiful, and above all, it is opening on schedule."[14]

There was to be one more moment of triumph during the West Coast tour. On March 2, while traveling south to Los Angeles on the train, Hallie heard an announcement on the radio: "The government's hit show, the Negro *Mikado*, . . . opened in New York to the plaudits of a distinguished audience, including the First Lady."[15]

The *Swing Mikado* was first performed by the Chicago Negro unit. The idea for it probably came from a couple of lead singers, who had "swung" a few numbers from the operetta in an earlier production. It was director Harry Minturn who picked up on the idea and expanded it, drawing on some prevalent stereotypes of the time. Minturn changed the setting from Japan to the South Sea islands, costumed his performers in generic "primitive" style, and got the singers and orchestra to introduce swing into some of the choruses.

The show opened fairly quietly, with mildly favorable reviews, but it soon became an enormous Chicago hit, breaking all-time house records at the Great Northern and selling out for weeks in advance. Hallie saw it and loved it when she stopped in Chicago on her trip west. She predicted in a letter to Phil that it would play forever: "Nothing so gusty, lusty and busty can possibly stop. It's crude, savage, funny, vulgar, beautiful, completely African in its pinks, reds and yellows. The scene with the moon, very round and yellow, rising over an ocean, violently in motion, bamboo trees in cellophane and a chorus of all shapes and sizes of Negroes starting romantic singing of 'The Flowers [That Bloom in the Spring]' and ending with the most abandoned truckin', cakewalk and swing is the top of Chicago." She added, "I think it would frighten Brooks [Atkinson] and John Mason Brown to death."[16]

But it turned out, when the Chicago troupe opened *Mikado* in New York on March 1, 1939, that Brooks and nearly all the other New York critics liked it just fine, as did the distinguished visitors, including not only Eleanor Roosevelt, but also Harry Hopkins and Mayor Fiorello LaGuardia. It was, wrote John Chapman in the *New York Daily News*, a "grand and genial show" and, in the words of Brooks Atkinson, "one of the most enjoyable nights [of] the Gotham season." As for Mrs. Roosevelt, whom one critic described as "the lady who thinks Marian Anderson should be allowed to sing anywhere she pleases,"[17] she told a reporter that she found it "very amusing," adding that the cast seemed to be having "such a good time."

Not long after she got the good news about *Mikado*, Hallie arrived in Los Angeles, where the situation had gone from bad to worse. The problem was finding a director who could manage the quarrelsome place. James Ullman, an experienced theatre man, had signed on for a while, but by the time Hallie got to Los Angeles in February, he had decided to resign. Afterward, he wrote a brilliant editorial piece in which he insisted there was absolutely nothing un-American about the Federal Theatre Project. "The Federal Theatre is *so* American that it hurts. It has tried so hard

to pattern itself on our democratic form of government and to do what its
workers and public want it to do that it is always within a hair's breadth of
sinking itself in the morass of its good intentions."[18]

Hallie herself surely agreed with this assessment. One of her reasons for
coming to California was to find a successor to Ullman. But the new WPA
administrator turned a deaf ear to all her suggestions. "On the last two
days of that visit," Hallie wrote her Los Angeles hosts afterward, "I felt like
a swimmer in water almost too deep . . . there is a very definite cabal
against putting in any person that I really want."[19] In the end, the WPA administrator ignored Hallie's suggestions and appointed his own man, who
promised a "housecleaning" and brought the lively Los Angeles project to
a dead stop. "It did not take an Act of Congress to end the Federal Theatre
for Southern California," Hallie wrote later. "It ended the day the local
WPA took over."[20]

Back in the East, it was looking more and more as though there *would* be
a lethal act of Congress. As Hallie had feared, the HUAC assault had made
the Federal Theatre Project a tempting target for other ambitious
anti–New Dealers. "Everyone [on the project] is scared," Hallie reported
from Washington in mid-March. "The Federal Theatre was attacked several times on the floor as an example of waste of money, inefficiency and
subversive propaganda. All the old lies are being told and no one disproves
them."[21]

Meanwhile, the Roosevelt administration was increasingly distracted
from the defense of the WPA by events on the world stage. On March 15,
1939, Hitler defied the Munich accords and annexed the last sections of
Czechoslovakia. Two weeks later, Franco declared victory in Spain,
strengthening the Fascist grip on Europe. Roosevelt was becoming preoccupied with the challenge of convincing an intensely isolationist nation
that the Nazi aggression in Europe and the Japanese aggression in the East
were threats that required American action. Astonishingly, however, the
Congress remained focused on the creeping Communist threat posed by
New Deal programs.

In early April, two new charges were brought by congressmen against
the Federal Theatre Project. One had to do with the unproductive history
of *Sing for Your Supper*, a musical revue that had been in rehearsal in New
York for over a year. The other was the charge of unfair competition: The
Federal Theatre, some argued, put commercial producers at a disadvantage
and refused, when opportunities arose, to turn over its productions to the
profit-making sector.

Charges of unfair competition had been in the air right from the start.

Most producers had come to believe that the Federal Theatre Project, with its low prices, brought in new theatregoers and stimulated business. But New York producer Brock Pemberton, a vocal Republican, had complained repeatedly of the project's incursion into the Broadway theatre district. And *Swing Mikado*, now a smash hit in New York, had raised the issue again. Several private producers, including Michael Todd, had offered to turn *Swing Mikado* into a commercial production in New York. But the Chicago cast had refused, for several reasons: They feared a private producer would cherry-pick the best performers from the cast and abandon the rest, and they feared the show wouldn't last when a commercial producer tripled the ticket price.

In early April, Democratic congressman Sol Bloom, an ally of New York commercial theatre, complained to the WPA's new director, Colonel Harrington, that the Federal Theatre Project had flouted congressional rules by refusing to accept offers from commercial producers, including Mike Todd, to mount *Mikado*. Harrington defended the project, explaining that no producer had come forth who promised to employ the complete Chicago cast. Within two weeks, however, the question became moot: Florence Kerr, who had taken over from Ellen Woodward as head of Federal One, announced that the *Swing Mikado* cast had accepted an offer of private employment. That, in turn, set up a head-to-head competition with *Hot Mikado*, a copy-cat production Todd had opened on Broadway after the Chicago troupe turned down his offer to produce *Swing Mikado*. *Swing Mikado*, with its new commercial producer, moved in across the street from *Hot Mikado*.

The battle of the two *Mikado*s created a stir on Broadway that was good for everyone's business. Todd had the more sophisticated costumes and the better-known performers, including Bojangles Robinson in a hilarious, freewheeling interpretation of the emperor Mikado. But the *Swing Mikado* had its own charms. And both, undeniably, came about because of a government-subsidized theatre, now in danger of extinction,

The *Sing for Your Supper* allegations were harder to deal with. *Sing for Your Supper* was planned as a lighthearted musical send-up of the Federal Theatre Project, similar to *O Say Can You Sing*, the revue that had been so popular in Chicago. But, as Hallie tried to explain to the Dies committee, the production had been plagued with problems, often related to the same issues that came up with *Swing Mikado*. A number of the leads, including Norman Lloyd of Living Newspaper fame, had been recruited for roles in commercial productions—roles that, according to congressional rules, they were obliged to accept. Along with the actors, four whole sketches had been lifted from *Sing for Your Supper* and put into other Broadway revues: The Federal Theatre, as a public entity, was defenseless against such piracies. Retraining in dance and singing was required for many of the cast, who were either rusty or untrained in musical theatre. What Hallie didn't say was that there was also a good deal of skittishness about some of the material, given the precarious situation the project was in. Hallie herself was watching nervously over the production, suggesting changes in lyrics and reminding the director that *Sing for Your Supper* had become "the narrow thread on which the fate of the entire Federal Theatre hangs."[22]

On April 7, Senator Robert R. Reynolds of North Carolina went after *Sing for Your Supper*, which he renamed *Bark for Your Food*, on the floor of the Senate. Reynolds cited a letter that was published in the Catholic magazine the *Tablet* charging that the revue was "a filthy thing" with a cast of "rank amateurs who seek between the downright filth to spread the leftist gospel and actually ridicule the United States Government." The letter went on to claim that top people in the project were getting huge salaries and chauffeurs, that rehearsals were costing enormous amounts in theatre rent, and that the lighting director, "a former electric appliance salesman named Abe Feder," had spent $40,000 to light the show with the result that you couldn't see anyone on the stage.

Anti-Semitism, in this letter as in others Hallie received, was blatant. The director of the show, Harold Hecht, was "a former Y.M.H.A. camp counselor, never had any connection with the theatre, but holds a degree from an East Side 'delicatessen college,' " the letter writer claimed. What's more, a "ghetto intellectual group" was responsible for throwing away the taxpayers' money.

The letter was unsigned, which prompted Senator James M. Mead, a Democrat from New York, to retort that "if I received a letter of this character, unsigned as it is, it would be immediately consigned to the wastebasket." Nonetheless, the attack was in the record, adding more fuel to the fire for those who wanted to believe the worst.[23] Twelve days later, South Carolina's James Byrnes introduced a bill in the Senate curtailing the WPA and sounding the "veritable death knell" for the Federal Theatre Project.[24]

In the House, a new and dangerous enemy of the Federal Theatre Project, a Democrat from Virginia named Clifton A. Woodrum, began an assault on the arts projects. Woodrum was head of the House Appropriations Committee and was crafting a bill that would return the WPA to the states. Following Dies's lead, the Woodrum committee embarked on an investigation targeting the arts projects.

On April 27, 1939, President Roosevelt sent a message to Congress that included a rather wordy defense of the "nonconstruction" programs, including Federal One. "I wish to state with emphasis," he told the Congress, "since the opposite view is frequently expressed, that the program of the Works Progress Administration should, as at present, include some projects of the non-construction type to meet the needs of those unemployed workers whose training is such that they are not adapted to employment on construction projects. The provision of work for those people at occupations which will conserve their skills is of prime importance." He concluded by expressing the hope that the House investigation of the WPA "will be guided along constructive lines, and if this is done I feel sure that its outcome will be to demonstrate the wisdom of the measures which have been adopted to meet the needs of the unemployed."

But destructive rather than constructive tactics were the rule in the Woodrum committee's investigation. An agent of the committee named H. Ralph Burton, an attorney for the DAR (Daughters of the American Revolution) and other right-wing groups, appeared in the New York offices of the Federal Writers' Project, where he distributed questionnaires to workers, then told them to list all affiliations and sign their names, certifying that all questions were answered honestly. Burton refused to comment on the character of his investigation, but those who were called to his suite for interrogation said that he was collecting data that would make it possible to abolish or drastically curtail the arts programs. He also seemed interested in evidence of amateurism on the projects and of failed theatrical productions.

Paradoxically, on the day after Burton came to New York City looking for Communist enemies of the state, the Fascist enemy Adolf Hitler delivered his most direct attack ever on the United States. Roosevelt had sent a cable to Hitler and Mussolini on April 15, naming thirty-one countries and asking for reassurance that they would not be attacked. Hitler responded with a speech in the Reichstag, heaping scorn on the president for two hours and hitting hard on the sensitive issue of recovery from the Depression.

"Mr. Roosevelt!" shouted the Führer. "I have conquered chaos in Germany, reestablished order and enormously increased production . . . I have succeeded in finding useful work once more for the whole of the seven million unemployed . . . You, Mr. Roosevelt, have a much easier task in comparison. You became President of the United States in 1933 when I became Chancellor of the Reich . . . Conditions prevailing in your country are on such a large scale that you can find time and leisure to give your attention to universal problems . . . My world, Mr. Roosevelt . . . is unfortunately much smaller."

In early May investigator Burton reported his "findings" to the Woodrum committee. According to Burton, *Androcles and the Lion*, *Prologue to Glory*, and *Haiti* were all box office failures, as was the much maligned *Sing for Your Supper*, which had finally opened. The opposite was true in every case, but the *New York Times* did not correct Burton's statement. Even *Sing for Your Supper*, which had been panned by the critics and which Burton described as "a sort of burlesque show" with a mixed black and white chorus, had actually turned into a hit at the box office.

Burton's lies did provoke a response from Brooks Atkinson, a response that is so thoughtful and complete in its understanding of the situation that it deserves to be quoted at length:

"Many things about the Federal Theatre are hard to defend," Atkinson wrote. "Being the most conspicuous of the WPA arts projects, it is the one Congress enjoys worrying most. Art seems like boondoggling to a Congressman who is looking for a club with which to belabor the administration, and there is always something in the Federal Theatre that can be blown up into a scandal. But for socially useful achievement it would be hard among the relief projects to beat the Federal Theatre, which has brought art and ideas within the range of millions of people all over the country and proved that the potential theatre audience is inexhaustible . . . the Federal Theatre has proved that people in general like the theatre and that plays with some sort of merit can run on indefinitely at $1.10. For half that price the Federal Theatre gave them last season one of the best performances of a play by George Bernard Shaw [*On the Rocks*] that this town has ever witnessed . . . Two million six hundred thousand people are employed on WPA projects throughout the country. Only 8040 of them are employed in the Federal Theatre—between one-third and one-quarter of 1 percent. Among the 2.6 million it would be hard to find another group of 8040 that has accomplished so much and given so rich a social return on the money . . . It has been the best friend the theatre as an institution has ever had in this country . . . In short, it deserves to be rescued from partisan politics which, on the one hand, are creeping into its administration, and on the other, are threatening to put it out of business."[25] Much of the Atkinson essay was later read into the *Congressional Record* by a defender of the project, Congressman Adolph J. Sabath, an Illinois Democrat.

At least as worrisome as the attacks of the Woodrum committee was the growing evidence that, as Atkinson hinted, WPA administrators wanted to wash their hands of the arts projects. On May 23, Hallie and her fellow arts directors were called into the office of Larry Morris, administrative supervisor of Federal One. Morris, a poet and editor himself, looked extremely uncomfortable as he prepared to give the directors the news. "Larry kept tearing up pieces of paper and putting them in little piles," Hallie reported. Then, after clearing his throat repeatedly, he told them that Colonel Harrington, current head of the WPA, was going to tell the Woodrum committee that the arts projects would be removed from federal jurisdiction on July 1. Harrington had decided, Morris explained, that the arts projects didn't need national guidance. He was also sick of the "headaches" the arts projects caused.

The arts directors drafted a letter of protest to the president and started making frantic phone calls to try to change Harrington's mind. "I kept thinking," Hallie said, "not with a bang but a whimper." Then she added characteristically, "But I'm not going to let it be a whimper. By tomorrow I'm going to try to fight again."[26]

The Woodrum committee continued to attack. On June 2, the committee claimed that 75 percent of those on the Federal Theatre Project and 50 percent of those on the Federal Writers' Project had no right to relief. On June 6, investigator Burton charged that there was so much lighting equipment used on *Sing for Your Supper* that the actors' ankles got sunburned. Charles Walton, the failed director who had testified before the Dies committee, told the Woodrum committee that New York theatrical people all believed Hallie Flanagan was a Communist and should be dismissed.

Finally, on June 15, the Woodrum committee produced a relief bill, giving President Roosevelt $1.7 billion but urging changes in the WPA that would undermine its effectiveness.[27] The bill stipulated, among other things, that all supervisory personnel on the WPA must swear allegiance to the Constitution. When Woodrum announced that the bill barred all funds for the Federal Theatre Project, there was a burst of applause from many congressmen. The Federal Theatre, Woodrum asserted, "has produced nothing of merit. Every theatrical critic of any note has expressed his disapproval of these productions," he said.[28]

By the time Woodrum made that claim, Hallie had decided that she had nothing to lose by going public, even if it meant defying her bosses. She was convinced, in any case, that they no longer supported the Federal Theatre Project. "Our enemies are within," she wrote Phil. "Harrington, Kerr, even Morris are all against us and secretly fighting us. It is open war and I am glad. We can and must win."[29]

The support Hallie Flanagan marshaled for the Federal Theatre Project over the next two weeks was astonishing. On June 17, the day the House was scheduled to vote on the relief bill, thirteen major New York drama critics wrote to Congress contradicting Woodrum. "If Mr. Woodrum had looked up the record he could not possibly have made his statements concerning critical reaction," wrote the critics. "We have had many occasions to praise productions of the Federal Theatre in New York, many of which have been distinguished contributions to the art of the theatre."

Eminent theatre people, including Lee Shubert, Richard Rodgers, Moss Hart, and Helen Hayes, protested to congressmen about the "grossly unfair" exclusion of the Federal Theatre, which had "brought economic relief and moral regeneration to thousands of theatre workers, who after a lifetime devoted to their art found themselves facing destitution." Eddie Cantor sent a message to the White House, praising the Federal Theatre Project as "one of the finest things this Administration has done." Even Colonel Harrington, whom Hallie suspected of desertion, came through with an announcement that twenty-five hundred actors had found their way back to regular paying jobs, thanks to the Federal Theatre Project. In Times Square, about one hundred Federal Theatre workers were out each day, on their own time, soliciting signatures on a petition to save the Federal Theatre Project.[30]

Hallie herself sent an open letter to Congressman Woodrum challenging the "inaccurate and often grossly untrue testimony given by your investigators" and expressing her concern about "the false impression given to the country by the repetition of so distorted a picture of a project which has since its inception employed thousands of professional theatre workers and which has . . . benefited millions of other Americans." The charge that the Federal Theatre had Communists on its rolls seemed to argue that "you have in your possession a record of the membership of the Communist Party. We have not. Nor according to rules which Congress has laid down are we at liberty to ask a relief client how he votes any more than we have a right to ask him what church, if any, he attends." She ended by countering the committee's accusations with a recitation of the Federal Theatre's accomplishments.[31]

The defense of the Federal Theatre Project came too late to influence the House. In the debate of the bill, Congressman Everett Dirksen of Illinois, who had once criticized a touring supervisor on the project for allowing blacks to sit in the orchestra seats in Peoria,[32] rose to attack the Federal Theatre. He claimed that the Federal Theatre had "prostituted" the theatre. *Sing for Your Supper*, he said, was "small, trashy kind of stuff . . .

"If there is anything in it . . . that contributes to the cultural or education benefit or uplift of America, I will eat the whole manuscript," Dirksen promised. In a raucous and lengthy session, in which amendments were shouted down before they could even be heard, the congressmen voted

373–21 to approve the Woodrum bill, cutting off funds to the Federal
Theatre Project and requiring the other Federal One programs to rely on
the states for much of their support.

"Any Congressman can move his colleagues to tears by talking of the
slaughter of little pigs under the New Deal," wrote Heywood Broun afterward, "but all eyes were dry as the vote rolled through to let undiscovered
writers, actors, playwrights and painters starve quietly and make no fuss
about it."[33]

The Senate was now the only hope, and Hallie sought support everywhere she could. Eleanor Roosevelt, after a meeting with Hallie in Hyde
Park, wrote in her column "My Day" that "I am just as concerned as she is
about the proposed ending of the federal theatre projects." She added with
surprising candor: "I know that this project is considered as dangerous because it may harbor some Communists, but I wonder if Communists occupied in producing plays are not safer than Communists starving to death . . .
I can only hope that in the Senate some changes may be deemed wise . . .
there are a great many who feel that we are sacrificing something which has
meant much to the development of culture in many parts of this country."[34]

In California, 850 members of the Screen Actors Guild, the Writers
Guild of America, and the Directors Guild of America gathered at the
Hollywood Playhouse for a national broadcast urging the senators to pass
the Wagner-Pepper-Downey amendment restoring the Federal Theatre
and the arts projects to the WPA budget. Lionel Barrymore and James
Cagney were among those who spoke, and Al Jolson sang the Depression
song "Brother, Can You Spare a Dime?" Then an all-star cast presented
Hallie Flanagan's dramatic narrative about a Federal Theatre touring company, entitled *The Florida Wheel*.[35] Hallie sent heartfelt letters of thanks to
all the participants.

Orson Welles, newly notorious after his *War of the Worlds* broadcast, defended the Federal Theatre Project on *American Forum of the Air*, a round-
table that included three representatives and a senator. "We feel in the
theatre that our very life's blood is the Federal Theatre," Orson told the
panel. "We believe that we depend upon the Federal Theatre not only for
new mediums but a new audience." He warned opponents that "you are
legislating against one of the most important things that ever happened in
a Democratic government."[36]

By far the most widely publicized event of the Federal Theatre Project
drive was the visit of the flamboyant actress Tallulah Bankhead to Capitol
Hill, where she attempted to persuade her uncle, Democratic senator John
H. Bankhead of Alabama, and her father, House Speaker William B.

Bankhead, also of Alabama, to support the Federal Theatre amendment. "Everybody in our family goes to Congress," Tallulah explained to Heywood Broun, "unless he'd rather raise cotton."[37]

Tallulah flew in from New York, where she was starring in Lillian Hellman's *The Little Foxes,* and greeted her uncle John with a big hug. "Uncle John," Tallulah said, "of course you'll vote to do something for the unemployed actors."

"No," answered Uncle John, "I don't think I will. These city fellows in Congress never vote to do anything for our farmers."

Tallulah started off her testimony before the Senate subcommittee with a flourish, tossing off her blue felt slouch hat and perching herself on the green baize-covered committee table. But her talk was serious. She credited the Federal Theatre Project with helping to revive the road and stimulating interest in the classics. And she argued that it had given "new life and hope and opportunity to earn their living in their own profession to thousands of actors, musicians, stage hands, scenic artists and other theatre workers." As she reached the end of her testimony, she burst into seemingly genuine tears. "I beg you from the bottom of my heart not to deprive these people of the chance to hold up their heads with the dignity and self-respect which is the badge of every American." The senators applauded the performance.[38]

"I don't know how much longer this will go on," Hallie wrote Phil two days after Tallulah's appearance. "It goes tomorrow to the Committee of the whole and by Monday may reach the House. We have to be on day and night duty. But darling, I really think we are going to get the project put back." Later in the letter she added, "But obviously we do not understand politics and may lose the whole thing. I feel as if I could not bear it if we did. We run out of money on June 30 and on that date, if the bill isn't through, everyone is out and the offices go under martial law."[39]

On June 28, Senator Robert Reynolds of North Carolina assailed the Federal Theatre Project once again on the Senate floor, warning of the "danger to America from the 'red' propaganda being broadcast by the majority of plays" and claiming that the American taxpayer was underwriting "dissemination of the revolution made in Russia." He claimed to know, too, that "real actors" were not employed. The actors play to empty houses, he informed the Senate, and he added, "I doubt that Mrs. Flanagan has ever had any real experience in the cold practicalities of presenting dramatic productions." Reynolds offered a list of titles of project plays, claiming they "bear the trade-mark of 'red' Russia in their titles." Among the offending titles were *Up in Mabel's Room, A New Deal for Mary, A New Kind of Love, A Boudoir Diplomat,* and *Cheating Husbands.*[40] Then he got to his real point: "Through such material the cardinal keystone of Communism—free love and racial equality—is being spread at the expense of the god-fearing, home-loving American taxpayer."

Once again, the story that Sally Saunders told the Dies committee, about being invited on a date by a black man, was introduced into the debate. Reynolds reminded his Senate colleagues that a woman named Trudy had said that the black man in question was entitled to life, liberty, and the pursuit of happiness, too. "Do you think the American taxpayers would approve of our financing Trudy in her pursuit of happiness with whatever men of whatever color she might choose, under whatever condition and in whichever gutter might please her?"

Despite Reynolds's long diatribe, on June 29 the Senate approved a bill that modified the House measure in several ways and continued limited funding for the Federal Theatre Project. But the victory was short-lived. When the Senate-House conference convened to draw up a compromise bill, House members refused to accept the Senate revision. Senator Alva Adams of Colorado said, when he returned to the Senate floor to report on the conference, that he was astounded by the hostility of the House members toward the theatre project. "I have never seen any conferees more anxious to eliminate something than were the House men about the theatre program. They put on a show of their own to get the project stricken out. We had to yield or the conference would still be going on."[41] The final bill, passed by House and Senate, once again eliminated the Federal Theatre Project.

Lee Simonson, theatre producer, designer, and writer, wrote Hallie after the vote that "the intellectuals of the Senate are evidently no match for the backwoods bigots of the House when they go into conference. Which is depressing enough, if the throttling of the real beginning of a National Theatre, which was of course what the FTP was, were not even more depressing. Millions of people. The common peepul that the same Congressmen bray their devotion to, were seeing and enjoying theatre for the first time at prices they could afford. So the benighted bastards had to deprive them of it."

Simonson added, "It's a great pity that terrorism has gone out of fashion. A single well-planted bomb scattering the entrails of the Woodrum Committee and their vestigial brains all over the floor, wainscoting and ceiling, would have had a salutary effect on their colleagues."[42]

Hallie Flanagan wrote back gratefully, "It was a magnificent fight in the Senate, but we drew the same horrible House Committee, and they put us out of business." She added, "You have no conception of how much vicarious satisfaction I got out of your remarks anent well-planted bombs."[43]

The WPA bill came over from the Congress to the White House on

June 30. Roosevelt objected to several provisions, including the elimination of the Federal Theatre Project, which, he said, "singles out a special group of professional people for a denial of work in their own profession."[44] But the president, with some reluctance, signed the bill into law.

On June 30, 1939, curtains came down for the last time in theatres all over America: on *The Merry Wives of Windsor* in Detroit, on *The Taming of the Shrew* in Seattle, on *Prelude to Swing*, which was turning people away in Philadelphia. In Chicago, the *Swing Mikado* troupe wanted to put on one final show but were told that it would be "criminal" to use government-owned sets and costumes. The thousand ticket holders for that night's show were given their money back.

In San Francisco, the cast of the vaudeville revue *Two a Day* sat in the dark in the front row of the Alcazar Theatre, listening to their piano player up onstage, running his fingers listlessly over the keyboard. A sign declaring NO SHOW TODAY had been hung outside the theatre, even though the performance had been selling out night after night. Only the technical staff was busy—tearing down the twenty-five sets and rolling up the thirty-five backdrops so that they could go into storage forever.

In New York, the cast of *Pinocchio* staged a new final scene. On other nights, the story ended happily when Pinocchio the puppet turned into a flesh-and-blood boy. On the final night, Pinocchio turned into a boy, but then he turned back into a puppet. A three-foot wooden figure, created especially for the occasion, was brought onto the stage and laid out on top of a coffin. The stagehands—all WPA employees—struck the sets in full view of the audience, and the actors gathered around the coffin and recited, "Thus passed Pinocchio. Born December 23, 1938 [the date of the show's opening], died June 30, 1939. Killed by an Act of Congress."[45]

A few days later, at the Adelphi Theatre on Broadway, a few dozen actors sat around and watched as the crew disassembled *Sing for Your Supper.* Up onstage, the workers piled up dozens and dozens of lights—the same lights that a congressman claimed had given the actors sunburn. A large truck pulled up to the dock on Fifty-third Street, and the crew loaded the pink-and-gray sets into it, piece by piece.

As the truck began to pull out, an emaciated old actor pointed to it with his bone-handled cane. "There goes our living," he told the others. "There's no hope now."[46]

FOUR FEBRILE YEARS

After it was all over, Hallie Flanagan wrote in the *New York Times* that the congressmen who went after the Federal Theatre were "afraid of the Project—but not for the reasons they mentioned on the floor of the Congress. They were afraid of the Federal Theatre because it was educating the people of its vast new audience to know more about government and politics and such vital issues of the day as housing, power, agriculture and labor. They were afraid, and rightly so, of thinking people."[1]

Hallie's analysis gave the congressmen too much credit. Of course they feared educating their constituents, but they also feared educating themselves. Over and over, Hallie pleaded with the congressmen to read her detailed brief, which completely discredited the witnesses brought up before the Dies and Woodrum committees and refuted their egregiously false charges. She also invited them to take in a Federal Theatre production.

But the congressmen who attacked the Federal Theatre Project didn't want to even imagine the kind of theatre Hallie Flanagan was working to create. "The truth is," Brooks Atkinson wrote, "that Congressmen as a lot do not like, respect or trust the theatre. To most of them the theatre will always be a leg show."[2] When theatre wasn't a leg show, it was the extreme opposite: high culture for the rich and comfortable, performed by a handful of elite artists like Katharine Cornell and Basil Rathbone. Theatre, as Hallie would say, for the penthouse class.

The contrast between this constricted view of theatre's possibilities and the alternative, as it unfolded during the reign of the Federal Theatre Project, could not have been greater. The project nurtured some very big talents, like Orson Welles, Marc Blitzstein, Arthur Miller, and Richard

Wright. But for many other working theatre people, the Federal Theatre was not a ticket to fame but a lifeline—a job which gave hope and, at the same time, opened up new artistic possibilities. It turned leg shows into satirical reviews. It gave vaudeville comedians a chance to play Shakespeare. And it taught old Shakespeareans new tricks.

For "four febrile years," in Brooks Atkinson's phrase, it seemed right and proper to send a troop of government-subsidized actors to entertain flood victims, to fashion a unique show to please the CCC boys, and to stage an all-black *Macbeth* for the residents of Harlem. It even seemed possible, within the Federal Theatre Project, to get past racism: to insist on integrated audiences, to put black and white actors together on a stage, and to agree, in the memorable words of *Haiti* director Maurice Clark, that "only nitwits take racism seriously."

But this idea of racial equity was the most alarming of all to many in Congress. Certainly, as Hallie noted in her *Times* piece, the congressmen were looking for "a way to hang the New Deal in effigy" and chose "for that purpose a project small and scattered enough so that protest would not cost too many votes, and yet potent enough to stir up prejudice."

Puritanism added fuel to the fire, as when Senator Dirksen went after the vaudeville humor in *Sing for Your Supper.* Charges of immorality and blasphemy went over well back home. So did the charge of communism. There *were* Communists in the Federal Theatre, especially in New York, and they made a convenient target.

But so many things were "Communist" in the minds of these congressional critics. They could have made a plausible case against such doctrinaire productions as *Injunction Granted* and *The Revolt of the Beavers.* But they put plays like *Up in Mabel's Room, A Boudoir Diplomat,* and *Cheating Husbands* on their "red" list as well, along with a play about the young Abe Lincoln. What truly scared the congressional attackers, much more than communism, was the racial cooperation that progressives, along with Communists, championed on the Federal Theatre Project. When opponents of the project got up to speak in the House and in the Senate, they might start off by talking about incompetence, or boondoggling, or communism, or immorality, but they wound up talking about race. Sally Saunders, with her story about being asked out on a date by a black man, trumped all the arguments that all the illustrious defenders of the Federal Theatre Project could muster.

For a while, Hallie Flanagan refused to quit. She told people that the end of the project was merely an "intermission," and continued to advocate for her dream of a nationally funded federation of theatres: three large city theatres to set standards for the country and four regional theatres, each with its own mission. But then came a lasting intermission: World War II. Many who lost their jobs on the Federal Theatre Project went to work for the USO, entertaining the troops. On Treasure Island in San Francisco Bay, one of Hallie's proudest achievements, the first and only theatre built for the project was transformed, along with the Tower of the Sun and Court of the Moon and Stars and all the other buildings of the Golden Gate International Exposition, into a naval base and military training school.

One piece of live theatre survives from the days of the Federal Theatre Project. *The Lost Colony*, the Paul Green pageant about Sir Walter Raleigh's failed attempt to establish a European foothold in the New World, continues to draw large crowds to Roanoke Island in North Carolina every summer. Otherwise, the Federal Theatre Project lives on only in the archives and in the stories of those who took part.

Hallie Flanagan coveted the stories. Once, after she learned about a lame barrel diver playing his first serious dramatic role, she wrote her colleague Howard Miller, "That's my story old dear, and don't you dare tell it—it's the whole Federal Theatre in a nutshell, or shall we say, in a barrel?"[3] The stories enlivened her book *Arena*, which came out to high praise in the year after the project ended. She wrote another book as well, entitled *Dynamo*, about her experimental work in college theatre before and after the project. The dynamo of the title was defined as a force which uses energy to produce power—an apt description of Hallie Flanagan herself. But Hallie's onstage successes were accompanied by private sorrow. In the winter of 1940, while she was still working on *Arena*, Phil Davis died of a stroke. And in 1946, after taking a dean's position at Smith College which turned out to be a mistake, Hallie began to notice the first symptoms of Parkinson's disease. She kept on working, but with diminishing energy. When asked about a future federal theatre, she answered, "I don't believe in revivals, in art or in life."[4]

A revival remains unlikely. Like the rest of the New Deal programs, the Federal Theatre Project could succeed because people believed that government was their best ally in a desperate time. "The Government employs us / Short hours and certain pay," sing the workers in *Power*, "Oh things are up and comin' / God bless the T.V.A." Very few Americans could now sing the government's praises with similar conviction. Neither they, nor their representatives, are likely to take a chance on government-sponsored art of any kind on a large scale.

Nor would the "free, adult and uncensored theatre" promised by Harry Hopkins be any easier to achieve now than it was then. Perhaps Brooks

Atkinson was right to conclude that a permanent, government-sponsored theatre is an impossibility in America. "To the official mind in general," he noted, "the theatre looks dangerous and depraved. Everything it does looks in advance like a threat against established institutions and standards of decency."[5] And that, Hallie Flanagan would surely say, is exactly as it should be.

And yet, for a brief time in our history, Americans had a vibrant national theatre almost by accident. What began as a relief project, without big names or one grand theatre, found a vast new audience, ready to laugh and cry and cheer and hiss and even, dangerously, to think.

ACKNOWLEDGMENTS

Thanks to all those who have helped me as readers and listeners: Sally Brady, Christopher Buchanan, Alison Cohen, Judith Cohen, Kathryn Kirshner, Paul Levy, Evy Megerman, Mary Mitchell, Fran Nason, Barbara Raives, Rich Remsberg, Judy Richardson, Mark Schneider, Peggy and Tom Simons, Marjorie Waters, and Nancy and Dennis Wynn. Thanks also to the members of my biography group, who challenged me to go deeper: Joyce Antler, Fran Malino, Megan Marshall, Lois Rudnick, Judith Tick, Roberta Wollons. Thanks to Gene Black especially, because he gave me the benefit of his wisdom as an American historian. Thanks to Joanne Bentley, for her trust. To Barbara Goldsmith, for a crucial intervention. To Betty Flanagan and her children, Hallie and Fred, for their insights, and to Robert Schnitzer and Eric Bentley for theirs. Thanks to Professor Bradley Bateman and Bill Menner, for helping me to understand Grinnell's history. To Merloyd Lawrence, for showing me Harry in a different light, and to the good work of my editor, Kathy Belden, and photo researcher Michael Dolan. To my dear children and grandchildren, who make me so happy, and to the memory of my mother, Esther Taft Quinn, who loved both books and the theatre.

Finally, I want to thank two people who have been looking over my shoulder throughout the writing of this book: my agent, Jill Kneerim, and my husband, Dan Jacobs. Jill had a vision for this book from the beginning that has made it so much more ambitious, and more fun, than it would have been otherwise. And Danny is my first and most important reader. He is present in all my books and in all the best moments of my life.

SELECTED BIBLIOGRAPHY

Most of the material for this book comes from the following sources: the Special Collections at Vassar College; the Hallie Flanagan papers in the Billy Rose Theatre Collection of the New York Public Library for the Performing Arts at Lincoln Center; the Federal Theatre Project Collections at the National Archives in College Park, Maryland, and the Library of Congress in Washington, D.C.; the Special Collection and Archives at George Mason University in Virginia; and the Hopkins papers at the Franklin D. Roosevelt Library in Hyde Park, New York.

The materials at George Mason require special comment. After the demise of the Federal Theatre Project, many documents, including photographs, posters, and programs, were left in boxes in an abandoned airport hangar in Baltimore for thirty-four years. Then two professors at George Mason, Lorraine Brown and John O'Connor, discovered the treasure and persuaded the Library of Congress, the putative custodians, to let them take the materials to George Mason. In 1992, the Library of Congress decided that they cared about the materials after all and took them back. But the lasting contribution of O'Connor and Brown is inestimable. Most important, they interviewed over 350 Federal Theatre Project personnel in the 1970s. Most of the people they interviewed are now dead, but they live on through those interviews, which have been invaluable to me in the writing of this book.

I have chosen not to annotate FDR's speeches and comments, as they are widely available from many sources.

BOOKS

Adams, Henry H. *Harry Hopkins: A Biography*. New York: G. P. Putnam's Sons, 1977.

Atkinson, Brooks. *Broadway*. New York: Macmillan, 1970.

Auerbach, Jerold S. *Labor and Liberty: The La Follette Committee and the New Deal*. Indianapolis: Bobbs-Merrill Co., Inc., 1966.

Bendiner, Robert. *Just Around the Corner*. New York: Harper & Row, 1967.

Bentley, Joanne. *Hallie Flanagan*. New York: Alfred A. Knopf, 1988.

Bernstein, Irving. *Turbulent Years: A History of the American Worker 1933–1941*. Boston: Houghton Mifflin Co., 1970.

Blitzstein, Marc. *The Cradle Will Rock*. New York: Random House, 1938.

Brinkley, Alan. *Voices of Protest: Huey Long, Father Coughlin, and the Great Depression*. New York: Knopf, 1982.

Buttita, Tony, and Barry Witham. *Uncle Sam Presents: A Memoir of the Federal Theatre, 1935–1939*. Philadelphia: University of Pennsylvania Press, 1982.

Callow, Simon. *Orson Welles: The Road to Xanadu*. New York: Viking, 1995.

Carlson, Oliver, and Ernest Sutherland Bates. *Hearst: Lord of San Simeon*. New York: Viking Press, 1936.

Childs, Marquis. *I Write from Washington*. New York: Harper & Brothers, 1942.

Clurman, Harold. *The Fervent Years: The Story of the Group Theatre & the 30's*. New York: Hill & Wang, 1957.

Countryman, Vern. *Un-American Activities in Washington State*. Ithaca: Cornell University Press, 1951.

Cowley, Malcolm. *The Dream of the Golden Mountains: Remembering the 1930s*. New York: Viking, 1964.

Crane, Milton, ed. *The Roosevelt Era*. New York: Boni & Gaer, 1947.

Denning, Michael. *The Cultural Front*. New York: Verso, 1996.

Dies, Martin. *The Trojan Horse in America*. New York: Arno Press, 1977.

Egan, Timothy. *The Worst Hard Time: The Untold Story of Those Who Survived the Great American Dust Bowl*. Boston: Houghton Mifflin Co., 2006.

Elam, Harry J., and David Krasner, eds. *African American Performance and Theatre History*. New York: Oxford University Press, 2001.

Ellis, Edward Robb. *A Nation in Torment: The Great American Depression, 1929–1939*. New York: Coward-McCann, 1970.

Engel, Lehman. *This Bright Day: An Autobiography*. New York: Macmillan Publishing Co., Inc., 1974.

Flanagan, Hallie. *Arena*. New York: Duell, Sloan and Pearce, 1940.

———. *Dynamo*. New York: Duell, Sloan and Pearce, 1943.

———. *Shifting Scenes of the Modern European Theatre*. New York: Coward-McCann Inc., 1928.

Fraden, Rena. *Blueprints for a Black Federal Theatre, 1935–39*. New York: Cambridge University Press, 1994.

France, Richard. *The Theatre of Orson Welles*. Lewisburg, Pa.: Bucknell University Press, 1977.

Freidel, Frank. *Roosevelt: A Rendezvous with Destiny*. Boston: Little, Brown & Co., 1990.

Gassner, John. *Dramatic Soundings: Evaluations and Retractions Culled from 30 Years of Dramatic Criticism*. New York: Crown, 1968.

Gelb, Arthur and Barbara. *O'Neill*. New York: Harper & Row, 1962.

Gellerman, William. *Martin Dies*. New York: John Day Company, 1944; reprinted by Da Capo, 1972.

Giffen, Allison, and June Hopkins, eds. *Jewish First Wife, Divorced.* Lanham, Md.: Lexington Books, 2003.

Gill, Glenda. *No Surrender! No Retreat!: African-American Pioneering Performers of 20th Century American Theatre.* New York: St. Martin's Press, 2000.

———. *White Grease Paint on Black Performers: A Study of Federal Theatre, 1935–39,* American University Press Series, vol. 40. New York: P. Lang, 1988.

Goldstein, Malcolm. *George S. Kaufman: His Life, His Theatre.* New York: Oxford University Press, 1979.

———. *The Political Stage.* New York: Oxford, 1974.

Goodman, Walter. *The Committee: The Extraordinary Career of the House Committee on Un-American Activities.* New York: Farrar, Straus & Giroux, 1968.

Goodwin, Doris Kearns. *No Ordinary Time.* New York: Simon & Schuster, 1994.

Gordon, Eric A. *Mark the Music: The Life and Work of Marc Blitzstein.* New York: St. Martin's Press, 1989.

Hair, William Ivy. *The Kingfish and His Realm: The Life and Times of Huey P. Long.* Baton Rouge: Louisiana State University Press, 1991.

Hamilton, Charles V., *Adam Clayton Powell, Jr.: The Political Biography of an American Dilemma.* New York: Atheneum, 1991.

Heller, Adele, and Lois Rudnick, eds. *1915: The Cultural Moment.* New Brunswick, N.J.: Rutgers University Press, 1991.

Henderson, Mary C. *The City and the Theatre: The History of New York Playhouses.* New York: Back Stage Books, 2004.

Hickey, Neil, and Ed Edwin. *Adam Clayton Powell and the Politics of Race.* New York: Fleet Publishing Corp., 1965.

Hickok, Lorena. *One Third of a Nation: Lorena Hickok Reports on the Great Depression.* Urbana: University of Illinois Press, 1981.

Hill, Edwin G. *In the Shadow of the Mountain: The Spirit of the CCC.* Pullman, Washington: Washington State University Press, 1990.

Hill, Errol G., and James V. Hatch. *A History of African American Theatre.* Cambridge: Cambridge University Press, 2003.

Himelstein, Morgan Y. *Drama Was a Weapon: The Left-Wing Theatre in New York, 1929–41.* New Brunswick, N.J.: Rutgers University Press, 1963.

Hopkins, Harry. *Spending to Save: The Complete Story of Relief.* New York: W. W. Norton, 1936.

Hopkins, June. *Harry Hopkins: Sudden Hero, Brash Reformer.* New York: St. Martin's Press, 1999.

Houseman, John. *Run-Through.* New York: Simon & Schuster, 1972.

Howe, Irving. *World of Our Fathers: The Journey of the East European Jews to America and the Life They Found and Made.* New York: Harcourt Brace Jovanovich, 1976.

Kazacoff, George. *Dangerous Theatre: The Federal Theatre Project as a Forum for New Plays.* New York: Lang, 1989.

Kazin, Alfred. *Starting Out in the Thirties.* Boston: Little, Brown & Co., 1962.

Kennedy, David M. *Freedom from Fear.* New York: Oxford University Press, 1999.

Kurth, Peter. *American Cassandra.* Boston: Little, Brown & Co., 1990.

Lacy, Leslie Alexander. *The Soil Soldiers: The Civilian Conservation Corps in the Great Depression*. Radnor, Pa.: Chilton Book Co., 1976.

Leaming, Barbara. *Orson Welles: A Biography*. New York: Penguin Books, 1985.

Levin, Meyer. *In Search: An Autobiography*. New York: Horizon Press, 1950.

————. *The New Bridge*. New York: Covici Friede, 1933.

Lewis, David Levering. *When Harlem Was in Vogue*. New York: Oxford University Press, 1989.

Lewis, Sinclair. *It Can't Happen Here*. New York: Doubleday, Doran & Co., Inc., 1935.

Loften, Mitchell. *Black Drama: The Story of the American Negro in the Theatre*. New York: Hawthorne Books, 1967.

Lowitt, Richard, and Maurine Beasley, eds. *One Third of a Nation: Lorena Hickok Reports on the Great Depression*. Urbana: University of Illinois Press, 1981.

Lynd, Alice and Staughton. *Rank and File*. Boston: Beacon Press, 1973.

Mangione, Jerry. *The Dream and the Deal: The Federal Writers' Project, 1935–43*. Boston: Little, Brown & Co., 1972.

Matthews, Jane deHart. *The Federal Theatre, 1935–39*. Princeton: Princeton University Press, 1967.

McJimsey, George. *Harry Hopkins: Ally of the Poor and Defender of Democracy*. Cambridge: Harvard University Press, 1987.

Morgan, Ted. *FDR: A Biography*. New York: Simon & Schuster, 1985.

————. *Reds*. New York: Random House, 2003.

Nasaw, David. *The Chief: The Life of William Randolph Hearst*. Boston: Houghton Mifflin Co., 2000.

Navasky, Victor S. *Naming Names*. New York: Penguin, 1981.

O'Connor, John, and Lorraine Brown. *Free Adult, Uncensored: The Living History of the Federal Theatre Project*. Washington, D.C.: New Republic Books, 1978.

Ogden, August Raymond. *The Dies Committee*. Westport, Ct.: Greenwood, 1984.

Perkins, Frances. *The Roosevelt I Knew*. New York: Viking Press, 1946.

Phillips, Cabell. *From the Crash to the Blitz: 1929–1939: The New York Times Chronicle of American Life*. New York: Macmillan, 1969.

Rice, Elmer. *Minority Report: An Autobiography*. New York: Simon & Schuster, 1963.

Schlesinger, Arthur M. *The Coming of the New Deal*. Boston: Houghton Mifflin, 1959.

————. *The Crisis of the Old Order, 1919–1933*. Boston: Houghton Mifflin, 1957.

————. *The Politics of Upheaval*. Boston: Houghton Mifflin, 1960.

Schoener, Allon, ed. *Portal to America: The Lower East Side 1870–1925*. New York: Holt, Rinehart & Winston, 1967.

————. *Harlem on My Mind: Cultural Capital of Black America, 1900–1968*. New York: Random House, 1968.

Schorer, Mark. *Sinclair Lewis: An American Life*. New York: McGraw-Hill Book Co., Inc., 1961.

Schwartz, Bonnie Nelson. *Voices from the Federal Theatre*. Madison: University of Wisconsin Press, 2003.

Sherwood, Robert E. *Roosevelt and Hopkins: An Intimate History*. New York: Grosset & Dunlap, 1950.

Smith, Mona. *Becoming Something: The Story of Canada Lee*. New York: Faber & Faber, 2004.

Steiner, Edward A. *From Alien to Citizen*. New York: Fleming H. Revell Co., 1914.

Thomson, Virgil. *Virgil Thomson*. New York: E. P. Dutton, 1985.

Tick, Judith, ed. *Music in the USA: A Documentary Companion*. New York: Oxford University Press, 2008.

Tully, Jim. *Beggars of Life: A Hobo Autobiography*. London: AK Press, 2004.

Turkel, Studs. *Hard Times*. New York: New Press, 1970.

Uys, Errol Lincoln. *Riding the Rails: Teenagers on the Move During the Great Depression*. New York: TV Books, 1999.

Warburg, James P. *Still Hell Bent*. New York: Doubleday, Doran & Co., Inc., 1936.

Warren, Donald. *Radio Priest: Charles Coughlin, the Father of Hate Radio*. New York: Free Press: 1996.

Watkins, T. H. *The Hungry Years: A Narrative History of the Great Depression in America*. New York: Henry Holt & Co., 1999.

Welles, Orson. *The Cradle Will Rock: An Original Screenplay*. Santa Barbara, Calif.: Santa Teresa Press, 1994.

Whitman, Willson. *Bread and Circuses: A Study of Federal Theatre*. New York: Oxford, 1937.

Williams, Jay. *Stage Left*. New York: Charles Scribner's Sons, 1974.

Witham, Barry B. *The Federal Theatre Project: A Case Study*. Cambridge: Cambridge University Press, 2003.

Woodruff, Nan Elizabeth. *As Rare as Rain: Federal Relief in the Great Southern Drought of 1930–31*. Urbana: University of Illinois Press, 1985.

ARTICLES

Arent, Arthur. "Ethiopia: The First 'Living Newspaper.'" *Educational Theatre Journal* 20, no. 1 (March 1968): 15–31. Introduction by Dan Isaac.

Blitzstein, Marc. "Out of the Cradle." *Opera News*, February 13, 1960.

Cornebise, Alfred Emile. "Heralds in New Deal America: Camp Newspapers of the Civilian Conservation Corps." *Media History Monographs* 1, no. 3.

Flanagan, Hallie. "A Theatre Is Born." *Theatre Arts Monthly* XV (November 1931): 908–915.

Macy, Jesse. "History from a Democratic Standpoint." *University Extension* 3 (March 1894): 293–302.

Plum, Jay. "Rose McClendon and the Black Units of the Federal Theatre Project: A Lost Contribution." *Theatre Survey* 33, no. 2 (November 1992): 144–153.

Ross, Ronald. "The Role of Blacks in the Federal Theatre, 1935–1939." In Errol Hill, ed., *The Theatre of Black Americans*, vol. 2 (Englewood Cliffs, N.J.: Prentice-Hall Inc., 1980).

Witham, Barry. "Backstage at *The Cradle Will Rock*." *Theatre History Studies* XII (1992).

PLAYS AND MUSICALS

DeRohan, Pierre. *Federal Theatre Plays* (includes *Haiti*, *One-Third of a Nation*, and *Prologue to Glory*). New York: Random House, 1938.

————. *Federal Theatre Plays* (includes *Power*, *Triple-A Plowed Under*, and *Spirochete*). New York: Da Capo Press, 1973.

Flanagan, Hallie. *Can You Hear Their Voices?* In ed. Judith A. Barlow, *Plays by American Women 1930–1960*. New York: Applause, 1994.

Eliot, T. S. *Murder in the Cathedral*. New York: Harcourt Brace and Co., 1935.

Johnson, Francis Hall. *Run, Little Chillun*. In James V. Hatch and Leo Hamalian, eds., *Lost Plays of the Harlem Renaissance, 1920–1940*. Detroit: Wayne State University Press, 1996.

Kaufman, George S., and Moss Hart. *I'd Rather Be Right: A Musical Revue*. Lyrics and music by Lorenz Hart and Richard Rodgers. New York: Random House, 1937.

Ward, Theodore. *Big White Fog*. In James V. Hatch, ed., *Black Theatre, U.S.A.: Forty-Five Plays by Black Americans, 1847–1974*. New York: The Free Press, 1974.

NOTES

I have used the following abbreviations to describe primary sources of material for this book:

GC Grinnell College Library
GMU George Mason University Special Collection and Archives
LC Billy Rose Theatre Collection at Lincoln Center, a division of the
   New York Public Library
LOC Library of Congress Federal Theatre Collection
NA National Archives; Record Group 69 (RG69) contains all the material
   relating to the Federal Theatre Project
FDRL Franklin D. Roosevelt Library, Hyde Park, New York
VC Vassar College Special Collections

PROLOGUE

1. Woodruff, *Rare as Rain*, 56.
2. Ibid., 57.
3. Ibid., 58.
4. January 4, 1931.
5. Woodruff, *Rare as Rain,* 61.
6. Ibid., 63.
7. Ibid., 62.
8. Flanagan, *Voices*, in Barlow, *Plays,* 3–48.
9. Press statement, *New York Times*, February 4, 1931.
10. *New York Times*, January 18, 1931.
11. Woodruff, *Rare as Rain*, 46.
12. Ibid.
13. *New York Times*, January 6, 1931.

14. Ibid., February 8, 1931.
15. Ibid., January 29, 1931.
16. Schlesinger, *Coming*, 22.
17. Cowley, *Dream*, 152.
18. Ibid., 156.

CHAPTER ONE: ON THE TRAIN

1. Uys, *Riding the Rails*, 262.
2. Schlesinger, *Coming*, 13.
3. The Civil Works Administration (CWA), which had power to hire the unemployed directly. This, too, was run by Harry Hopkins and employed four million at its height in January 1934. Roosevelt decided the CWA, which could be viewed as a forerunner of WPA, was too expensive and ended it in 1934.
4. *Philadelphia Inquirer*, October 13, 1936.
5. Schlesinger, *Coming*, 270.
6. I have decided to use the word *Negro*, which was the respectful word for identifying African Americans in the 1930s, when it is the word that fits the context (as here, when I am conveying Harry's and Hallie's ideas). When I am writing in the authorial voice, I will use "black" or "African American."
7. Melville House, Detroit, December 26, 1933, FDRL.
8. Schlesinger, *Upheaval*, 521.
9. *New York Post*, March 30, 1936.
10. Flanagan, *Arena*, 24–27.
11. *Baltimore Sun*, May 6, 1935.
12. *Literary Digest*, Current Opinion. Cartoons from the *Newark Evening News* and *Brooklyn Daily Eagle*, June 29, 1935.
13. *Des Moines Register*, September 18, 1935.
14. Lowitt, *One Third*.
15. Flanagan, *Arena*, 28.
16. *Des Moines Register*, July 27, 1935.
17. Flanagan, *Arena*, 28.

CHAPTER TWO: HARRY

1. Childs, *I Write*, 19.
2. *Scarlet and Black*, June 12, 1912.
3. McJimsey Papers, GC. Communication with E. T. Baker, a friend of Al Hopkins.
4. McJimsey, *Hopkins*, 8. Quotes from McJimsey Papers.
5. Macy, Jesse, *University Extension*.
6. Steiner, *From Alien to Citizen*.

7. *Scarlet and Black*, May 11, 1912.

8. Sherwood, *Roosevelt and Hopkins*.

9. McJimsey Papers, GC.

10. Hopkins, *Hopkins,* 87.

11. Ibid., 50.

12. Harry Hopkins, "Report on Unemployment Department," undated, probably 1913–1914, from Archives of the Community Service Society, as quoted in Hopkins, *Hopkins,* 64.

13. Hopkins, *Hopkins,* 152.

14. Giffen, *Jewish First Wife,* September 15, 1918.

15. Six years after they married, she told a reporter that Harry "simply hasn't one single fault."

16. Notes made by John Kingsbury, in the John A. Kingsbury Papers, Library of Congress, Washington, D.C.

17. Schlesinger, *Crisis,* 381.

18. Phillips, *Crash to the Blitz*.

19. Hopkins, *Hopkins*, 160.

20. Schlesinger, *Coming*, 264.

21. Sherwood, *Roosevelt*, 43.

CHAPTER THREE: HALLIE

1. Flanagan, Hallie, "Notes on My Life," VC.

2. Flanagan Journal, 1904, VC.

3. Grinnell *Cyclone*, 1909–10, GC.

4. *Scarlet and Black*, February 4, 1911, GC.

5. Ibid., October 12, 1907.

6. Hallie Flanagan, Scrapbook of Grinnell, VC.

7. *Scarlet and Black*, June 3, 1911.

8. Ibid., February 25, 1911.

9. Flanagan, "Notes."

10. *Scarlet and Black*, January 11, 1908; December 9, 1908.

11. Murray Flanagan diary, 1909. In the possession of Betty Flanagan.

12. Ibid.

13. Hallie Flanagan scrapbook, 1914, VC.

14. Bentley, *Flanagan*.

15. Flanagan, "Notes."

16. Letters to Deborah Wiley. Letters undated, but clearly 1917–18, VC.

17. Flanagan, "Notes."

18. Flanagan, *Curtain*.

19. Ibid.

20. Bentley, *Flanagan*, 19.

21. Dolan, Marc J., "The Art of His Technique," Harvard honors thesis, 1983.
22. n.d., LC.
23. Baker to "Miss Reed," January 16, 1925, VC.
24. Bentley, *Flanagan*, 44.
25. Cyclone, 1926, GC.
26. Flanagan, "Notes."
27. HF claimed she was "the first woman to receive a Guggenheim." This was not quite true.
28. October 14, 1926, LC.
29. Travel diary, 1926, VC.
30. Ibid.
31. Travel diary, 1926–1927, VC.
32. Letter from Berlin, December 27, 1926, LC.
33. Travel diary, 1926, VC.
34. Craig's comments, written on a draft of Hallie Flanagan article about him, 1928, LC.
35. 1928, LC.
36. April 2, 1934, LC.
37. Journal, July 21, 1934, VC.
38. Hopkins personal letters and papers, FDRL.
39. HF notes, VC.
40. *Arena*, 3.
41. Flanagan, "Notes."
42. Irwin Rhodes (Rubinstein), Joanne Bentley interview, VC.
43. Othello in the final act, actually "richer" than all his tribe.
44. Flanagan, "Notes."
45. Letter to students, April 30, 1934, VC.
46. Travel diary, March–April, 1934, VC.
47. Bentley, "Notes."
48. Flanagan, *Dynamo*.
49. "Notes."
50. Flanagan, *Arena*.
51. "Notes."

CHAPTER FOUR: GREAT PLANS FOR MILLIONS

1. Flanagan to Davis (hereafter "F–D"), September 4, 1935.
2. From a group of retyped, undated letters, F–D, VC.
3. Flanagan, "Notes."
4. F–D, October 8, 1935.
5. F–D, September 4, 1935.
6. F–D, September 9, 1935.

7. Flanagan, *Arena,* 35–36.

8. F–D, September 11, 1935.

9. F–D, September 18, 1935.

10. F–D, September 11, 1935.

11. F–D, September 18, 1935.

12. Flanagan, *Arena,* 40.

13. F–D, September 22, 1935.

14. F–D, October 1, 1935.

15. Flanagan, *Arena,* 41

16. October 1, 1935.

17. "Chronicle of a Trouper," *Sunday New York Times,* November 8, 1936.

18. F–D, September 9, 1935.

19. The actual quote is: "You must have chaos within you to give birth to a dancing star."

20. Federal Theatre press release, November 25, 1935, LC.

21. Drew Pearson in *Washington Herald,* January 1936.

22. F–D, September 26, 1935.

23. F–D, September 9, 1935.

24. FDRL.

25. Goodwin, *No Ordinary Time,* 209.

26. F–D, September 26, 1935. For some reason, perhaps a request from Eleanor, Hallie Flanagan never talked or wrote about this incident. The page in her letters to Phil that probably deals with it has been removed. A telegram at the Roosevelt Library and this reference at the end of a letter have allowed me to piece it together.

CHAPTER FIVE: *ETHIOPIA*

1. Hopkins journal, FDRL.

2. Hopkins telegram, Hopkins papers, FDRL.

3. Hopkins papers, FDRL.

4. Hopkins journal, FDRL.

5. Ayn Rand, *Night of January 16.* New York: World Publishing Co., 1968.

6. F–D.

7. Burns Mantle, *The Best Plays of 1934–35.*

8. Ibid.

9. HF to Elmer Rice, September 24, 1934, VC.

10. Typed notes, May 17, 1935, FDRL.

11. Introduction, *Federal Theatre Plays.*

12. Douglas McDermott, "The Living Newspaper as a Dramatic Form," *Modern Drama,* 1965.

13. Introduction, *Federal Theatre Plays.*

14. Rice to Flanagan, November 19, 1935, FDRL.

15. Francis Bosworth, GMU interview.
16. Motherwell memo to HF, LC.
17. Motherwell memo, January 18, 1936, FDRL.
18. Address to regional directors, September 8, 1935, FDRL.
19. Interview with Esther Porter Lane, GMU.
20. Schwartz, *Voices*.
21. Interview with Bud Fishel, GMU.
22. Schwartz, *Voices*.
23. "Report of Federal Theatre Project as Released to Various Theatrical Publications," December 23, 1935," FDRL.
24. F–D, November 8, 1935.
25. Now the Manhattan Theatre Club.
26. *New York Times*, January 5, 1936.
27. This occurred, as Hallie Flanagan explains in *Arena*, before there was a prohibition against hiring noncitizens onto the Federal Theatre Project.
28. Hill and Hatch, *History of African American Theatre*, 371.
29. Arthur Arent, "Ethiopia."
30. January 11, 1936, LC.
31. January 15, 1936, LC.
32. Memo from Mary Cox to Jake Baker, January 16, 1936, LC.
33. HF notes on January 17, 1936, meeting with Eleanor Roosevelt, LC.
34. January 18, 1936, LC.
35. January 21, 1936. HF notes on phone conversation, dictated from memory, LC.
36. LC.
37. Flanagan, *Arena*, 56.
38. Esther Porter Lane interview, GMU.
39. F–D, n.d.
40. F–D, March 3, 1936.
41. Rice, *Minority Report*, 357–358.
42. *New York Times,* January 25, 1936.
43. *Sunday Mirror* magazine, March 8, 1936.
44. Aubrey Williams to Eleanor Roosevelt, January 25, 1936, LC.

CHAPTER SIX: *TRIPLE-A PLOWED UNDER*

1. Schlesinger, *Coming*, 35, 36, 39, 40.
2. Ibid., 71.
3. Ibid., 375–378.
4. Kennedy, *Freedom*, 329.
5. Morgan, *Reds*, 431.
6. *Federal Theatre Plays* (New York: Random House, 1938).
7. Thomson, *Thomson*, 263.

8. Morgan, *Reds*, 167.
9. Cowley, *Dream*, 315.
10. Morgan, *Reds*, 167.
11. Flanagan to directors, September 9, 1935.
12. Philip Barber interview, GMU. *New York Times*, March 17, 1936.
13. *New York American*, March 21, 1936.
14. F–D, March 17, 1936.
15. Ibid.
16. *New York Times*, March 15, 1936.
17. Barber interview, GMU.
18. *New York Times*, March 15, 1936.
19. F–D, March 17, 1936.

ENTR'ACTE ONE: *THE CCC MURDER MYSTERY*

1. Perkins, *Roosevelt*, 113.
2. Quotes from CCCers are taken from the James F. Justin Civilian Conservation Corps Museum, a Web site where corps members share their stories.
3. Tony March, included in a report from the Los Angeles Federal Theatre unit, NA.
4. F–D, March 24, 1936.
5. NA.
6. *Federal Theatre Bulletin* 2, no. 1, LOC.
7. HF memo to regional directors, February 12, 1936, VC.
8. Taken from 1931 song "Brother, Can You Spare a Dime?" with words by Yip Harburg and lyrics by Jay Gorney.
9. Cornebise, "Heralds in New Deal America."
10. September 11, 1936.
11. September 20, 1936.
12. Flanagan, *Arena,* 242–243.
13. NA.

CHAPTER SEVEN: THE SIMPLE AND THE DIFFICULT

1. Flanagan, *Dynamo*.
2. Eliot to HF, March 18, 1933, VC.
3. The Liberty League was organized by a group of wealthy right-wing opponents of FDR. Al Smith became an unlikely ally.
4. *New York Times*, March 15, 1936.
5. *New Republic,* April 8, 1936.
6. *New York Herald Tribune*, March 29, 1936.
7. *New Yorker*, March 28, 1936.

8. *Daily Worker*, March 26, 1936.

9. *New York Post*, March 30, 1936.

10. Norman Lloyd interview, GMU.

11. Letter from Halstead Welles to Joanne Bentley, October 25, 1988. Courtesy of Joanne Bentley.

12. *Nation*, March 23, 1936.

13. *New York Herald Tribune*, March 29, 1936.

14. Memo from Hallie Flanagan, April 2, 1936, NA.

15. F–D, March 24, 1936.

CHAPTER EIGHT: DO YOU VOODOO?

1. Clurman, *Fervent Years*.

2. October 2, 1934.

3. Smith, *Canada*, 48.

4. Now the Al Hirschfeld Theatre.

5. Houseman, *Run-Through*, 144.

6. Ross, "The Role," 38.

7. Fraden, *Blueprints*, 198.

8. Flanagan, *Arena*, 63.

9. Carlton Moss interview, GMU.

10. *Variety* as quoted by the *Amsterdam News*, October 23, 1929.

11. Lewis, *Harlem*, 209.

12. Hickey, *Powell,* 36.

13. Hamilton, *Powell*, 60.

14. Schoener, *Harlem*, 137.

15. Ibid., 135.

16. Houseman, *Run-Through,* 179.

17. Leonard de Paur interview, GMU.

18. Houseman, *Run-Through*, 182.

19. Ibid., 183–189.

20. *New York Times*, April 26, 1936.

21. Callow, *Welles*, 243.

22. Ibid., 233.

23. Tommy Anderson interview, GMU.

24. Callow, *Welles*, 225–226.

25. Edward Dudley interview, GMU.

26. Houseman, *Run-Through,* 196–197.

27. Tommy Anderson interview, GMU.

28. Virgil Thomson interview, GMU.

29. Houseman, *Run-Through*, 193.

30. Callow, *Welles*, 230, 231.

31. Flanagan, *Arena*, 74.

32. F–D, April 1936.

33. April 16, 1936.

34. April 15, 1936.

35. Houseman, *Run-Through*, 202.

36. Edward Dudley interview, GMU.

37. Smith, *Canada*, 54.

CHAPTER NINE: *IT CAN'T HAPPEN HERE*

1. FBI documents, from an informant's testimony.

2. Flanagan notes, FDRL.

3. Warren, *Radio Priest*.

4. Ibid., 25.

5. Lewis, *It Can't*.

6. Kurth, *American Cassandra*, 186–187.

7. Schorer, *Lewis*, 577.

8. Kurth, *American Cassandra,* 166.

9. Ibid., 205.

10. Schorer, *Lewis*, 608.

11. *Motion Picture Herald*, August 29, 1936.

12. Francis Bosworth interview, GMU.

13. Flanagan, *Shifting Scenes*, 257.

14. *Federal Theatre Bulletin* 2, no. 2, November/December, 1936, LOC.

15. *New York Times*, July 25, 1936.

16. Flanagan, *Arena*, 72.

17. Matthews, *Federal*, 110.

18. *Federal Theatre Bulletin* 2, no. 1, LOC, n.d.

19. *Harper's*.

20. Matthews, *Federal*, 111–112.

21. *New York Journal*.

22. *Saturday Evening Post*, August 1, 1936.

23. *New York Times* interview, as quoted in the West Coast *Federal Theatre Bulletin*, November 1936.

24. *Federal Theatre Bulletin* 2, no. 2., November/December, 1935. LOC.

25. Ibid.

26. August 31, 1936, VC.

27. Schorer, *Lewis*, 592.

28. Kurth, *Cassandra*, 210.

29. October 1935.

30. *New Yorker*, November 21, 1936.

31. Flanagan, *Arena*, 116.

32. November 21, 1936.

33. F–D, September 23, 1936.

34. Playscript in NA, dated September 18, 1936.

35. Matthews, *Federal,* 97–98.

36. Flanagan, *Arena,* 122–123.

37. Bud Fishel interview, GMU.

38. *New Yorker*, October 31, 1936.

39. *New York Evening Journal,* October 28, 1936.

40. *New Republic,* November 11, 1936.

41. *New York Times*, November 8, 1936.

42. Ibid.

43. October 28, 1936.

44. *Commonwealth News*, October 31, 1936.

45. Flyer in NA.

46. *San Francisco Chronicle*, October 28, 1936.

47. NA.

48. *Daily Times*, October 28, 1936.

49. Mencken in Crane, *Roosevelt*, 193.

50. Schlesinger, *Politics*, 574.

51. *Philadelphia Inquirer*, October 13, 1936.

52. *Washington Post*, August 21, 1936.

53. Warburg, *Still Hell Bent,* 87.

54. Kurth, *Cassandra*, 208.

55. Freidel, *Roosevelt*, 207.

56. Adams, *Hopkins*, 108–109.

57. F–D November 8, 1936.

ENTR'ACTE TWO: AFTER THE FLOOD

1. HF to Phil, February 4, 1937.

2. Report by Herbert A. Price, LC.

CHAPTER TEN: UNDER A POWERFUL STAR

1. Freidel, *Roosevelt*, 226.

2. Ibid., 249.

3. Houseman, *Run-Through*, 202–203.

4. Filed under "unique letters" in the correspondence of HF, LC.

5. *Federal Theatre Bulletin* 2, no. 1. n.d.

6. *Fortune*, May 1937.

7. *Variety*, March 17, 1937.

8. *Billboard*, May 1, 1937.

9. Ibid., January 30, 1937.

10. Minutes of D.C. meeting, March 13, 14, 1937, FDRL.

11. Ibid.

12. 109 W. Thirty-ninth, demolished in 1959.

13. Title in translation, *The Italian Straw Hat* (in French, *Un chapeau de paille d'Italie*).

14. Houseman, *Run-Through,* 212.

15. Ibid., 221.

16. Bil Baird interview, GMU.

17. Variations and original music for the show were written by Paul Bowles, orchestrated by Virgil Thomson.

18. Callow, *Welles*, 257.

19. Houseman, *Run-Through*, 221.

20. Stark Young, *New Republic*, October 14, 1936.

21. Houseman, *Run-Through,* 223.

22. Callow, *Welles*, 257.

23. Flanagan, *Arena*, 78.

24. Thomson, *Thomson*, 266.

25. Flanagan, *Arena*, 78.

26. F–D, January 15, 1937.

27. Houseman, *Run-Through*, 231.

28. Ibid., 235, 236.

29. *New Republic*, February 17, 1937.

30. Herald *Tribune*, January 24, 1937.

31. *Bachelor*, May 1937.

32. Letter to the regional directors, February 12, 1936, NA.

33. *New Republic*, February 17, 1937.

34. *New York Times*, January 9, 1937.

35. F–D, January 15, 1937.

36. Houseman, *Run-Through*, 241.

37. Matthews, 112. Joe Losey did leave the project over *Injunction*, but Morris Watson stayed on and was running *Power.*

38. Flanagan to Walter Hart, February 17, 1937, NA.

39. *New York Evening Journal*, February 24, 1937.

40. February 24, 1937.

41. As quoted in *Time*, March 8, 1937.

42. *Catholic World*, March 1937.

43. Jean Thomas, who played a farm wife in *Power,* had spent some time collecting folk songs and provided this TVA song to the show. Modern scholars have criticized her romanticized renderings of Appalachian songs.

44. In the end, FDR failed to pack the Supreme Court, but he got a New Deal majority through attrition and appointments.

45. *Life,* March 22, 1937.

46. Flanagan, *Arena,* 115.
47. Witham, *Federal*, 85.
48. *Seattle Times*, July 7, 1937.
49. *Seattle Post-Intelligencer*, July 7, 1937.
50. Memo from Hiram Motherwell to HF, January 18, 1936.
51. *New York Times*, September 19, 1937.
52. F–D, January 15, 1937.
53. Bill Farnsworth interview, GMU.
54. HF to Hopkins.
55. F–D, April 18, 1937.
56. April 21, 1937, NA.
57. *World Telegram,* April 30, 1937.
58. G. B. Shaw to Hallie Flanagan, May 22, 1937, NA.
59. Kennedy, *Freedom*, 331.
60. Childs, *I Write,* 129.
61. *New York Times*, May 4, 1937.
62. Ibid., May 6, 1937.
63. *New York Times*, May 4, 1937.
64. Ibid., May 6, 1937.
65. *Billboard*, May 1, 1937.
66. May 2, 1937.
67. *New York Times*, May 14, 1937.
68. Ibid., May 15, 1937.
69. Transcribed conversation, VC.
70. NA.
71. *Collier's*, October 9, 1937.
72. Matthews, 116–117.
73. Houseman, *Run-Through*, 254.

CHAPTER ELEVEN: *THE CRADLE WILL ROCK*

1. Callow, *Welles*, 290.
2. Leaming, *Welles*, 130.
3. Welles, *Cradle*.
4. Houseman, *Run-Through*, 247.
5. Flanagan, *Arena*, 199.
6. Houseman, *Run-Through*, 248.
7. Gordon, *Mark*, 113.
8. *New York Times*, June 18, 1937.
9. Houseman, *Run-Through*, 247.
10. HF speech before American Federation of Arts, Washington, D.C., May 12, 1937, NA.

11. John Anderson in Lynd, *Rank and File.*

12. Auerbach, *Labor*, 133–134.

13. Ibid., 103.

14. Howard Da Silva interview, GMU.

15. Engel, *Bright Day*, 81.

16. Leaming, *Welles*, 132.

17. Engel, *Bright Day*, 81.

18. *New York Times*, May 28, 1937.

19. Auerbach, *Labor.*

20. Ibid., 140.

21. Ibid., 101.

22. Lynd, *Rank and File*, 96.

23. Watkins, *Hungry Years*, 286.

24. Auerbach, *Labor*, 127.

25. Houseman, *Run-Through,* 254.

26. Flanagan, *Arena*, 314.

27. Bill Farnsworth interview, GMU.

28. *New Republic*, July 21, 1937.

29. Matthews, *Federal Theatre*, 123.

30. Howard Bay interview, GMU.

31. Houseman, *Run-Through*, 257.

32. Ibid., 260.

33. Ibid., 261.

34. Houseman says Hiram Sherman, but Da Silva remembers him and Geer coming out. See GMU interview with Da Silva.

35. There are varying stories about the piano—Houseman makes much of Jean Rosenthal's traveling around Manhattan on the back of a truck with the piano, waiting for orders, then recruiting some helpful firemen to haul it onto the Venice stage. But other accounts are less dramatic.

36. *Opera News,* February 13, 1960.

37. Houseman, *Run-Through*, 268–269.

38. *Opera News,* February 13, 1960.

39. Houseman, *Run-Through,* 271–274.

40. *New York Times*, June 17, 1937.

41. Memo with verbatim account of interview between David Niles, Ellen Woodward, Orson Welles, and a Miss Cronin, June 17, 1937, NA.

42. Houseman, *Run-Through*, 255, 258.

43. *World Telegram,* September 14, 1937.

44. *New York Times*, August 29, 1937.

45. Interview with Robert Schnitzer by author.

46. Flanagan to Hopkins, January 28, 1938, NA. Handwritten at the top are the words *Not Sent.*

47. Flanagan, *Arena*, 203.
48. Gordon, *Blitzstein*, 162.

ENTR'ACTE THREE: *I'D RATHER BE RIGHT*

1. *New Yorker*, September 26, 1936.
2. *World Telegram,* November 5, 1937.
3. *Federal Theatre Bulletin* 2, no. 5, n.d.
4. According to Flanagan in *Arena*, de Rohan was a Democrat recommended to the project by vice president John Nance Garner.
5. "To each his need; from each his power."
6. Flanagan, *Arena*, 204–205.
7. Freidel, *Roosevelt,* 252.
8. F–D, October 7, 1937.
9. F–D, October 14, 1937.

CHAPTER TWELVE: CHANTS OF THE PRAIRIES

1. F–D, December 17, 1937.
2. F–D, December 19, 1937. From the poem "Starting from Paumanok."
3. Flanagan speech to staff, March 13–14, 1937, FDRL.
4. Flanagan to Dorothea Thomas Lynch, state supervisor, and Josef Lentz, state technical supervisor, April 8, 1936, NA.
5. Flanagan, *Arena*, 89.
6. *New York Times*, August 15, 1937. *Lost Colony* is the one remnant of the Federal Theatre Project that continues to play even now on Roanoke Island.
7. *Tampa Morning Tribune*, October 2, 1936.
8. *Jacksonville Journal*, April 25, 1939.
9. Flanagan, *Arena*, 131.
10. *Minneapolis Journal*, January 12, 1936.
11. It turned out that she had given the photographer permission to fetch the rubber dress and fans at her apartment.
12. Flanagan to E. C. Mabie, January 10, 1936.
13. Speech by HF, "Federal Theatre 1937," NA.
14. F–D, October 20, 1935.
15. Levin, *The New Bridge*.
16. Levin, *In Search*, 80.
17. Meyer Levin to President Roosevelt, February 12, 1936, NA.
18. Howard O. Hunter, field representative, to Jacob Baker, assistant administrator, WPA, January 16, 1936, NA.
19. Flanagan, *Arena*, 136.
20. Flanagan memo, May 4, 1936.

21. Thomas Wood Stevens to HF, April 29, 1936.

22. F–D, May 1936 (letter undated).

23. Record of Chicago trip, April–May 1937, FDRL.

24. F–D, May 1936.

25. Record of Chicago trip.

26. Selected verses from script of *O Say Can You Sing*, NA.

27. *Chicago Tribune*, December 12, 1936.

28. Claudia Cassidy, *Chicago Journal of Commerce and LaSalle St. Journal*, December 14, 1936.

29. Flanagan, *Arena*, 140.

30. *Billboard*, June 19, 1937.

31. Kondolf to HF, June 7, 1936.

32. *Variety*, September 13, 1937.

33. F–D, October 1937.

34. Meyer Zolotareff, newspaper unidentified, NA.

35. Gelb, *O'Neill*, 483.

36. F–D, October 1937.

CHAPTER THIRTEEN: THE WEST

1. HF to Phil, October 31, 1937.

2. HF to Phil, November 1, 1937.

3. Report on the Federal Theatre Project, Seattle, Washington, November 4, 1937. From Flanagan to Ellen Woodward et al., FDRL.

4. *Register Guard*, September 19, 1936.

5. Script in NA, II-27.

6. Howard J. Miller to HF, September 26, 1936.

7. *Seattle Star*, September 18, 1936.

8. Guy Williams, state director of the Federal Theatre Project, to Hallie Flanagan, September 19, 1936.

9. *District Herald*, September 18, 1936.

10. Robert St. Clair to HF, September 19, 1936.

11. *Seattle Star*, September 22, 1936.

12. Transcript of telephone conversation between Bill Farnsworth and Guy Williams, September 23, 1936.

13. Howard J. Miller to HF, September 26, 1936, NA.

14. HF to Howard J. Miller, October 5, 1936, VC.

15. Flanagan, *Arena,* 226.

16. F–D, November 2, 1937.

17. Report on the Federal Theatre Project, Seattle, Washington, November 4, 1937.

18. Ibid.

19. F–D, no date.

20. *San Francisco News,* September 4, 1936.

21. *Times-Delta,* May 4, 1937.

22. *San Francisco Chronicle,* September 5, 1936.

23. Flanagan, *Arena,* 281.

24. August 6, 1936, LC.

25. *Los Angeles Herald-Express,* December 8, 1935.

26. *Variety,* August 31, 1936.

27. *Los Angeles Daily News,* December 10, 1935.

28. *Variety,* August 31, 1936.

29. *Variety,* September 2, 1936.

30. *Variety,* September 16, 1936; *Hollywood Citizen News,* December 3, 1936; *Variety,* September 3, 1936; *Los Angeles Evening News,* January 20, 1937.

31. Ellen Woodward to Byron Scott et al., April 30, 1937, NA.

32. *Los Angeles Evening News,* February 11, 1937.

33. *Hollywood Citizen-News,* March 3, 1937.

34. April 18, 1937.

35. *Variety,* May 20, 1936.

36. "Winchell's Daily Chatter," *Los Angeles Evening Herald and Express,* February 6, 1937.

37. *Long Beach Sun,* June 11, 1937.

38. F–D, November 13, 1937.

39. Flanagan, *Arena,* 299.

40. Ibid., 283.

41. Frank's *Pinocchio* became the basis of the Disney movie.

42. F–D, November 21, 1937.

43. *Los Angeles Examiner,* November 18, 1937.

44. *Hollywood Citizen News,* November 18, 1937.

45. *Los Angeles Evening News,* November 22, 1937.

46. *Hollywood Citizen News,* November 22, 1937.

47. Flanagan, *Arena,* 285–286.

48. F–D, December 9, 1937.

CHAPTER FOURTEEN: PAST IS PRESENT

1. *Time* magazine, April 26, 1937.

2. September 2, 1937, LC.

3. George Kondolf interview, GMU.

4. Ibid.

5. Walter Goodman to HF, February 1, 1938, VC.

6. *New York Times,* February 20, 1938.

7. F–D, January 11, 1938.

8. F–D, January 1938.

9. HF to Connolly, January 12, 1938.

10. HF to Hopkins, January 29, 1938.

11. *World Telegram*, February 7, 1938.

12. F–D, January 1938. Six weeks later, Connolly's office announced that *Judgment Day* would open in Los Angeles that May. *Stevedore* was still a question mark.

13. *New York Times*, February 9, 1938.

14. F–D, February 8, 1938.

15. Flanagan, *Arena*, 326.

16. *Commonweal*, February 4, 1938.

17. *New York Post,* January 21, 1938.

18. *Daily News*, January 18, 1938.

19. *Herald Tribune*, January 18, 1938.

20. *One Act Play Magazine*, February 1938.

21. *New York Post*, January 18, 1938.

22. Flanagan, *Arena,* 218.

23. Ibid., 213.

24. Howard Bay interview, GMU.

25. *New York Herald Tribune,* February 7, 1938.

26. *Daily News*, February 8, 1938.

27. *New York Post*, February 9, 1938.

28. *New York Herald Tribune*, February 23, 1938.

29. *Sunday News,* April 11, 1938.

30. March 12, 1938, editorial.

31. *New York Post*, February 9, 1938.

32. *Herald Tribune* May 11, 1938.

33. *New York Herald Tribune*, March 1, 1938.

34. *New York Times*, March 1, 1938.

35. Flanagan, *Arena*, 326.

36. *New York Post*, March 19, 1938.

37. Flanagan, *Arena*, 326.

38. Samuel Chotzinoff, New York newspaper unidentified, June 20, 1938.

39. *New York Post*, June 17, 1938.

40. Ironically, playwright William DuBois, who came from the South, condemned miscegenation in the original script.

41. Maurice Clark interview, GMU.

42. Leonard de Paur interview, GMU.

43. Gill, *White Grease Paint*, 99.

44. Facts on syphilis from Witham, *Federal Theatre Project*.

45. *Billboard*, May 7, 1938.

46. *Chicago American*, April 30, 1938. Later, the Knights of Columbus objected—not to the candid treatment of syphilis, but to the mention of Christopher Columbus as the carrier of the disease from Europe. In a number of productions, the name Columbus was stricken and replaced with "a sea captain."

47. Richard Wright, *American Hunger* (New York: Harper & Row, 1944).

48. Fraden, *Blueprints*, 118–119.

49. Ward, *Big White Fog*.

50. Hill, *History*, 324.

51. Fraden, *Blueprints*, 118 and following.

52. Introduction, *Big White Fog*, in Hatch, ed., *Black Theatre, U.S.A. Forty-Five Plays by Black Americans, 1847–1974*, 279–280.

53. *New York Daily Worker*, April 28, 1938.

54. F–D, May 19, 1938.

55. F–D. This is a retyped letter. I have used context to determine its date.

CHAPTER FIFTEEN: ENTER HUAC

1. Freidel, *Roosevelt*, 281.

2. Kennedy, *Freedom,* 345.

3. Goodman, *Committee*, 15.

4. Ibid.

5. Childs, *I Write*, 91–92.

6. Morgan, *Reds*, 184–185. Taken from a PhD thesis by Dennis Kay McDaniel, "Martin Dies of Un-American Activities: Life and Times," University of Houston, 1988.

7. Ibid., 186.

8. Ironically, it was Congressman Sam Dickstein, a strident foe of fascism, who suggested the word. But HUAC did not turn out to be the kind of investigating committee he wished for. His initiative had begun as a proposal to investigate the Black Legion.

9. Goodman, *Committee*, 22.

10. *New York Times*, July 27, 1938.

11. *New York Herald Tribune*, August 11, 1938.

12. Childs, *I Write*, 92.

13. Goodman, *Committee*, 25.

14. Ibid., 34.

15. *New York Post*, August 19, 1938.

16. *New York Sun*, August 20, 1938.

17. *Journal American,* August 21, 1938.

18. Morgan, *Reds*, 192.

19. Gellerman, *Dies*, 75.

20. Ibid., 181.

21. Goodman, *Committee*, 21.

22. *New York Telegraph*, September 2, 1938.

23. *New York Times*, September 2, 1938.

24. Ibid., September 4, 1938.

25. Ibid., September 17, 1938.

26. Goodman, *Committee*, 37–39.
27. HF to Phil, in retyped letters, dated only November 1938.

CHAPTER SIXTEEN: MARLOWE'S GHOST

1. Hopkins to FDR, December 24, 1938, FDRL.
2. Mangione, *Dream*, 287.
3. Flanagan to Burns Mantle, December 2, 1938, NA.
4. Mangione, *The Dream*, 225.
5. Woodward testimony taken from *New York Times*, December 5, 1938; *New York Herald Tribune*, December 6, 1938. The Wright passage is taken from Morgan, *Reds*, 197.
6. All quotes from Hallie Flanagan's appearance are taken from the *Congressional Record*, "Investigation of Un-American Propaganda Activities in the United States," Hearings Before a Special Committee on Un-American Activities, House of Representatives, Seventy-fifth Congress, Third Session, November 19–28, December 1–14, 1938.
7. *Washington Daily News*, December 7, 1938.
8. HF to Pepper, January 13, 1939, VC.

CHAPTER SEVENTEEN: AN ACT OF CONGRESS

1. Agnes Sanford to HF, January 21, 1939, NA.
2. *New York Times*, December 17, 1938.
3. *New York Post*, December 24, 1938.
4. *New York Times*, December 30, 1938.
5. F–D, January 24, 1939.
6. F–D, February 3, 1939.
7. Telegram to Phil, February 12, 1939.
8. F–D, February 3, 1939.
9. F–D, February 9, 1939.
10. F–D, February 13, 1939.
11. *San Francisco Chronicle,* January 14, 1939.
12. Flanagan, *Arena*, 290.
13. F–D, February 18, 1939.
14. Flanagan to directors, February 16, 1939, NA.
15. F–D, March 2, 1939.
16. F–D, February 5, 1939.
17. Because of Eleanor's intervention, after Marian Anderson was rejected by the DAR, she sang on the Washington Mall on April 9, 1939.
18. This essay, "Report on Democracy Versus the Theatre," is in the Vassar collection but has no date. However, Ullman resigned on February 12, 1939.
19. Flanagan to Herbert Biberman, March 22, 1939, VC.
20. Flanagan, *Arena,* 294.

21. F–D, March 6, 1939.

22. Flanagan to Morris Ankrum, April 19, 1939, FDRL.

23. Unless otherwise indicated, remarks of congressmen and senators are taken from the *Congressional Record.*

24. *Variety,* April 19, 1929.

25. *New York Times,* May 28, 1939.

26. F–D, May 23, 1939.

27. Among other things, the WPA directorship would be divided among three people, and people on relief would be taken off for two months.

28. *New York Daily News,* June 15, 1939.

29. F–D, June 1939. Retyped letter, no exact date.

30. *New York Times,* June 17, 1939.

31. Ibid., June 18, 1939.

32. *Voices,* interview with Alan Peters, 39.

33. *World Telegram,* June 19, 1939.

34. *World Telegram,* June 20, 1939.

35. *California Citizen News,* June 27, 1939.

36. Transcript from FDRL.

37. *World Telegram,* June 22, 1939.

38. *New York Times,* June 22, 1939.

39. F–D, June 23, 1939.

40. As with every other charge, the Federal Theatre staff prepared a detailed refutation of Reynolds's claims about these plays, all of which were, ironically enough, the kind of trivial and completely apolitical entertainment that Hallie was trying to discourage on the project.

41. *New York Post,* July 5, 1939.

42. Lee Simonson to Flanagan, July 16, 1939, LC.

43. Flanagan to Simonson, July 27, 1939, LC.

44. *California Herald,* July 1, 1939.

45. *Washington Post,* July 2, 1939.

46. *New York Daily News,* July 11, 1939.

EPILOGUE

1. *New York Times,* August 20, 1939.

2. *New York Times,* December 29, 1940.

3. HF Report on Federal Theatre Project, Seattle, Washington, November 4, 1937, FDRL.

4. HF to Max Shohet, August 29, 1947, LC.

5. *New York Times,* December 29, 1940.

INDEX